OUR SERVER IS DOWN!

DIDN'T YOU ASK MOMMY TO BRING US SOME POPCORN?
YEAH. A LONG TIME AGO.
AND YOU ASKED HER TO BRING US SOME JUICE BEFORE THE PROGRAM STARTED.
I'D BETTER GO SEE WHAT'S WRONG.
A-HA. I SEE THE PROBLEM.
WHAT IS IT?
ZZZ.
Z
OUR SERVER IS DOWN.
KIRKMAN & SCOTT

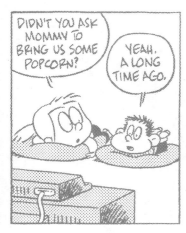

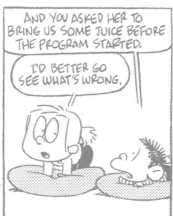

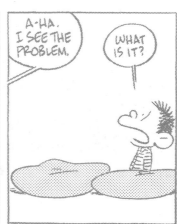

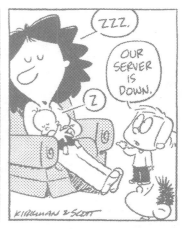

Other *Baby Blues*® Books from Andrews McMeel Publishing

Guess Who Didn't Take a Nap?
I Thought Labor Ended When the Baby Was Born
We Are Experiencing Parental Difficulties . . . Please Stand By
Night of the Living Dad
I Saw Elvis in My Ultrasound
One More and We're Outnumbered!
Check, Please . . .
threats, bribes & videotape
If I'm a Stay-at-Home Mom, Why Am I Always in the Car?
Lift and Separate
I Shouldn't Have to Scream More Than Once!
Motherhood Is Not for Wimps
Baby Blues®: Unplugged
Dad to the Bone
Never a Dry Moment
Two Plus One Is Enough
Playdate: Category 5

Treasuries

The Super-Absorbent Biodegradable Family-Size Baby Blues®
Baby Blues®: Ten Years and Still in Diapers
Butt-Naked Baby Blues®
Wall-to-Wall Baby Blues®
Driving Under the Influence of Children

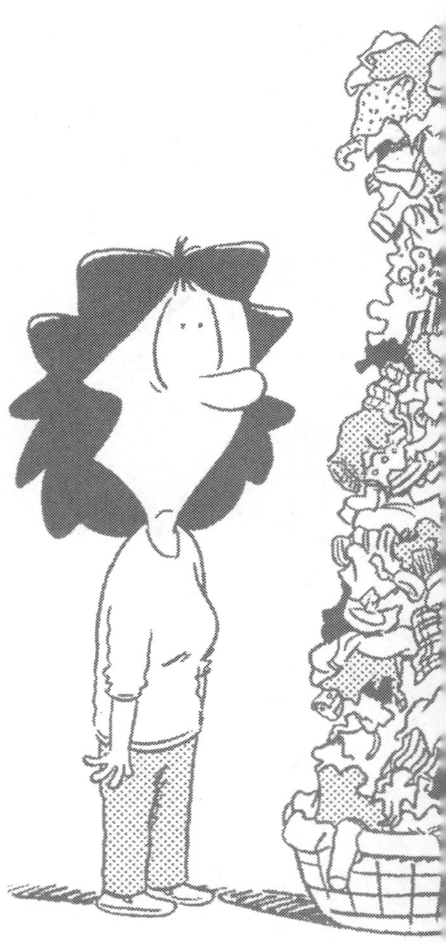

Baby Blues® 20 Scrapbook

OUR SERVER IS DOWN!

By Rick Kirkman & Jerry Scott

Andrews McMeel
Publishing

Kansas City

Baby Blues® is syndicated internationally by King Features Syndicate, Inc. For information, write King Features Syndicate, Inc., 888 Seventh Avenue, New York, New York 10019.

Our Server Is Down copyright © 2005 by Baby Blues Partnership. All rights reserved. Printed in the United States of America. No part of this book may be used or reproduced in any manner whatsoever without written permission except in the case of reprints in the context of reviews. For information, write Andrews McMeel Publishing, an Andrews McMeel Universal company, 4520 Main Street, Kansas City, Missouri 64111.

05 06 07 08 09 BBG 10 9 8 7 6 5 4 3 2 1

ISBN-13: 978-0-7407-5445-6
ISBN-10: 0-7407-5445-9

Library of Congress Catalog Card Number: 2005925659

Find *Baby Blues*® on the Web at
www.babyblues.com.

www.andrewsmcmeel.com

————— **ATTENTION: SCHOOLS AND BUSINESSES** —————

Andrews McMeel books are available at quantity discounts with bulk purchase for educational, business, or sales promotional use. For information, please write to: Special Sales Department, Andrews McMeel Publishing, 4520 Main Street, Kansas City, Missouri 64111.

For Maddie, on your new super-fantastic, super smash-hit adventure. YAAAAHHH.
With love from your very proud dad.

—R.K.

To Shari Latta and all the teachers at Children's Creative Workshop. Thank you.

—J.S.

BABY BLUES®
BY RICK KIRKMAN / JERRY SCOTT

WHERE ARE THE KIDS?
IN THE LIVING ROOM.
THEY'RE BEING AWFULLY QUIET.
THAT'S BECAUSE THEY'RE WATCHING TV.
IT'S WEIRD... AS SOON AS THE TELEVISION IS TURNED ON, THEY JUST STOP.
THEY SURE DO.
KIRKMAN & SCOTT
AND THEY'LL JUST SIT AND STARE AT IT, NOT MAKING A SOUND, FOR AS LONG AS IT'S ON!
SHOULD WE HAVE THE CABLE COMPANY DISCONNECT US?
ACTUALLY, I WAS THINKING OF SENDING THEM A FRUIT BASKET AND A THANK-YOU CARD.

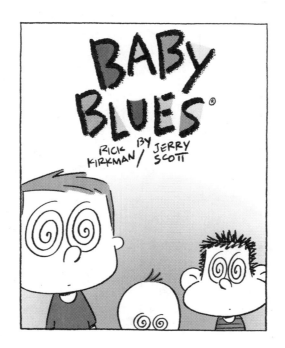

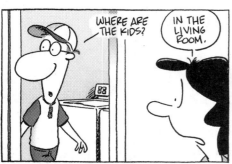

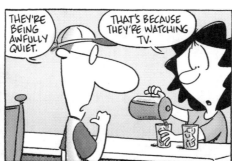

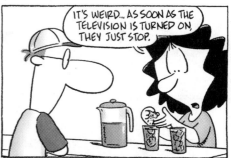

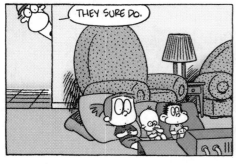

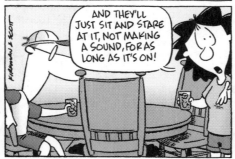

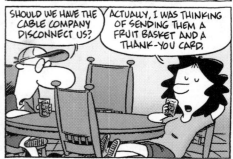

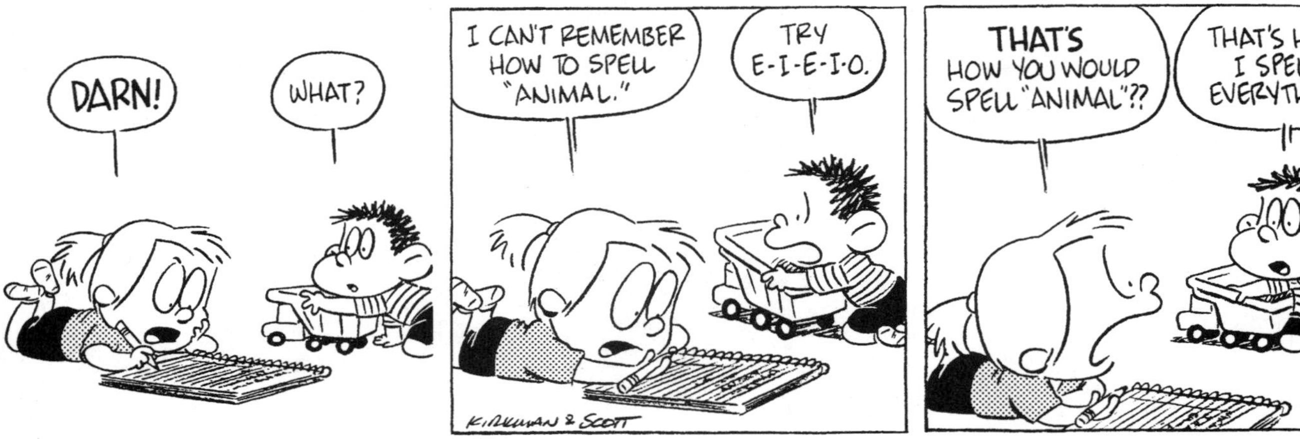
DARN!
WHAT?
I CAN'T REMEMBER HOW TO SPELL "ANIMAL."
TRY E-I-E-I-O.
KIRKMAN & SCOTT
THAT'S HOW YOU WOULD SPELL "ANIMAL"??
THAT'S HOW I SPELL EVERYTHING.

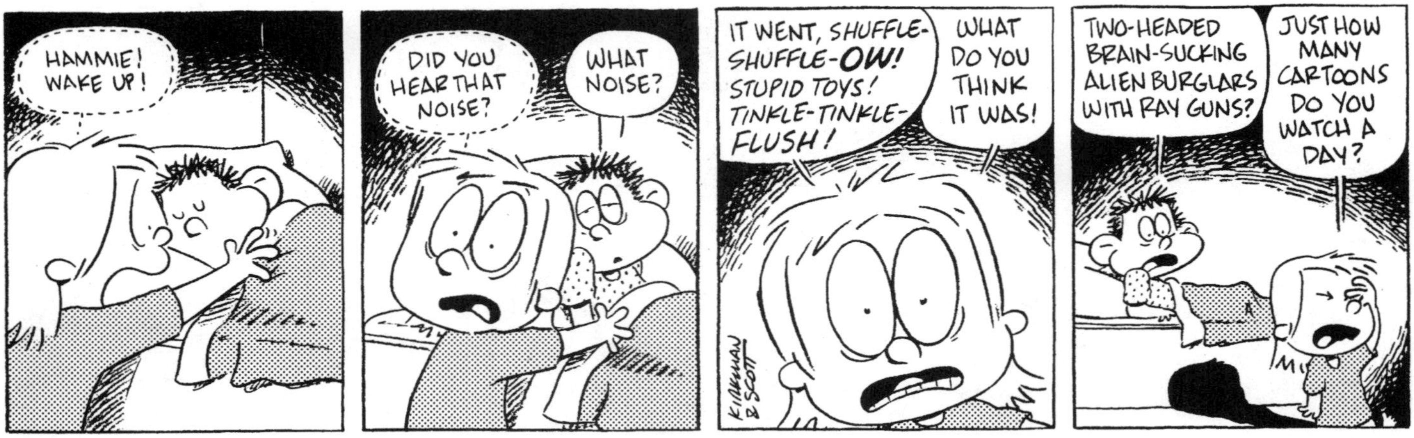
HAMMIE! WAKE UP!
DID YOU HEAR THAT NOISE?
WHAT NOISE?
IT WENT, SHUFFLE-SHUFFLE-OW! STUPID TOYS! TINKLE-TINKLE-FLUSH!
WHAT DO YOU THINK IT WAS!
KIRKMAN & SCOTT
TWO-HEADED BRAIN-SUCKING ALIEN BURGLARS WITH RAY GUNS?
JUST HOW MANY CARTOONS DO YOU WATCH A DAY?

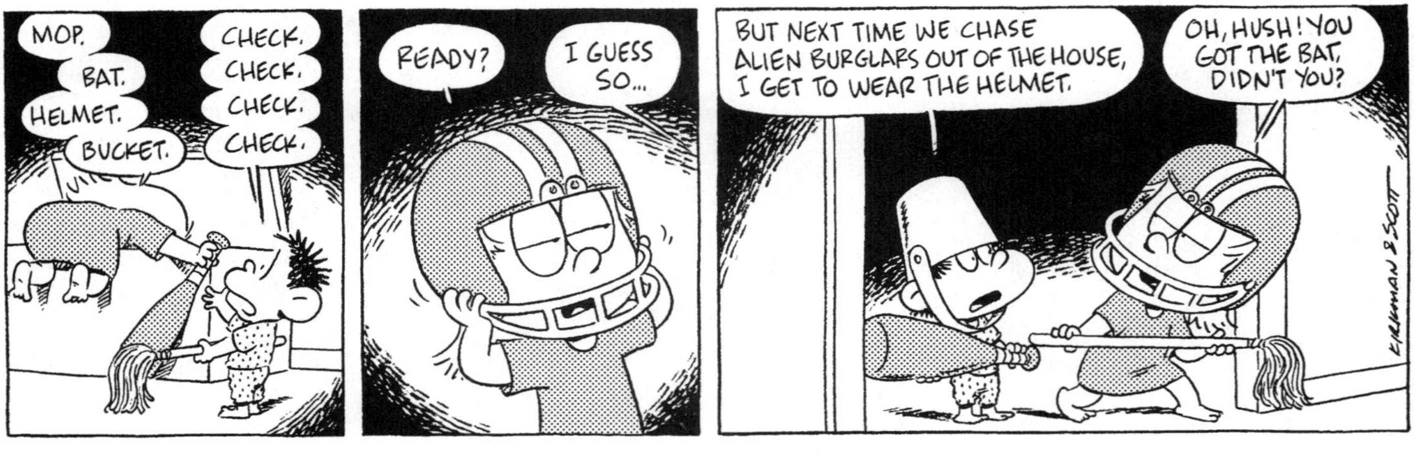
MOP.
BAT.
HELMET.
BUCKET.
CHECK.
CHECK.
CHECK.
CHECK.
READY?
I GUESS SO...
BUT NEXT TIME WE CHASE ALIEN BURGLARS OUT OF THE HOUSE, I GET TO WEAR THE HELMET.
OH, HUSH! YOU GOT THE BAT, DIDN'T YOU?
KIRKMAN & SCOTT

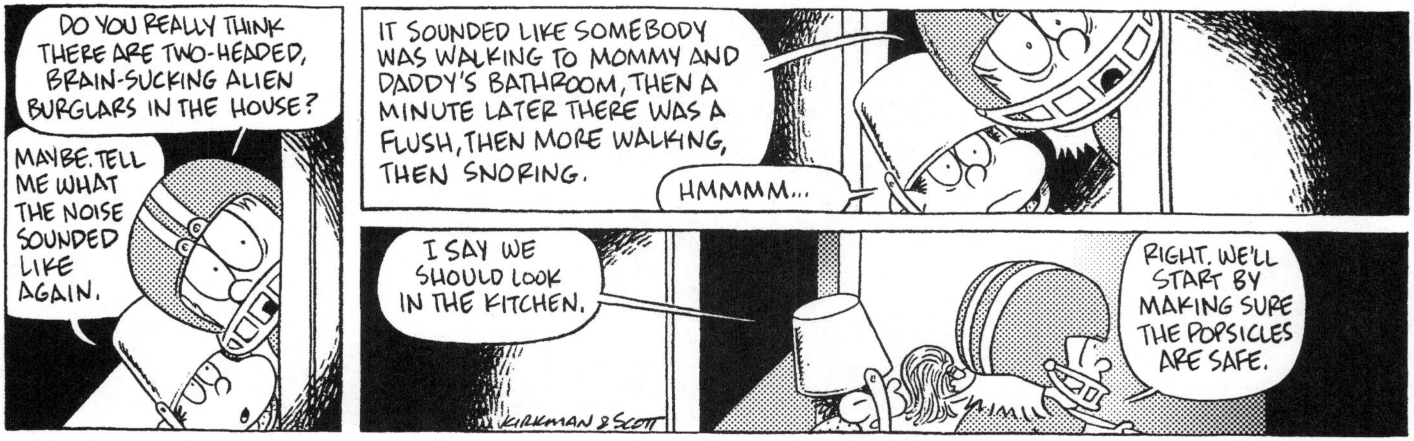
DO YOU REALLY THINK THERE ARE TWO-HEADED, BRAIN-SUCKING ALIEN BURGLARS IN THE HOUSE?
MAYBE. TELL ME WHAT THE NOISE SOUNDED LIKE AGAIN.
IT SOUNDED LIKE SOMEBODY WAS WALKING TO MOMMY AND DADDY'S BATHROOM, THEN A MINUTE LATER THERE WAS A FLUSH, THEN MORE WALKING, THEN SNORING.
HMMMM...
I SAY WE SHOULD LOOK IN THE KITCHEN.
RIGHT. WE'LL START BY MAKING SURE THE POPSICLES ARE SAFE.
KIRKMAN & SCOTT

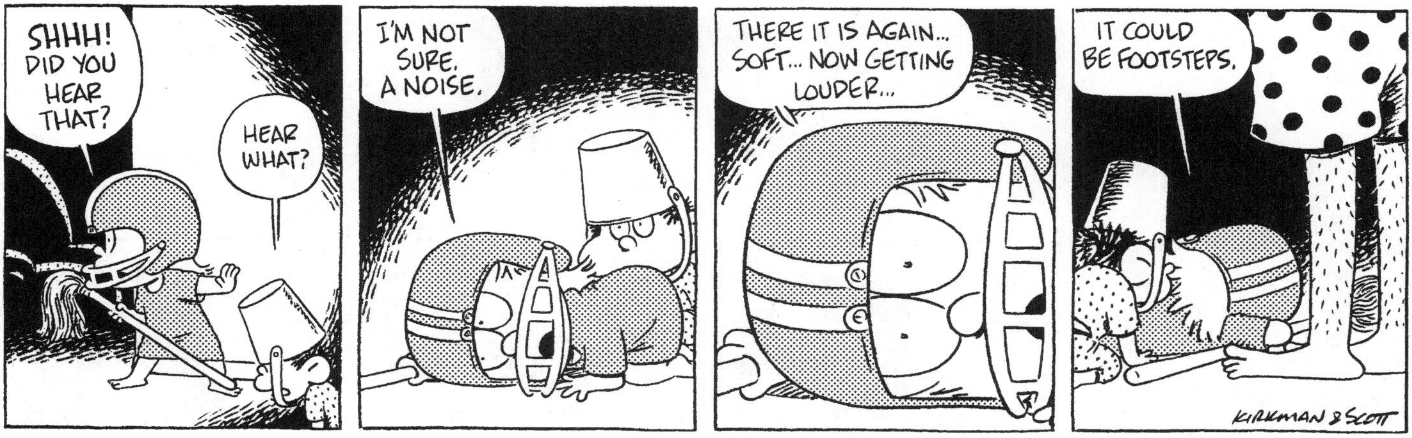
SHHH! DID YOU HEAR THAT?
HEAR WHAT?
I'M NOT SURE. A NOISE.
THERE IT IS AGAIN... SOFT... NOW GETTING LOUDER...
IT COULD BE FOOTSTEPS.
KIRKMAN & SCOTT

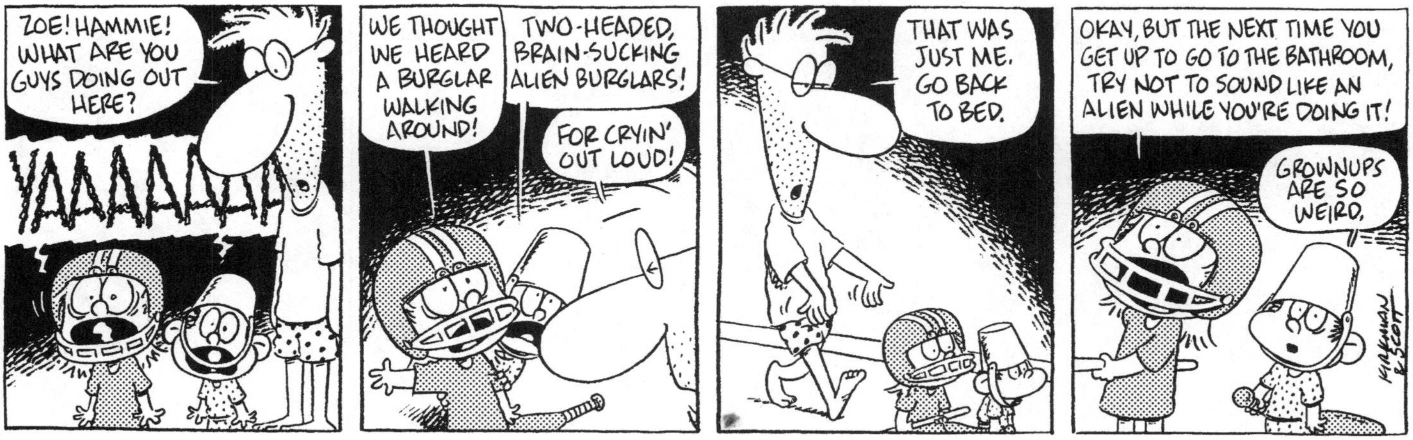
ZOE! HAMMIE! WHAT ARE YOU GUYS DOING OUT HERE?
YAAAAAAA
WE THOUGHT WE HEARD A BURGLAR WALKING AROUND!
TWO-HEADED, BRAIN-SUCKING ALIEN BURGLARS!
FOR CRYIN' OUT LOUD!
THAT WAS JUST ME. GO BACK TO BED.
OKAY, BUT THE NEXT TIME YOU GET UP TO GO TO THE BATHROOM, TRY NOT TO SOUND LIKE AN ALIEN WHILE YOU'RE DOING IT!
GROWNUPS ARE SO WEIRD.
KIRKMAN & SCOTT

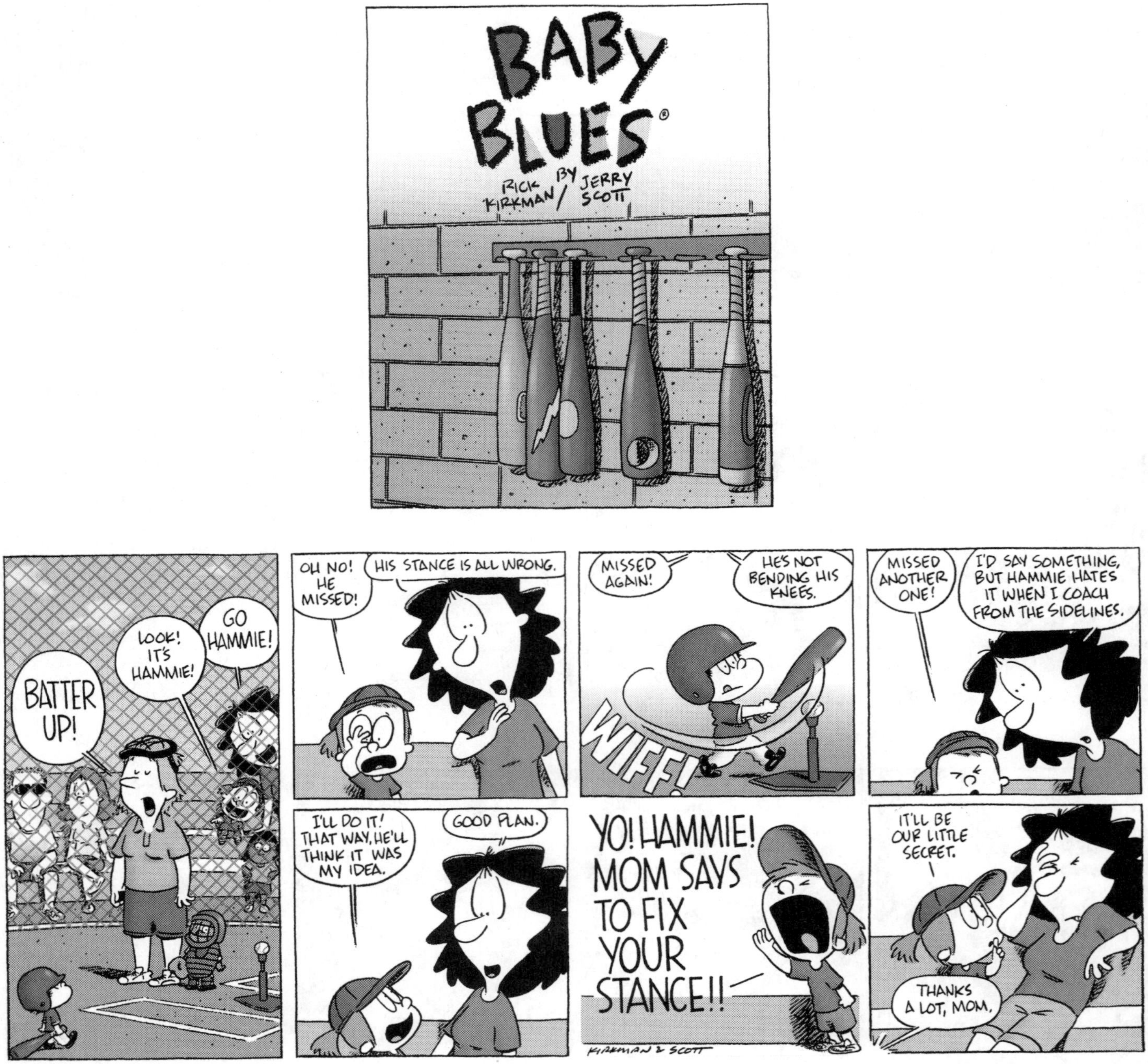
BABY BLUES®
BY RICK KIRKMAN / JERRY SCOTT
BATTER UP!
LOOK! IT'S HAMMIE!
GO HAMMIE!
OH NO! HE MISSED!
HIS STANCE IS ALL WRONG.
MISSED AGAIN!
HE'S NOT BENDING HIS KNEES.
WIFF!
MISSED ANOTHER ONE!
I'D SAY SOMETHING, BUT HAMMIE HATES IT WHEN I COACH FROM THE SIDELINES.
I'LL DO IT! THAT WAY, HE'LL THINK IT WAS MY IDEA.
GOOD PLAN.
YO! HAMMIE! MOM SAYS TO FIX YOUR STANCE!!
IT'LL BE OUR LITTLE SECRET.
THANKS A LOT, MOM.
KIRKMAN & SCOTT

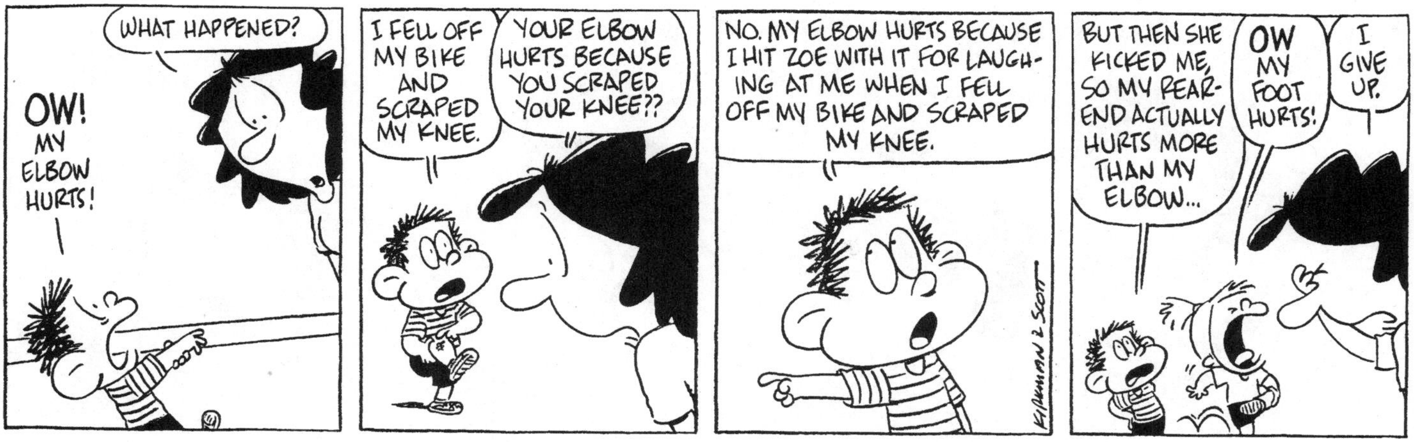
OW! MY ELBOW HURTS!
WHAT HAPPENED?
I FELL OFF MY BIKE AND SCRAPED MY KNEE.
YOUR ELBOW HURTS BECAUSE YOU SCRAPED YOUR KNEE??
NO. MY ELBOW HURTS BECAUSE I HIT ZOE WITH IT FOR LAUGHING AT ME WHEN I FELL OFF MY BIKE AND SCRAPED MY KNEE.
KIRKMAN & SCOTT
BUT THEN SHE KICKED ME, SO MY REAR-END ACTUALLY HURTS MORE THAN MY ELBOW...
OW MY FOOT HURTS!
I GIVE UP.

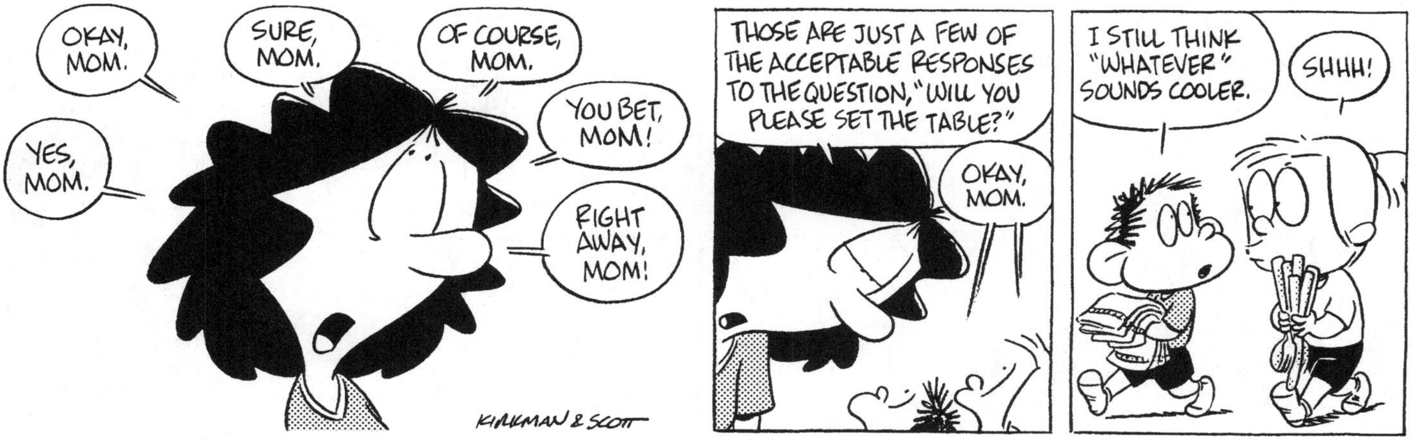
OKAY, MOM.
SURE, MOM.
OF COURSE, MOM.
YES, MOM.
YOU BET, MOM!
RIGHT AWAY, MOM!
KIRKMAN & SCOTT
THOSE ARE JUST A FEW OF THE ACCEPTABLE RESPONSES TO THE QUESTION, "WILL YOU PLEASE SET THE TABLE?"
OKAY, MOM.
I STILL THINK "WHATEVER" SOUNDS COOLER.
SHHH!

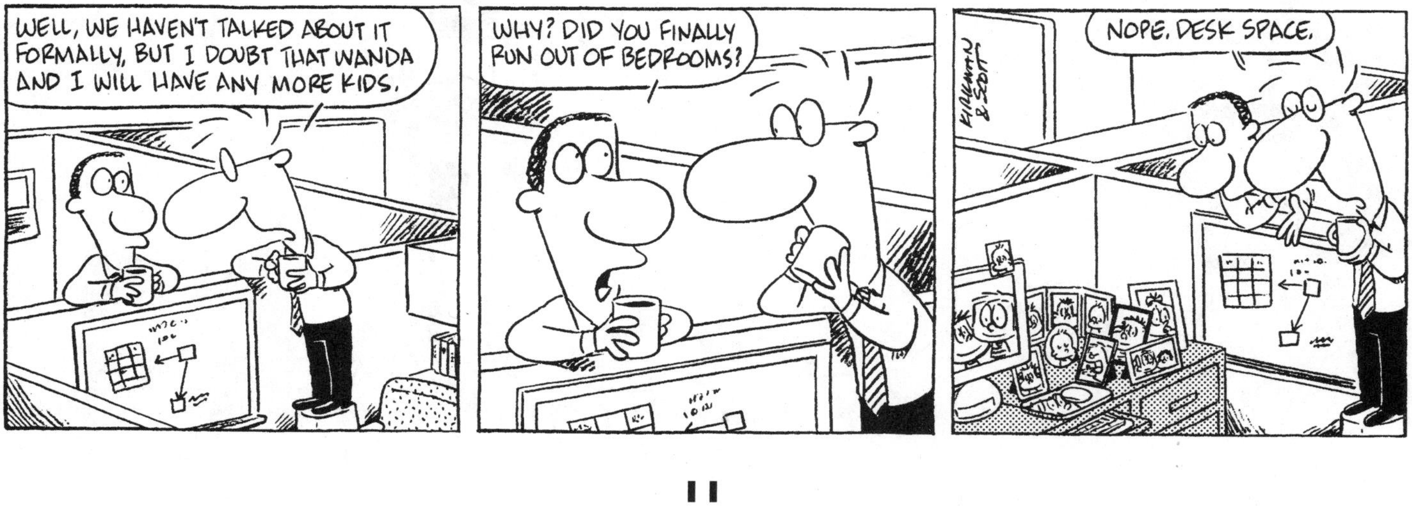
WELL, WE HAVEN'T TALKED ABOUT IT FORMALLY, BUT I DOUBT THAT WANDA AND I WILL HAVE ANY MORE KIDS.
WHY? DID YOU FINALLY RUN OUT OF BEDROOMS?
KIRKMAN & SCOTT
NOPE. DESK SPACE.

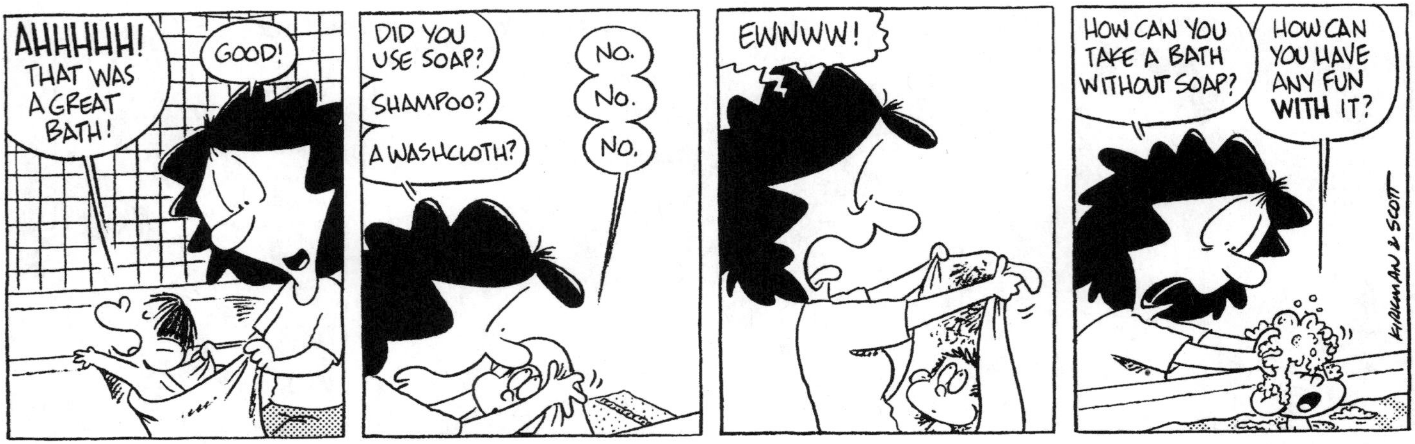
AHHHHH! THAT WAS A GREAT BATH!
GOOD!
DID YOU USE SOAP?
NO.
SHAMPOO?
NO.
A WASHCLOTH?
NO.
EWWWW!
HOW CAN YOU TAKE A BATH WITHOUT SOAP?
HOW CAN YOU HAVE ANY FUN WITH IT?
KIRKMAN & SCOTT

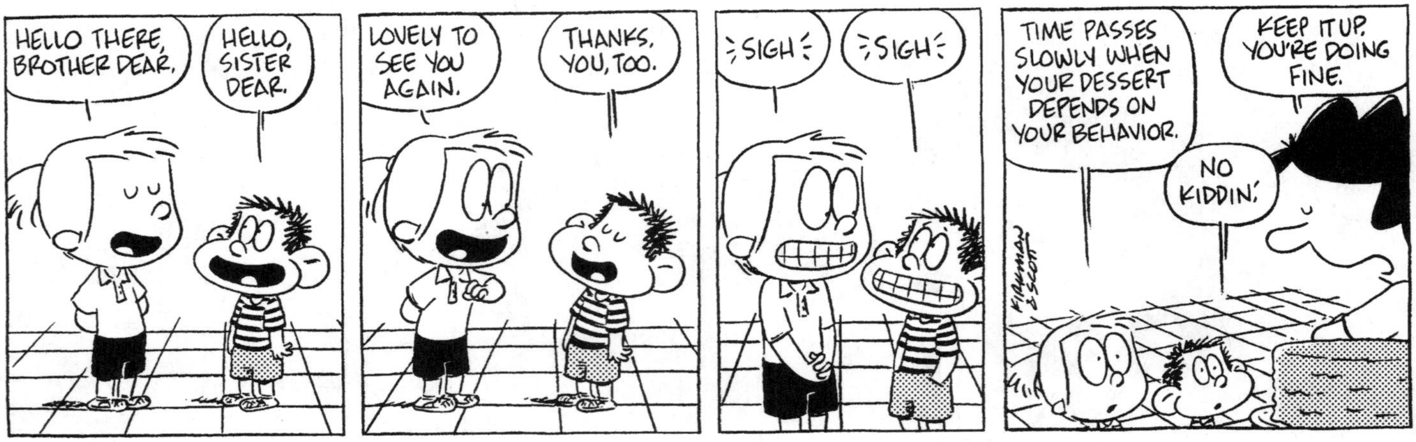
HELLO THERE, BROTHER DEAR.
HELLO, SISTER DEAR.
LOVELY TO SEE YOU AGAIN.
THANKS. YOU, TOO.
SIGH
SIGH
KIRKMAN & SCOTT
TIME PASSES SLOWLY WHEN YOUR DESSERT DEPENDS ON YOUR BEHAVIOR.
KEEP IT UP. YOU'RE DOING FINE.
NO KIDDIN'.

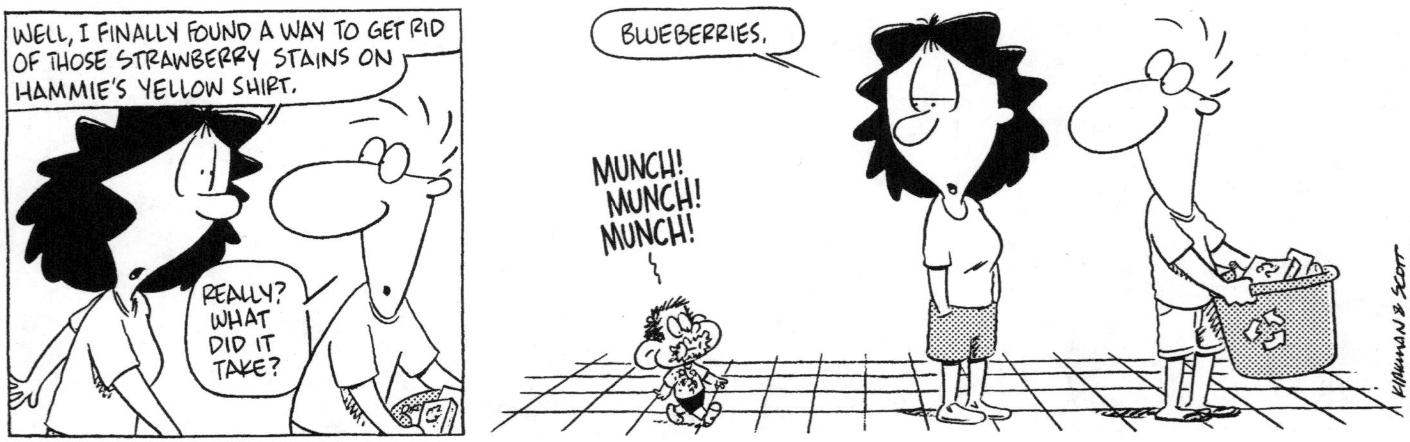
WELL, I FINALLY FOUND A WAY TO GET RID OF THOSE STRAWBERRY STAINS ON HAMMIE'S YELLOW SHIRT.
REALLY? WHAT DID IT TAKE?
BLUEBERRIES.
MUNCH! MUNCH! MUNCH!
KIRKMAN & SCOTT

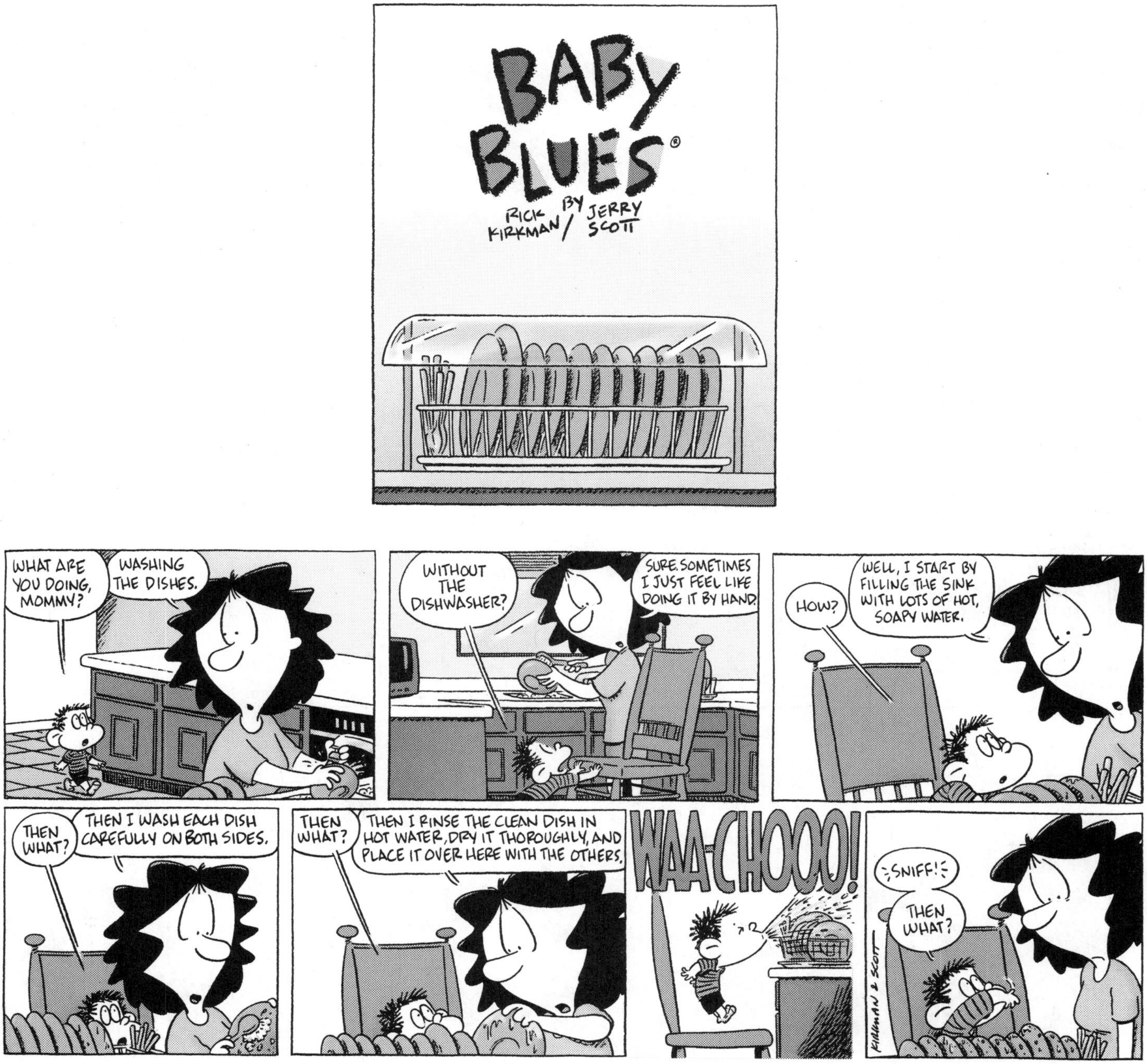
BABY BLUES®
BY RICK KIRKMAN / JERRY SCOTT
WHAT ARE YOU DOING, MOMMY?
WASHING THE DISHES.
WITHOUT THE DISHWASHER?
SURE. SOMETIMES I JUST FEEL LIKE DOING IT BY HAND.
HOW?
WELL, I START BY FILLING THE SINK WITH LOTS OF HOT, SOAPY WATER.
THEN WHAT?
THEN I WASH EACH DISH CAREFULLY ON BOTH SIDES.
THEN WHAT?
THEN I RINSE THE CLEAN DISH IN HOT WATER, DRY IT THOROUGHLY, AND PLACE IT OVER HERE WITH THE OTHERS.
WAA-CHOOO!
KIRKMAN & SCOTT
SNIFF!
THEN WHAT?

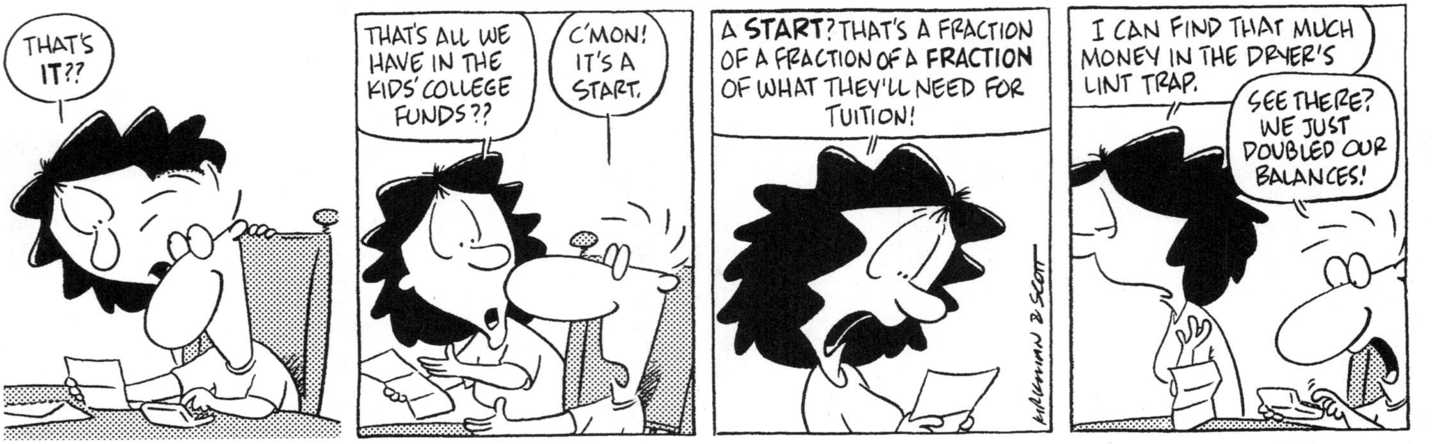
THAT'S IT??
THAT'S ALL WE HAVE IN THE KIDS' COLLEGE FUNDS??
C'MON! IT'S A START.
A START? THAT'S A FRACTION OF A FRACTION OF A FRACTION OF WHAT THEY'LL NEED FOR TUITION!
KIRKMAN & SCOTT
I CAN FIND THAT MUCH MONEY IN THE DRYER'S LINT TRAP.
SEE THERE? WE JUST DOUBLED OUR BALANCES!

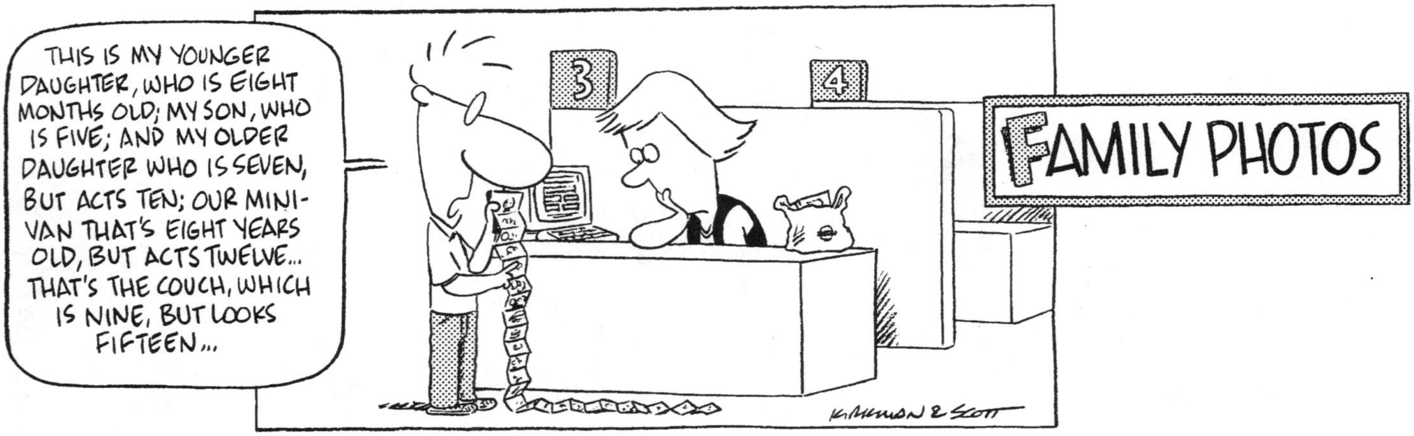
FAMILY PHOTOS
THIS IS MY YOUNGER DAUGHTER, WHO IS EIGHT MONTHS OLD; MY SON, WHO IS FIVE; AND MY OLDER DAUGHTER WHO IS SEVEN, BUT ACTS TEN; OUR MINI-VAN THAT'S EIGHT YEARS OLD, BUT ACTS TWELVE... THAT'S THE COUCH, WHICH IS NINE, BUT LOOKS FIFTEEN...
3
4
KIRKMAN & SCOTT

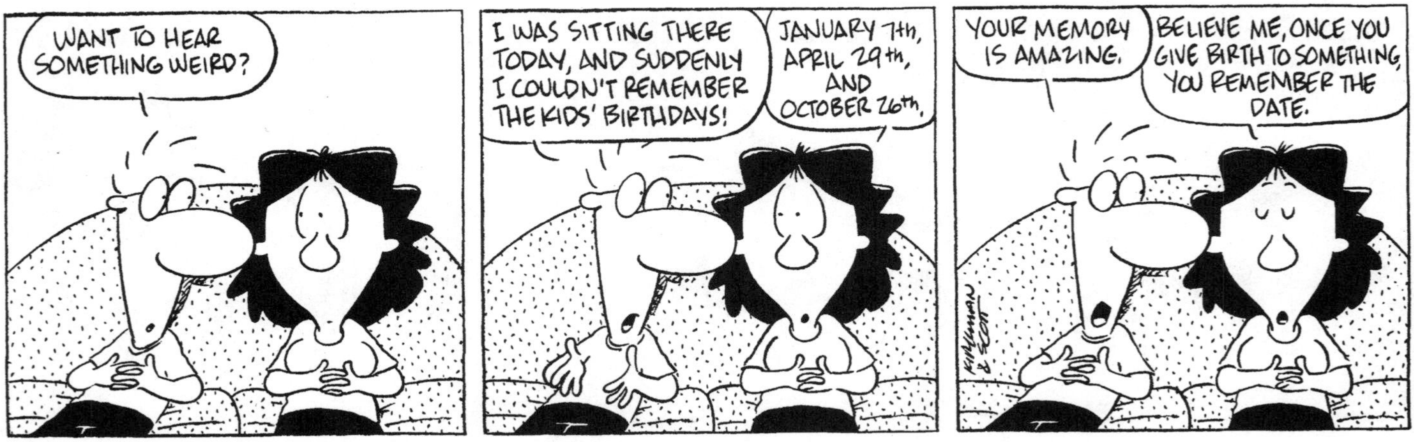
WANT TO HEAR SOMETHING WEIRD?
I WAS SITTING THERE TODAY, AND SUDDENLY I COULDN'T REMEMBER THE KIDS' BIRTHDAYS!
JANUARY 7th, APRIL 29th, AND OCTOBER 26th.
YOUR MEMORY IS AMAZING.
BELIEVE ME, ONCE YOU GIVE BIRTH TO SOMETHING, YOU REMEMBER THE DATE.
KIRKMAN & SCOTT

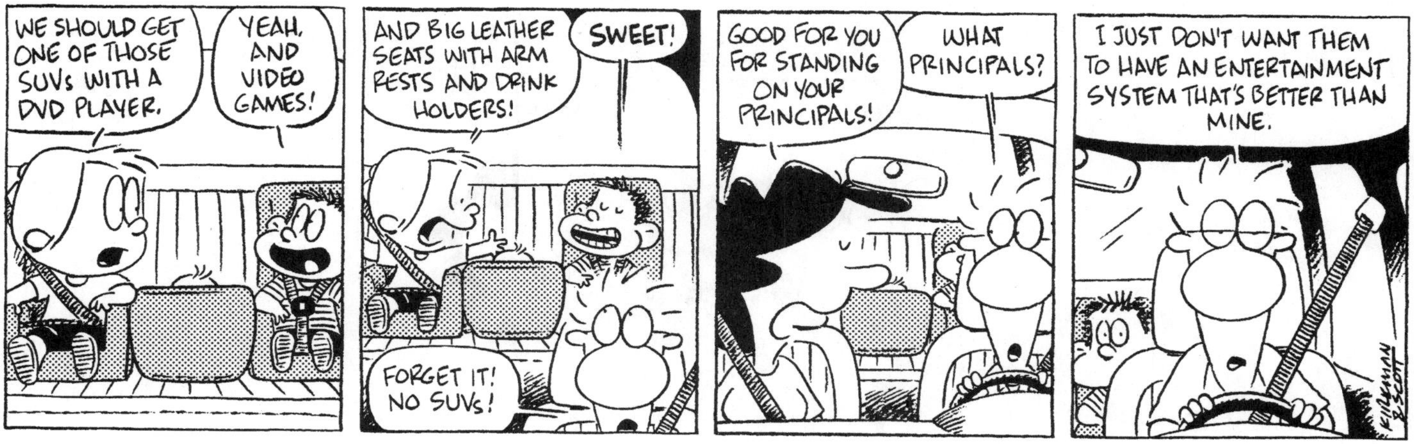
WE SHOULD GET ONE OF THOSE SUVs WITH A DVD PLAYER.
YEAH, AND VIDEO GAMES!
AND BIG LEATHER SEATS WITH ARM RESTS AND DRINK HOLDERS!
SWEET!
FORGET IT! NO SUVs!
GOOD FOR YOU FOR STANDING ON YOUR PRINCIPALS!
WHAT PRINCIPALS?
I JUST DON'T WANT THEM TO HAVE AN ENTERTAINMENT SYSTEM THAT'S BETTER THAN MINE.

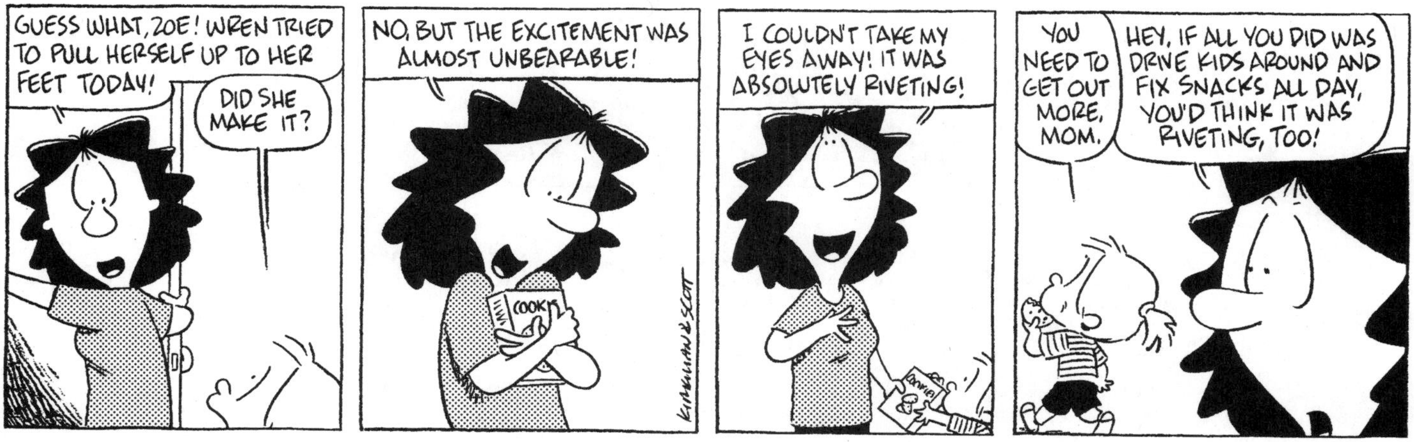
GUESS WHAT, ZOE! WREN TRIED TO PULL HERSELF UP TO HER FEET TODAY!
DID SHE MAKE IT?
NO, BUT THE EXCITEMENT WAS ALMOST UNBEARABLE!
I COULDN'T TAKE MY EYES AWAY! IT WAS ABSOLUTELY RIVETING!
YOU NEED TO GET OUT MORE, MOM.
HEY, IF ALL YOU DID WAS DRIVE KIDS AROUND AND FIX SNACKS ALL DAY, YOU'D THINK IT WAS RIVETING, TOO!

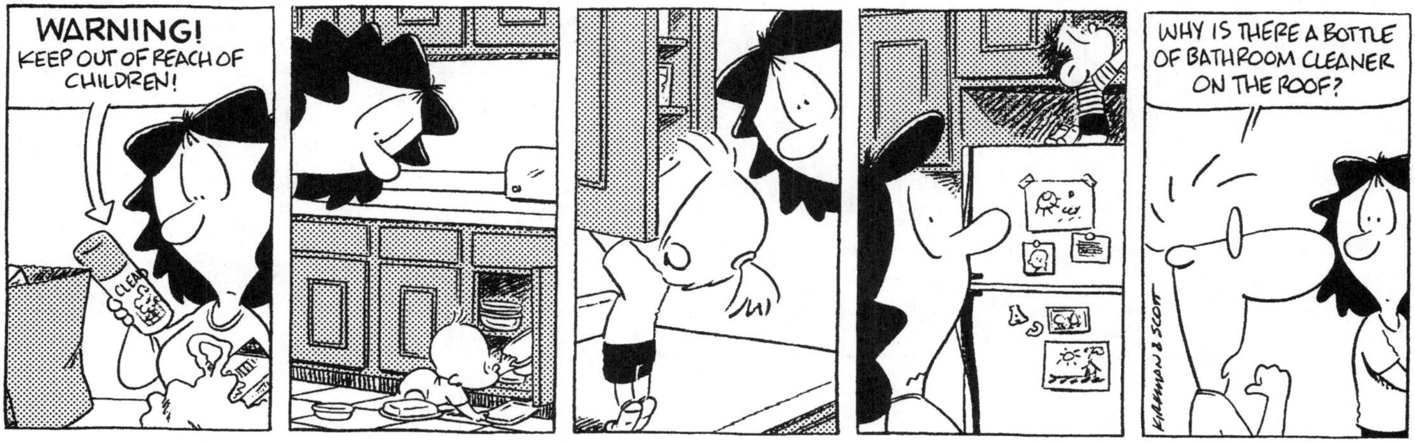
WARNING!
KEEP OUT OF REACH OF CHILDREN!
WHY IS THERE A BOTTLE OF BATHROOM CLEANER ON THE ROOF?

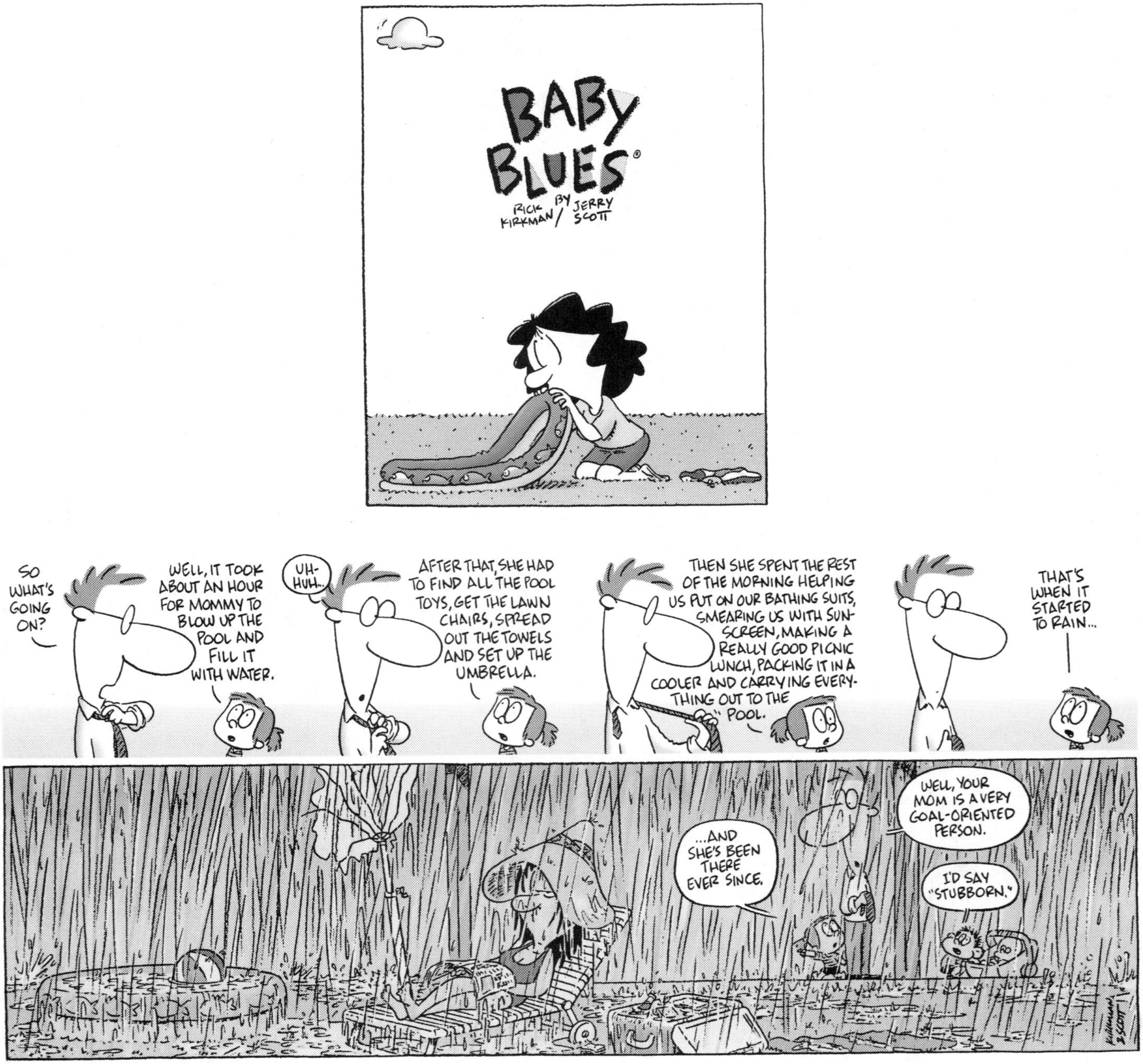
BABY BLUES®
BY RICK KIRKMAN / JERRY SCOTT
SO WHAT'S GOING ON?
WELL, IT TOOK ABOUT AN HOUR FOR MOMMY TO BLOW UP THE POOL AND FILL IT WITH WATER.
UH-HUH...
AFTER THAT, SHE HAD TO FIND ALL THE POOL TOYS, GET THE LAWN CHAIRS, SPREAD OUT THE TOWELS AND SET UP THE UMBRELLA.
THEN SHE SPENT THE REST OF THE MORNING HELPING US PUT ON OUR BATHING SUITS, SMEARING US WITH SUN-SCREEN, MAKING A REALLY GOOD PICNIC LUNCH, PACKING IT IN A COOLER AND CARRYING EVERY-THING OUT TO THE POOL.
THAT'S WHEN IT STARTED TO RAIN...
...AND SHE'S BEEN THERE EVER SINCE.
WELL, YOUR MOM IS A VERY GOAL-ORIENTED PERSON.
I'D SAY "STUBBORN."

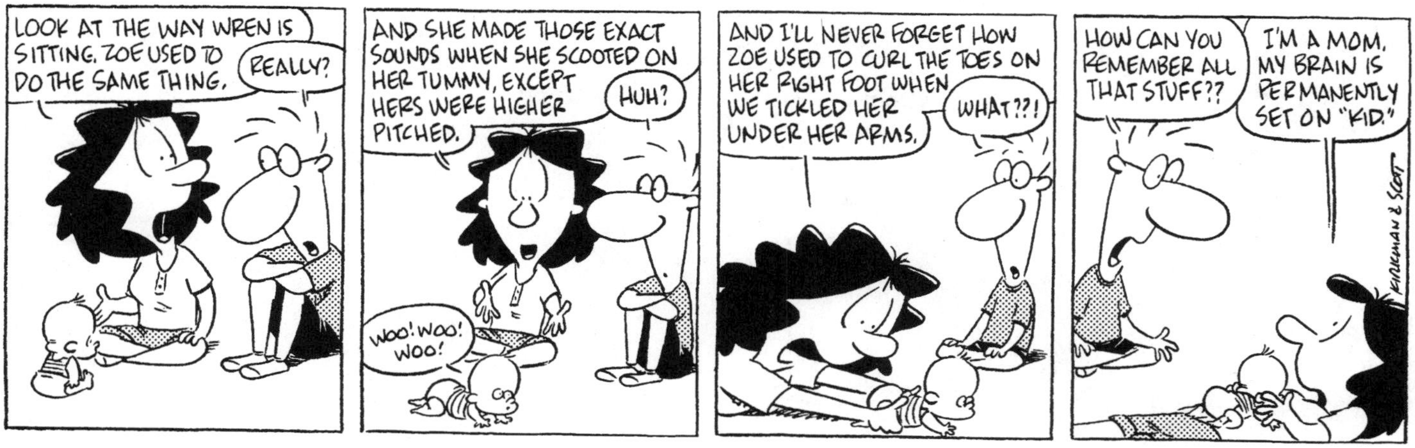
LOOK AT THE WAY WREN IS SITTING. ZOE USED TO DO THE SAME THING.
REALLY?
AND SHE MADE THOSE EXACT SOUNDS WHEN SHE SCOOTED ON HER TUMMY, EXCEPT HERS WERE HIGHER PITCHED.
HUH?
WOO! WOO! WOO!
AND I'LL NEVER FORGET HOW ZOE USED TO CURL THE TOES ON HER RIGHT FOOT WHEN WE TICKLED HER UNDER HER ARMS.
WHAT??!
HOW CAN YOU REMEMBER ALL THAT STUFF??
I'M A MOM. MY BRAIN IS PERMANENTLY SET ON "KID."
KIRKMAN & SCOTT

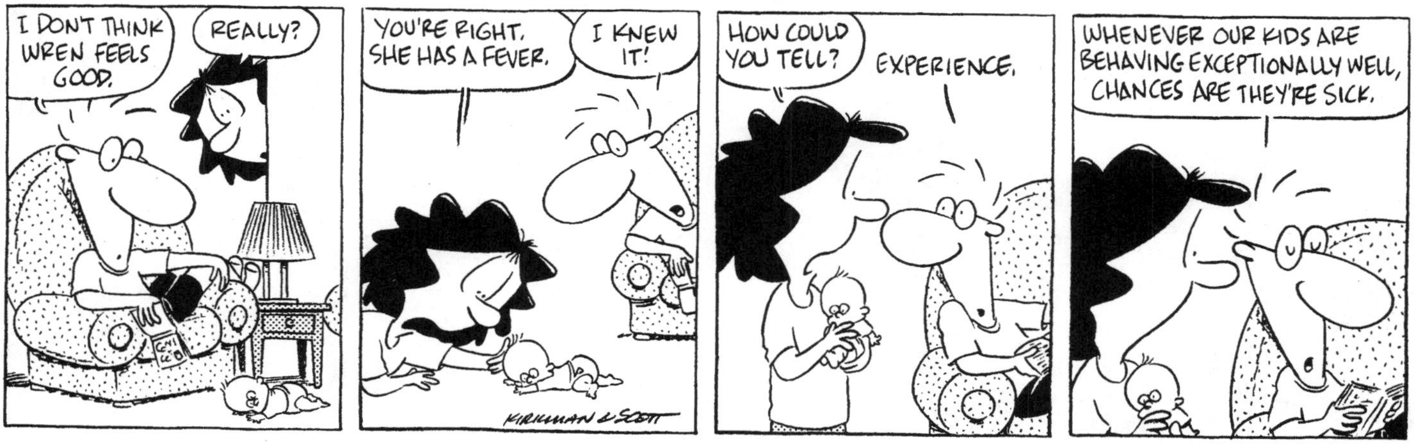
I DON'T THINK WREN FEELS GOOD.
REALLY?
YOU'RE RIGHT. SHE HAS A FEVER.
I KNEW IT!
KIRKMAN & SCOTT
HOW COULD YOU TELL?
EXPERIENCE.
WHENEVER OUR KIDS ARE BEHAVING EXCEPTIONALLY WELL, CHANCES ARE THEY'RE SICK.

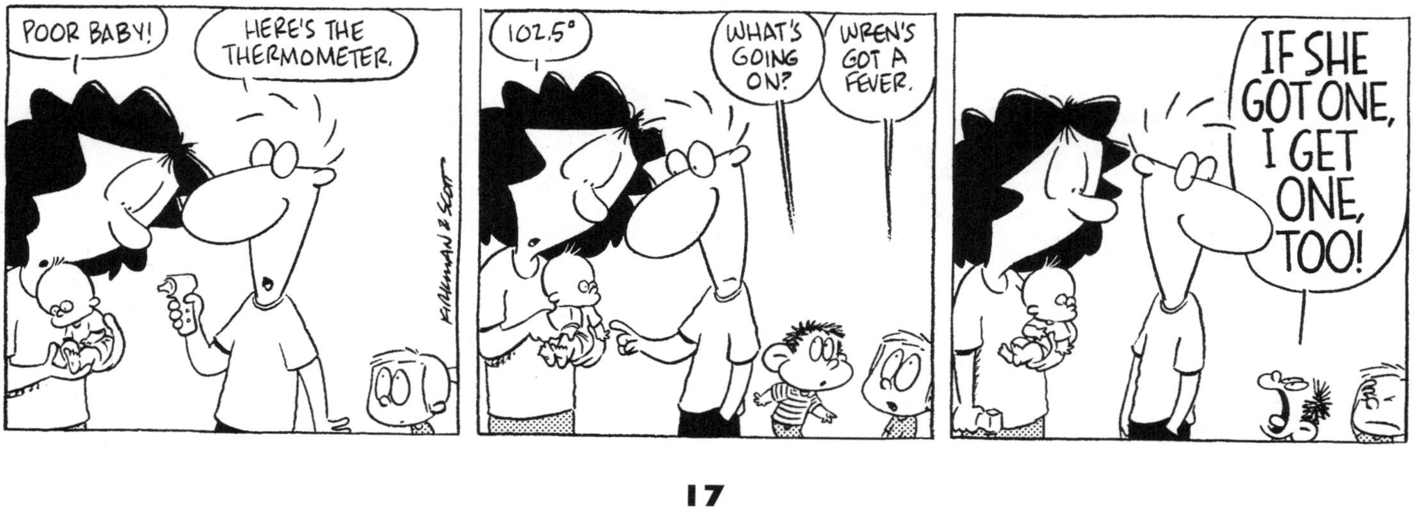
POOR BABY!
HERE'S THE THERMOMETER.
KIRKMAN & SCOTT
102.5°
WHAT'S GOING ON?
WREN'S GOT A FEVER.
IF SHE GOT ONE, I GET ONE, TOO!

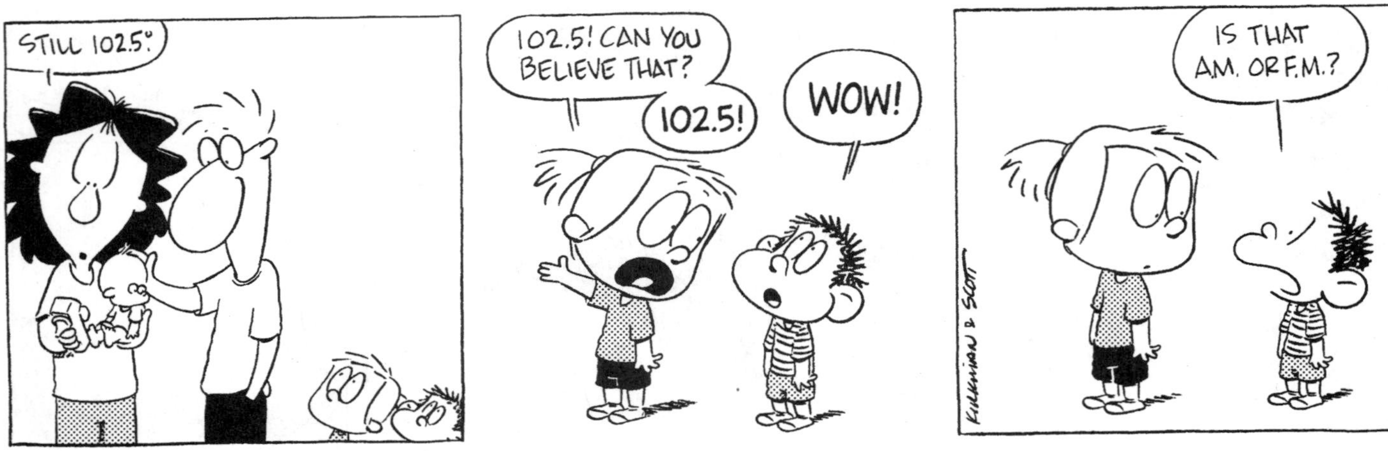
STILL 102.5°
102.5! CAN YOU BELIEVE THAT?
102.5!
WOW!
IS THAT A.M. OR F.M.?
KIRKMAN & SCOTT

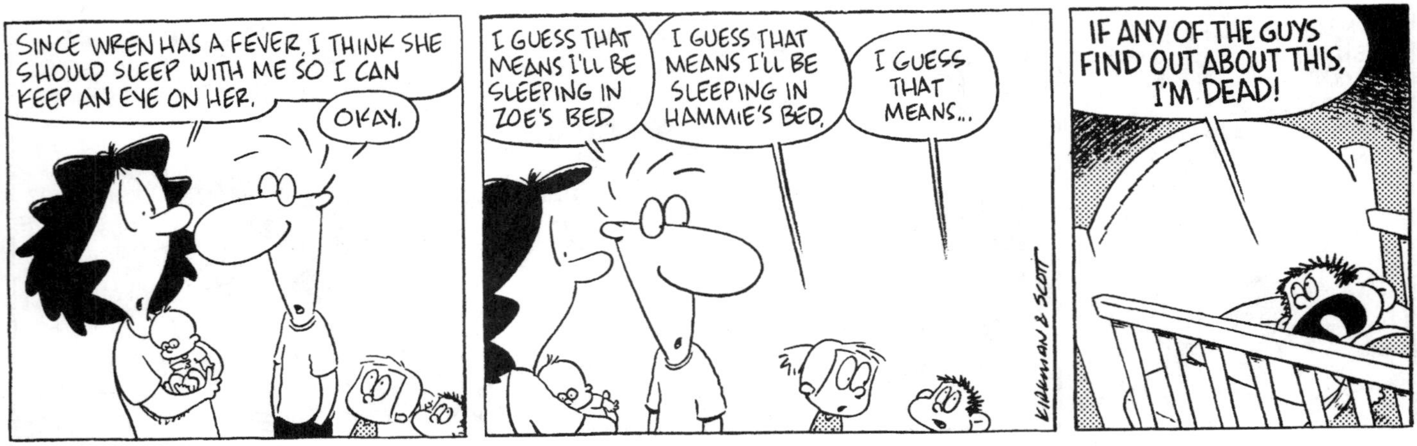
SINCE WREN HAS A FEVER, I THINK SHE SHOULD SLEEP WITH ME SO I CAN KEEP AN EYE ON HER.
OKAY.
I GUESS THAT MEANS I'LL BE SLEEPING IN ZOE'S BED.
I GUESS THAT MEANS I'LL BE SLEEPING IN HAMMIE'S BED.
I GUESS THAT MEANS...
KIRKMAN & SCOTT
IF ANY OF THE GUYS FIND OUT ABOUT THIS, I'M DEAD!

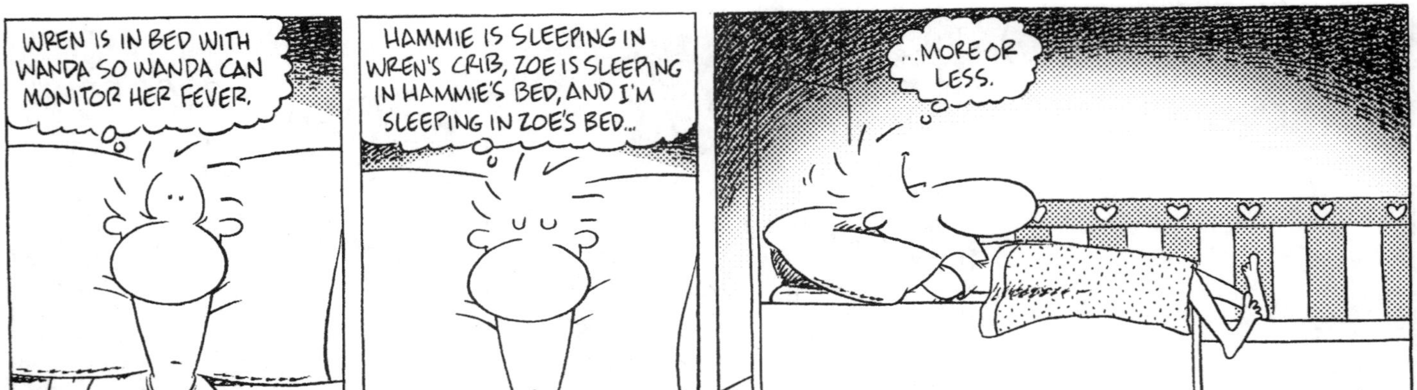
WREN IS IN BED WITH WANDA SO WANDA CAN MONITOR HER FEVER.
HAMMIE IS SLEEPING IN WREN'S CRIB, ZOE IS SLEEPING IN HAMMIE'S BED, AND I'M SLEEPING IN ZOE'S BED...
...MORE OR LESS.
KIRKMAN & SCOTT

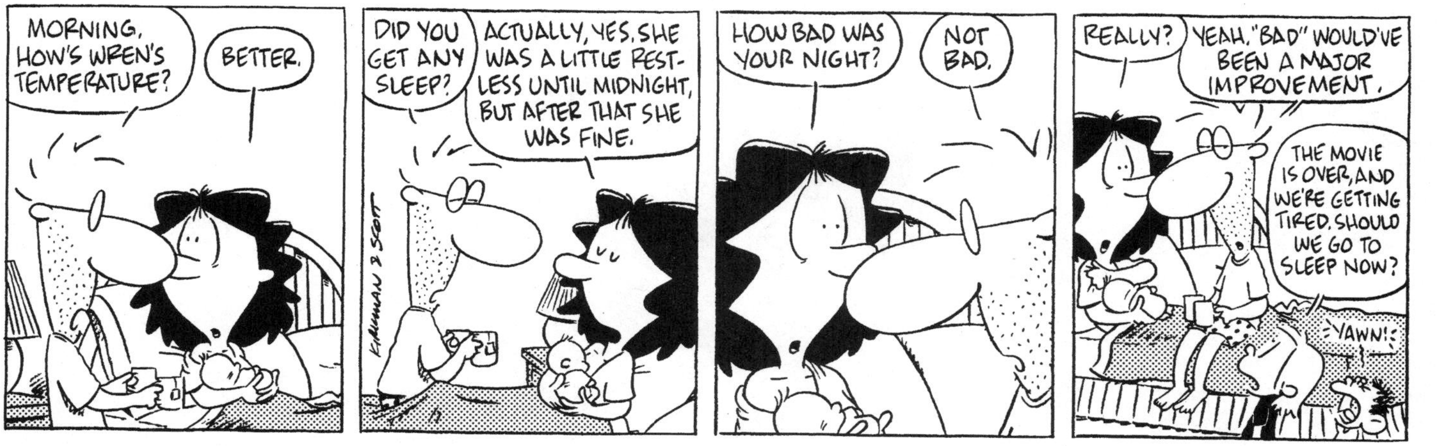
MORNING. HOW'S WREN'S TEMPERATURE?
BETTER.
DID YOU GET ANY SLEEP?
ACTUALLY, YES. SHE WAS A LITTLE REST-LESS UNTIL MIDNIGHT, BUT AFTER THAT SHE WAS FINE.
KIRKMAN & SCOTT
HOW BAD WAS YOUR NIGHT?
NOT BAD.
REALLY?
YEAH. "BAD" WOULD'VE BEEN A MAJOR IMPROVEMENT.
THE MOVIE IS OVER, AND WE'RE GETTING TIRED. SHOULD WE GO TO SLEEP NOW?
YAWN!

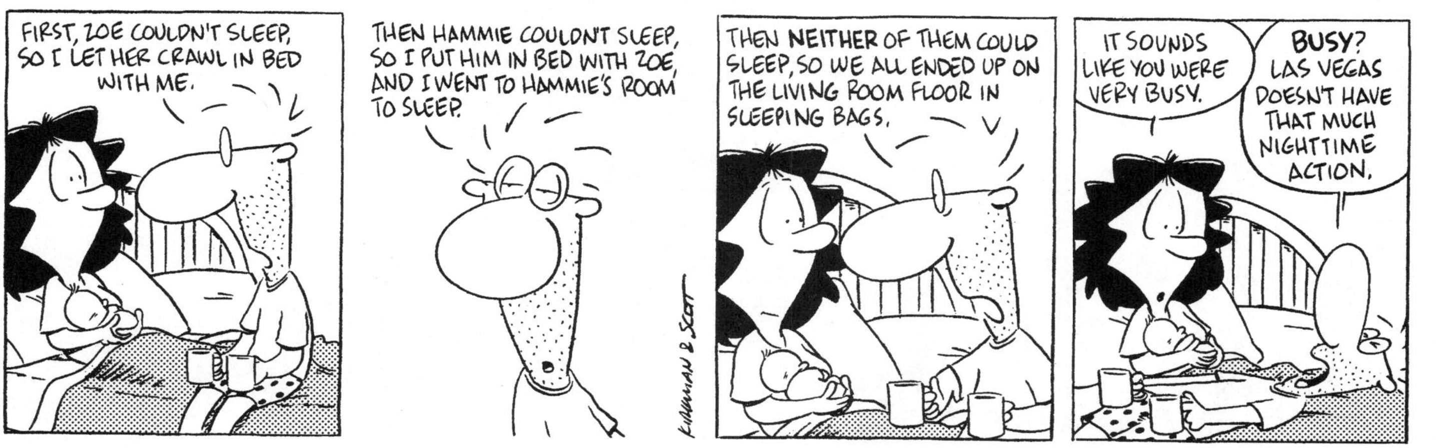
FIRST, ZOE COULDN'T SLEEP, SO I LET HER CRAWL IN BED WITH ME.
THEN HAMMIE COULDN'T SLEEP, SO I PUT HIM IN BED WITH ZOE, AND I WENT TO HAMMIE'S ROOM TO SLEEP.
KIRKMAN & SCOTT
THEN **NEITHER** OF THEM COULD SLEEP, SO WE ALL ENDED UP ON THE LIVING ROOM FLOOR IN SLEEPING BAGS.
IT SOUNDS LIKE YOU WERE VERY BUSY.
BUSY? LAS VEGAS DOESN'T HAVE THAT MUCH NIGHTTIME ACTION.

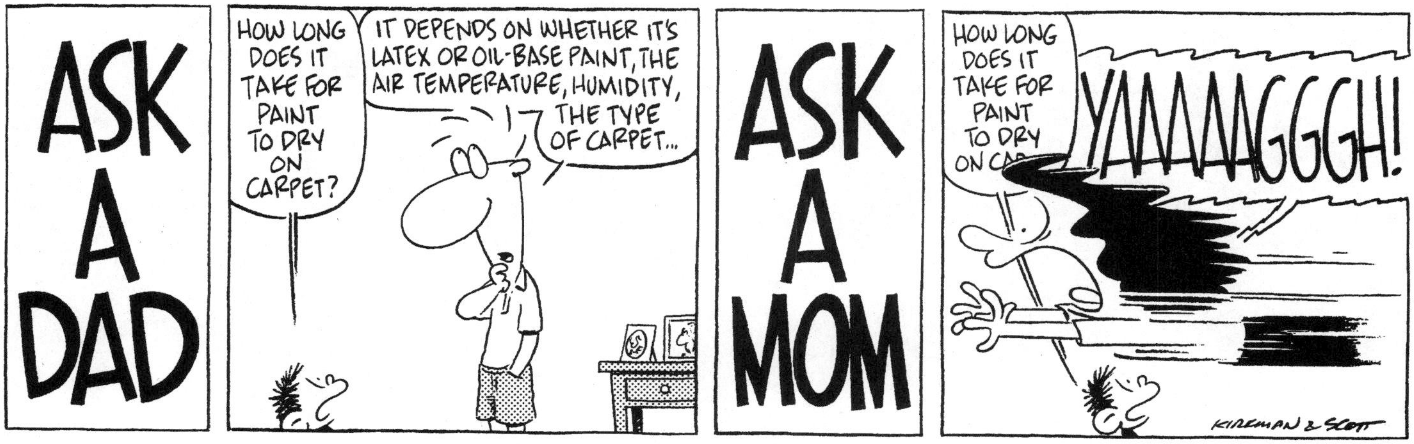
ASK A DAD
HOW LONG DOES IT TAKE FOR PAINT TO DRY ON CARPET?
IT DEPENDS ON WHETHER IT'S LATEX OR OIL-BASE PAINT, THE AIR TEMPERATURE, HUMIDITY, THE TYPE OF CARPET...
ASK A MOM
HOW LONG DOES IT TAKE FOR PAINT TO DRY ON CA
YAAAAAGGGH!
KIRKMAN & SCOTT

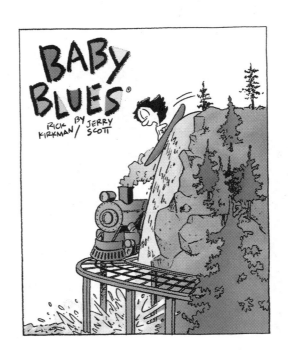

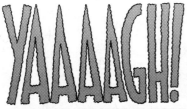

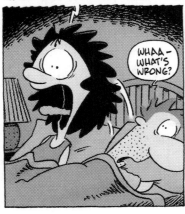

BABY BLUES®
BY RICK KIRKMAN / JERRY SCOTT

YAAAAGH!
WHAA-WHAT'S WRONG?
UNH! I HAD THAT DREAM AGAIN!
THE ONE WHERE YOU TUMBLE OVER A HUGE WATERFALL IN A CANOE?
NO.
THE ONE WHERE YOU NARROWLY AVOID A COLLISION WITH A SPEEDING FREIGHT TRAIN?
NO.
THE ONE WHERE YOU FIND YOURSELF NAKED IN A ROOMFUL OF PEOPLE?
NO. WORSE THAN THAT.
IT WAS THE ONE WHERE I GIVE UP MY CAREER TO BECOME A STAY-AT-HOME MOM WITH THREE UNGRATEFUL KIDS, A BIG MORTGAGE, FLABBY THIGHS, AND NO TIME TO MYSELF.
IT ALL SEEMED SO REAL!
WHAT SEEMED SO REAL?
SHHH! NOTHING... MOMMY JUST NEEDS A LITTLE MORE SLEEP.

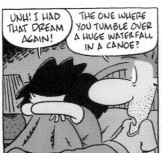

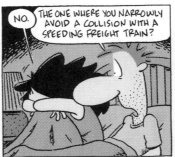

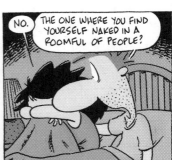

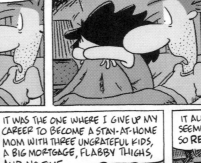

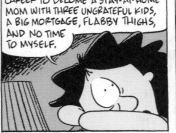

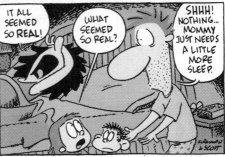

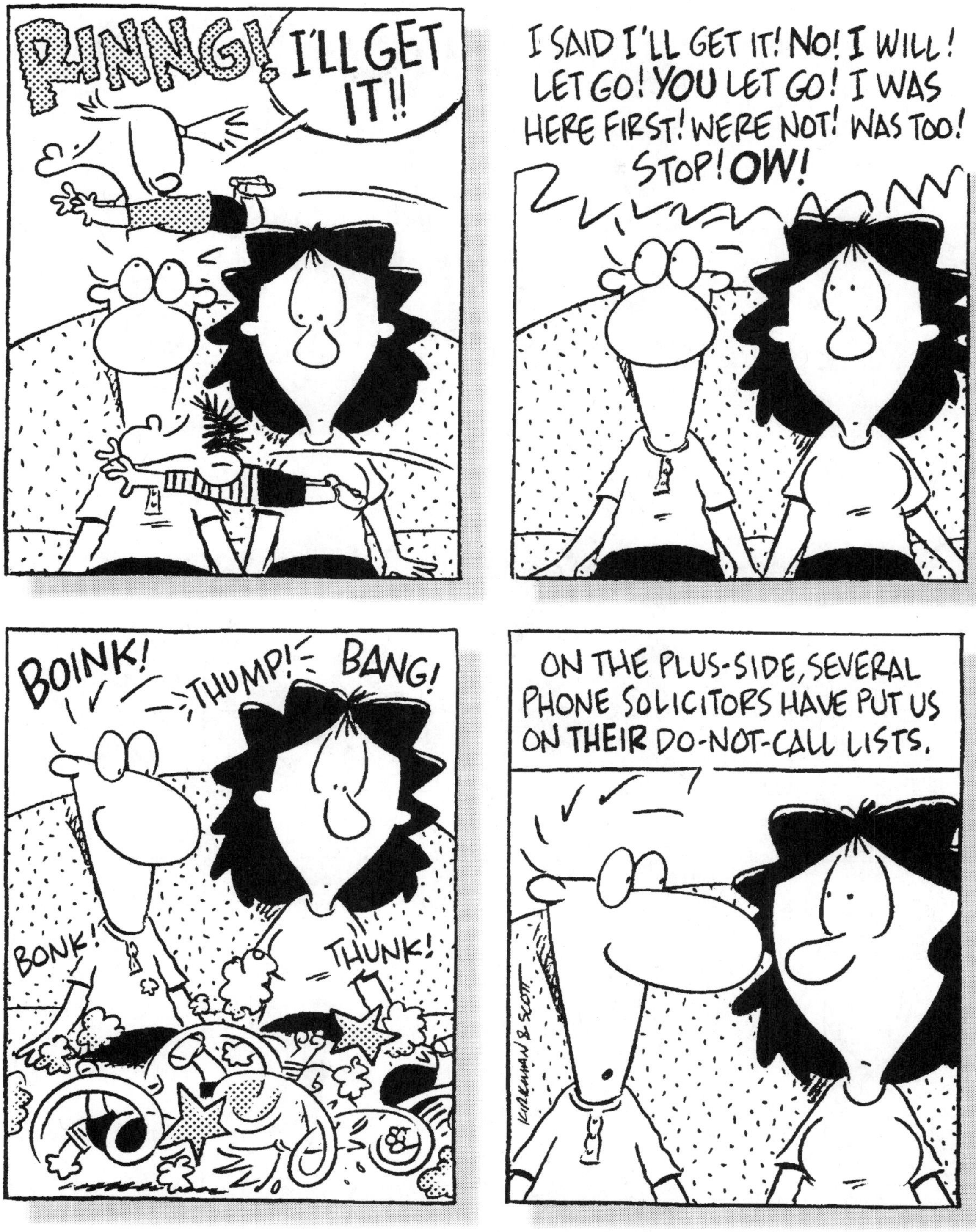
RINNG!
I'LL GET IT!!
I SAID I'LL GET IT! NO! I WILL! LET GO! YOU LET GO! I WAS HERE FIRST! WERE NOT! WAS TOO! STOP! OW!
BOINK!
THUMP!
BANG!
BONK!
THUNK!
ON THE PLUS-SIDE, SEVERAL PHONE SOLICITORS HAVE PUT US ON THEIR DO-NOT-CALL LISTS.
KIRKMAN & SCOTT

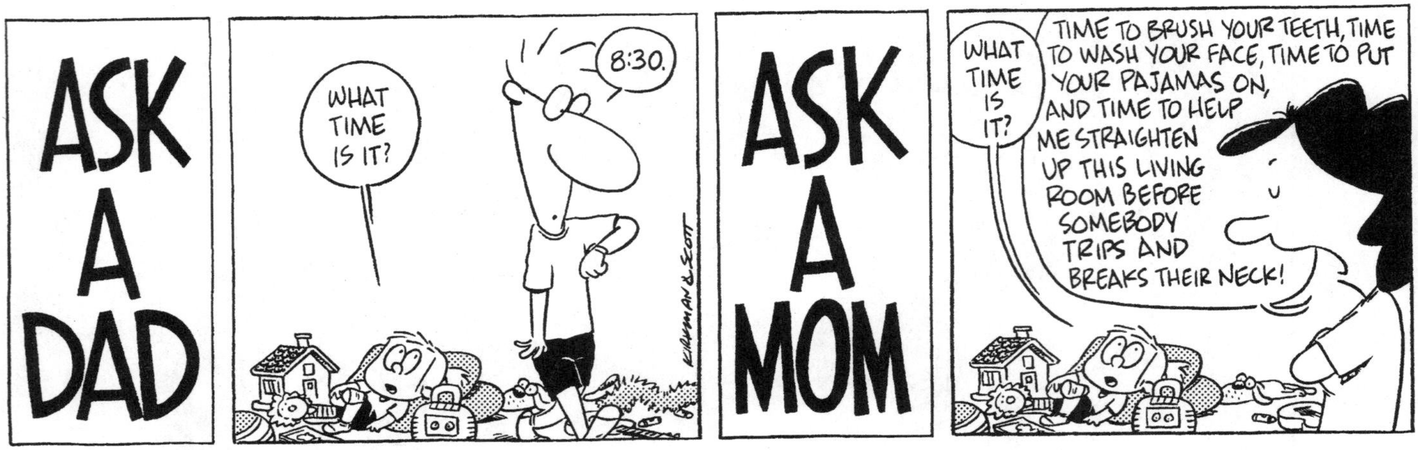
ASK A DAD
WHAT TIME IS IT?
8:30.
KIRKMAN & SCOTT
ASK A MOM
WHAT TIME IS IT?
TIME TO BRUSH YOUR TEETH, TIME TO WASH YOUR FACE, TIME TO PUT YOUR PAJAMAS ON, AND TIME TO HELP ME STRAIGHTEN UP THIS LIVING ROOM BEFORE SOMEBODY TRIPS AND BREAKS THEIR NECK!

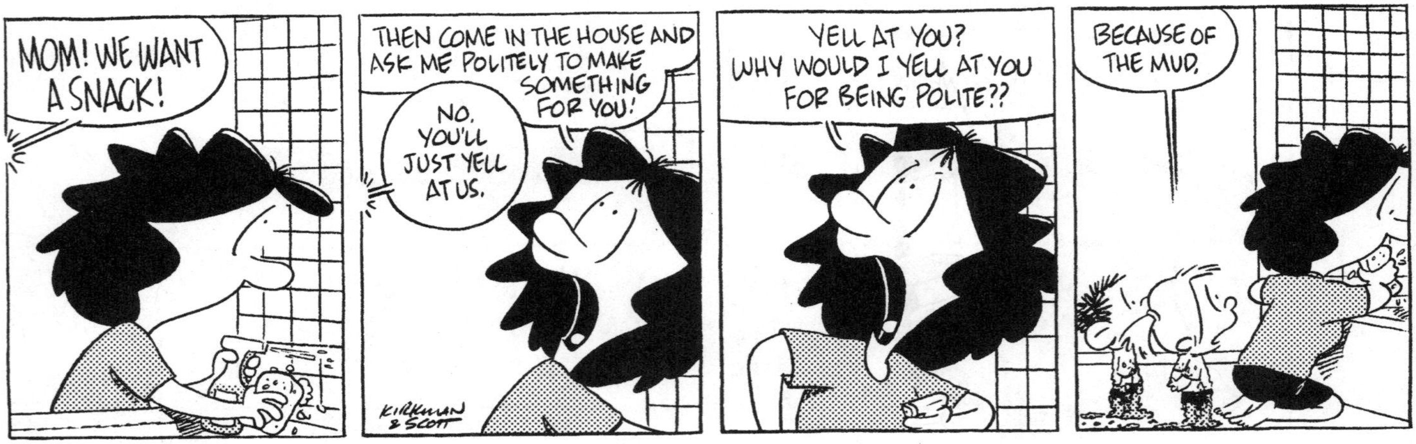
MOM! WE WANT A SNACK!
THEN COME IN THE HOUSE AND ASK ME POLITELY TO MAKE SOMETHING FOR YOU!
NO. YOU'LL JUST YELL AT US.
KIRKMAN & SCOTT
YELL AT YOU? WHY WOULD I YELL AT YOU FOR BEING POLITE??
BECAUSE OF THE MUD.

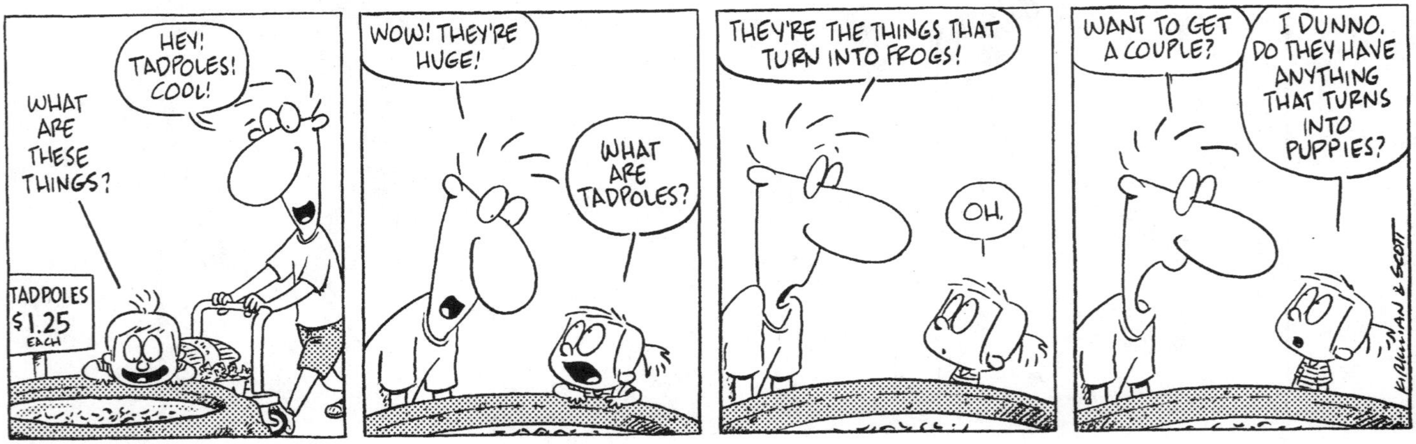
WHAT ARE THESE THINGS?
HEY! TADPOLES! COOL!
TADPOLES $1.25 EACH
WOW! THEY'RE HUGE!
WHAT ARE TADPOLES?
THEY'RE THE THINGS THAT TURN INTO FROGS!
OH.
WANT TO GET A COUPLE?
I DUNNO. DO THEY HAVE ANYTHING THAT TURNS INTO PUPPIES?
KIRKMAN & SCOTT

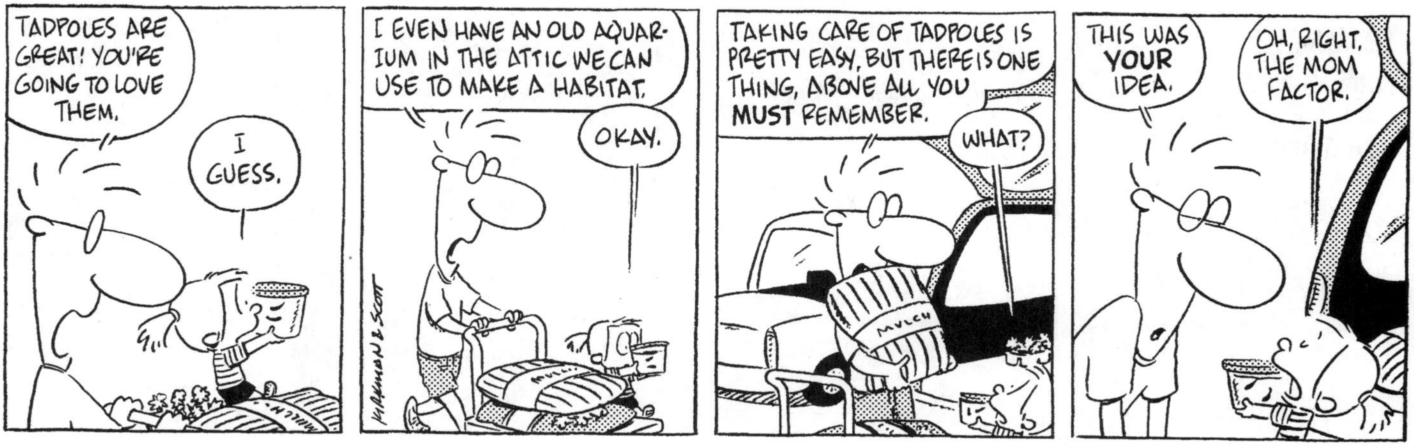
TADPOLES ARE GREAT! YOU'RE GOING TO LOVE THEM.
I GUESS.
I EVEN HAVE AN OLD AQUARIUM IN THE ATTIC WE CAN USE TO MAKE A HABITAT.
OKAY.
KIRKMAN & SCOTT
MULCH
TAKING CARE OF TADPOLES IS PRETTY EASY, BUT THERE IS ONE THING, ABOVE ALL YOU **MUST** REMEMBER.
WHAT?
THIS WAS **YOUR** IDEA.
OH, RIGHT. THE MOM FACTOR.

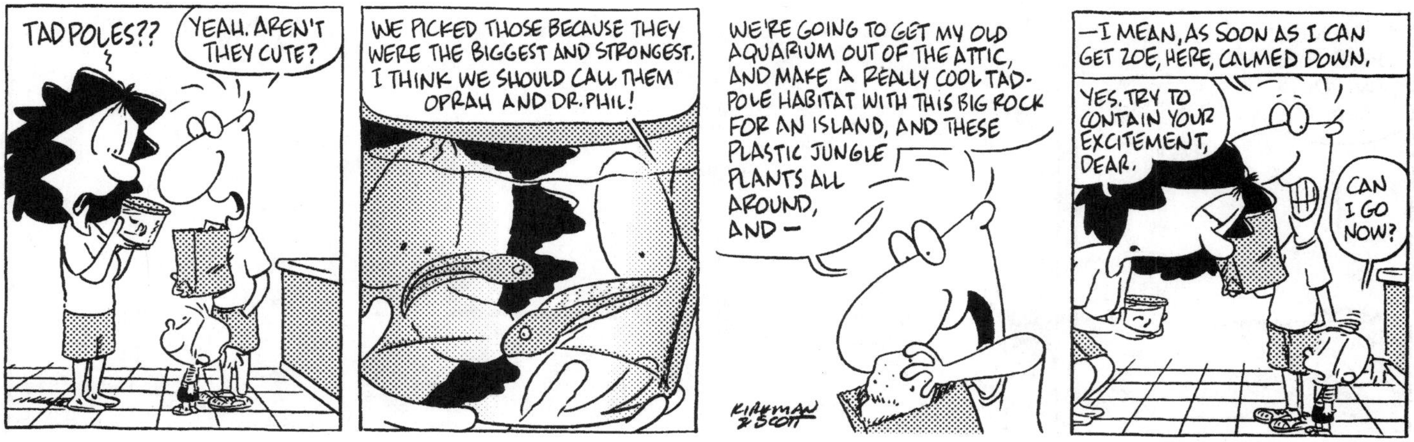
TADPOLES??
YEAH. AREN'T THEY CUTE?
WE PICKED THOSE BECAUSE THEY WERE THE BIGGEST AND STRONGEST. I THINK WE SHOULD CALL THEM OPRAH AND DR. PHIL!
WE'RE GOING TO GET MY OLD AQUARIUM OUT OF THE ATTIC, AND MAKE A REALLY COOL TADPOLE HABITAT WITH THIS BIG ROCK FOR AN ISLAND, AND THESE PLASTIC JUNGLE PLANTS ALL AROUND, AND —
KIRKMAN & SCOTT
—I MEAN, AS SOON AS I CAN GET ZOE, HERE, CALMED DOWN.
YES. TRY TO CONTAIN YOUR EXCITEMENT, DEAR.
CAN I GO NOW?

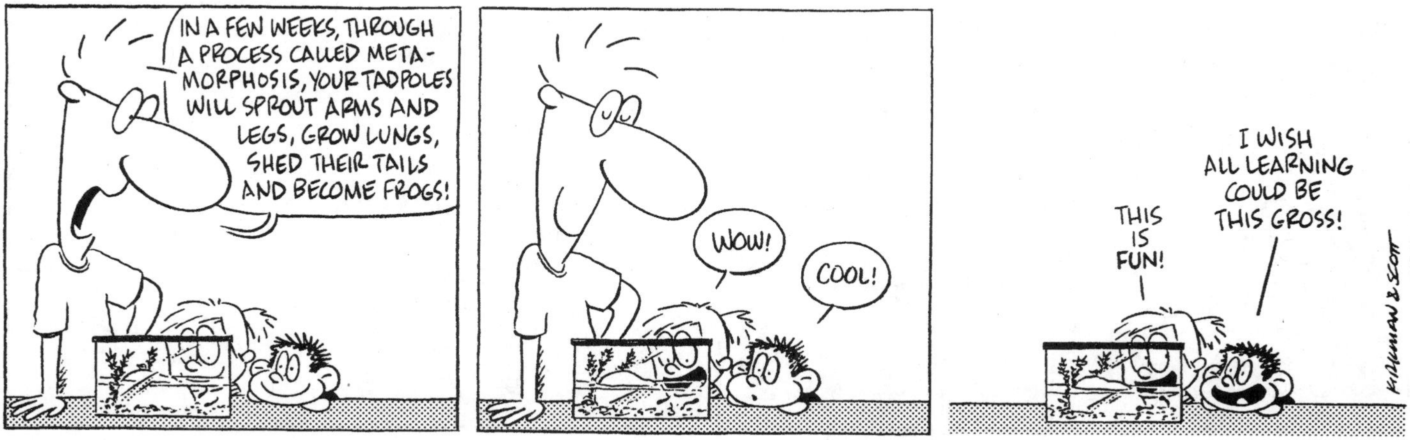
IN A FEW WEEKS, THROUGH A PROCESS CALLED METAMORPHOSIS, YOUR TADPOLES WILL SPROUT ARMS AND LEGS, GROW LUNGS, SHED THEIR TAILS AND BECOME FROGS!
WOW!
COOL!
THIS IS **FUN!**
I WISH ALL LEARNING COULD BE THIS GROSS!
KIRKMAN & SCOTT

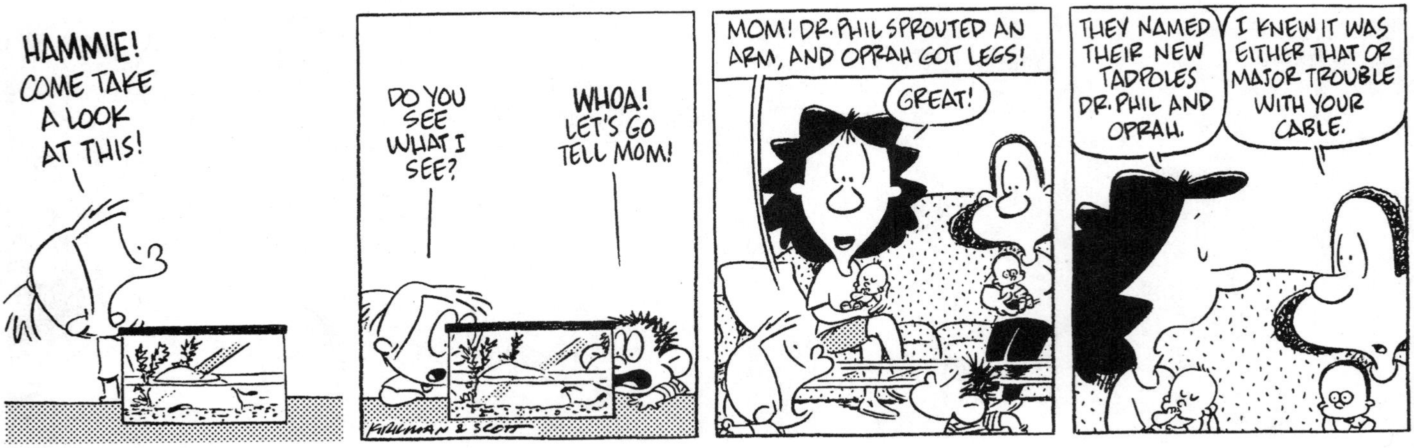
HAMMIE! COME TAKE A LOOK AT THIS!
DO YOU SEE WHAT I SEE?
WHOA! LET'S GO TELL MOM!
KIRKMAN & SCOTT
MOM! DR. PHIL SPROUTED AN ARM, AND OPRAH GOT LEGS!
GREAT!
THEY NAMED THEIR NEW TADPOLES DR. PHIL AND OPRAH.
I KNEW IT WAS EITHER THAT OR MAJOR TROUBLE WITH YOUR CABLE.

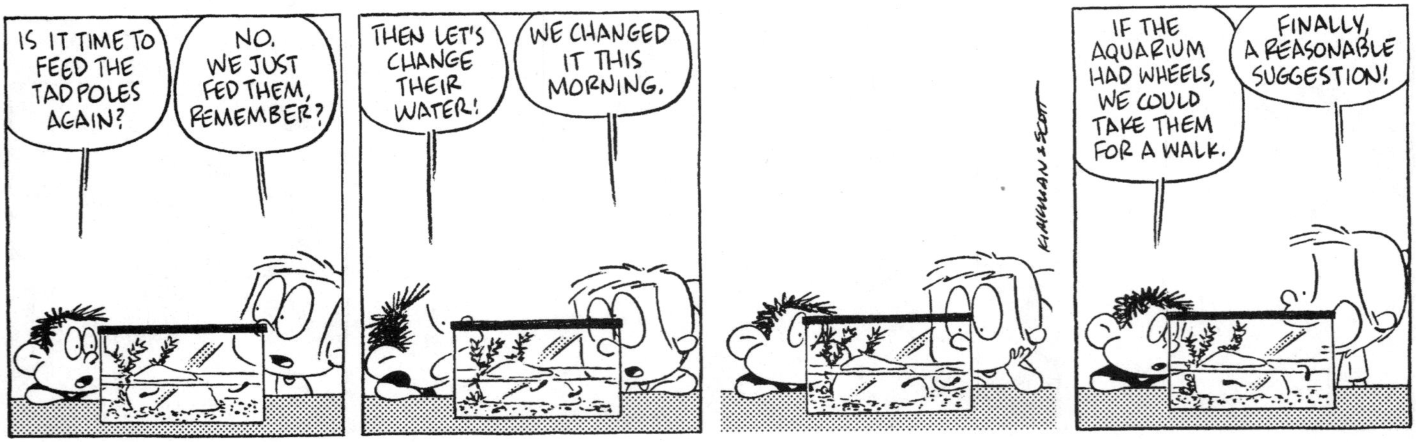
IS IT TIME TO FEED THE TADPOLES AGAIN?
NO. WE JUST FED THEM, REMEMBER?
THEN LET'S CHANGE THEIR WATER!
WE CHANGED IT THIS MORNING.
KIRKMAN & SCOTT
IF THE AQUARIUM HAD WHEELS, WE COULD TAKE THEM FOR A WALK.
FINALLY, A REASONABLE SUGGESTION!

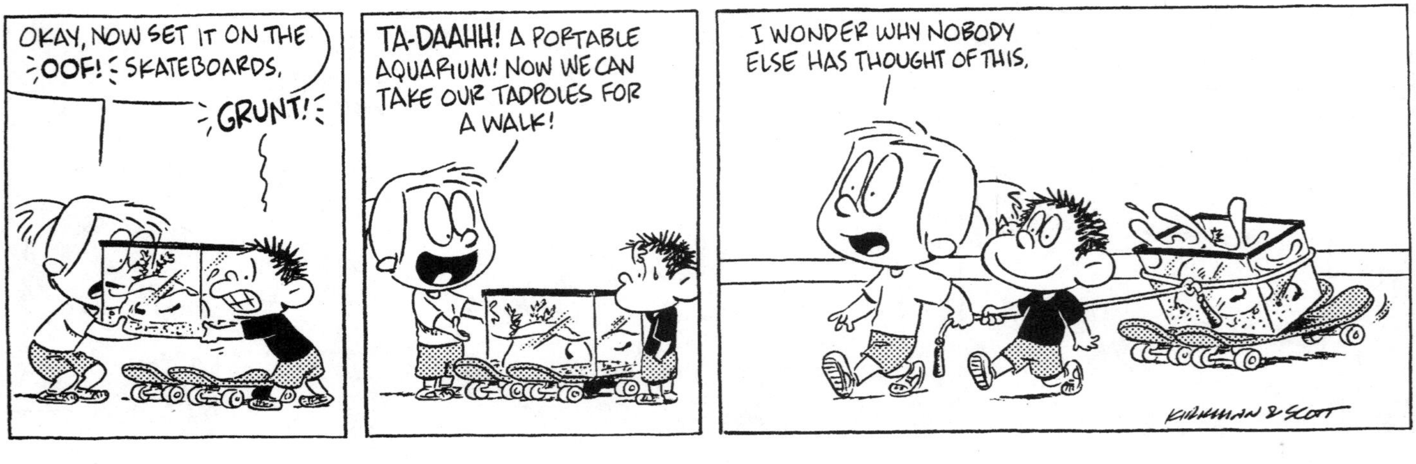
OKAY, NOW SET IT ON THE OOF! SKATEBOARDS.
GRUNT!
TA-DAAHH! A PORTABLE AQUARIUM! NOW WE CAN TAKE OUR TADPOLES FOR A WALK!
I WONDER WHY NOBODY ELSE HAS THOUGHT OF THIS.
KIRKMAN & SCOTT

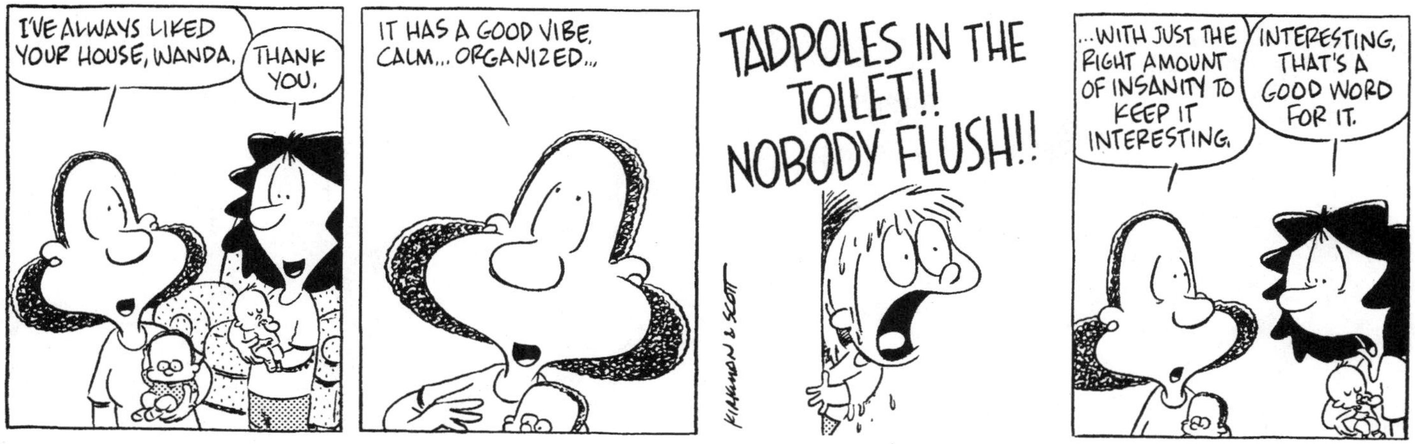
I'VE ALWAYS LIKED YOUR HOUSE, WANDA.
THANK YOU.
IT HAS A GOOD VIBE. CALM... ORGANIZED...
TADPOLES IN THE TOILET!! NOBODY FLUSH!!
KIRKMAN & SCOTT
...WITH JUST THE RIGHT AMOUNT OF INSANITY TO KEEP IT INTERESTING.
INTERESTING, THAT'S A GOOD WORD FOR IT.

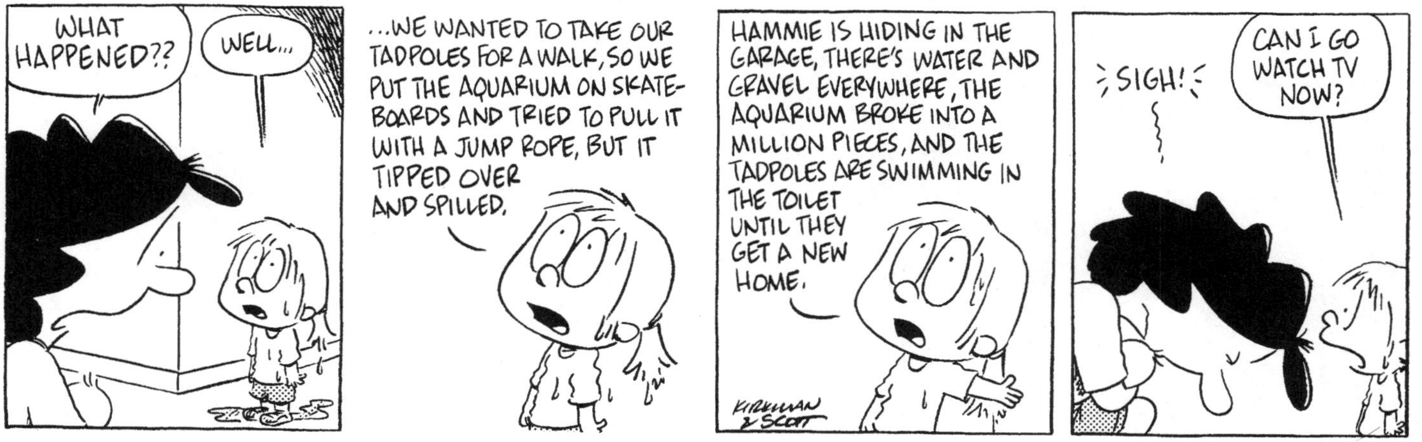
WHAT HAPPENED??
WELL...
...WE WANTED TO TAKE OUR TADPOLES FOR A WALK, SO WE PUT THE AQUARIUM ON SKATEBOARDS AND TRIED TO PULL IT WITH A JUMP ROPE, BUT IT TIPPED OVER AND SPILLED.
HAMMIE IS HIDING IN THE GARAGE, THERE'S WATER AND GRAVEL EVERYWHERE, THE AQUARIUM BROKE INTO A MILLION PIECES, AND THE TADPOLES ARE SWIMMING IN THE TOILET UNTIL THEY GET A NEW HOME.
KIRKMAN & SCOTT
SIGH!
CAN I GO WATCH TV NOW?

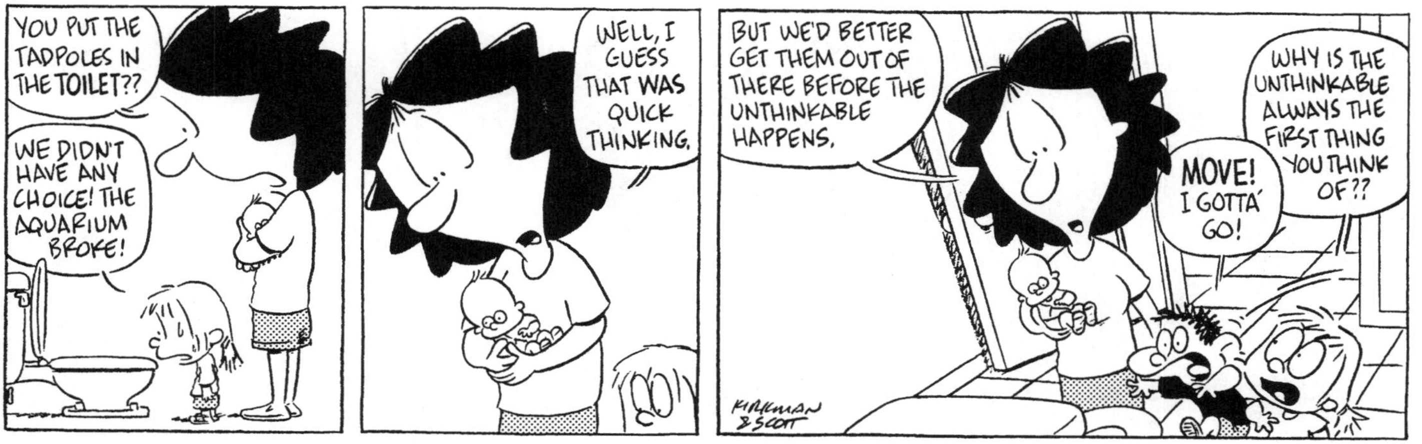
YOU PUT THE TADPOLES IN THE TOILET??
WE DIDN'T HAVE ANY CHOICE! THE AQUARIUM BROKE!
WELL, I GUESS THAT WAS QUICK THINKING.
BUT WE'D BETTER GET THEM OUT OF THERE BEFORE THE UNTHINKABLE HAPPENS.
MOVE! I GOTTA' GO!
WHY IS THE UNTHINKABLE ALWAYS THE FIRST THING YOU THINK OF??
KIRKMAN & SCOTT

Panel 1: $136.00 TO EXTRACT THE WATER AND CLEAN THE CARPET?? — YUP.

Panel 2: ADD THE $70 YOU JUST SPENT ON A NEW AQUARIUM, AND THAT COMES TO $103 APIECE WE'VE INVESTED IN THOSE STUPID TADPOLES.

Panel 3: WELL, I GUESS IT'S WORTH IT IF THE KIDS LEARN SOMETHING ABOUT NATURE. — AAAAGHH! THE HERTZ'S CAT EATS TADPOLES!

Panel 4: ZOE, WOULD YOU LIKE AN APPLE? — NO. APPLES MAKE ME CRANKY.

Panel 5: OH. HOW ABOUT A BANANA THEN? — NO. BANANAS ANNOY ME THIS WEEK.

Panel 6: PEACHES ARE UNDEPENDABLE, PEARS ARE SNEAKY, AND DON'T EVEN GET ME STARTED ON MANGOES!

Panel 7: ARE THERE ANY FRUITS THAT YOU **DO** GET ALONG WITH? — WHAT DO YOU HAVE THAT'S CHOCOLATE-COVERED?

Panel 8: !!BANG!! — DARRYL, GO TELL ZOE AND HAMMIE TO TURN THE TV DOWN.

Panel 9: GUYS!! TURN DOWN THE TV! — !! BAM!

Panel 10: THE TV IS ON?? — TURN IT UP! I CAN'T HEAR IT!

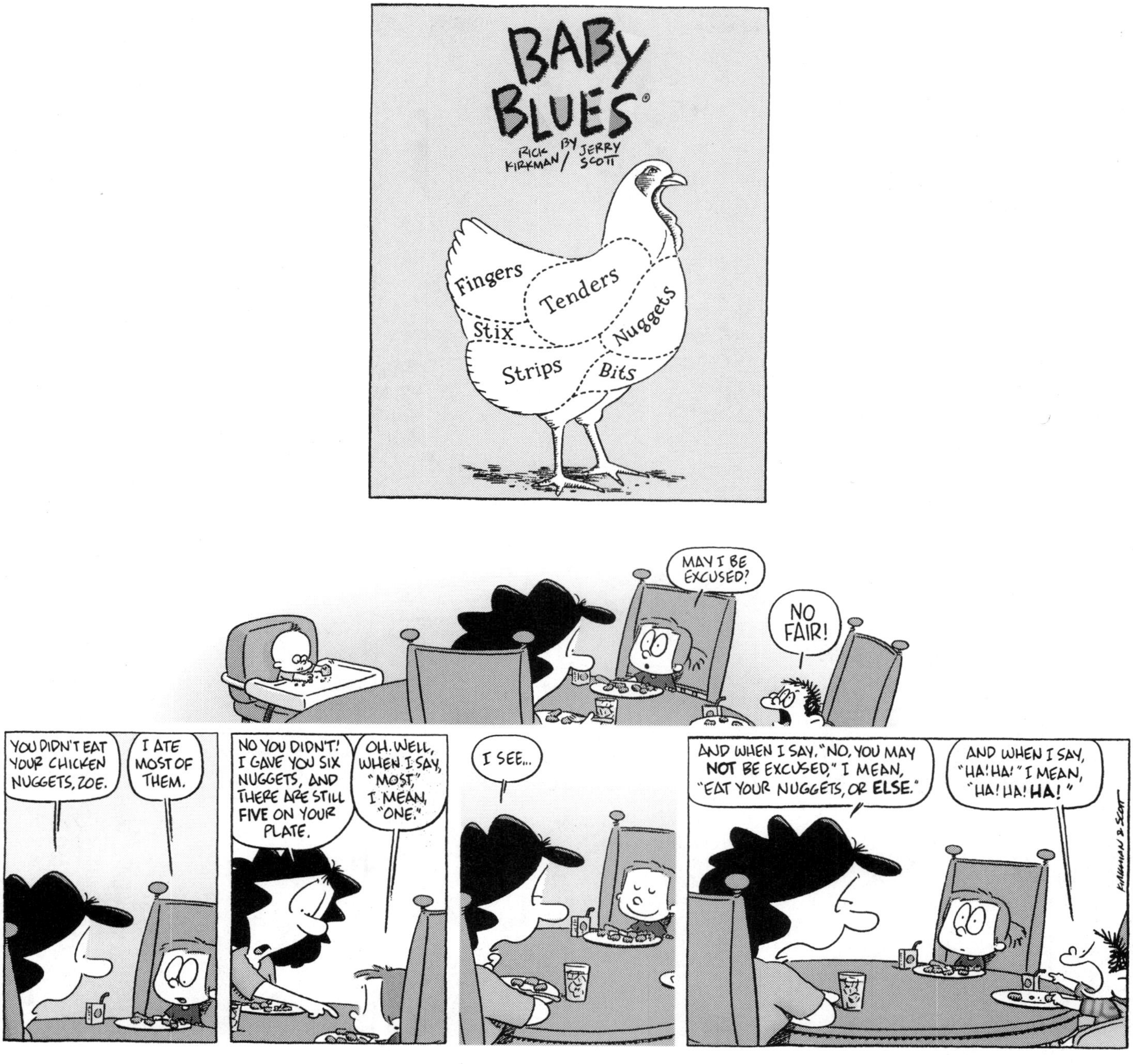
BABY BLUES®
BY RICK KIRKMAN / JERRY SCOTT
Fingers
Tenders
Stix
Nuggets
Strips
Bits
MAY I BE EXCUSED?
NO FAIR!
YOU DIDN'T EAT YOUR CHICKEN NUGGETS, ZOE.
I ATE MOST OF THEM.
NO YOU DIDN'T! I GAVE YOU SIX NUGGETS, AND THERE ARE STILL **FIVE** ON YOUR PLATE.
OH. WELL, WHEN I SAY, "MOST," I MEAN, "ONE."
I SEE...
AND WHEN I SAY, "NO, YOU MAY **NOT** BE EXCUSED," I MEAN, "EAT YOUR NUGGETS, OR **ELSE**."
AND WHEN I SAY, "HA! HA!" I MEAN, "HA! HA! **HA!**"

BABY BLUES®
BY RICK KIRKMAN / JERRY SCOTT

OKAY!
THIS ISN'T WORKING.
ZOE, KEEP AN EYE ON WREN SO I CAN GET DINNER READY.
HAMMIE! KEEP AN EYE ON WREN WHILE I FINISH THIS CHAPTER!
DADDY, KEEP AN EYE ON WREN WHILE I PRACTICE MY SWING.
WANDA, KEEP AN EYE ON WREN WHILE I TIGHTEN THIS FAUCET.
KIRKMAN & SCOTT
BY THE WAY, WHEN IS DINNER GOING TO BE READY?

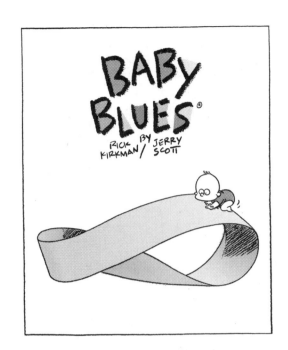

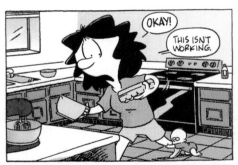

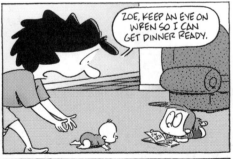

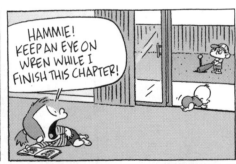

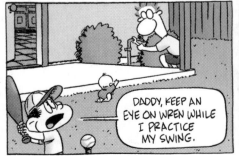

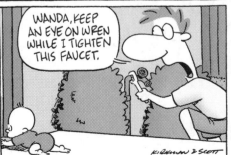

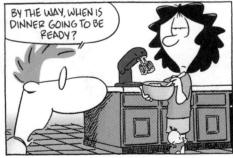

BABY BLUES®
BY RICK KIRKMAN / JERRY SCOTT

THWOK!
KA-THWOK!
KIRKMAN & SCOTT

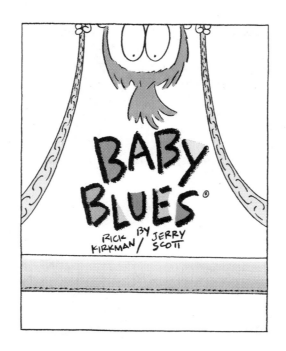

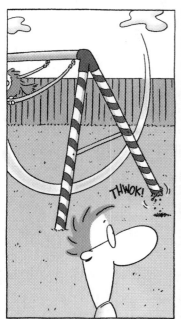

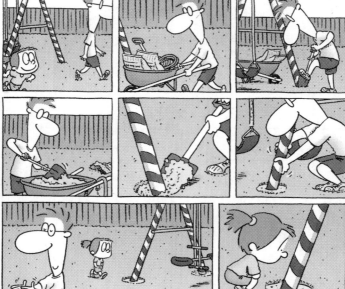

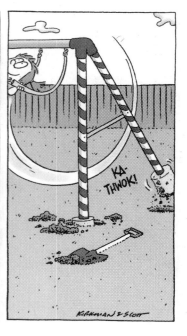

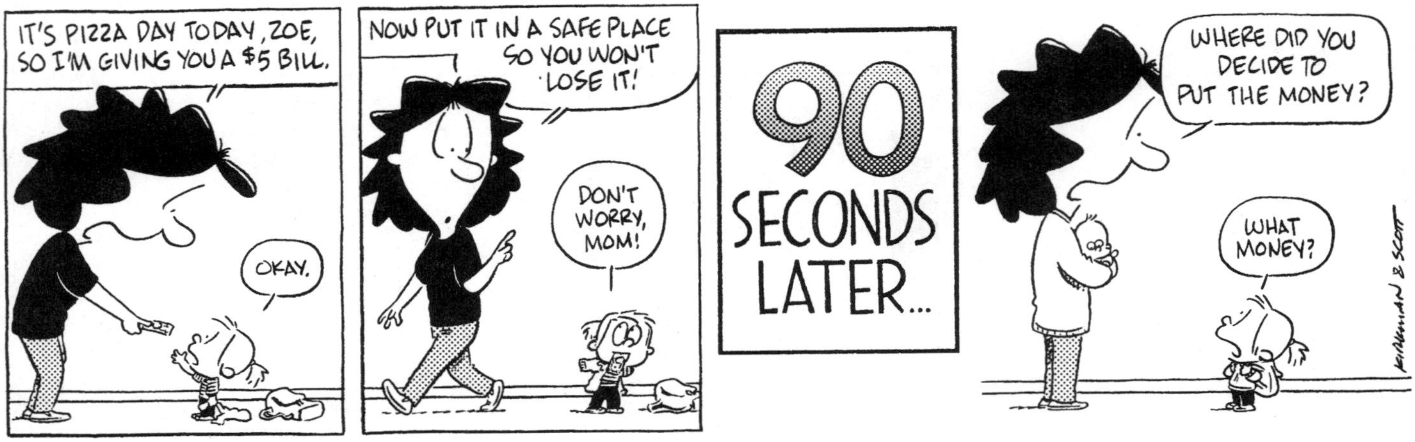
IT'S PIZZA DAY TODAY, ZOE, SO I'M GIVING YOU A $5 BILL.
OKAY.
NOW PUT IT IN A SAFE PLACE SO YOU WON'T LOSE IT!
DON'T WORRY, MOM!
90 SECONDS LATER...
WHERE DID YOU DECIDE TO PUT THE MONEY?
WHAT MONEY?
KIRKMAN & SCOTT

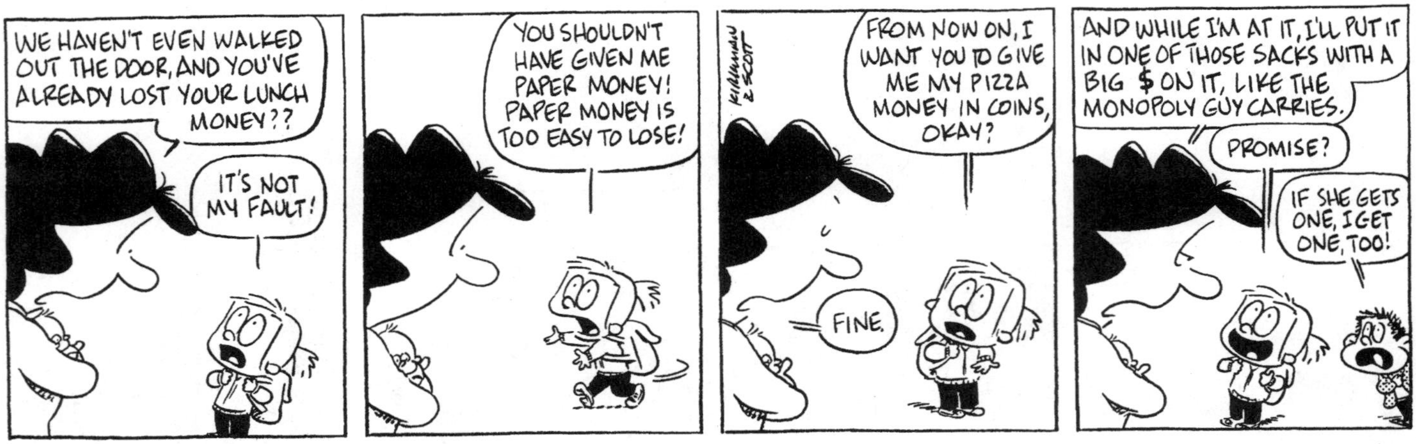
WE HAVEN'T EVEN WALKED OUT THE DOOR, AND YOU'VE ALREADY LOST YOUR LUNCH MONEY??
IT'S NOT MY FAULT!
YOU SHOULDN'T HAVE GIVEN ME PAPER MONEY! PAPER MONEY IS TOO EASY TO LOSE!
KIRKMAN & SCOTT
FROM NOW ON, I WANT YOU TO GIVE ME MY PIZZA MONEY IN COINS, OKAY?
FINE.
AND WHILE I'M AT IT, I'LL PUT IT IN ONE OF THOSE SACKS WITH A BIG $ ON IT, LIKE THE MONOPOLY GUY CARRIES.
PROMISE?
IF SHE GETS ONE, I GET ONE, TOO!

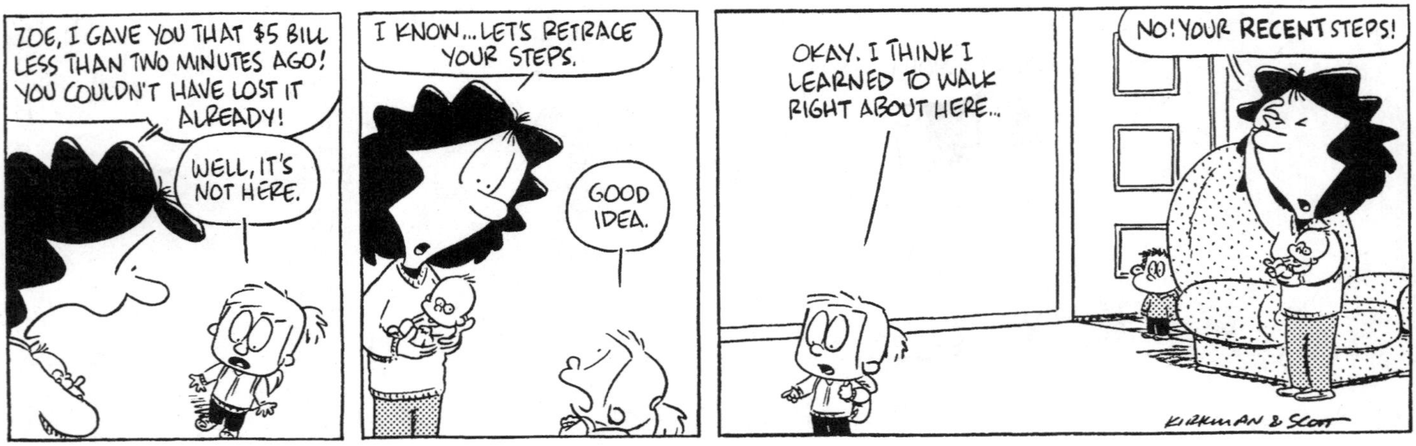
ZOE, I GAVE YOU THAT $5 BILL LESS THAN TWO MINUTES AGO! YOU COULDN'T HAVE LOST IT ALREADY!
WELL, IT'S NOT HERE.
I KNOW... LET'S RETRACE YOUR STEPS.
GOOD IDEA.
OKAY. I THINK I LEARNED TO WALK RIGHT ABOUT HERE...
NO! YOUR RECENT STEPS!
KIRKMAN & SCOTT

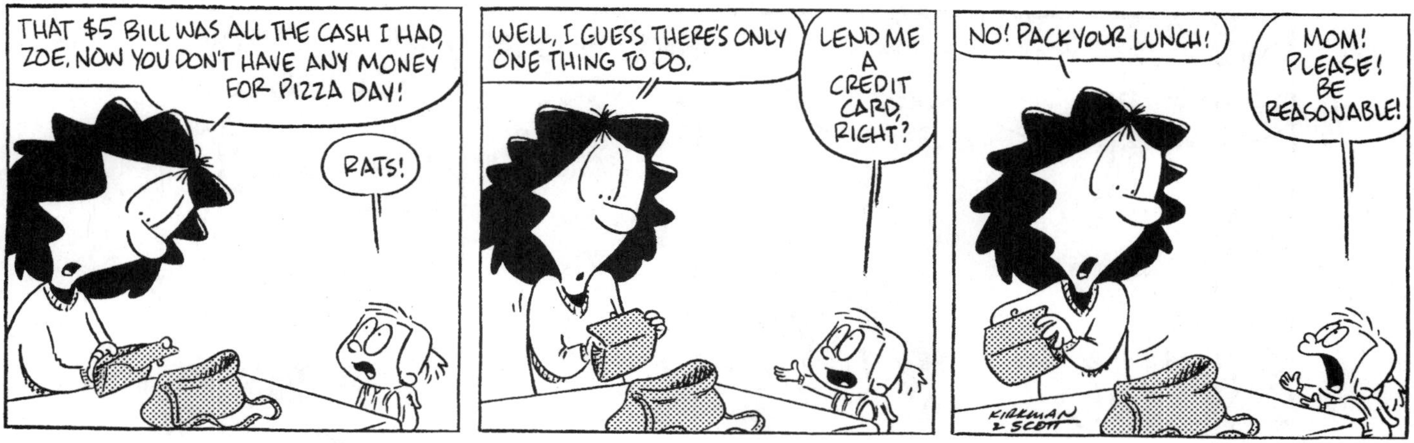
THAT $5 BILL WAS ALL THE CASH I HAD, ZOE. NOW YOU DON'T HAVE ANY MONEY FOR PIZZA DAY!
RATS!
WELL, I GUESS THERE'S ONLY ONE THING TO DO.
LEND ME A CREDIT CARD, RIGHT?
NO! PACK YOUR LUNCH!
MOM! PLEASE! BE REASONABLE!
KIRKMAN & SCOTT

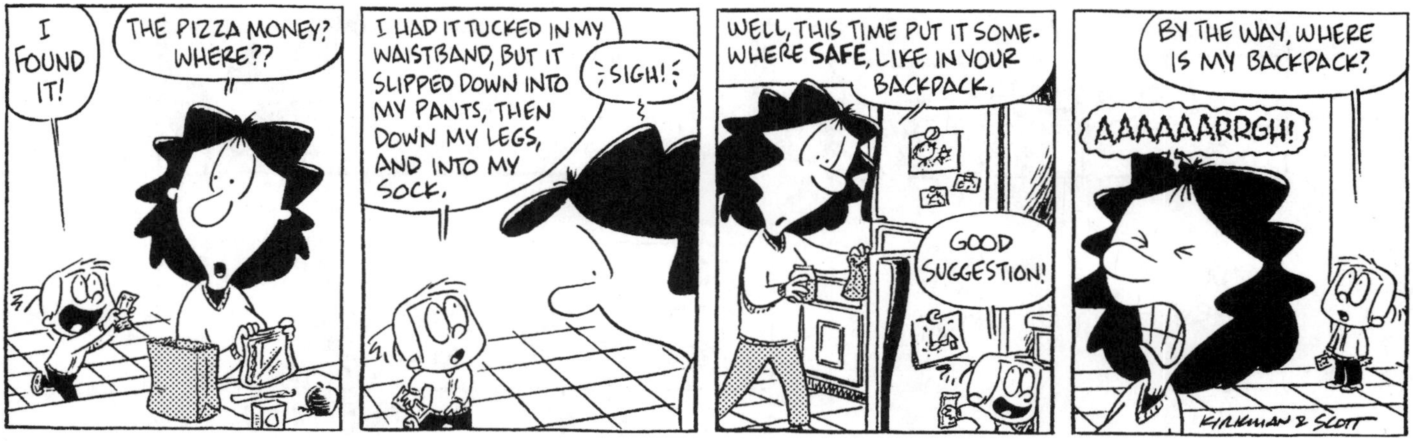
I FOUND IT!
THE PIZZA MONEY? WHERE??
I HAD IT TUCKED IN MY WAISTBAND, BUT IT SLIPPED DOWN INTO MY PANTS, THEN DOWN MY LEGS, AND INTO MY SOCK.
SIGH!
WELL, THIS TIME PUT IT SOMEWHERE SAFE, LIKE IN YOUR BACKPACK.
GOOD SUGGESTION!
BY THE WAY, WHERE IS MY BACKPACK?
AAAAAARRGH!
KIRKMAN & SCOTT

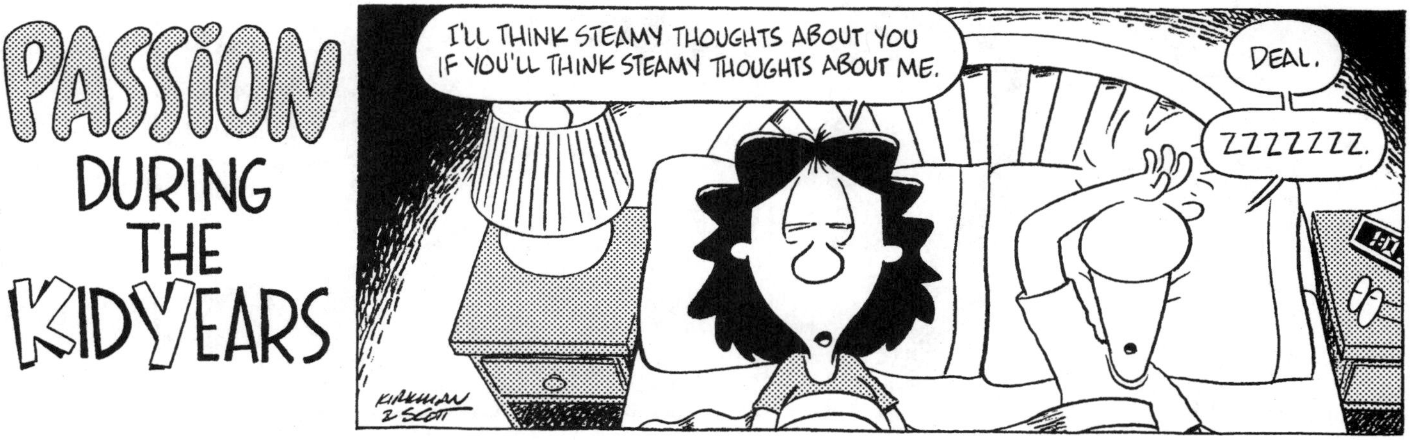
PASSION DURING THE KID YEARS
I'LL THINK STEAMY THOUGHTS ABOUT YOU IF YOU'LL THINK STEAMY THOUGHTS ABOUT ME.
DEAL.
ZZZZZZZ.
KIRKMAN & SCOTT

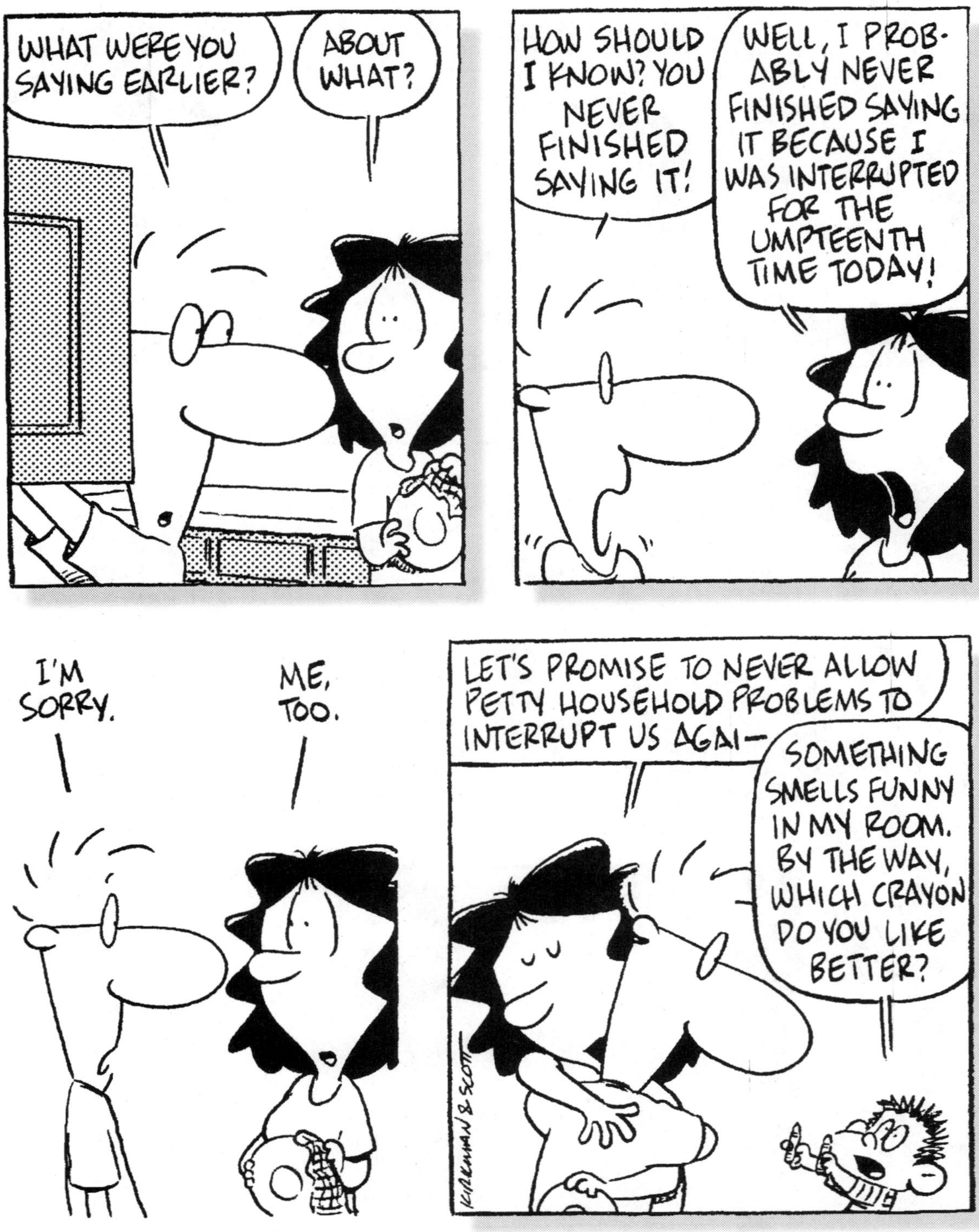
WHAT WERE YOU SAYING EARLIER?
ABOUT WHAT?
HOW SHOULD I KNOW? YOU NEVER FINISHED SAYING IT!
WELL, I PROBABLY NEVER FINISHED SAYING IT BECAUSE I WAS INTERRUPTED FOR THE UMPTEENTH TIME TODAY!
I'M SORRY.
ME, TOO.
LET'S PROMISE TO NEVER ALLOW PETTY HOUSEHOLD PROBLEMS TO INTERRUPT US AGAI—
SOMETHING SMELLS FUNNY IN MY ROOM. BY THE WAY, WHICH CRAYON DO YOU LIKE BETTER?
KIRKMAN & SCOTT

BABY BLUES©
GOODBYE SUMMER!

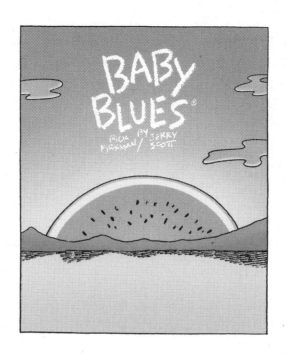

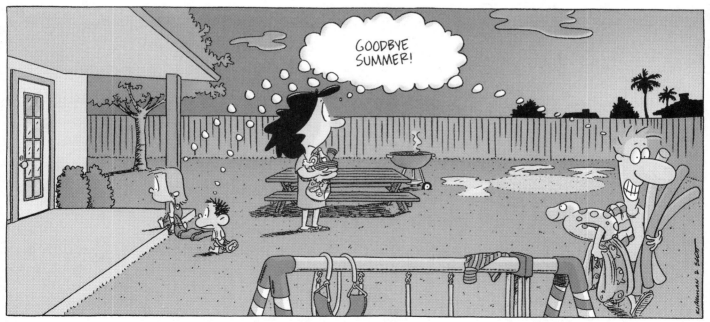

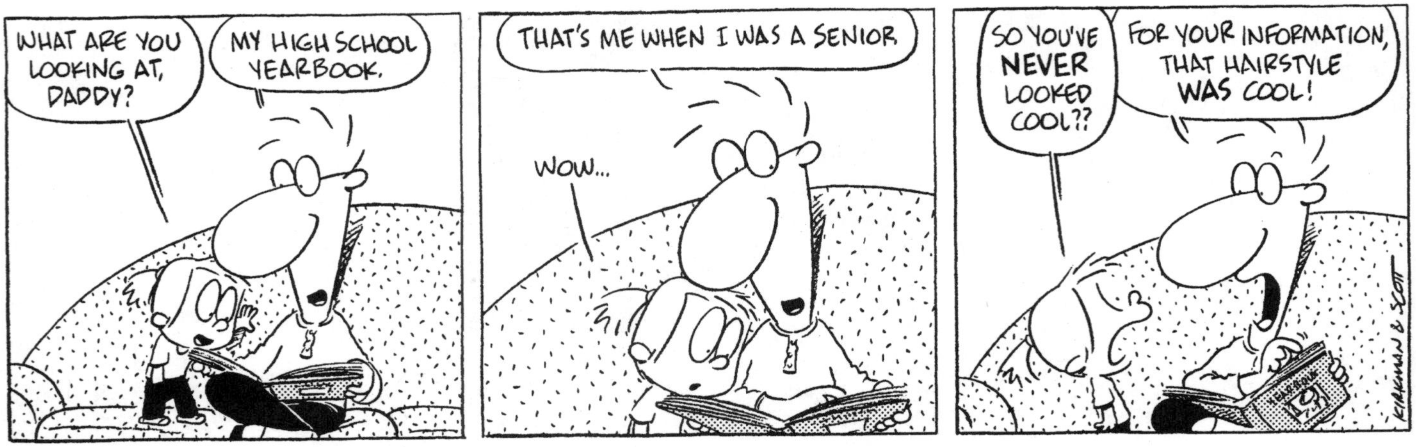
WHAT ARE YOU LOOKING AT, DADDY?
MY HIGH SCHOOL YEARBOOK.
THAT'S ME WHEN I WAS A SENIOR.
WOW...
SO YOU'VE NEVER LOOKED COOL??
FOR YOUR INFORMATION, THAT HAIRSTYLE WAS COOL!
KIRKMAN & SCOTT

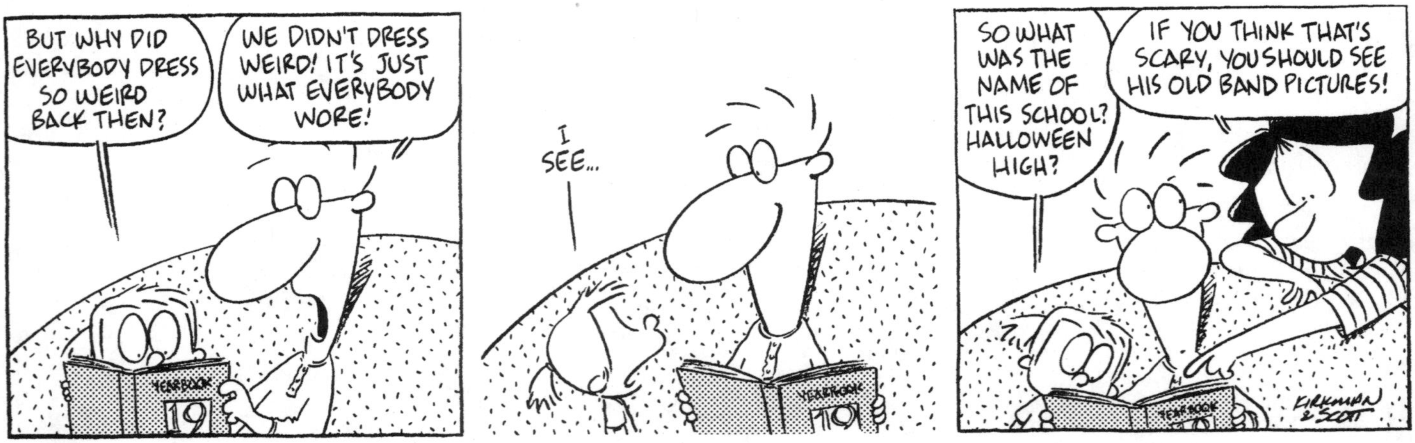
BUT WHY DID EVERYBODY DRESS SO WEIRD BACK THEN?
WE DIDN'T DRESS WEIRD! IT'S JUST WHAT EVERYBODY WORE!
I SEE...
SO WHAT WAS THE NAME OF THIS SCHOOL? HALLOWEEN HIGH?
IF YOU THINK THAT'S SCARY, YOU SHOULD SEE HIS OLD BAND PICTURES!
KIRKMAN & SCOTT

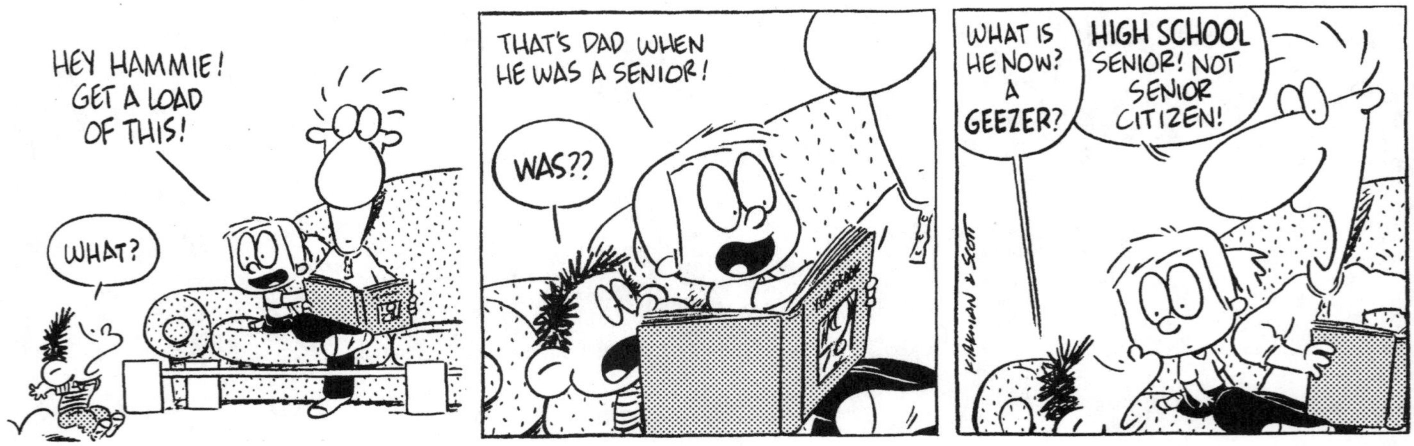
HEY HAMMIE! GET A LOAD OF THIS!
WHAT?
THAT'S DAD WHEN HE WAS A SENIOR!
WAS??
WHAT IS HE NOW? A GEEZER?
HIGH SCHOOL SENIOR! NOT SENIOR CITIZEN!
KIRKMAN & SCOTT

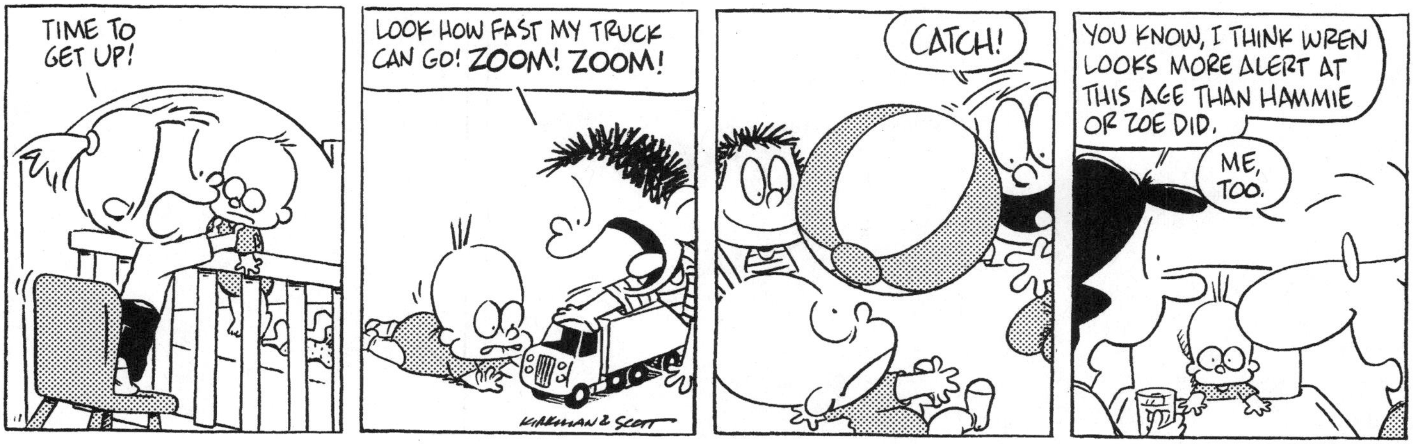
TIME TO GET UP!
LOOK HOW FAST MY TRUCK CAN GO! ZOOM! ZOOM!
KIRKMAN & SCOTT
CATCH!
YOU KNOW, I THINK WREN LOOKS MORE ALERT AT THIS AGE THAN HAMMIE OR ZOE DID.
ME, TOO.

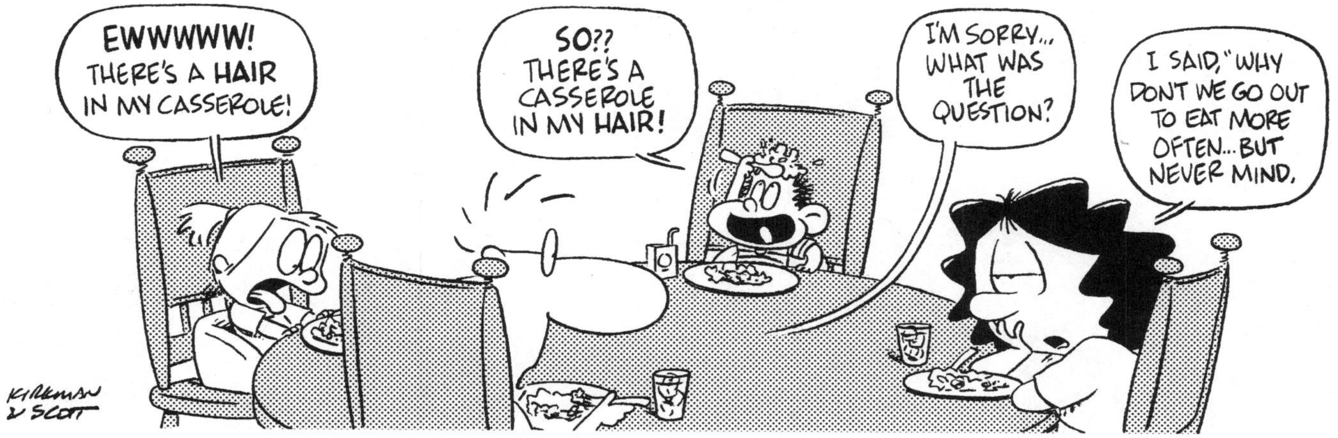
EWWWWW! THERE'S A HAIR IN MY CASSEROLE!
SO?? THERE'S A CASSEROLE IN MY HAIR!
I'M SORRY... WHAT WAS THE QUESTION?
I SAID, "WHY DON'T WE GO OUT TO EAT MORE OFTEN... BUT NEVER MIND.
KIRKMAN & SCOTT

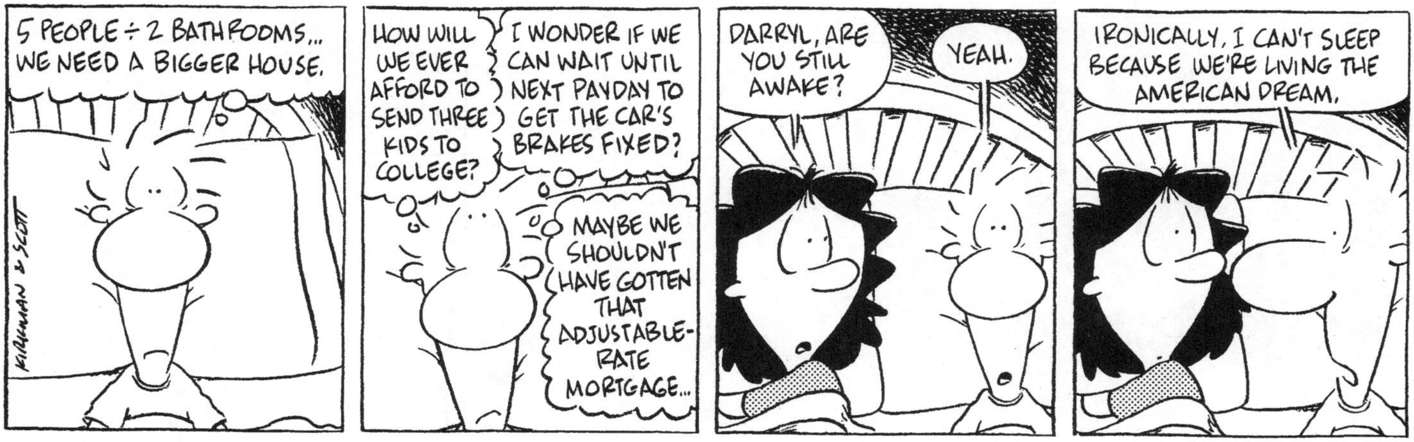
5 PEOPLE ÷ 2 BATHROOMS... WE NEED A BIGGER HOUSE.
KIRKMAN & SCOTT
HOW WILL WE EVER AFFORD TO SEND THREE KIDS TO COLLEGE?
I WONDER IF WE CAN WAIT UNTIL NEXT PAYDAY TO GET THE CAR'S BRAKES FIXED?
MAYBE WE SHOULDN'T HAVE GOTTEN THAT ADJUSTABLE-RATE MORTGAGE...
DARRYL, ARE YOU STILL AWAKE?
YEAH.
IRONICALLY, I CAN'T SLEEP BECAUSE WE'RE LIVING THE AMERICAN DREAM.

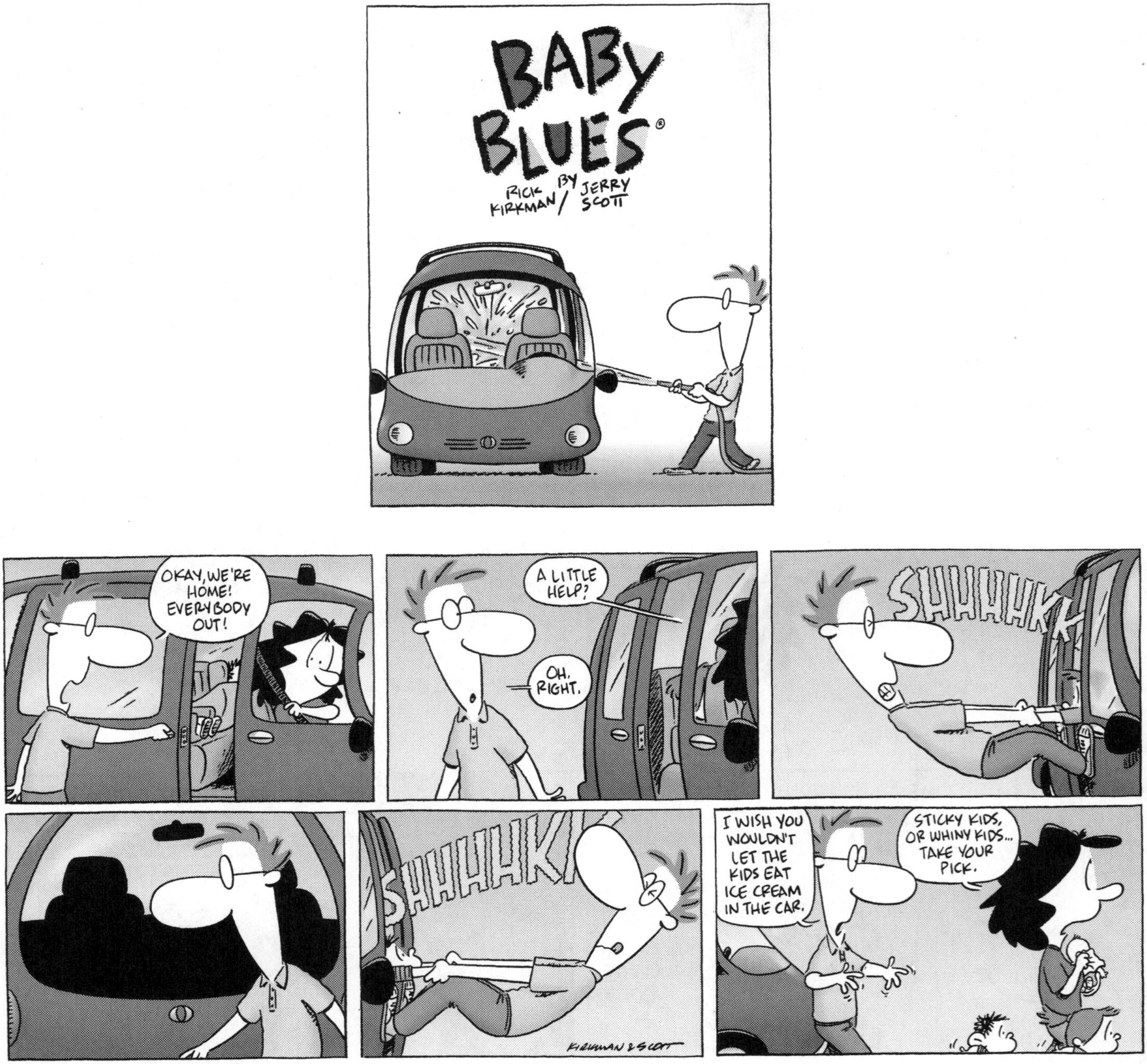
BABY BLUES®
BY RICK KIRKMAN / JERRY SCOTT
OKAY, WE'RE HOME! EVERYBODY OUT!
A LITTLE HELP?
OH. RIGHT.
SHHHHKK!
SHHHHKK!
KIRKMAN & SCOTT
I WISH YOU WOULDN'T LET THE KIDS EAT ICE CREAM IN THE CAR.
STICKY KIDS, OR WHINY KIDS... TAKE YOUR PICK.

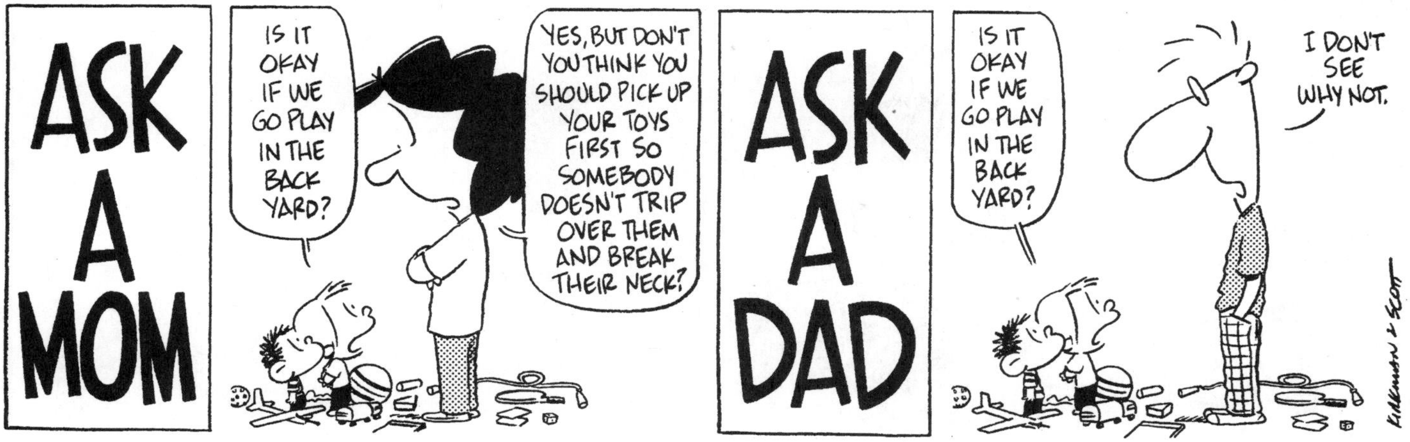
ASK A MOM
IS IT OKAY IF WE GO PLAY IN THE BACK YARD?
YES, BUT DON'T YOU THINK YOU SHOULD PICK UP YOUR TOYS FIRST SO SOMEBODY DOESN'T TRIP OVER THEM AND BREAK THEIR NECK?
ASK A DAD
IS IT OKAY IF WE GO PLAY IN THE BACK YARD?
I DON'T SEE WHY NOT.
KIRKMAN & SCOTT

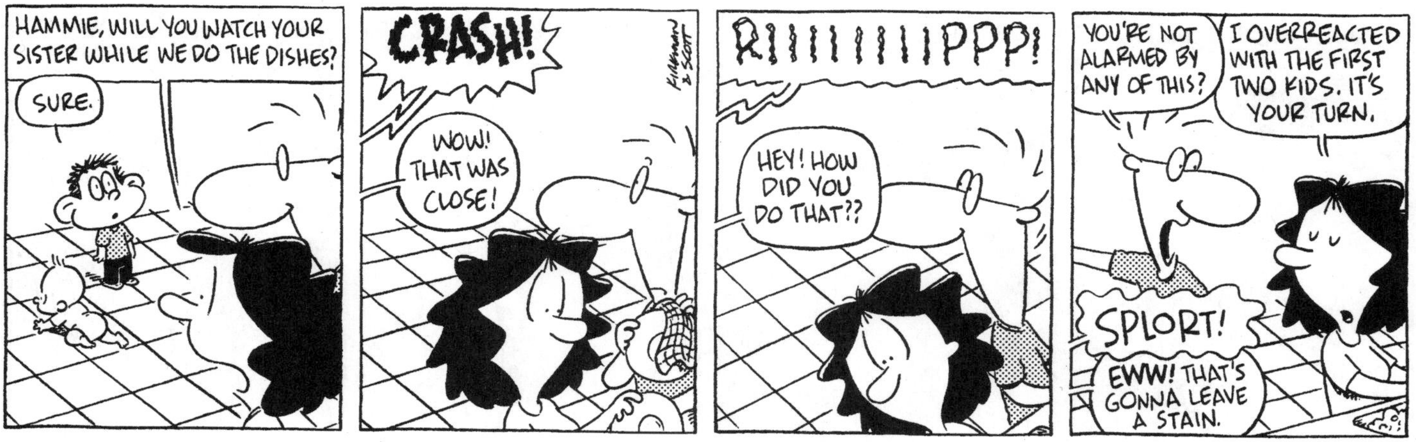
HAMMIE, WILL YOU WATCH YOUR SISTER WHILE WE DO THE DISHES?
SURE.
CRASH!
WOW! THAT WAS CLOSE!
KIRKMAN & SCOTT
RIIIIIIIIPPP!
HEY! HOW DID YOU DO THAT??
YOU'RE NOT ALARMED BY ANY OF THIS?
I OVERREACTED WITH THE FIRST TWO KIDS. IT'S YOUR TURN.
SPLORT!
EWW! THAT'S GONNA LEAVE A STAIN.

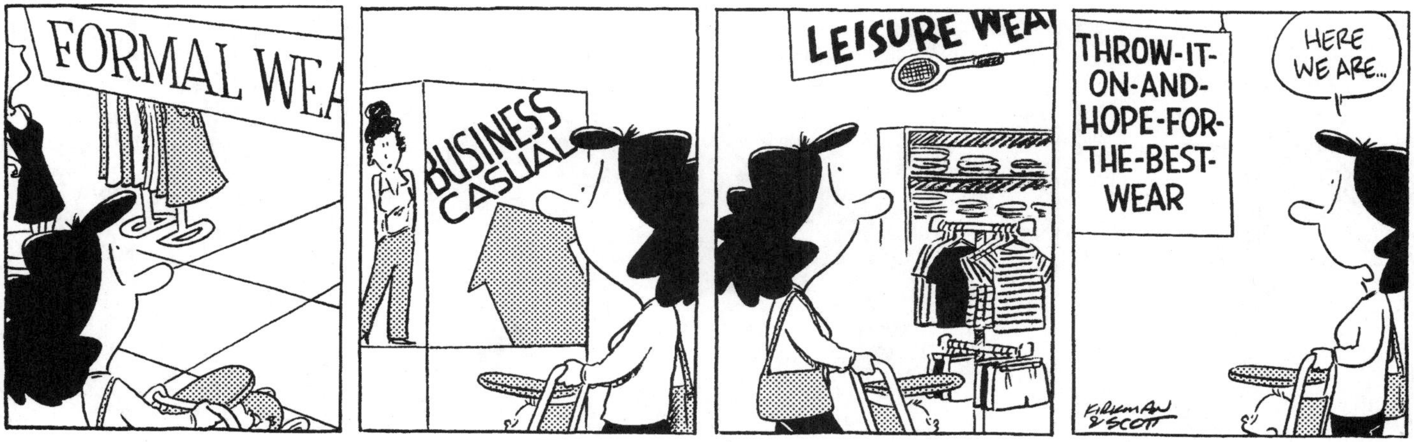
FORMAL WEA
BUSINESS CASUAL
LEISURE WEA
THROW-IT-ON-AND-HOPE-FOR-THE-BEST-WEAR
HERE WE ARE...
KIRKMAN & SCOTT

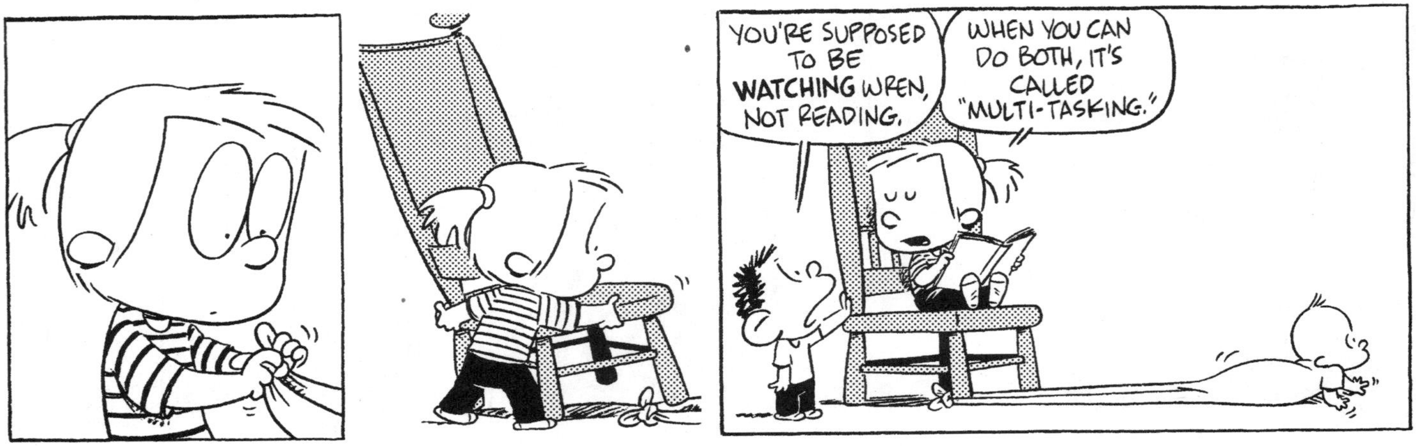
YOU'RE SUPPOSED TO BE **WATCHING** WREN, NOT READING.
WHEN YOU CAN DO BOTH, IT'S CALLED "MULTI-TASKING."

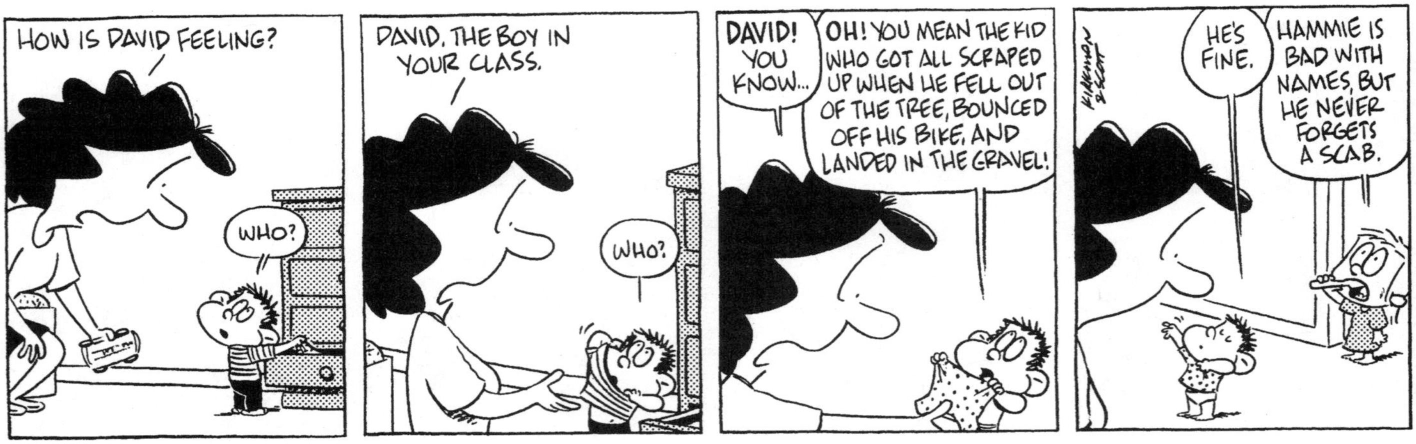
HOW IS DAVID FEELING?
WHO?
DAVID. THE BOY IN YOUR CLASS.
WHO?
DAVID! YOU KNOW...
OH! YOU MEAN THE KID WHO GOT ALL SCRAPED UP WHEN HE FELL OUT OF THE TREE, BOUNCED OFF HIS BIKE, AND LANDED IN THE GRAVEL!
HE'S FINE.
HAMMIE IS BAD WITH NAMES, BUT HE NEVER FORGETS A SCAB.

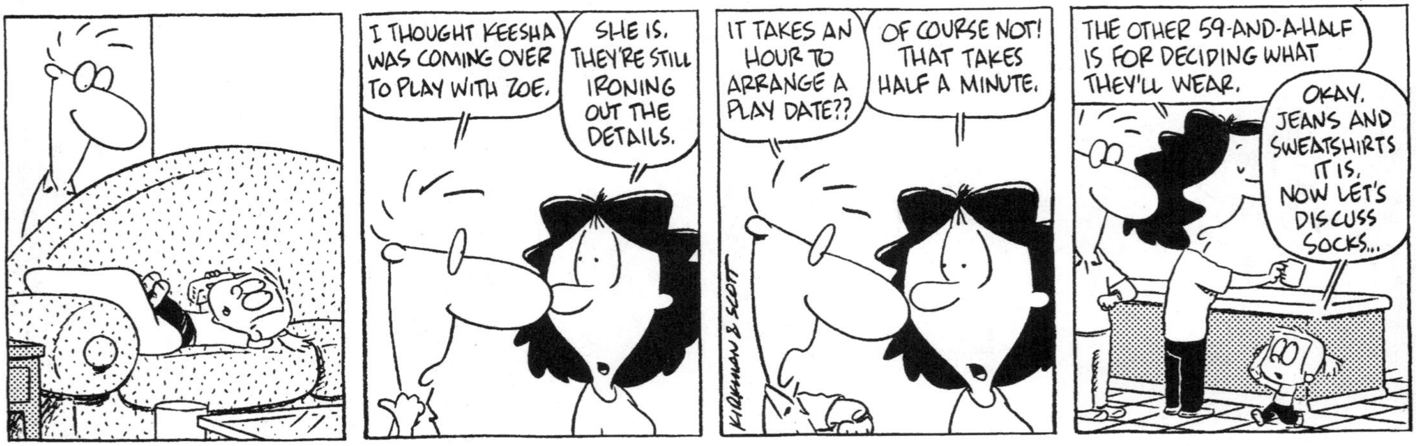
I THOUGHT KEESHA WAS COMING OVER TO PLAY WITH ZOE.
SHE IS. THEY'RE STILL IRONING OUT THE DETAILS.
KIRKMAN & SCOTT
IT TAKES AN HOUR TO ARRANGE A PLAY DATE??
OF COURSE NOT! THAT TAKES HALF A MINUTE.
THE OTHER 59-AND-A-HALF IS FOR DECIDING WHAT THEY'LL WEAR.
OKAY. JEANS AND SWEATSHIRTS IT IS. NOW LET'S DISCUSS SOCKS...

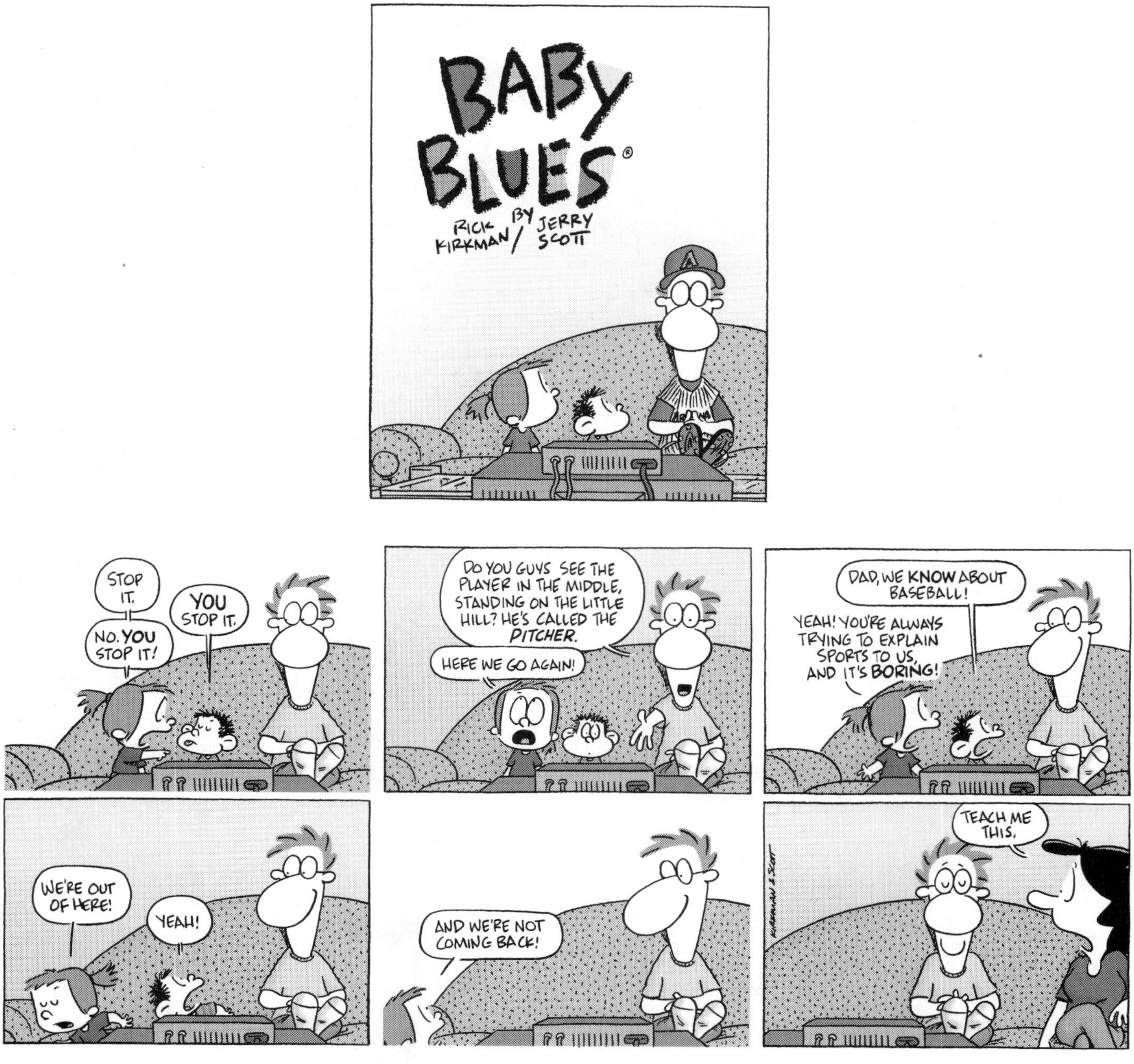
BABY BLUES®
BY RICK KIRKMAN / JERRY SCOTT
STOP IT.
NO. YOU STOP IT!
YOU STOP IT.
DO YOU GUYS SEE THE PLAYER IN THE MIDDLE, STANDING ON THE LITTLE HILL? HE'S CALLED THE PITCHER.
HERE WE GO AGAIN!
DAD, WE KNOW ABOUT BASEBALL!
YEAH! YOU'RE ALWAYS TRYING TO EXPLAIN SPORTS TO US, AND IT'S BORING!
WE'RE OUT OF HERE!
YEAH!
AND WE'RE NOT COMING BACK!
TEACH ME THIS.

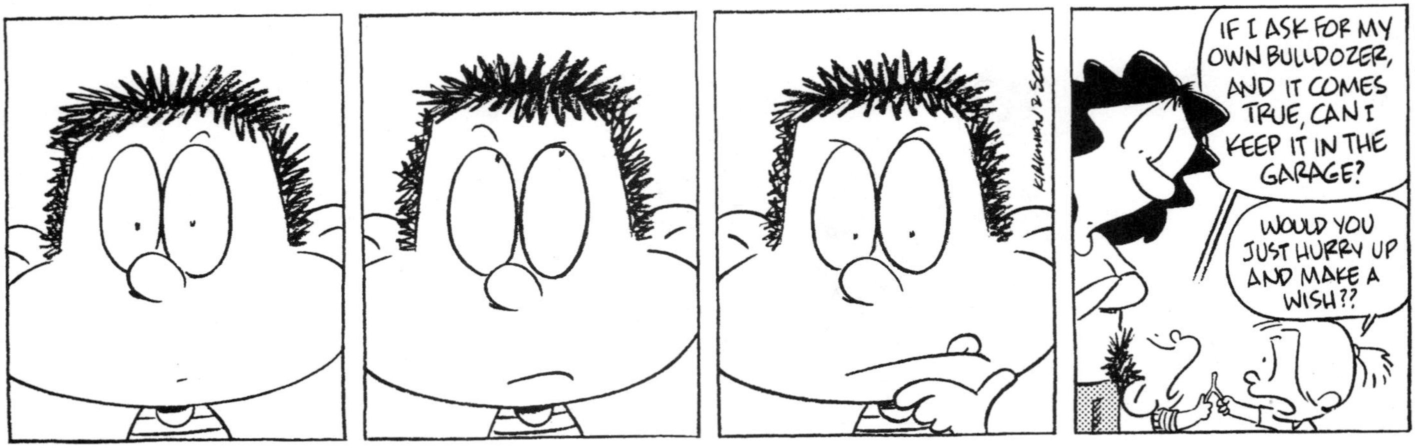
KIRKMAN & SCOTT
IF I ASK FOR MY OWN BULLDOZER, AND IT COMES TRUE, CAN I KEEP IT IN THE GARAGE?
WOULD YOU JUST HURRY UP AND MAKE A WISH??

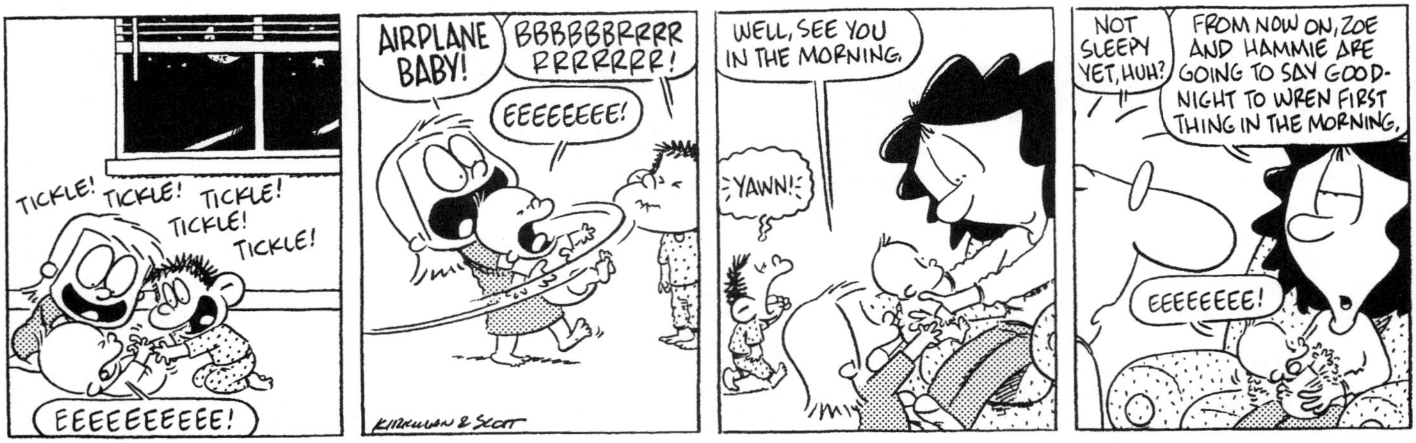
TICKLE! TICKLE! TICKLE! TICKLE! TICKLE!
EEEEEEEEEE!
AIRPLANE BABY!
BBBBBBRRRR RRRRRRR!
EEEEEEEE!
KIRKMAN & SCOTT
WELL, SEE YOU IN THE MORNING.
YAWN!
NOT SLEEPY YET, HUH?
FROM NOW ON, ZOE AND HAMMIE ARE GOING TO SAY GOOD-NIGHT TO WREN FIRST THING IN THE MORNING.
EEEEEEEE!

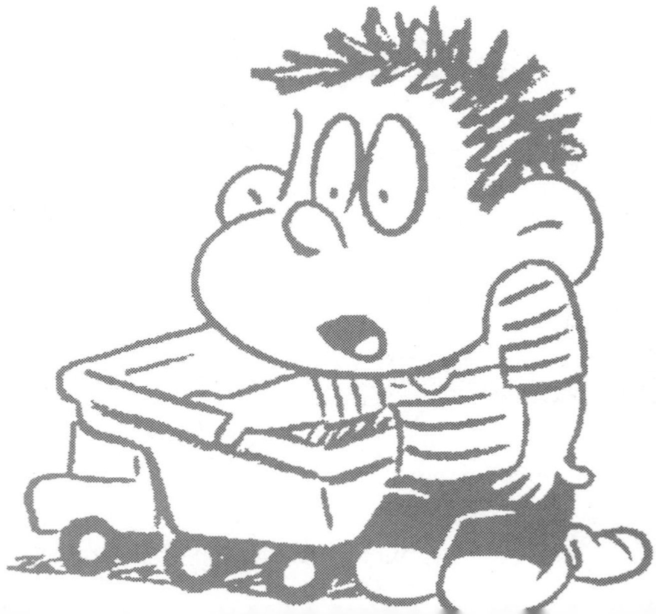

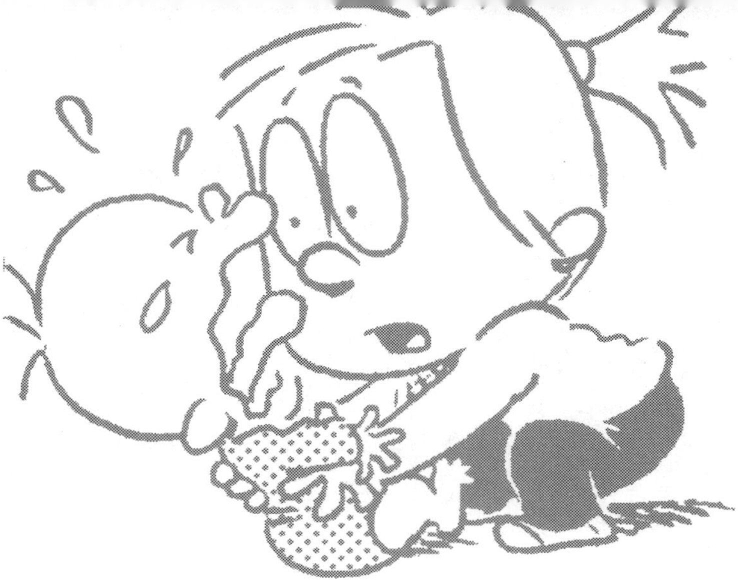

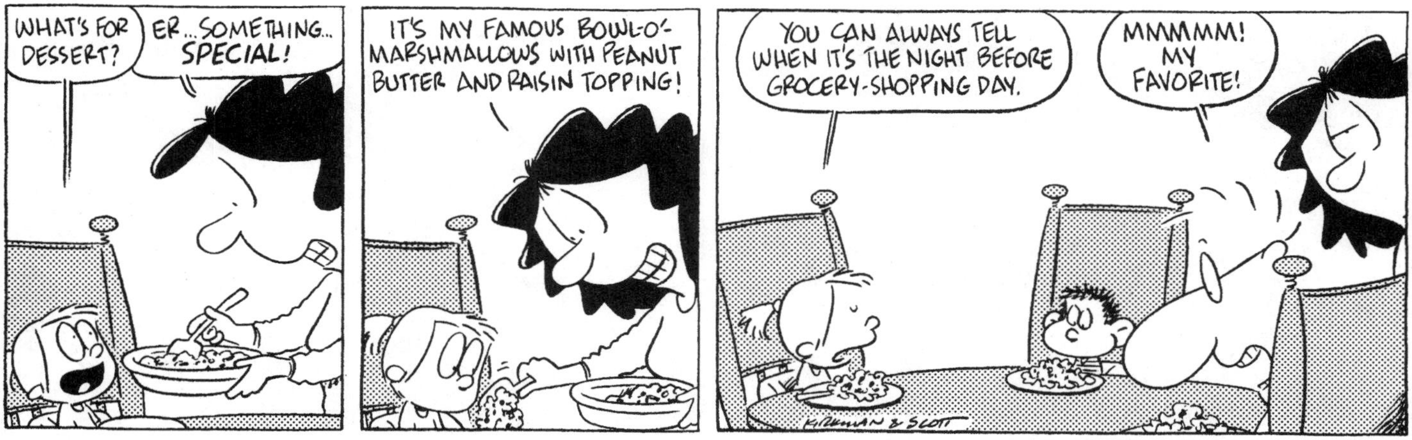

WHAT'S FOR DESSERT?
ER...SOMETHING... SPECIAL!
IT'S MY FAMOUS BOWL-O'-MARSHMALLOWS WITH PEANUT BUTTER AND RAISIN TOPPING!
YOU CAN ALWAYS TELL WHEN IT'S THE NIGHT BEFORE GROCERY-SHOPPING DAY.
MMMMM! MY FAVORITE!
KIRKMAN & SCOTT

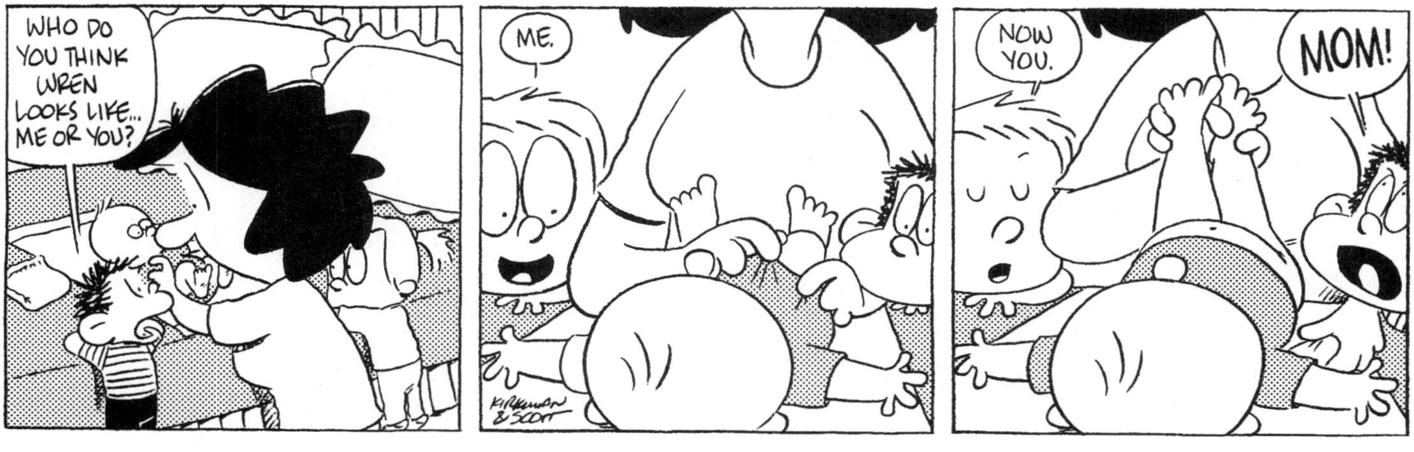

WHO DO YOU THINK WREN LOOKS LIKE... ME OR YOU?
ME.
KIRKMAN & SCOTT
NOW YOU.
MOM!

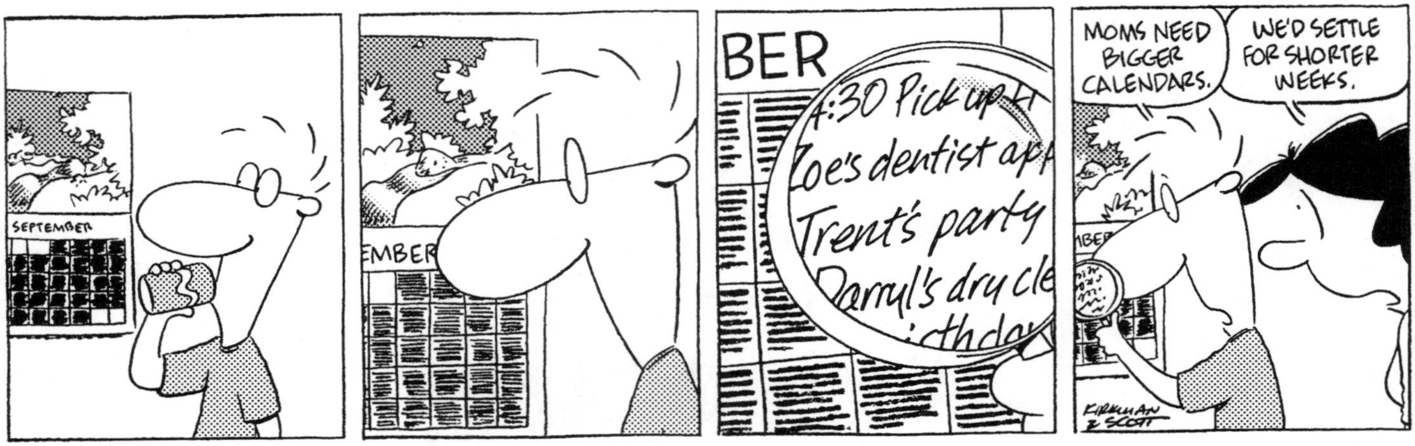
SEPTEMBER
Trent's party
MOMS NEED BIGGER CALENDARS.
WE'D SETTLE FOR SHORTER WEEKS.
KIRKMAN & SCOTT

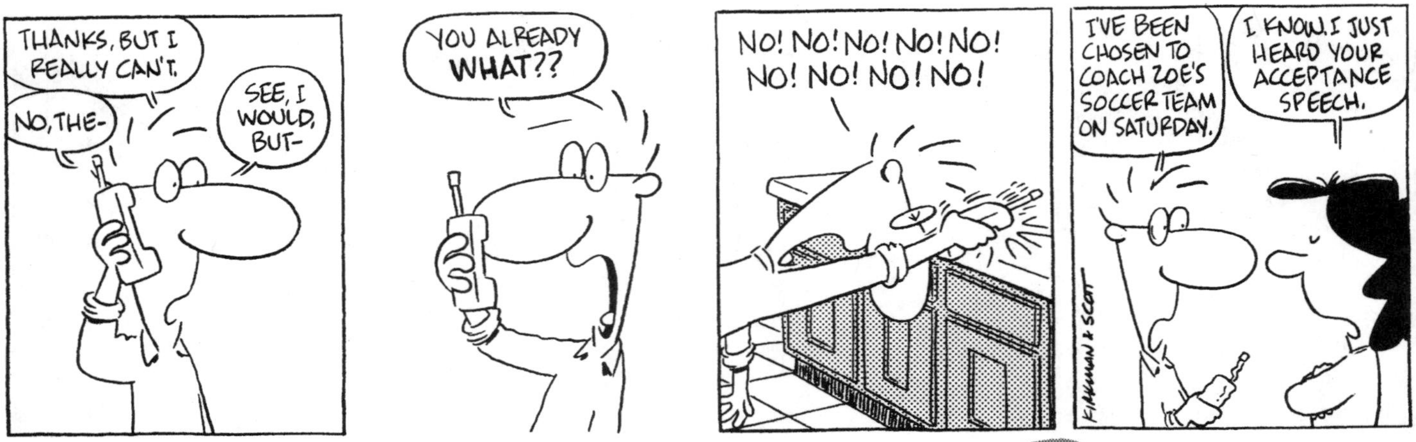
THANKS, BUT I REALLY CAN'T.
NO, THE-
SEE, I WOULD, BUT-
YOU ALREADY WHAT??
NO! NO! NO! NO! NO! NO! NO! NO! NO!
KIRKMAN & SCOTT
I'VE BEEN CHOSEN TO COACH ZOE'S SOCCER TEAM ON SATURDAY.
I KNOW. I JUST HEARD YOUR ACCEPTANCE SPEECH.

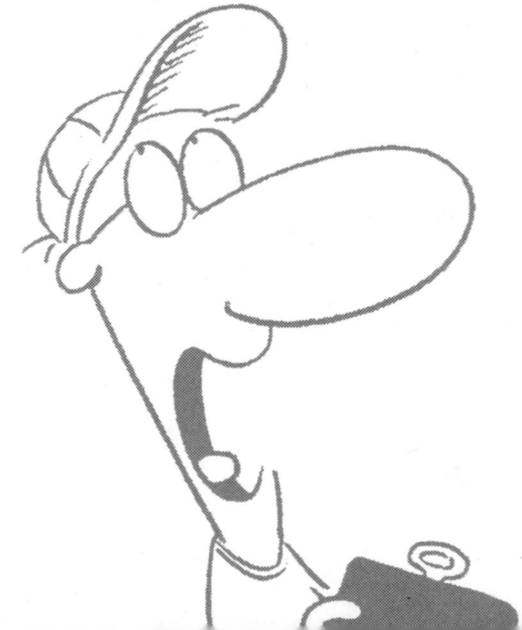

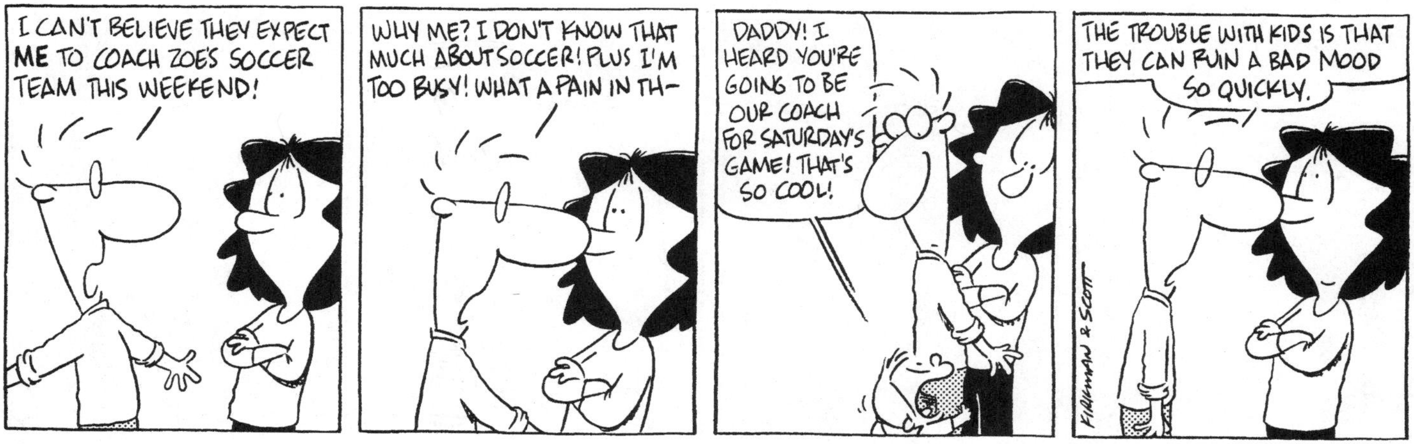
I CAN'T BELIEVE THEY EXPECT **ME** TO COACH ZOE'S SOCCER TEAM THIS WEEKEND!
WHY ME? I DON'T KNOW THAT MUCH ABOUT SOCCER! PLUS I'M TOO BUSY! WHAT A PAIN IN TH-
DADDY! I HEARD YOU'RE GOING TO BE OUR COACH FOR SATURDAY'S GAME! THAT'S SO COOL!
THE TROUBLE WITH KIDS IS THAT THEY CAN RUIN A BAD MOOD SO QUICKLY.
KIRKMAN & SCOTT

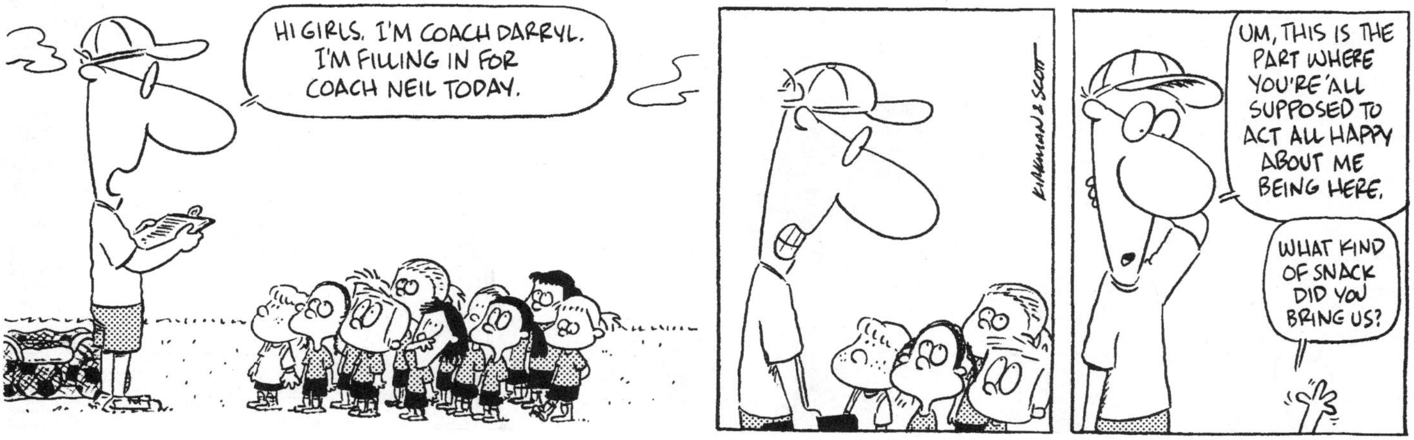
HI GIRLS. I'M COACH DARRYL. I'M FILLING IN FOR COACH NEIL TODAY.
KIRKMAN & SCOTT
UM, THIS IS THE PART WHERE YOU'RE ALL SUPPOSED TO ACT ALL HAPPY ABOUT ME BEING HERE.
WHAT KIND OF SNACK DID YOU BRING US?

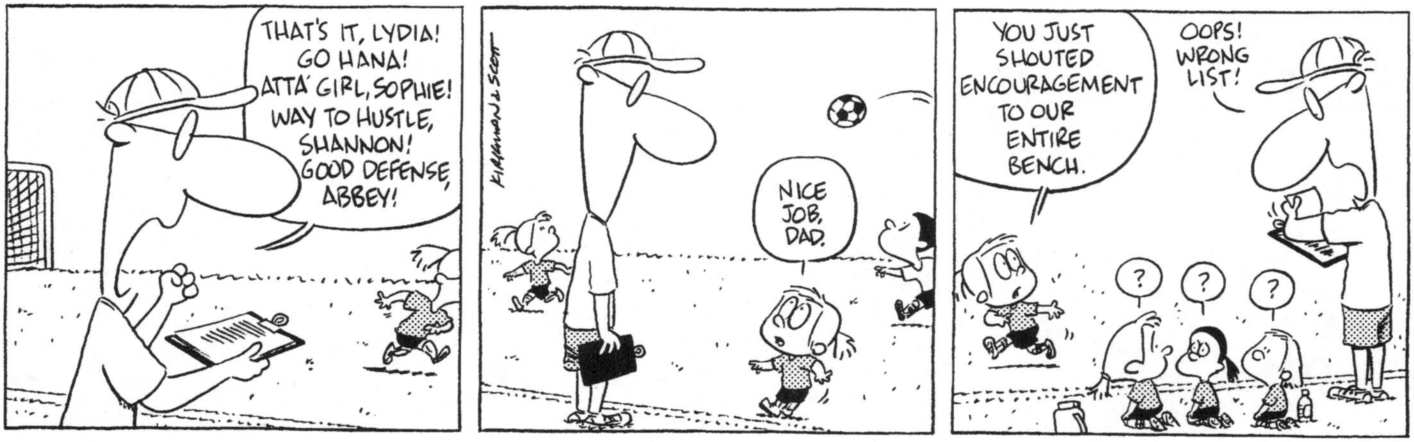
THAT'S IT, LYDIA! GO HANA! ATTA' GIRL, SOPHIE! WAY TO HUSTLE, SHANNON! GOOD DEFENSE, ABBEY!
KIRKMAN & SCOTT
NICE JOB, DAD.
YOU JUST SHOUTED ENCOURAGEMENT TO OUR ENTIRE BENCH.
OOPS! WRONG LIST!
?
?
?

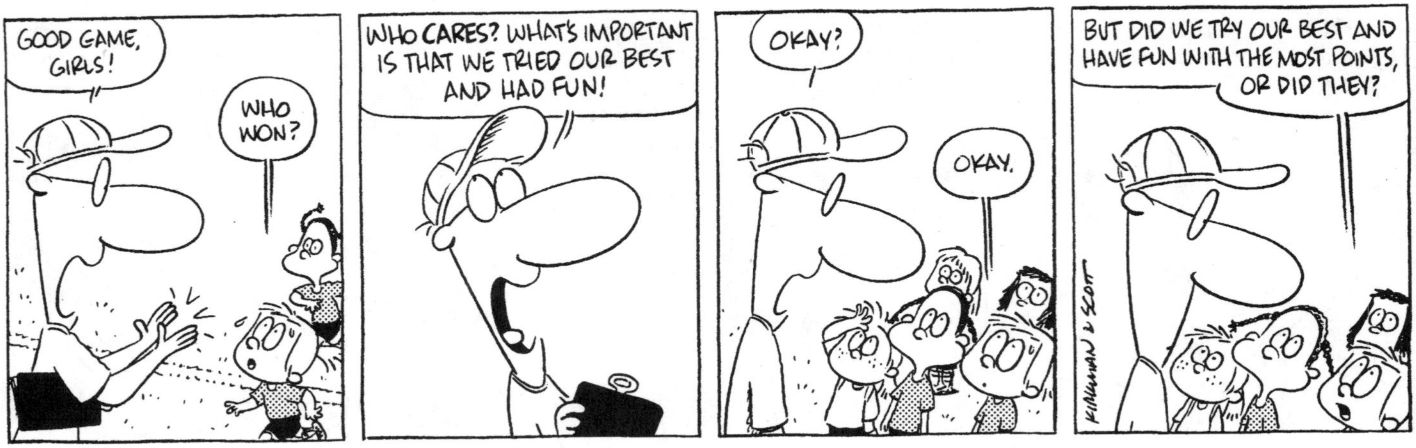
GOOD GAME, GIRLS!
WHO WON?
WHO CARES? WHAT'S IMPORTANT IS THAT WE TRIED OUR BEST AND HAD FUN!
OKAY?
OKAY.
BUT DID WE TRY OUR BEST AND HAVE FUN WITH THE MOST POINTS, OR DID THEY?
KIRKMAN & SCOTT

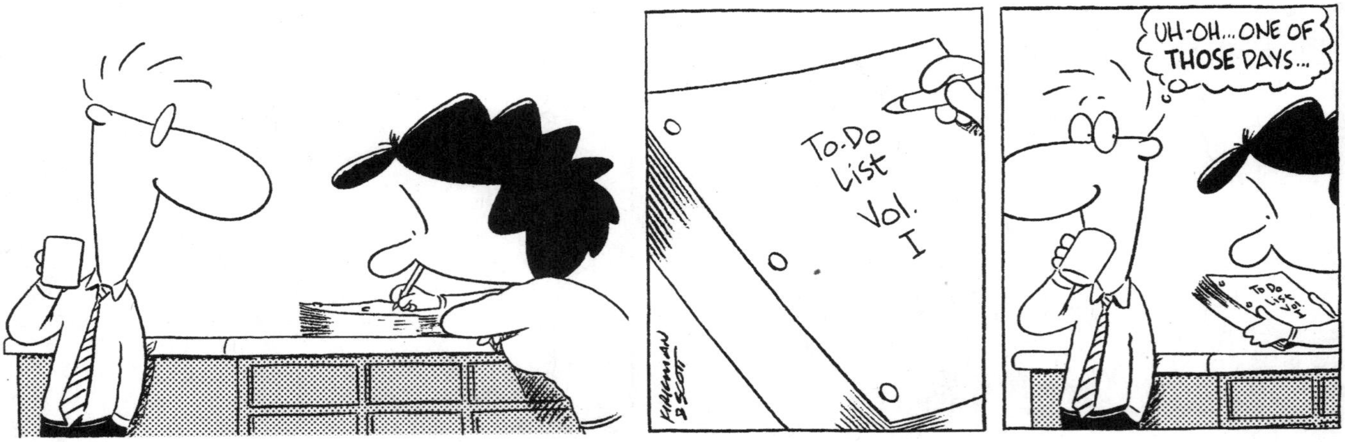
KIRKMAN & SCOTT
To-Do List Vol. I
UH-OH... ONE OF THOSE DAYS...

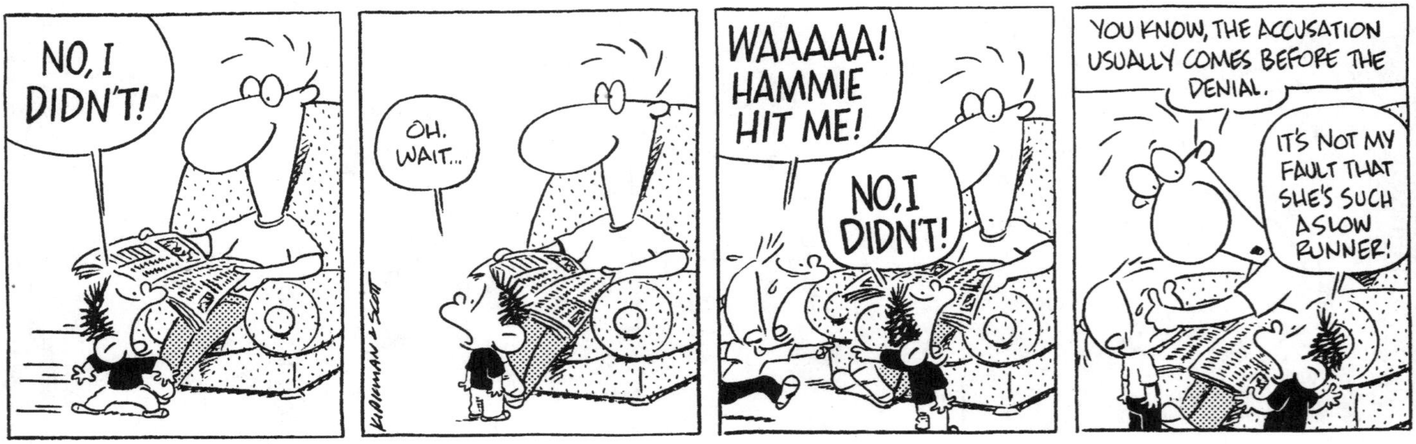
NO, I DIDN'T!
OH. WAIT...
KIRKMAN & SCOTT
WAAAAA! HAMMIE HIT ME!
NO, I DIDN'T!
YOU KNOW, THE ACCUSATION USUALLY COMES BEFORE THE DENIAL.
IT'S NOT MY FAULT THAT SHE'S SUCH A SLOW RUNNER!

lue
baby blues
ocean blue
eriwinkle blue
sky blue

I HAVE HOMEWORK!
THAT'S RIGHT... HOMEWORK!
I'D BETTER EAT A GOOD DINNER BECAUSE I HAVE HOMEWORK!
AS SOON AS WE CLEAR THE TABLE, I CAN DO MY HOMEWORK!
QUIET EVERYBODY! I'M STARTING MY HOMEWORK!
SCRIBBLE! SCRIBBLE! SCRIBBLE!
DONE!
COLORING THREE SHAPES IS HOME-WORK??
I COULD USE A LITTLE NECK RUB TO EASE THE TENSION.
KIRKMAN & SCOTT

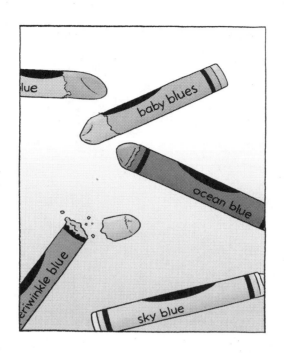

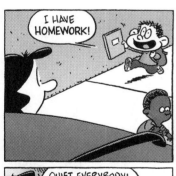

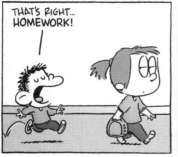

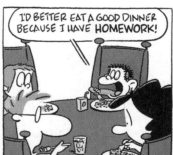

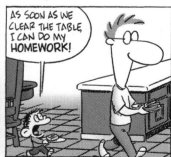

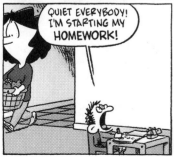

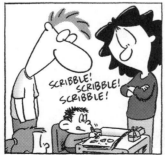

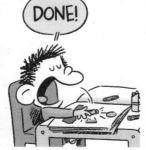

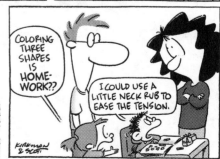

BABY BLUES®
BY
RICK KIRKMAN / JERRY SCOTT

WOW! TAKE A LOOK AT THIS ARTICLE, HONEY!
LIVING
GOSH! HOW...
LIVING
...INTERESTING!
IF YOU NEED THE READING GLASSES, JUST WEAR THEM.
NO WAY... THOSE THINGS ARE FOR OLD PEOPLE.
KIRKMAN & SCOTT

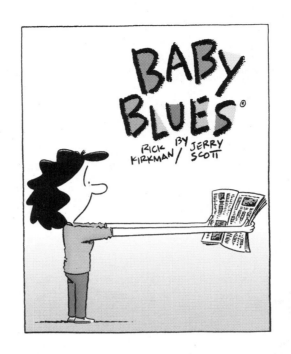

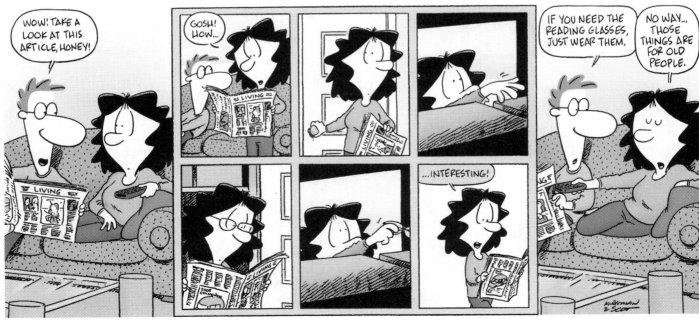

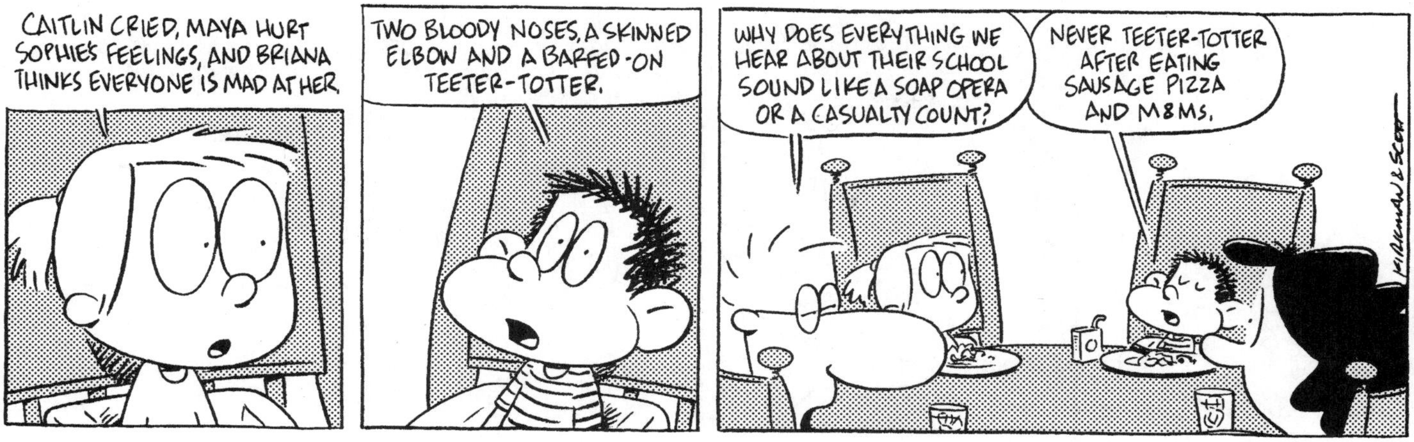
CAITLIN CRIED, MAYA HURT SOPHIE'S FEELINGS, AND BRIANA THINKS EVERYONE IS MAD AT HER.
TWO BLOODY NOSES, A SKINNED ELBOW AND A BARFED-ON TEETER-TOTTER.
WHY DOES EVERYTHING WE HEAR ABOUT THEIR SCHOOL SOUND LIKE A SOAP OPERA OR A CASUALTY COUNT?
NEVER TEETER-TOTTER AFTER EATING SAUSAGE PIZZA AND M&MS.
KIRKMAN & SCOTT

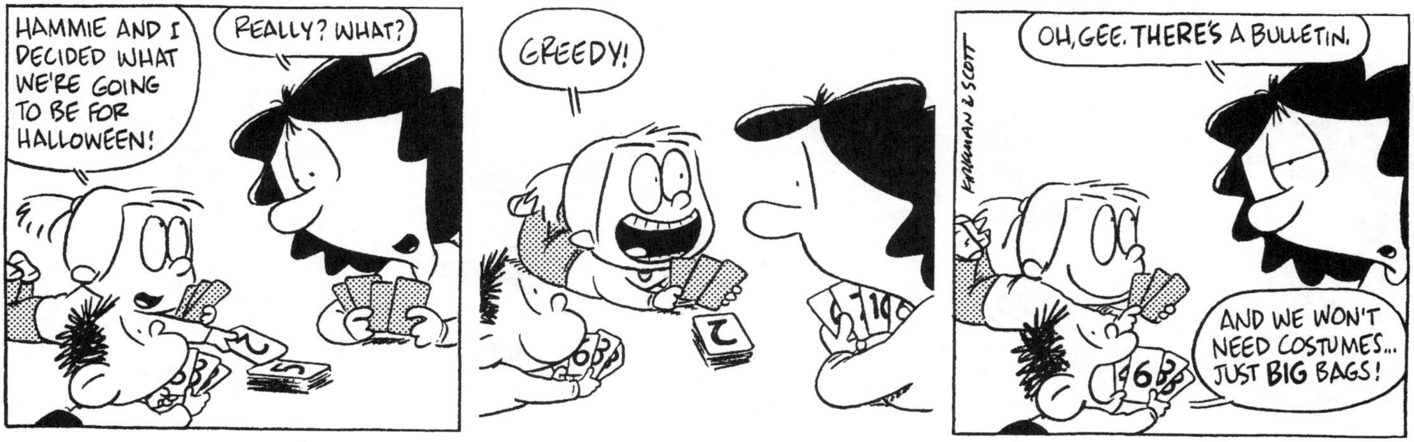
HAMMIE AND I DECIDED WHAT WE'RE GOING TO BE FOR HALLOWEEN!
REALLY? WHAT?
GREEDY!
KIRKMAN & SCOTT
OH, GEE. THERE'S A BULLETIN.
AND WE WON'T NEED COSTUMES... JUST BIG BAGS!

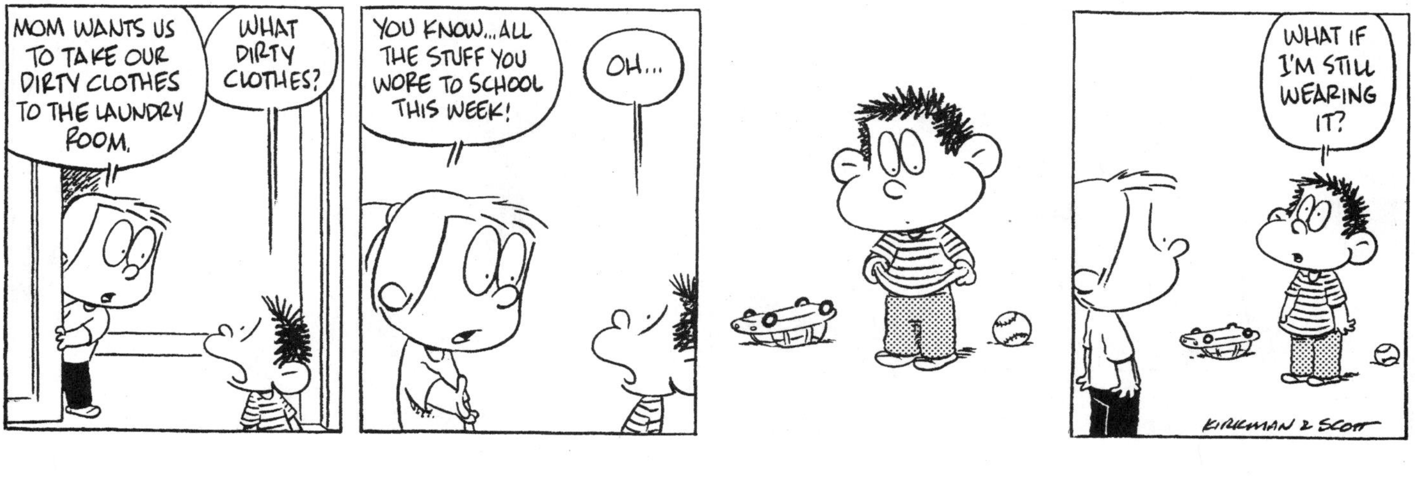
MOM WANTS US TO TAKE OUR DIRTY CLOTHES TO THE LAUNDRY ROOM.
WHAT DIRTY CLOTHES?
YOU KNOW... ALL THE STUFF YOU WORE TO SCHOOL THIS WEEK!
OH...
WHAT IF I'M STILL WEARING IT?
KIRKMAN & SCOTT

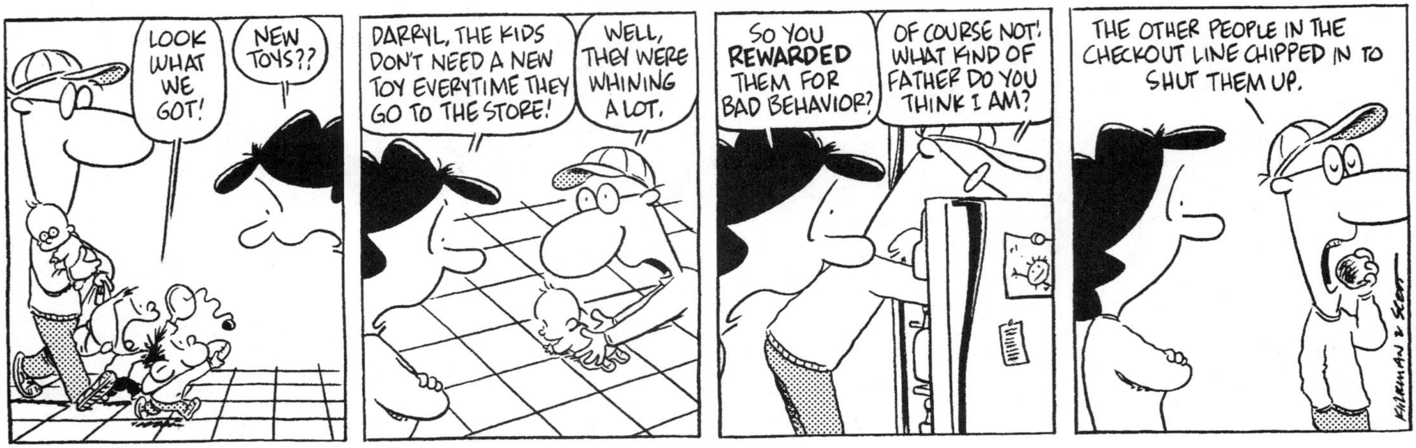
LOOK WHAT WE GOT!
NEW TOYS??
DARRYL, THE KIDS DON'T NEED A NEW TOY EVERYTIME THEY GO TO THE STORE!
WELL, THEY WERE WHINING A LOT.
SO YOU **REWARDED** THEM FOR BAD BEHAVIOR?
OF COURSE NOT! WHAT KIND OF FATHER DO YOU THINK I AM?
THE OTHER PEOPLE IN THE CHECKOUT LINE CHIPPED IN TO SHUT THEM UP.
KIRKMAN & SCOTT

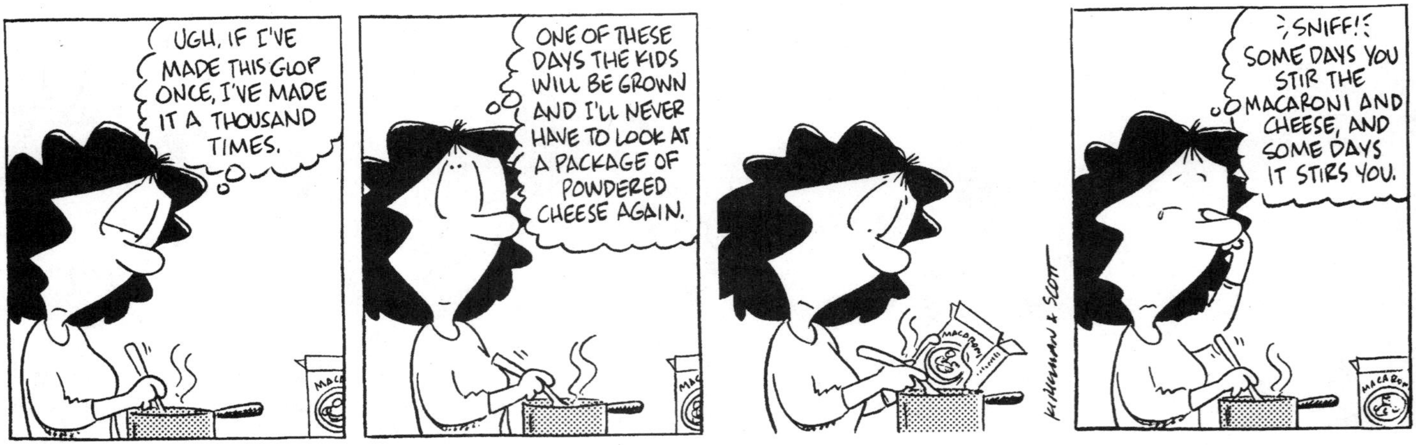
UGH, IF I'VE MADE THIS GLOP ONCE, I'VE MADE IT A THOUSAND TIMES.
ONE OF THESE DAYS THE KIDS WILL BE GROWN AND I'LL NEVER HAVE TO LOOK AT A PACKAGE OF POWDERED CHEESE AGAIN.
KIRKMAN & SCOTT
SNIFF!
SOME DAYS YOU STIR THE MACARONI AND CHEESE, AND SOME DAYS IT STIRS YOU.

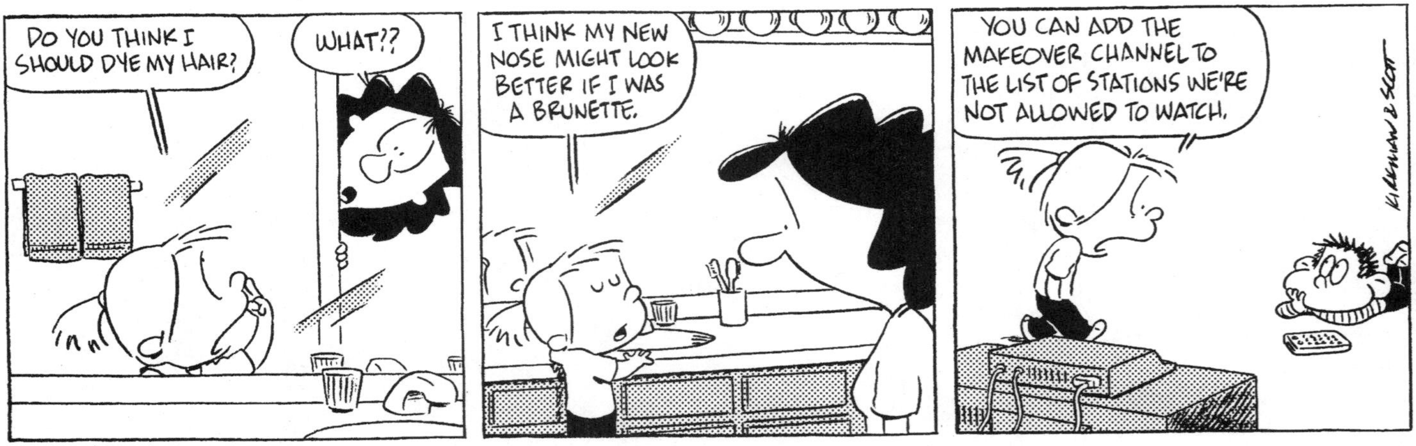
DO YOU THINK I SHOULD DYE MY HAIR?
WHAT??
I THINK MY NEW NOSE MIGHT LOOK BETTER IF I WAS A BRUNETTE.
YOU CAN ADD THE MAKEOVER CHANNEL TO THE LIST OF STATIONS WE'RE NOT ALLOWED TO WATCH.
KIRKMAN & SCOTT

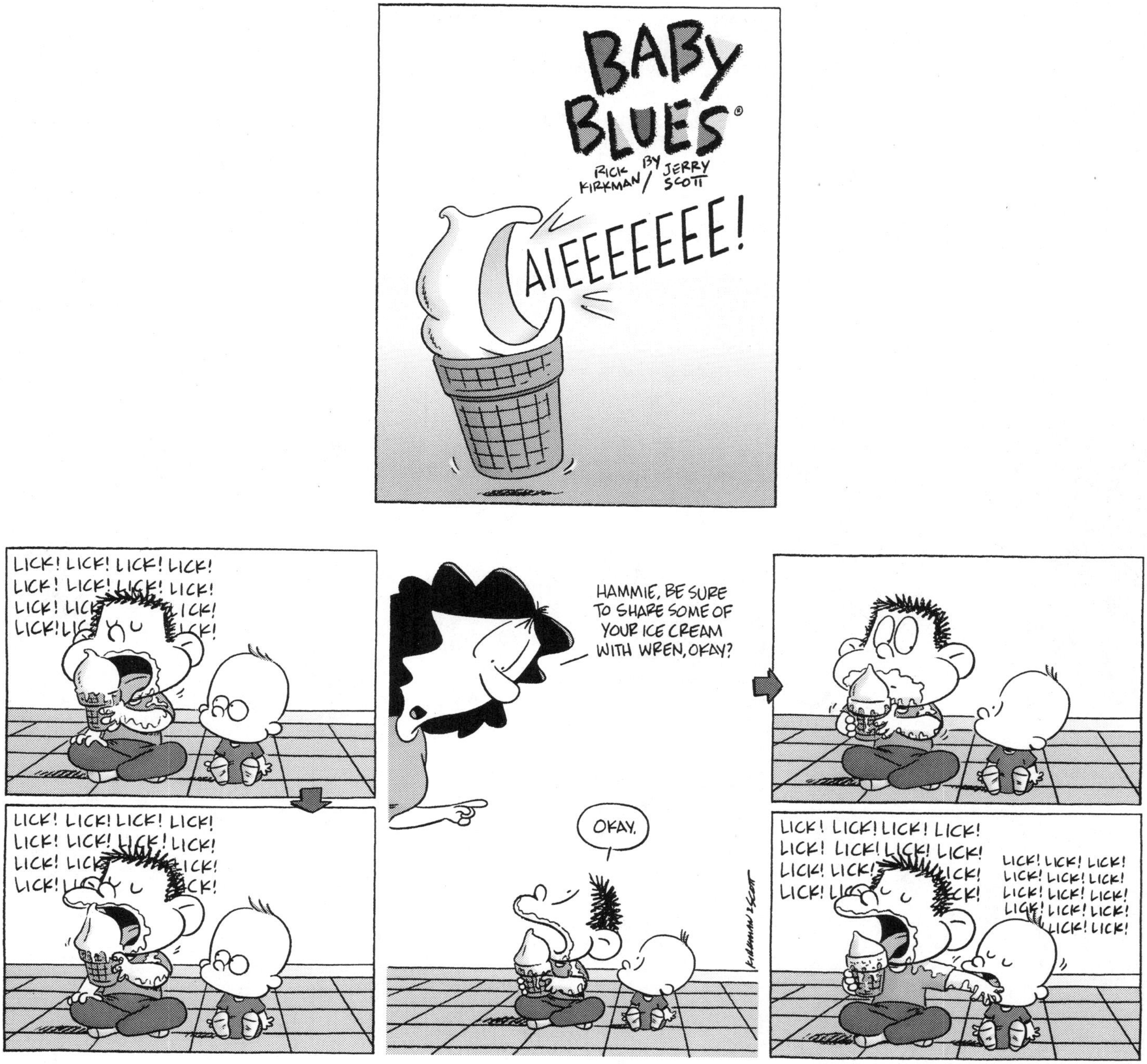
BABY BLUES®
BY RICK KIRKMAN / JERRY SCOTT
AIEEEEEEE!
LICK! LICK! LICK! LICK!
HAMMIE, BE SURE TO SHARE SOME OF YOUR ICE CREAM WITH WREN, OKAY?
OKAY.
KIRKMAN & SCOTT
LICK! LICK! LICK!

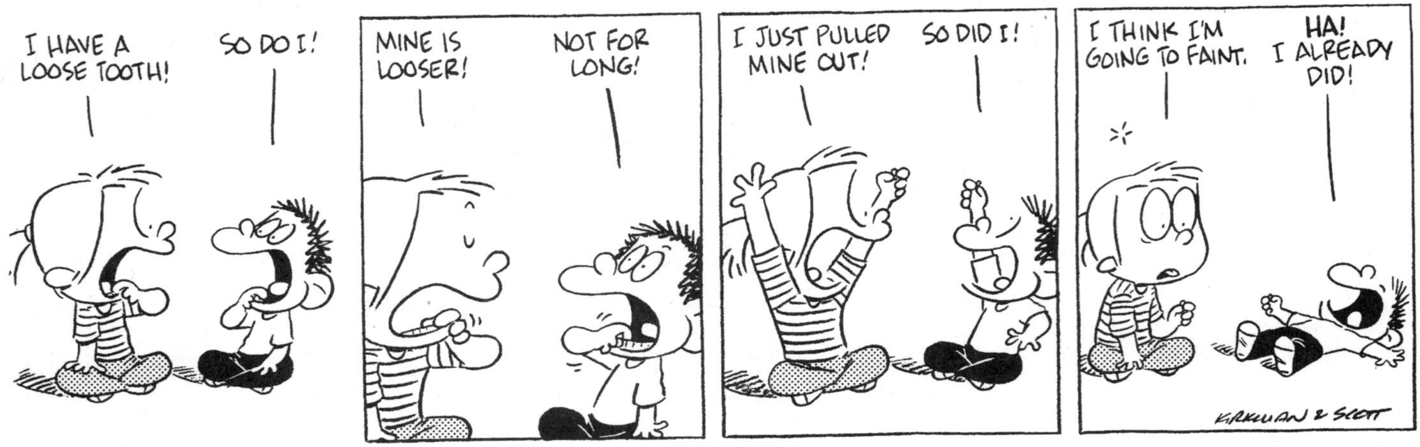
I HAVE A LOOSE TOOTH!
SO DO I!
MINE IS LOOSER!
NOT FOR LONG!
I JUST PULLED MINE OUT!
SO DID I!
I THINK I'M GOING TO FAINT.
HA! I ALREADY DID!
KIRKMAN & SCOTT

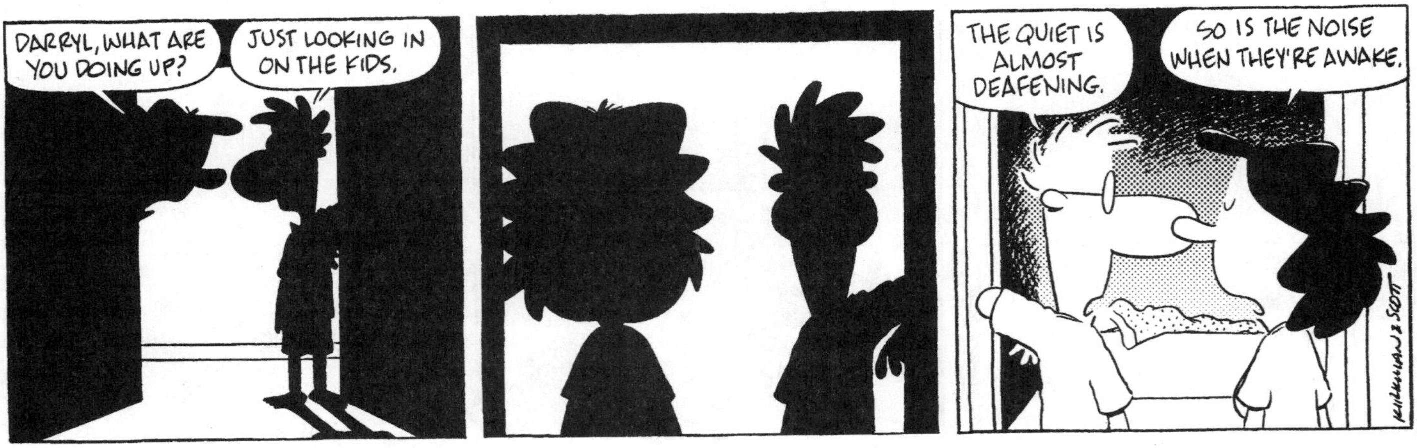
DARRYL, WHAT ARE YOU DOING UP?
JUST LOOKING IN ON THE KIDS.
THE QUIET IS ALMOST DEAFENING.
SO IS THE NOISE WHEN THEY'RE AWAKE.
KIRKMAN & SCOTT

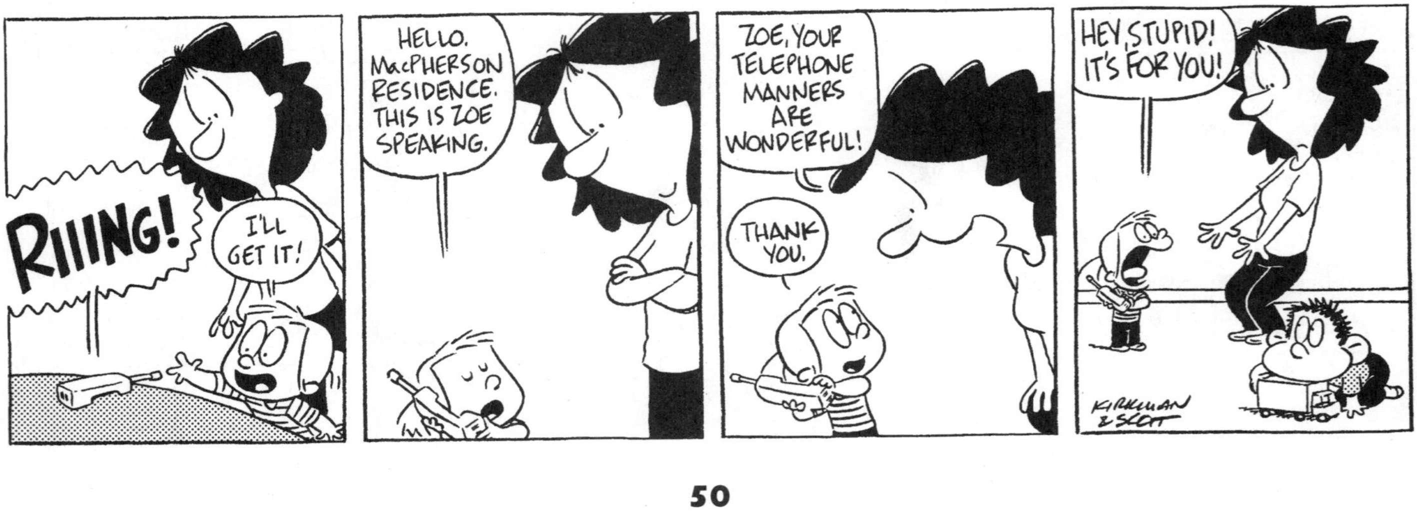
RIIING!
I'LL GET IT!
HELLO. MacPHERSON RESIDENCE. THIS IS ZOE SPEAKING.
ZOE, YOUR TELEPHONE MANNERS ARE WONDERFUL!
THANK YOU.
HEY, STUPID! IT'S FOR YOU!
KIRKMAN & SCOTT

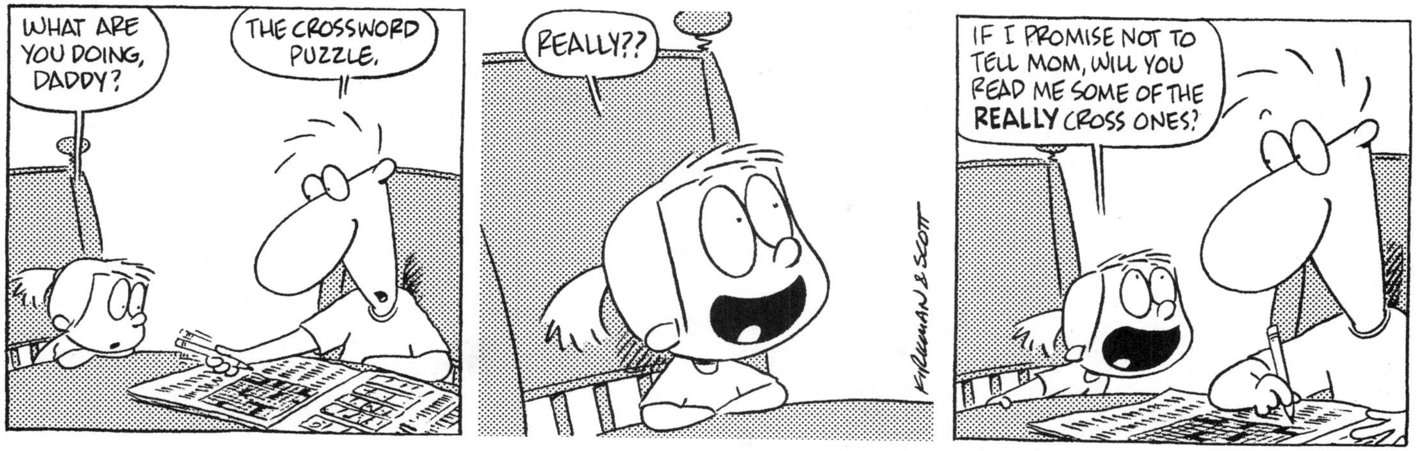
WHAT ARE YOU DOING, DADDY?
THE CROSSWORD PUZZLE.
REALLY??
KIRKMAN & SCOTT
IF I PROMISE NOT TO TELL MOM, WILL YOU READ ME SOME OF THE **REALLY** CROSS ONES?

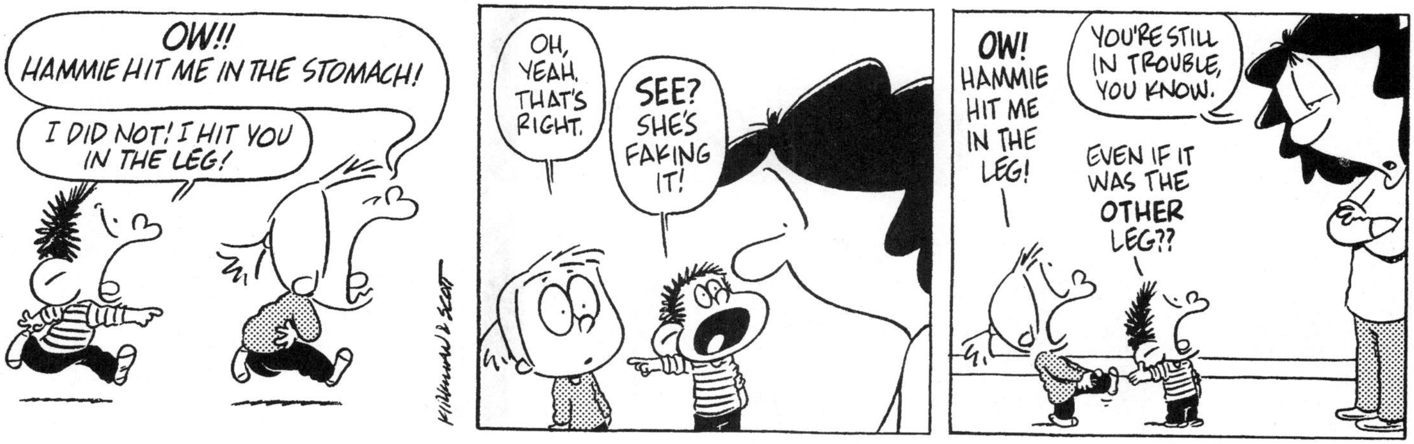
OW!! HAMMIE HIT ME IN THE STOMACH!
I DID NOT! I HIT YOU IN THE LEG!
KIRKMAN & SCOTT
OH, YEAH. THAT'S RIGHT.
SEE? SHE'S FAKING IT!
OW! HAMMIE HIT ME IN THE LEG!
YOU'RE STILL IN TROUBLE, YOU KNOW.
EVEN IF IT WAS THE **OTHER** LEG??

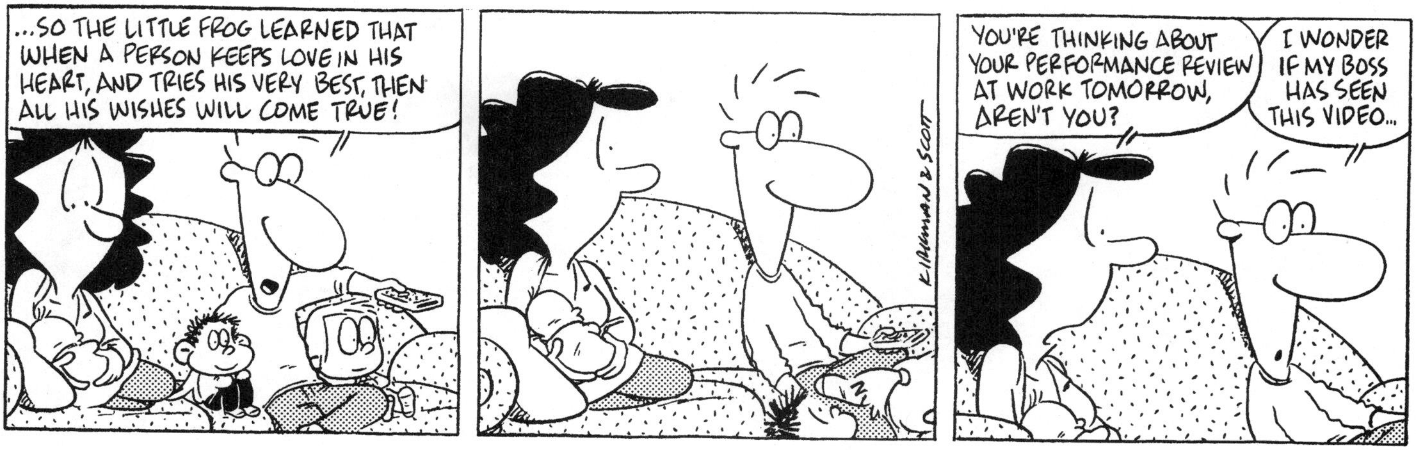
...SO THE LITTLE FROG LEARNED THAT WHEN A PERSON KEEPS LOVE IN HIS HEART, AND TRIES HIS VERY BEST, THEN ALL HIS WISHES WILL COME TRUE!
KIRKMAN & SCOTT
YOU'RE THINKING ABOUT YOUR PERFORMANCE REVIEW AT WORK TOMORROW, AREN'T YOU?
I WONDER IF MY BOSS HAS SEEN THIS VIDEO...

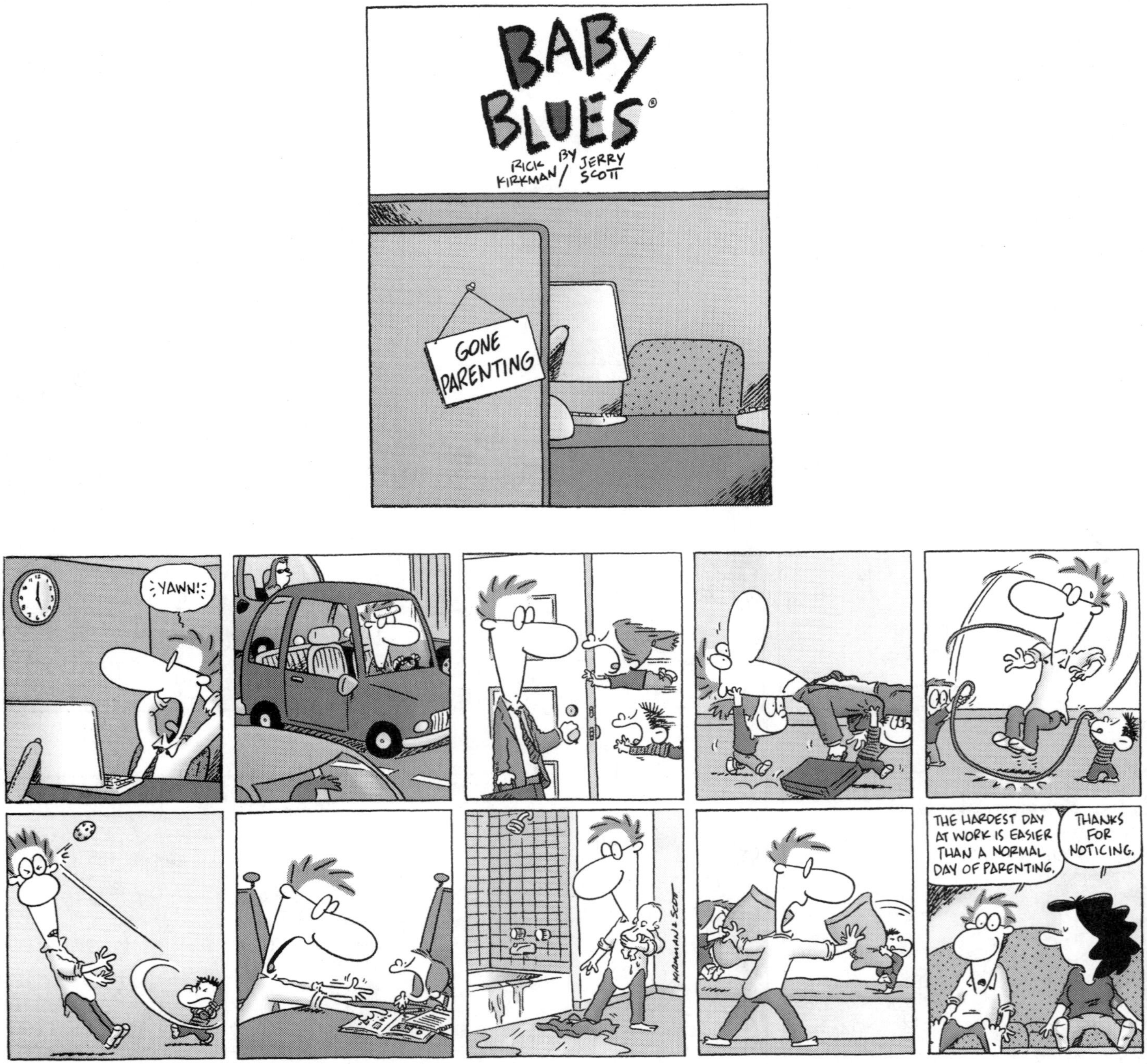
BABY BLUES®
BY RICK KIRKMAN / JERRY SCOTT
GONE PARENTING
YAWN!
THE HARDEST DAY AT WORK IS EASIER THAN A NORMAL DAY OF PARENTING.
THANKS FOR NOTICING.

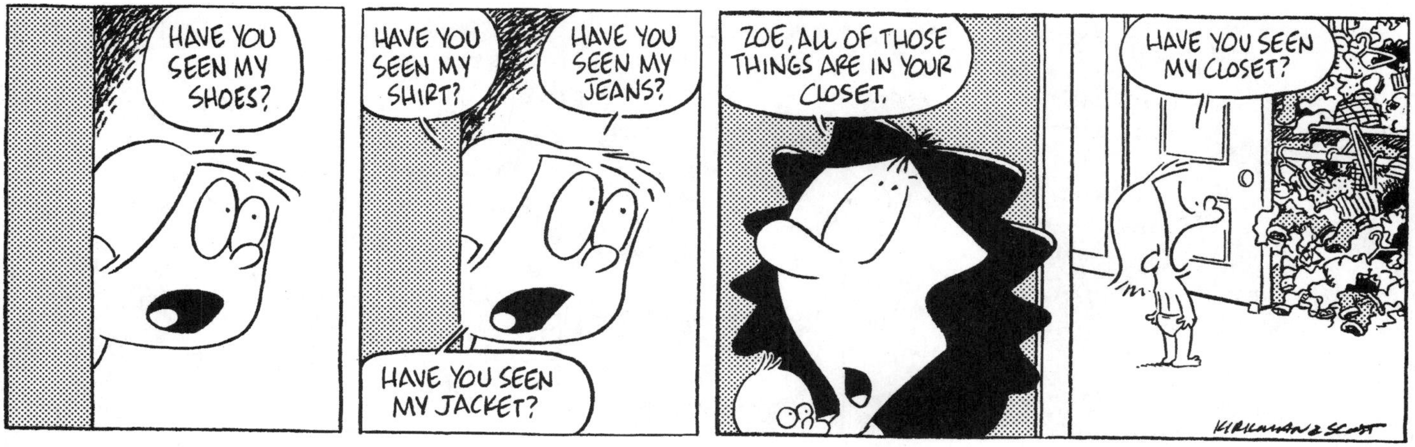
HAVE YOU SEEN MY SHOES?
HAVE YOU SEEN MY SHIRT?
HAVE YOU SEEN MY JEANS?
HAVE YOU SEEN MY JACKET?
ZOE, ALL OF THOSE THINGS ARE IN YOUR CLOSET.
HAVE YOU SEEN MY CLOSET?
KIRKMAN & SCOTT

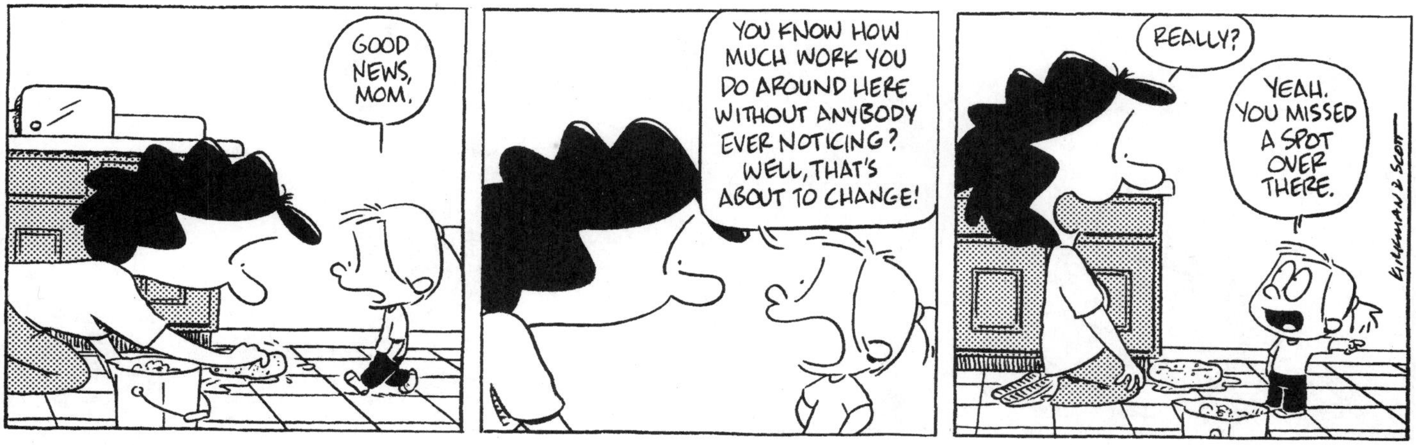
GOOD NEWS, MOM.
YOU KNOW HOW MUCH WORK YOU DO AROUND HERE WITHOUT ANYBODY EVER NOTICING? WELL, THAT'S ABOUT TO CHANGE!
REALLY?
YEAH. YOU MISSED A SPOT OVER THERE.
KIRKMAN & SCOTT

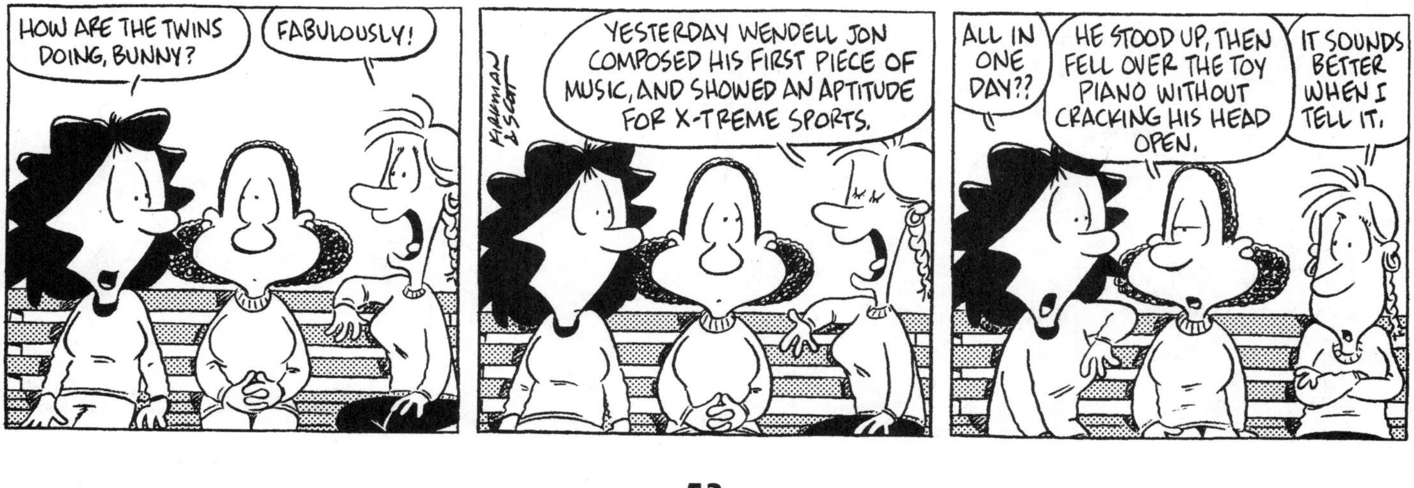
HOW ARE THE TWINS DOING, BUNNY?
FABULOUSLY!
KIRKMAN & SCOTT
YESTERDAY WENDELL JON COMPOSED HIS FIRST PIECE OF MUSIC, AND SHOWED AN APTITUDE FOR X-TREME SPORTS.
ALL IN ONE DAY??
HE STOOD UP, THEN FELL OVER THE TOY PIANO WITHOUT CRACKING HIS HEAD OPEN.
IT SOUNDS BETTER WHEN I TELL IT.

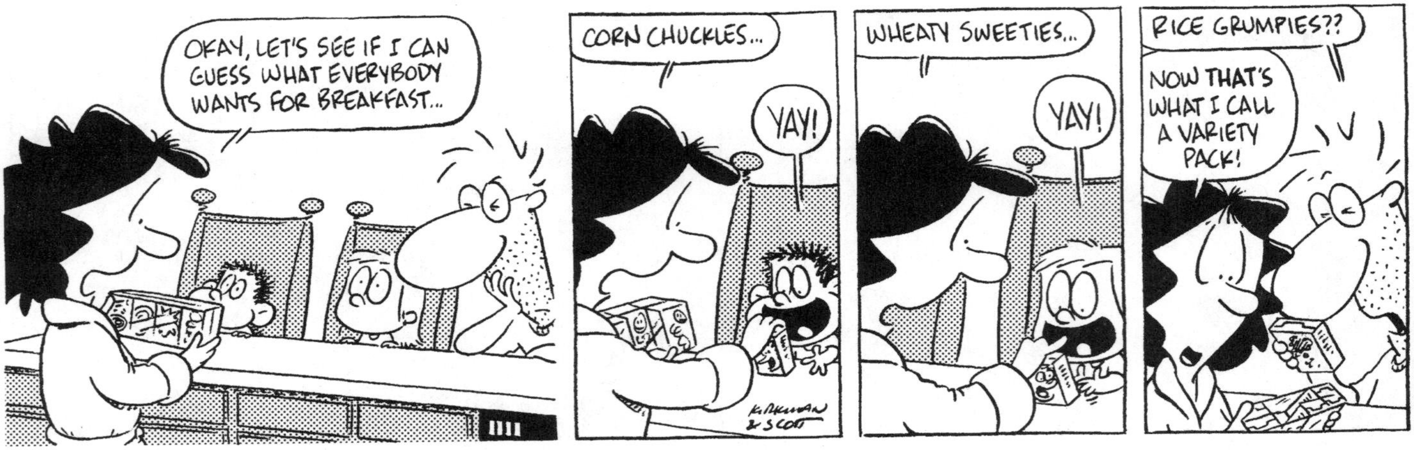

OKAY, LET'S SEE IF I CAN GUESS WHAT EVERYBODY WANTS FOR BREAKFAST...
CORN CHUCKLES...
YAY!
WHEATY SWEETIES...
YAY!
RICE GRUMPIES??
NOW THAT'S WHAT I CALL A VARIETY PACK!
KIRKMAN & SCOTT

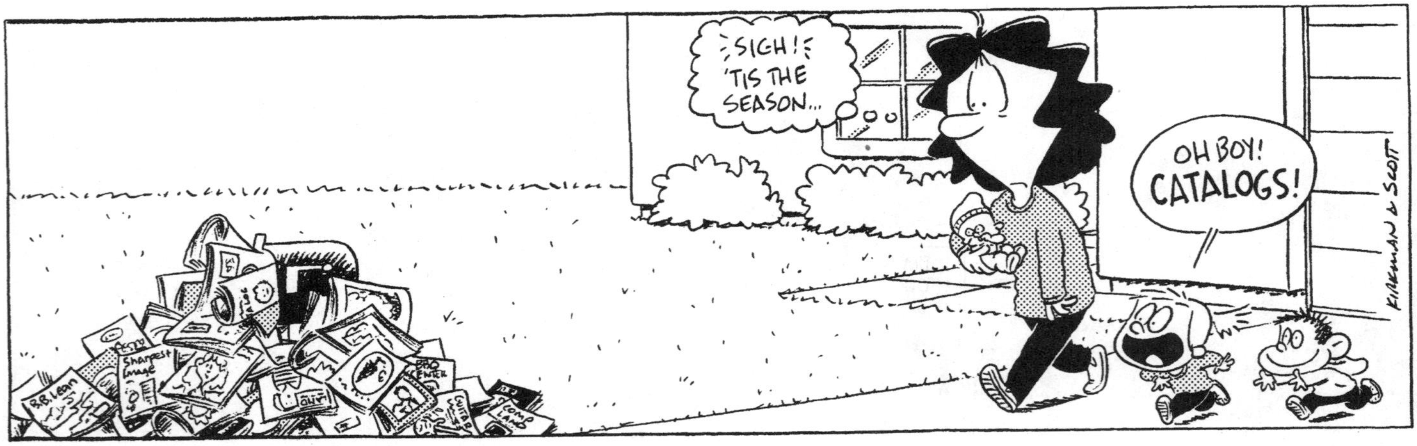

SIGH! 'TIS THE SEASON...
OH BOY! CATALOGS!
KIRKMAN & SCOTT

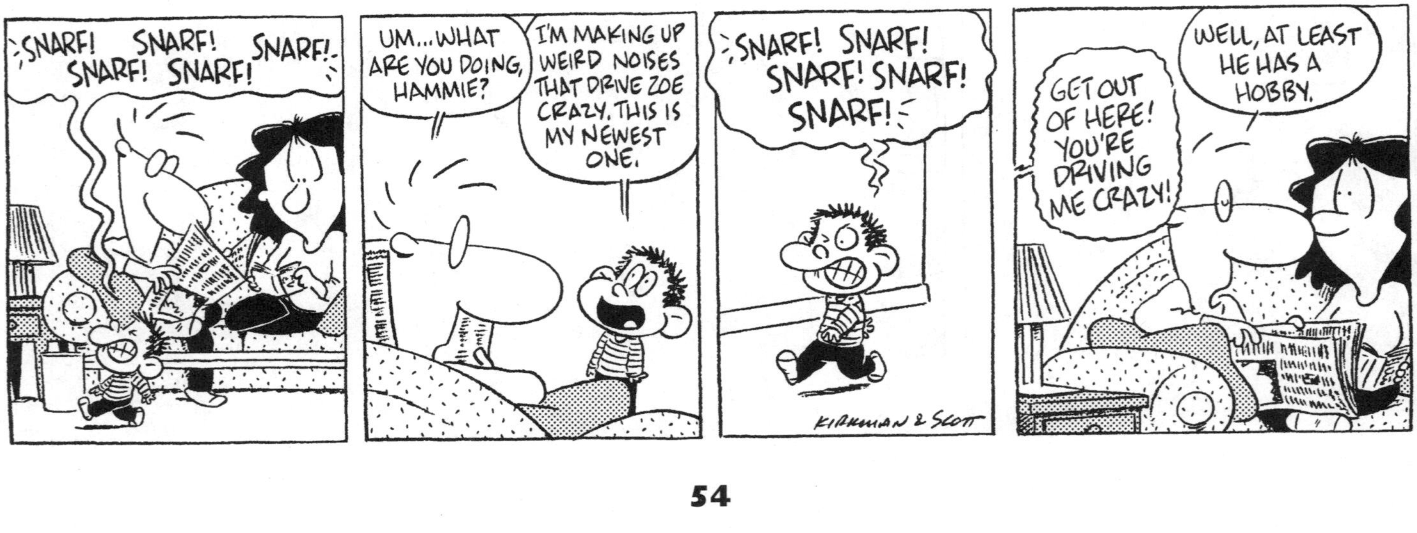

SNARF! SNARF! SNARF! SNARF! SNARF!
UM... WHAT ARE YOU DOING, HAMMIE?
I'M MAKING UP WEIRD NOISES THAT DRIVE ZOE CRAZY. THIS IS MY NEWEST ONE.
SNARF! SNARF! SNARF! SNARF! SNARF!
KIRKMAN & SCOTT
GET OUT OF HERE! YOU'RE DRIVING ME CRAZY!
WELL, AT LEAST HE HAS A HOBBY.

BABY BLUES®
RICK KIRKMAN / BY JERRY SCOTT

I'M NOT TOUCHING YOU.
I'M NOT TOUCHING YOU, EITHER.
I'M STILL NOT TOUCHING YOU.
I'M STILL NOT TOUCHING YOU, EITHER.
I'M NOT TOUCHING YOU WAY CLOSER THAN YOU'RE NOT TOUCHING ME.
NO YOU'RE NOT.
YES I AM.
NO YOU'RE NOT.
YES I AM.
NO YOU'RE NOT.
THAT'S ENOUGH!
YOU TWO STOP NOT TOUCHING EACH OTHER!
OKAY.
OW!
HE HIT ME!
SLAP!
DID NOT!
SMACK!
SLAP!
THWACK!
BRILLIANT SOLUTION.
SIGH!
KIRKMAN & SCOTT

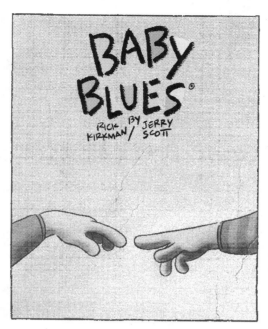

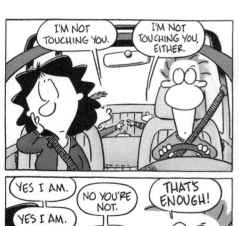

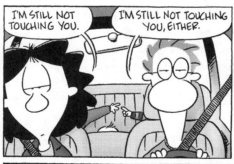

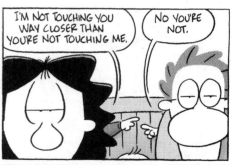

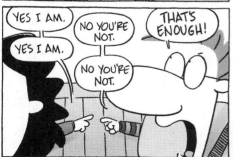

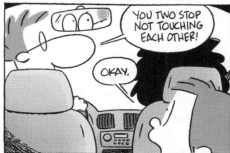

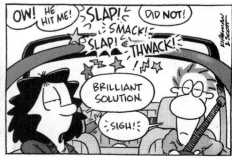

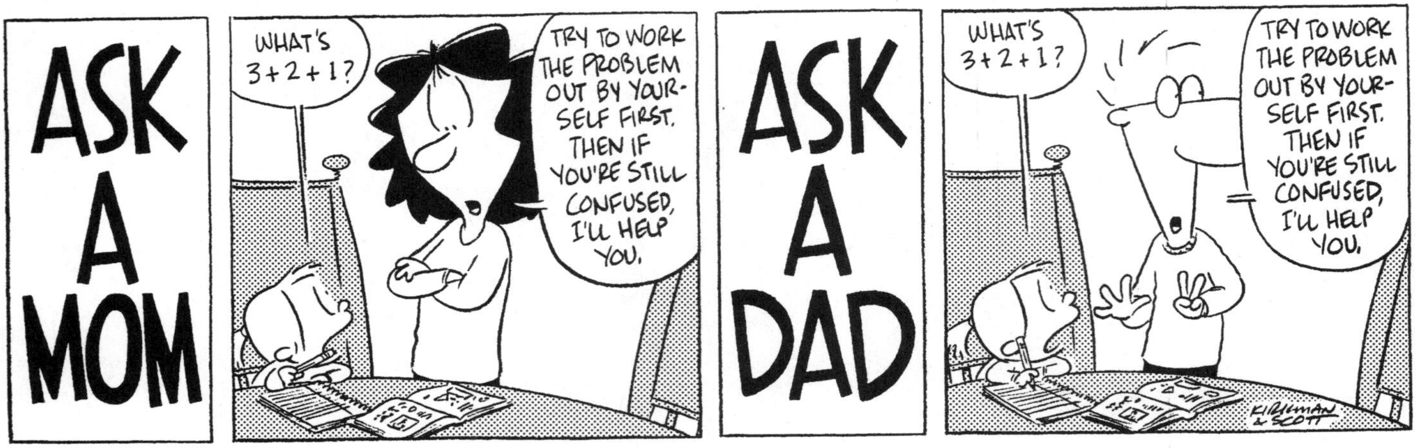
ASK A MOM
WHAT'S 3+2+1?
TRY TO WORK THE PROBLEM OUT BY YOURSELF FIRST. THEN IF YOU'RE STILL CONFUSED, I'LL HELP YOU.
ASK A DAD
WHAT'S 3+2+1?
TRY TO WORK THE PROBLEM OUT BY YOURSELF FIRST. THEN IF YOU'RE STILL CONFUSED, I'LL HELP YOU.
KIRKMAN & SCOTT

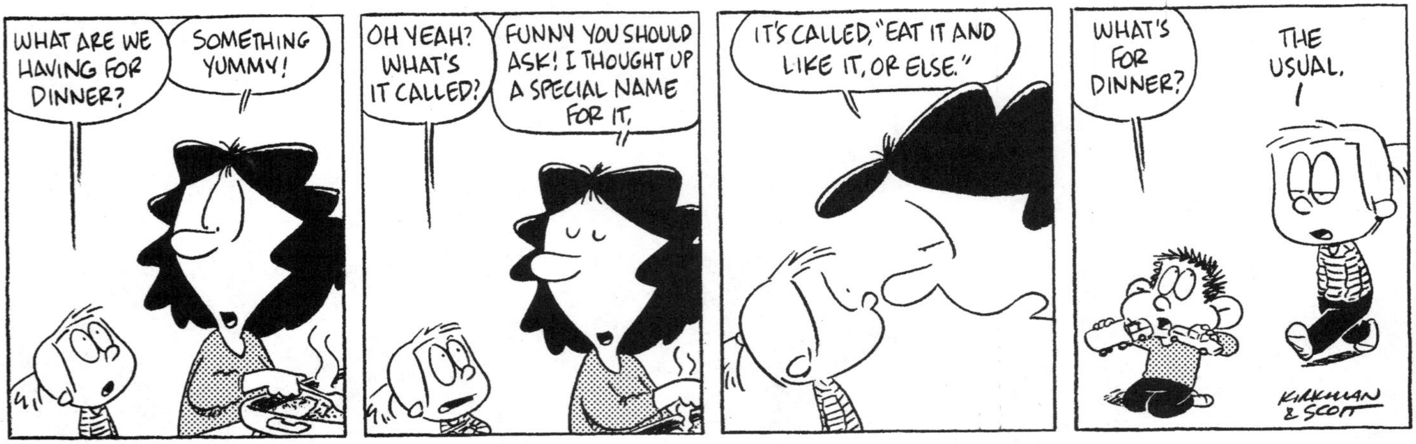
WHAT ARE WE HAVING FOR DINNER?
SOMETHING YUMMY!
OH YEAH? WHAT'S IT CALLED?
FUNNY YOU SHOULD ASK! I THOUGHT UP A SPECIAL NAME FOR IT.
IT'S CALLED, "EAT IT AND LIKE IT, OR ELSE."
WHAT'S FOR DINNER?
THE USUAL.
KIRKMAN & SCOTT

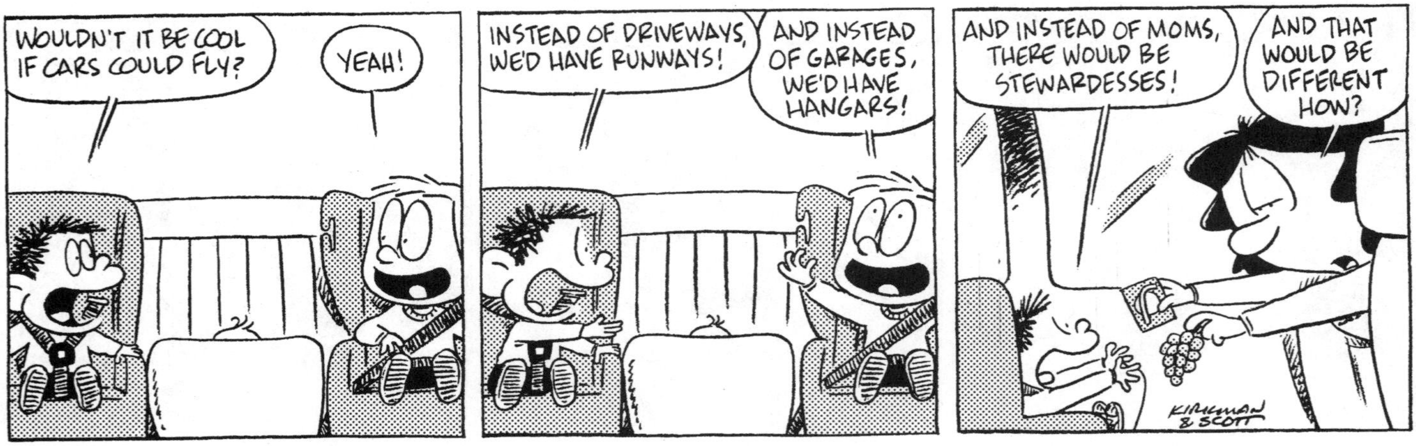
WOULDN'T IT BE COOL IF CARS COULD FLY?
YEAH!
INSTEAD OF DRIVEWAYS, WE'D HAVE RUNWAYS!
AND INSTEAD OF GARAGES, WE'D HAVE HANGARS!
AND INSTEAD OF MOMS, THERE WOULD BE STEWARDESSES!
AND THAT WOULD BE DIFFERENT HOW?
KIRKMAN & SCOTT

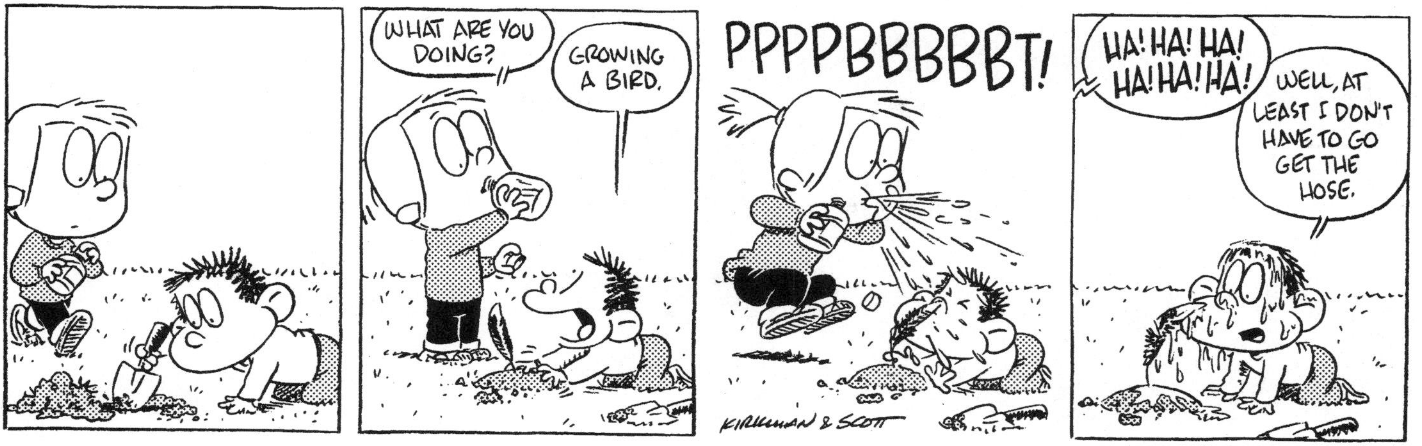
WHAT ARE YOU DOING?
GROWING A BIRD.
PPPPBBBBBT!
HA! HA! HA! HA! HA! HA!
WELL, AT LEAST I DON'T HAVE TO GO GET THE HOSE.
KIRKMAN & SCOTT

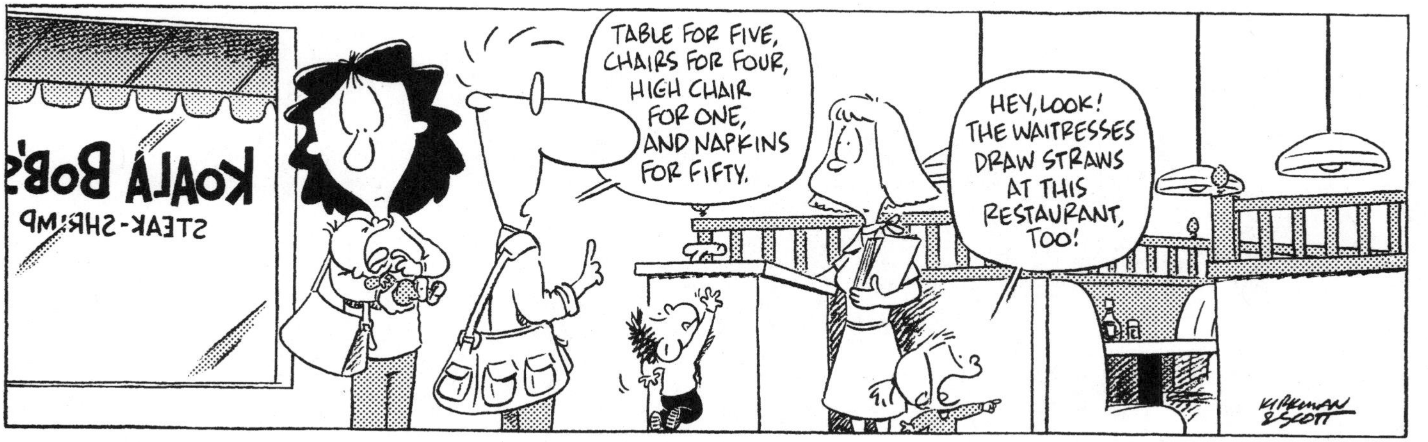
KOALA BOB'S
STEAK-SHRIMP
TABLE FOR FIVE, CHAIRS FOR FOUR, HIGH CHAIR FOR ONE, AND NAPKINS FOR FIFTY.
HEY, LOOK! THE WAITRESSES DRAW STRAWS AT THIS RESTAURANT, TOO!
KIRKMAN & SCOTT

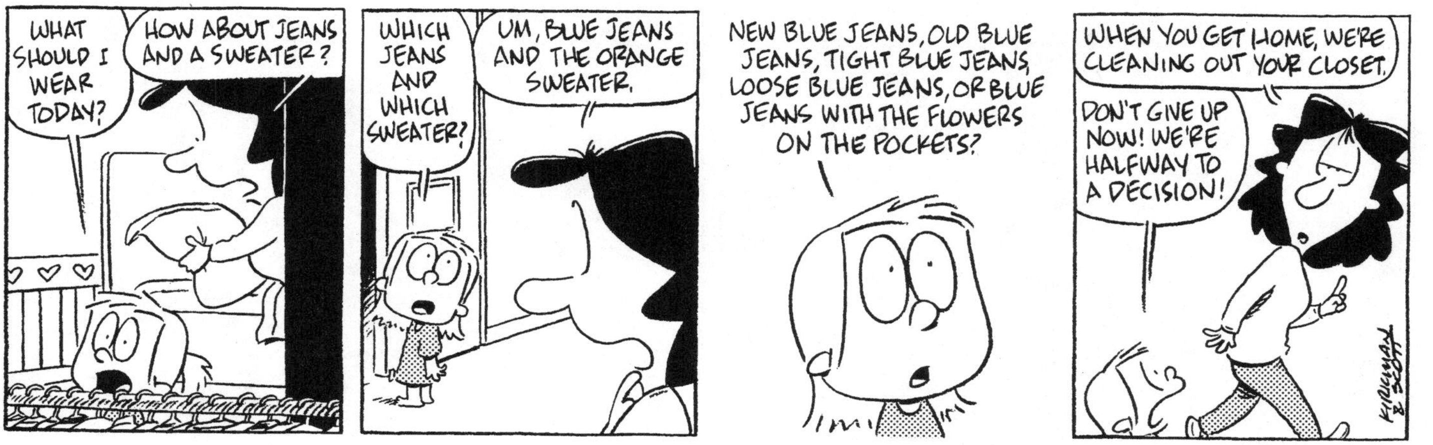
WHAT SHOULD I WEAR TODAY?
HOW ABOUT JEANS AND A SWEATER?
WHICH JEANS AND WHICH SWEATER?
UM, BLUE JEANS AND THE ORANGE SWEATER.
NEW BLUE JEANS, OLD BLUE JEANS, TIGHT BLUE JEANS, LOOSE BLUE JEANS, OR BLUE JEANS WITH THE FLOWERS ON THE POCKETS?
WHEN YOU GET HOME, WE'RE CLEANING OUT YOUR CLOSET.
DON'T GIVE UP NOW! WE'RE HALFWAY TO A DECISION!
KIRKMAN & SCOTT

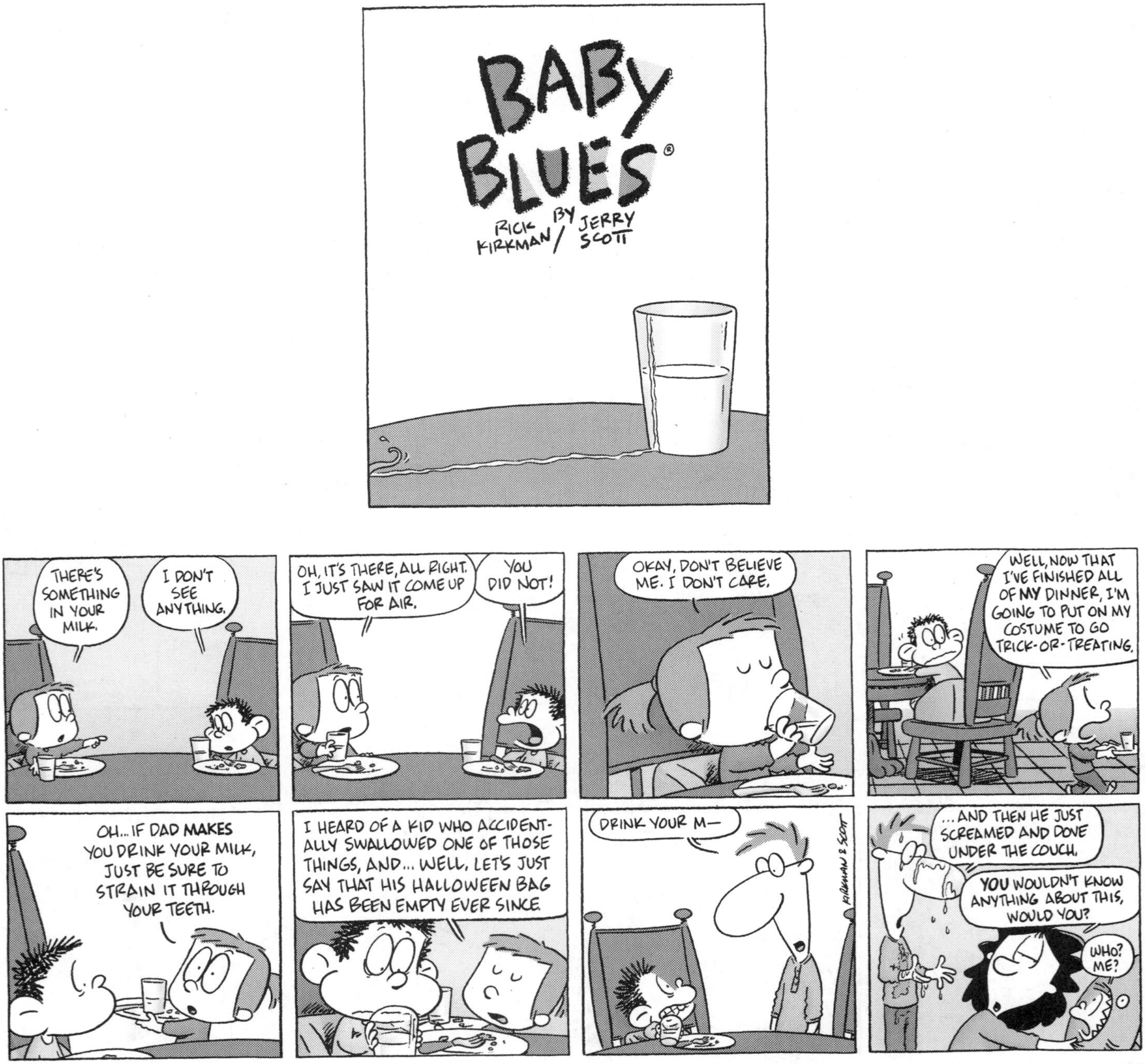
BABY BLUES®
BY RICK KIRKMAN / JERRY SCOTT
THERE'S SOMETHING IN YOUR MILK.
I DON'T SEE ANYTHING.
OH, IT'S THERE, ALL RIGHT. I JUST SAW IT COME UP FOR AIR.
YOU DID NOT!
OKAY, DON'T BELIEVE ME. I DON'T CARE.
WELL, NOW THAT I'VE FINISHED ALL OF MY DINNER, I'M GOING TO PUT ON MY COSTUME TO GO TRICK-OR-TREATING.
OH... IF DAD MAKES YOU DRINK YOUR MILK, JUST BE SURE TO STRAIN IT THROUGH YOUR TEETH.
I HEARD OF A KID WHO ACCIDENTALLY SWALLOWED ONE OF THOSE THINGS, AND... WELL, LET'S JUST SAY THAT HIS HALLOWEEN BAG HAS BEEN EMPTY EVER SINCE.
DRINK YOUR M—
KIRKMAN & SCOTT
...AND THEN HE JUST SCREAMED AND DOVE UNDER THE COUCH.
YOU WOULDN'T KNOW ANYTHING ABOUT THIS, WOULD YOU?
WHO? ME?

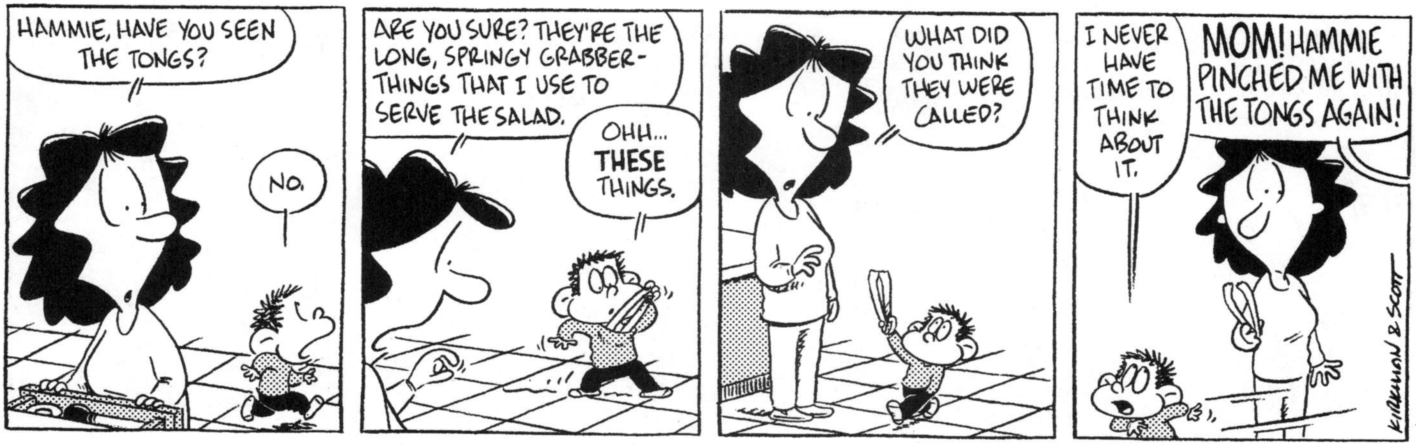
HAMMIE, HAVE YOU SEEN THE TONGS?
NO.
ARE YOU SURE? THEY'RE THE LONG, SPRINGY GRABBER-THINGS THAT I USE TO SERVE THE SALAD.
OHH... THESE THINGS.
WHAT DID YOU THINK THEY WERE CALLED?
I NEVER HAVE TIME TO THINK ABOUT IT.
MOM! HAMMIE PINCHED ME WITH THE TONGS AGAIN!
KIRKMAN & SCOTT

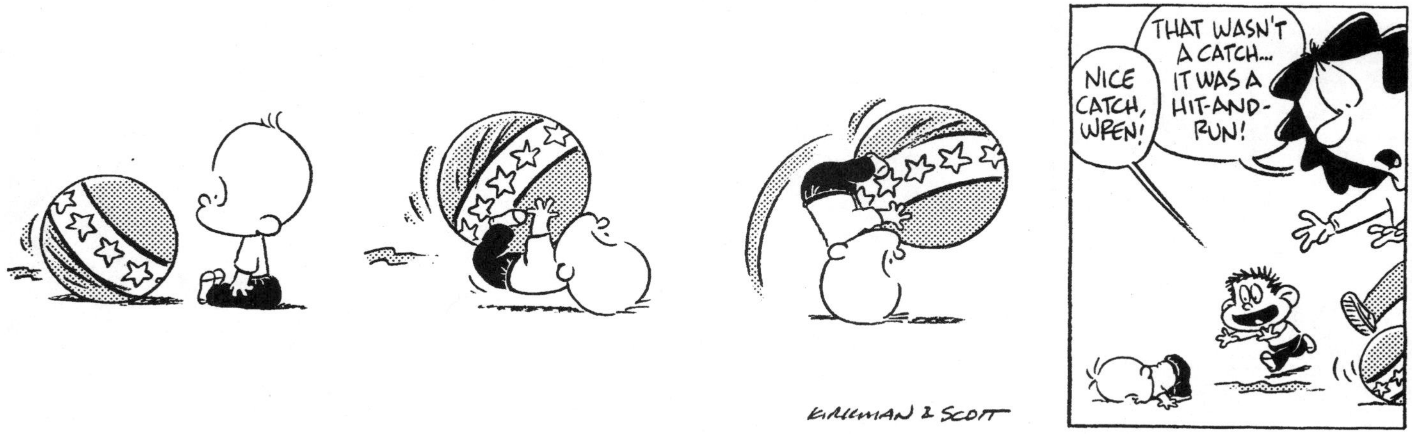
KIRKMAN & SCOTT
NICE CATCH, WREN!
THAT WASN'T A CATCH... IT WAS A HIT-AND-RUN!

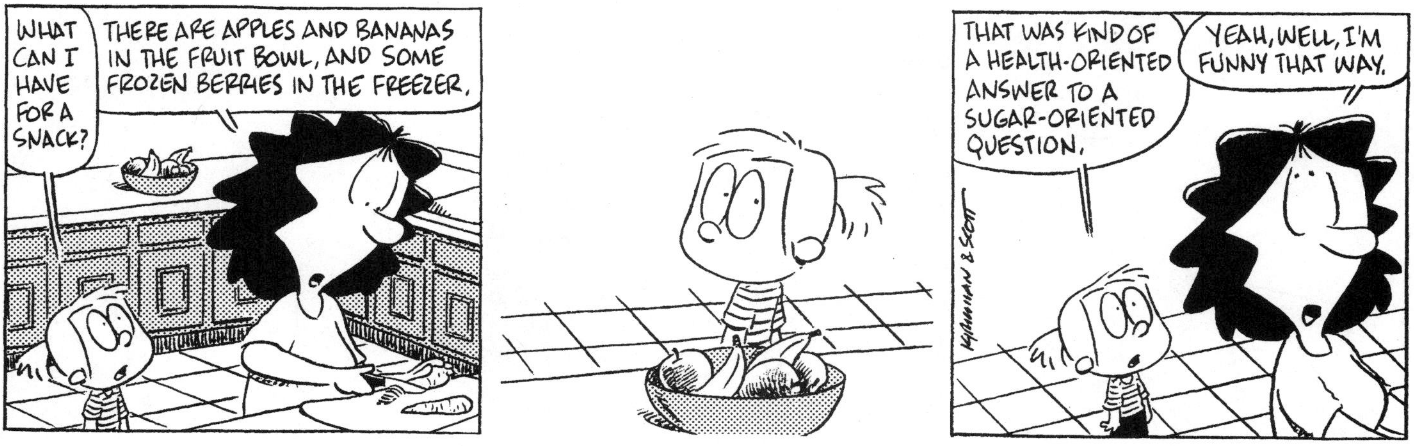
WHAT CAN I HAVE FOR A SNACK?
THERE ARE APPLES AND BANANAS IN THE FRUIT BOWL, AND SOME FROZEN BERRIES IN THE FREEZER.
KIRKMAN & SCOTT
THAT WAS KIND OF A HEALTH-ORIENTED ANSWER TO A SUGAR-ORIENTED QUESTION.
YEAH, WELL, I'M FUNNY THAT WAY.

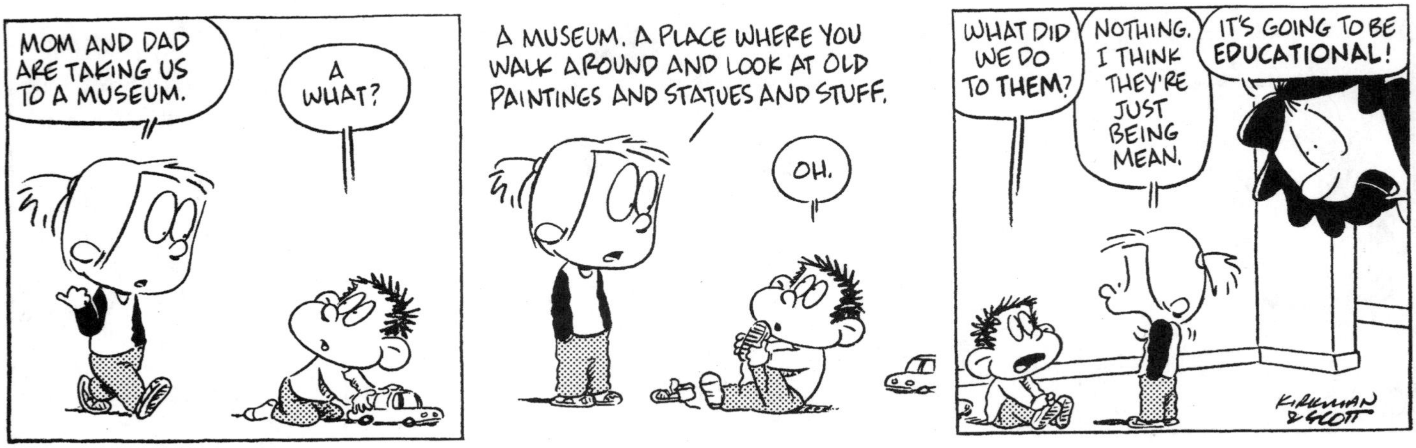
MOM AND DAD ARE TAKING US TO A MUSEUM.
A WHAT?
A MUSEUM. A PLACE WHERE YOU WALK AROUND AND LOOK AT OLD PAINTINGS AND STATUES AND STUFF.
OH.
WHAT DID WE DO TO **THEM**?
NOTHING. I THINK THEY'RE JUST BEING MEAN.
IT'S GOING TO BE **EDUCATIONAL**!
KIRKMAN & SCOTT

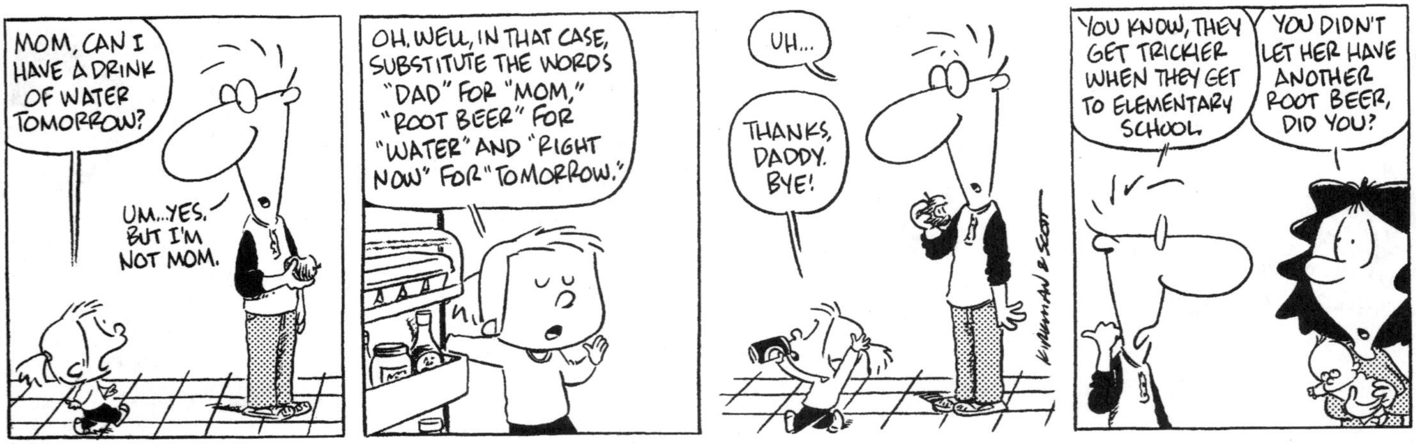
MOM, CAN I HAVE A DRINK OF WATER TOMORROW?
UM...YES. BUT I'M NOT MOM.
OH. WELL, IN THAT CASE, SUBSTITUTE THE WORDS "DAD" FOR "MOM," "ROOT BEER" FOR "WATER" AND "RIGHT NOW" FOR "TOMORROW."
UH...
THANKS, DADDY. BYE!
KIRKMAN & SCOTT
YOU KNOW, THEY GET TRICKIER WHEN THEY GET TO ELEMENTARY SCHOOL.
YOU DIDN'T LET HER HAVE ANOTHER ROOT BEER, DID YOU?

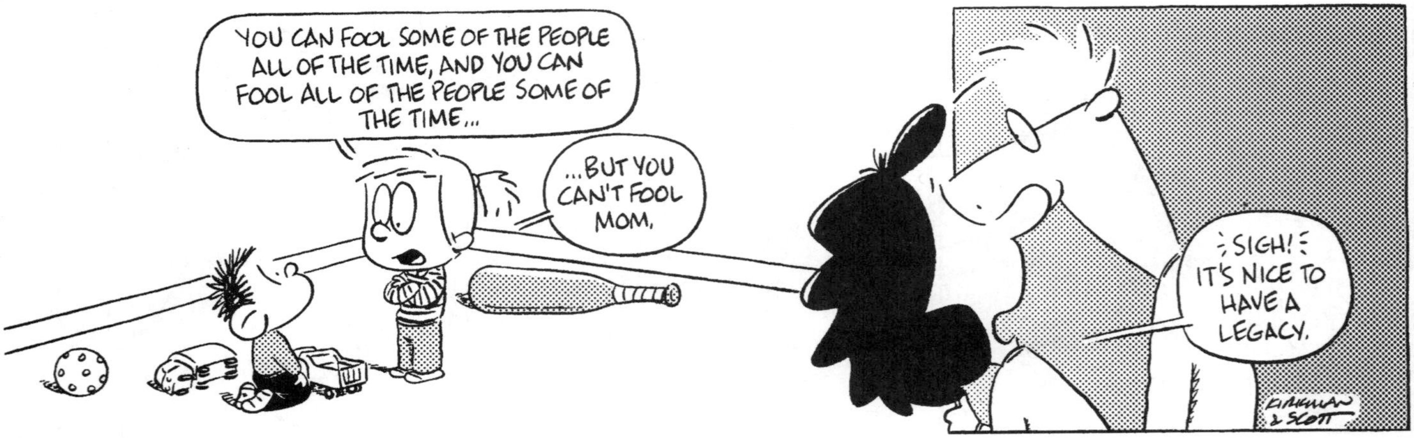
YOU CAN FOOL SOME OF THE PEOPLE ALL OF THE TIME, AND YOU CAN FOOL ALL OF THE PEOPLE SOME OF THE TIME...
...BUT YOU CAN'T FOOL MOM.
SIGH! IT'S NICE TO HAVE A LEGACY.
KIRKMAN & SCOTT

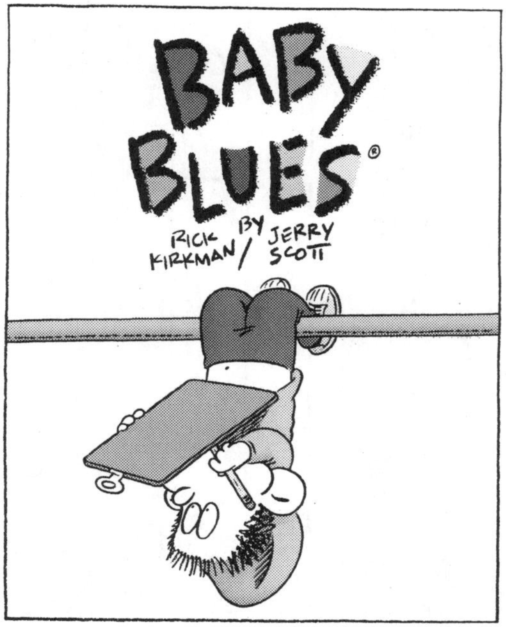
BABY BLUES®
BY RICK KIRKMAN / JERRY SCOTT

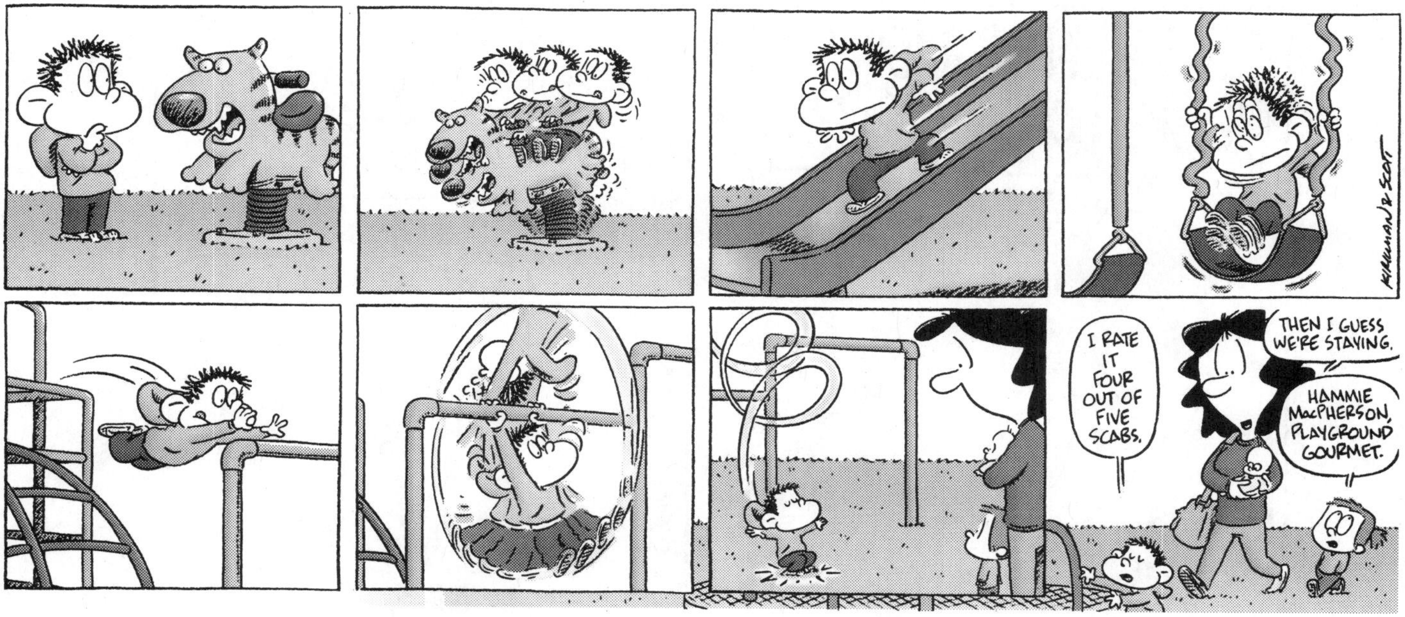
KIRKMAN & SCOTT
I RATE IT FOUR OUT OF FIVE SCABS.
THEN I GUESS WE'RE STAYING.
HAMMIE MacPHERSON, PLAYGROUND GOURMET.

PUPPIES!!
ETS
AWWW! AREN'T THEY CUTE?
I WISH WE COULD GET ONE.
ARE THEY EXPENSIVE?
SIXTEEN HUNDRED BUCKS FOR A PUPPY??
IS THAT A LOT?
LET ME PUT IT THIS WAY... IT'S MORE THAN WE PAID THE HOSPITAL WHEN YOU WERE BORN.
YEAH. BUT YOU GET WHAT YOU PAY FOR.
KIRKMAN & SCOTT

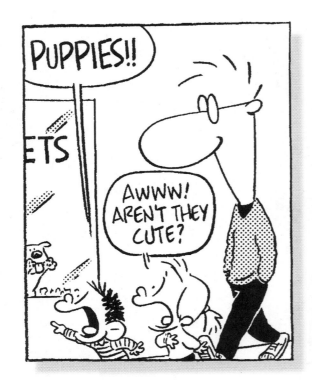

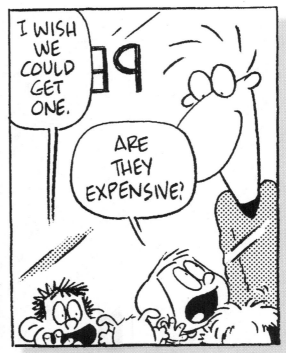

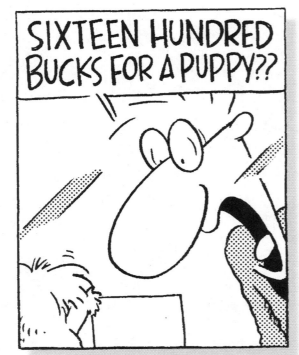

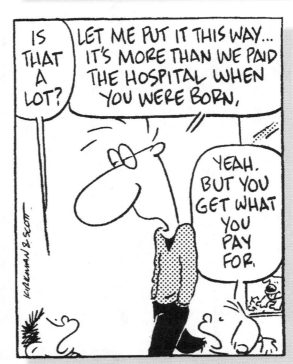

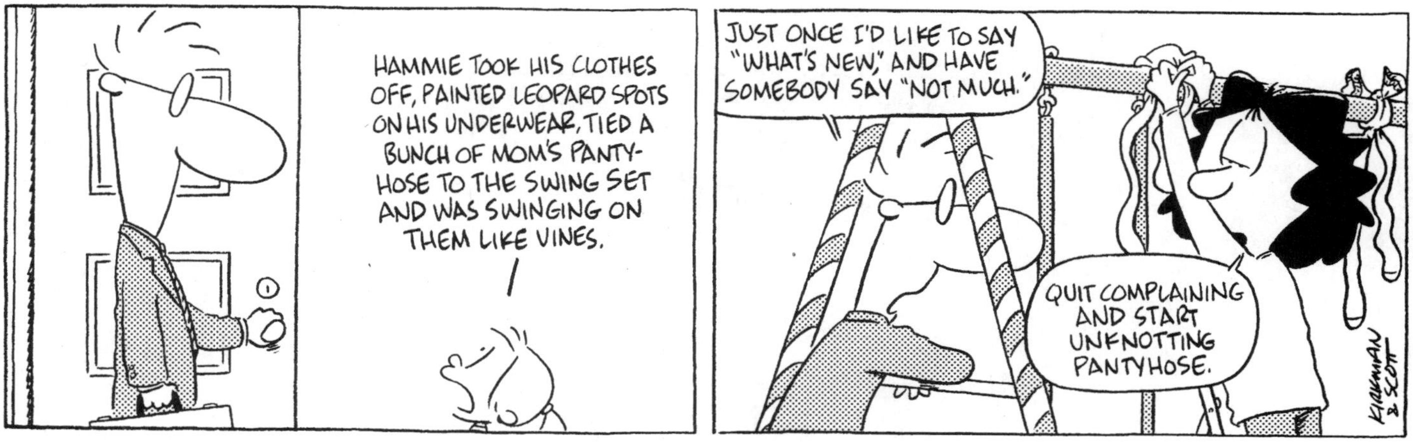
HAMMIE TOOK HIS CLOTHES OFF, PAINTED LEOPARD SPOTS ON HIS UNDERWEAR, TIED A BUNCH OF MOM'S PANTY-HOSE TO THE SWING SET AND WAS SWINGING ON THEM LIKE VINES.
JUST ONCE I'D LIKE TO SAY "WHAT'S NEW," AND HAVE SOMEBODY SAY "NOT MUCH."
QUIT COMPLAINING AND START UNKNOTTING PANTYHOSE.
KIRKMAN & SCOTT

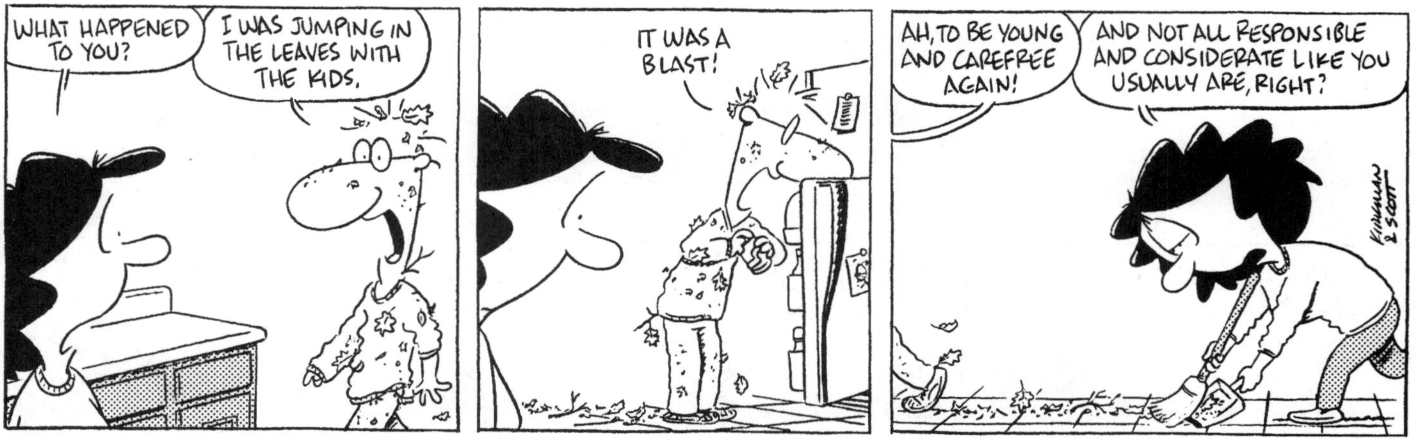
WHAT HAPPENED TO YOU?
I WAS JUMPING IN THE LEAVES WITH THE KIDS.
IT WAS A BLAST!
AH, TO BE YOUNG AND CAREFREE AGAIN!
AND NOT ALL RESPONSIBLE AND CONSIDERATE LIKE YOU USUALLY ARE, RIGHT?
KIRKMAN & SCOTT

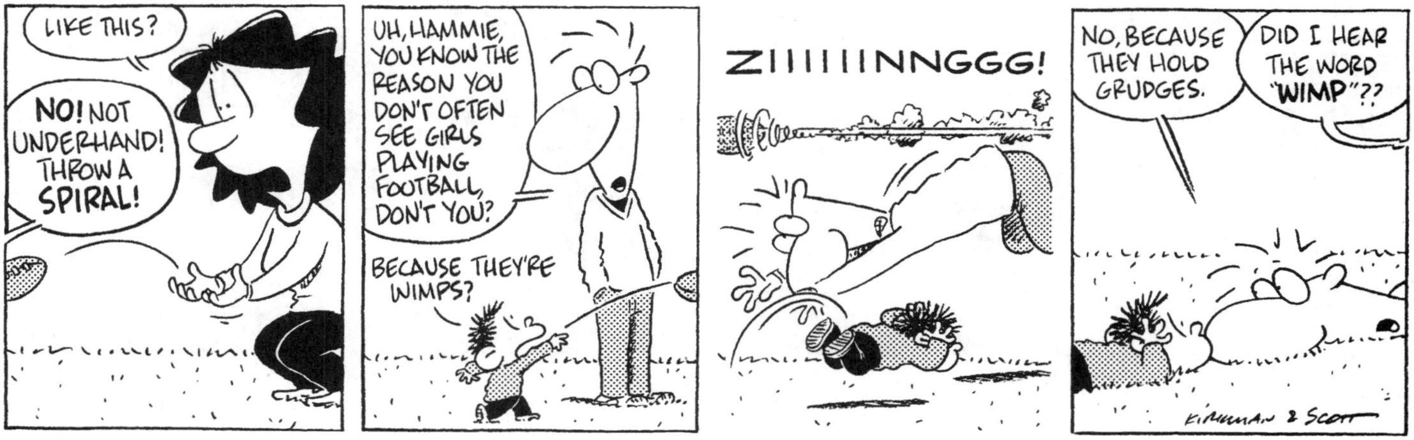
LIKE THIS?
NO! NOT UNDERHAND! THROW A **SPIRAL!**
UH, HAMMIE, YOU KNOW THE REASON YOU DON'T OFTEN SEE GIRLS PLAYING FOOTBALL, DON'T YOU?
BECAUSE THEY'RE WIMPS?
ZIIIIIINNGGG!
NO, BECAUSE THEY HOLD GRUDGES.
DID I HEAR THE WORD "**WIMP**"??
KIRKMAN & SCOTT

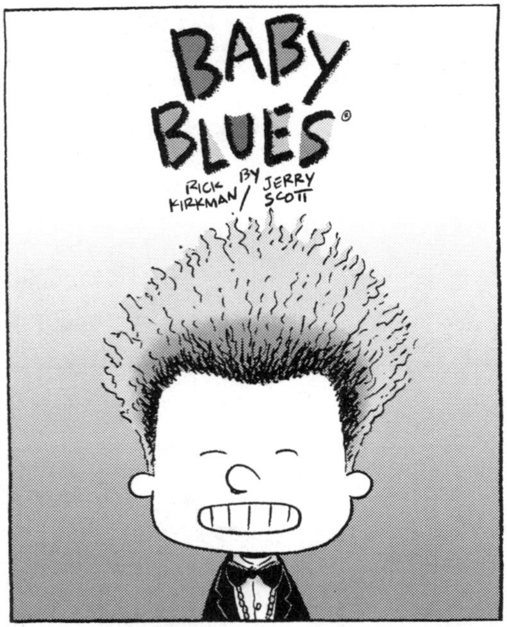
BABY BLUES®
BY RICK KIRKMAN / JERRY SCOTT

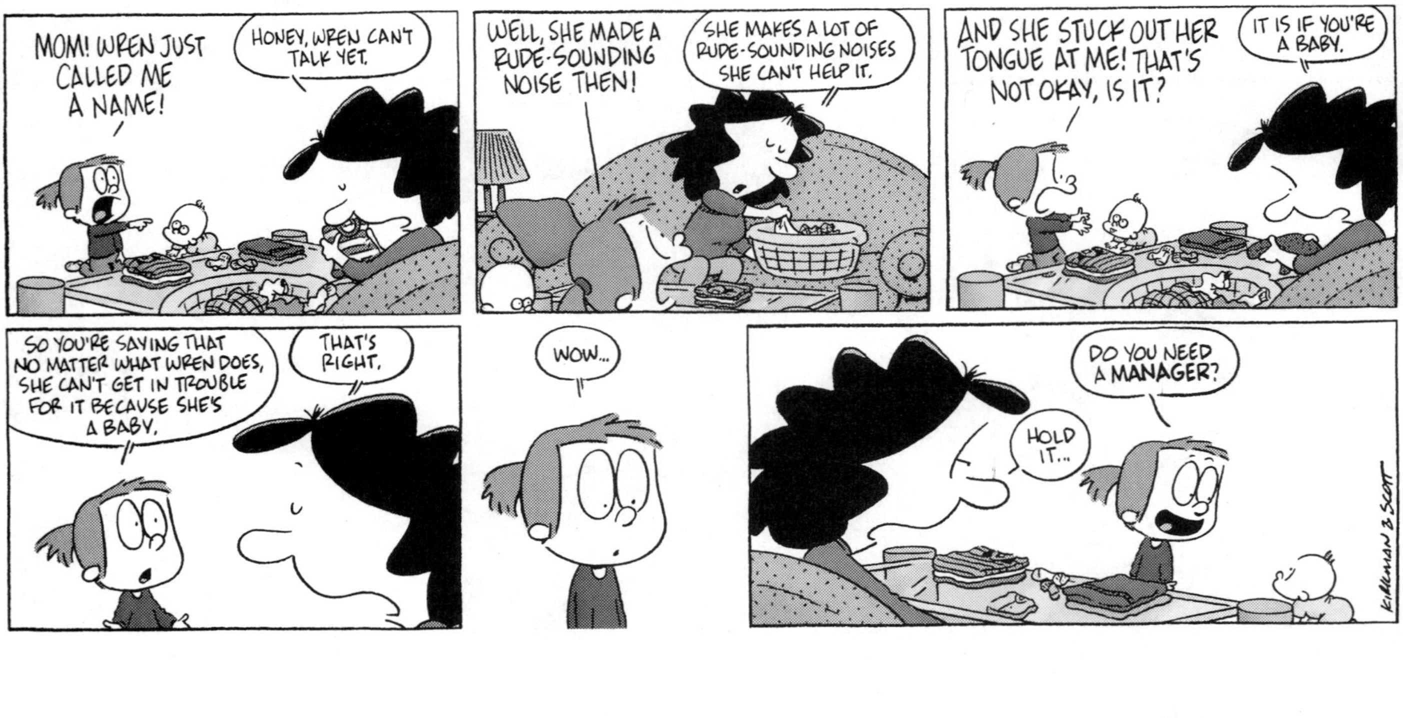
MOM! WREN JUST CALLED ME A NAME!
HONEY, WREN CAN'T TALK YET.
WELL, SHE MADE A RUDE-SOUNDING NOISE THEN!
SHE MAKES A LOT OF RUDE-SOUNDING NOISES SHE CAN'T HELP IT.
AND SHE STUCK OUT HER TONGUE AT ME! THAT'S NOT OKAY, IS IT?
IT IS IF YOU'RE A BABY.
SO YOU'RE SAYING THAT NO MATTER WHAT WREN DOES, SHE CAN'T GET IN TROUBLE FOR IT BECAUSE SHE'S A BABY.
THAT'S RIGHT.
WOW...
DO YOU NEED A **MANAGER**?
HOLD IT...
KIRKMAN & SCOTT

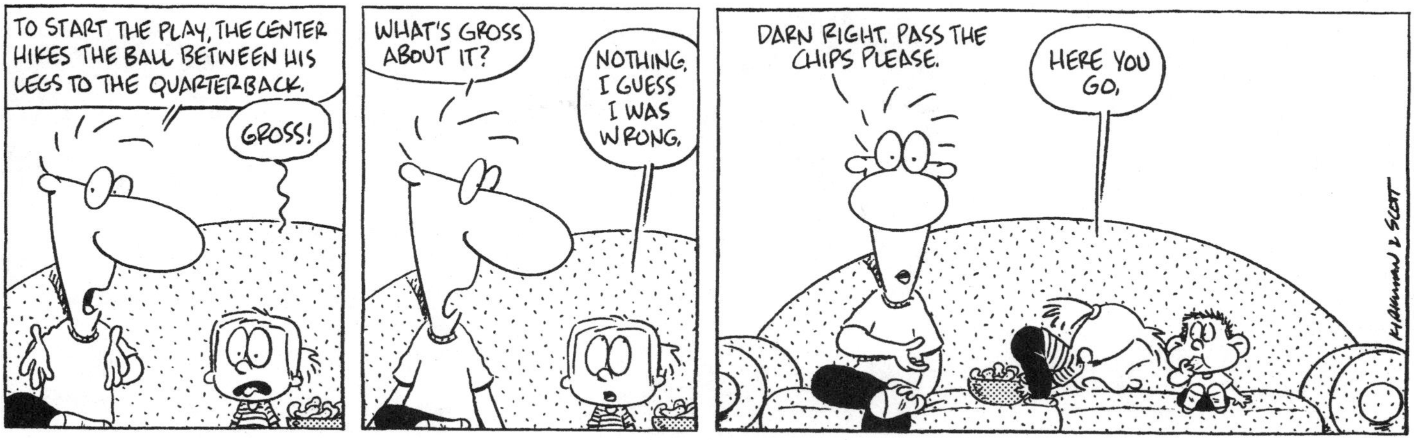
TO START THE PLAY, THE CENTER HIKES THE BALL BETWEEN HIS LEGS TO THE QUARTERBACK.
GROSS!
WHAT'S GROSS ABOUT IT?
NOTHING. I GUESS I WAS WRONG.
DARN RIGHT. PASS THE CHIPS PLEASE.
HERE YOU GO.
KIRKMAN & SCOTT

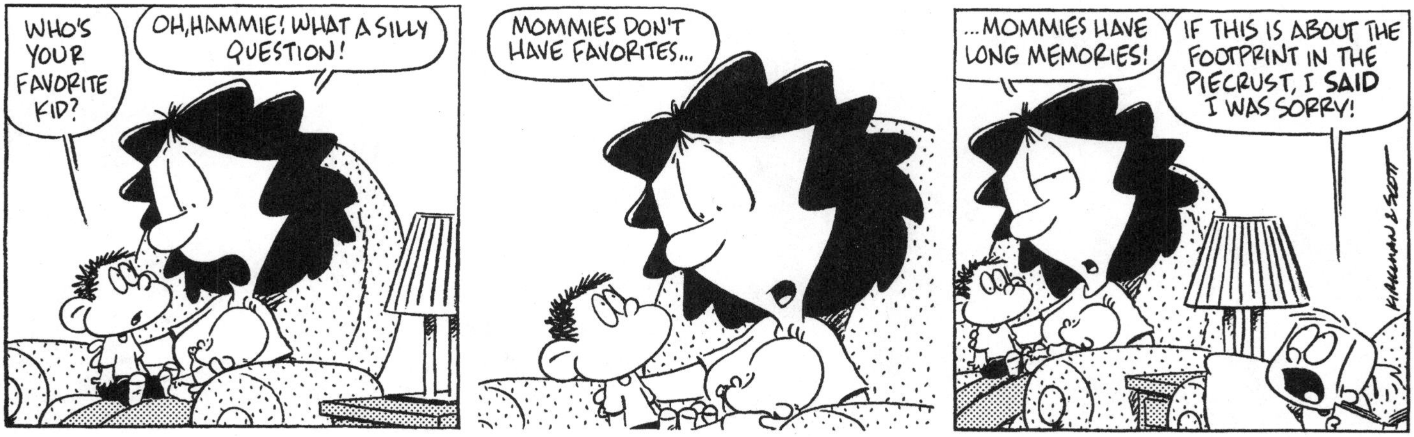
WHO'S YOUR FAVORITE KID?
OH, HAMMIE! WHAT A SILLY QUESTION!
MOMMIES DON'T HAVE FAVORITES...
...MOMMIES HAVE LONG MEMORIES!
IF THIS IS ABOUT THE FOOTPRINT IN THE PIECRUST, I **SAID** I WAS SORRY!
KIRKMAN & SCOTT

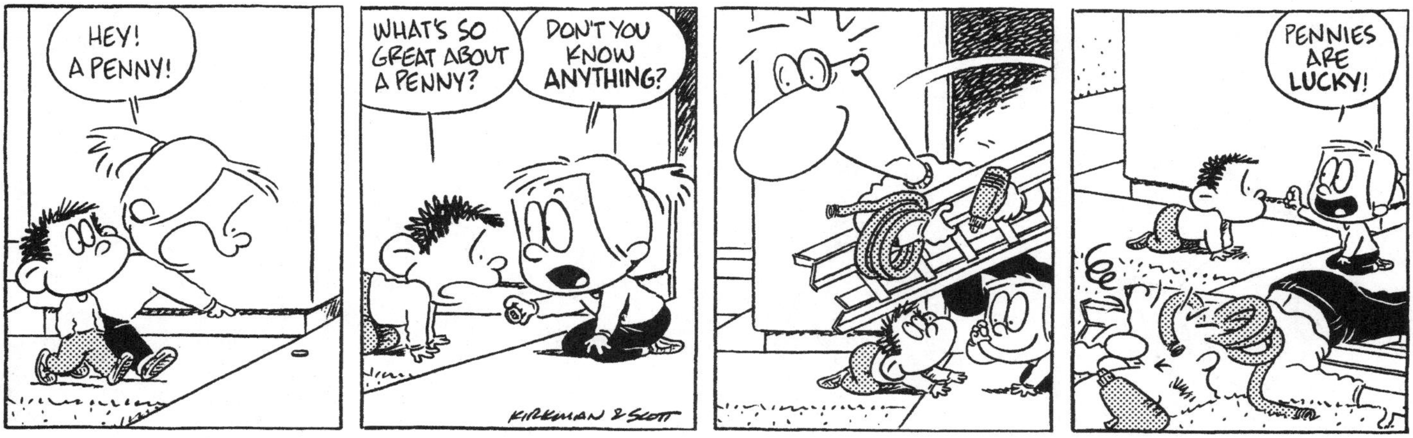
HEY! A PENNY!
WHAT'S SO GREAT ABOUT A PENNY?
DON'T YOU KNOW **ANYTHING**?
KIRKMAN & SCOTT
PENNIES ARE **LUCKY**!

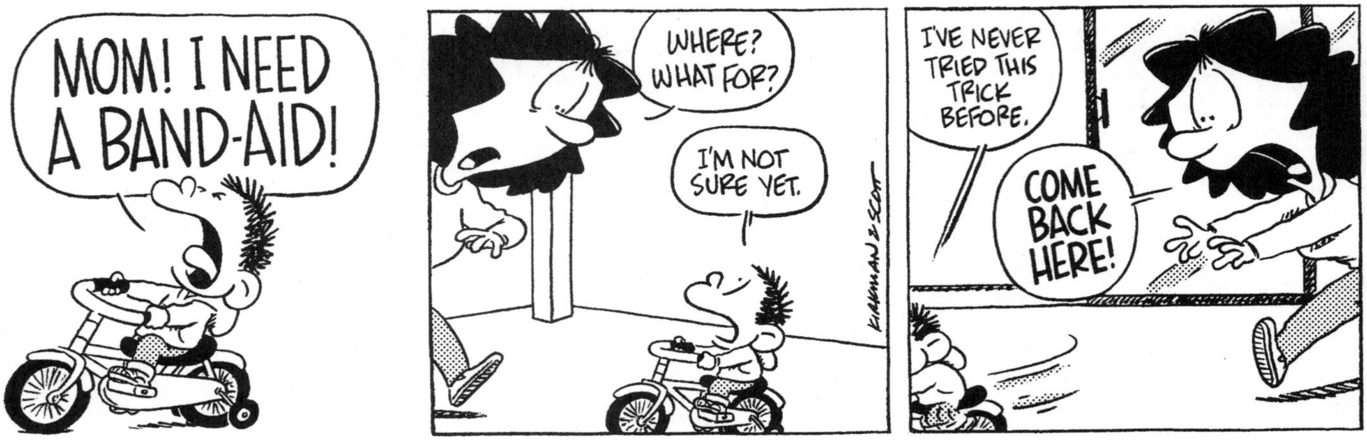
MOM! I NEED A BAND-AID!
WHERE? WHAT FOR?
I'M NOT SURE YET.
KIRKMAN & SCOTT
I'VE NEVER TRIED THIS TRICK BEFORE.
COME BACK HERE!

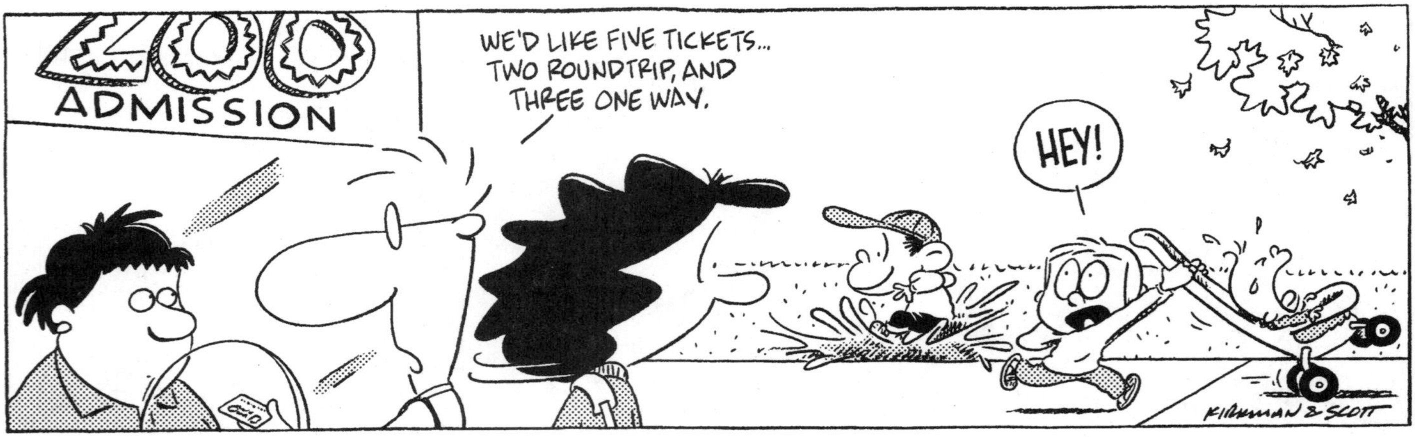
ZOO
ADMISSION
WE'D LIKE FIVE TICKETS... TWO ROUNDTRIP, AND THREE ONE WAY.
HEY!
KIRKMAN & SCOTT

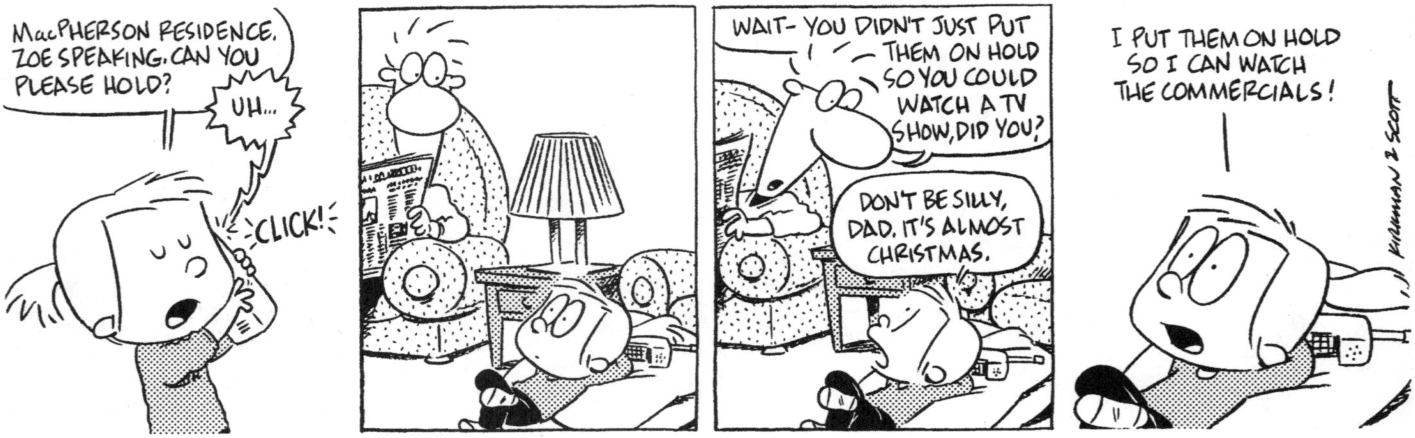
MacPHERSON RESIDENCE. ZOE SPEAKING. CAN YOU PLEASE HOLD?
UH...
CLICK!
WAIT- YOU DIDN'T JUST PUT THEM ON HOLD SO YOU COULD WATCH A TV SHOW, DID YOU?
DON'T BE SILLY, DAD. IT'S ALMOST CHRISTMAS.
I PUT THEM ON HOLD SO I CAN WATCH THE COMMERCIALS!
KIRKMAN & SCOTT

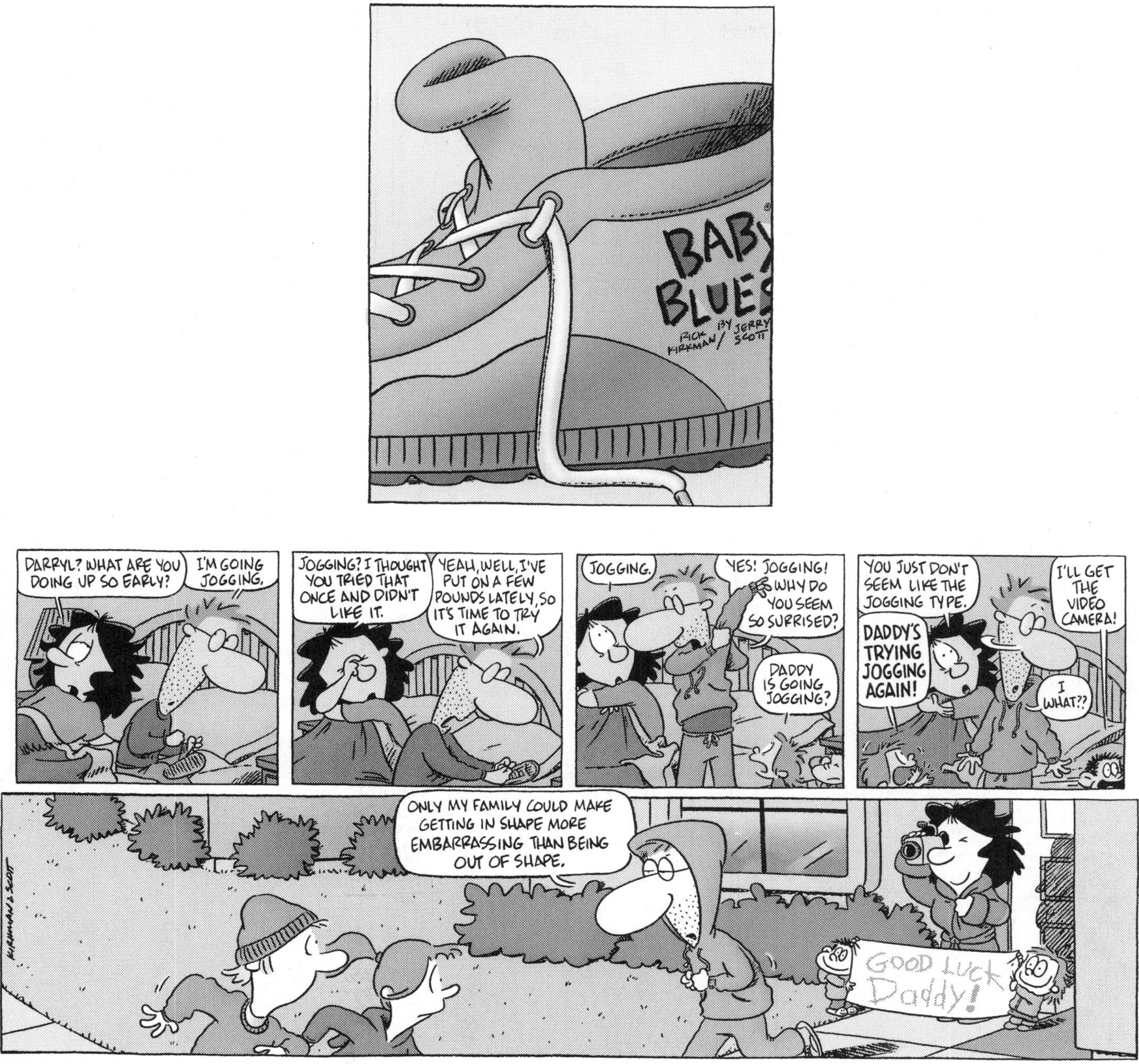
BABY BLUES®
BY RICK KIRKMAN / JERRY SCOTT
DARRYL? WHAT ARE YOU DOING UP SO EARLY?
I'M GOING JOGGING.
JOGGING? I THOUGHT YOU TRIED THAT ONCE AND DIDN'T LIKE IT.
YEAH, WELL, I'VE PUT ON A FEW POUNDS LATELY, SO IT'S TIME TO TRY IT AGAIN.
JOGGING.
YES! JOGGING! WHY DO YOU SEEM SO SURPRISED?
DADDY IS GOING JOGGING?
YOU JUST DON'T SEEM LIKE THE JOGGING TYPE.
I'LL GET THE VIDEO CAMERA!
DADDY'S TRYING JOGGING AGAIN!
I WHAT??
ONLY MY FAMILY COULD MAKE GETTING IN SHAPE MORE EMBARRASSING THAN BEING OUT OF SHAPE.
GOOD LUCK Daddy!
KIRKMAN & SCOTT

A Really, Really, Really Bad Answer:

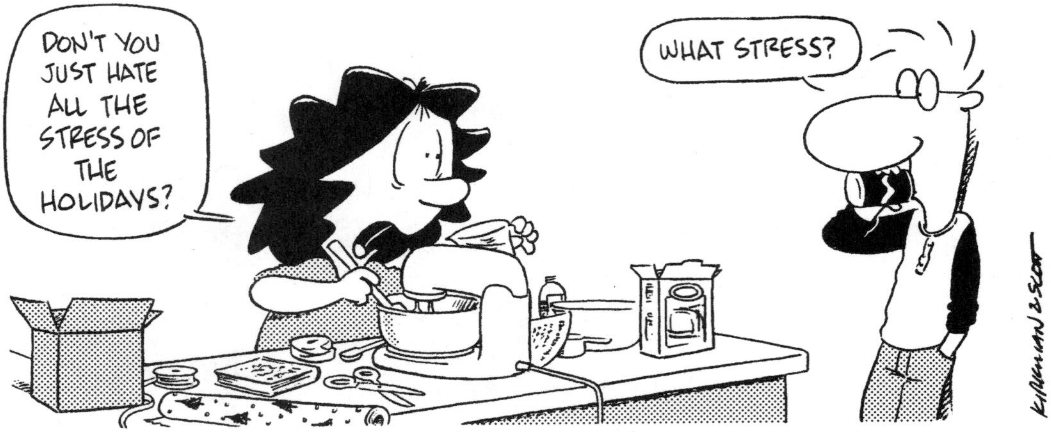
DON'T YOU JUST HATE ALL THE STRESS OF THE HOLIDAYS?
WHAT STRESS?

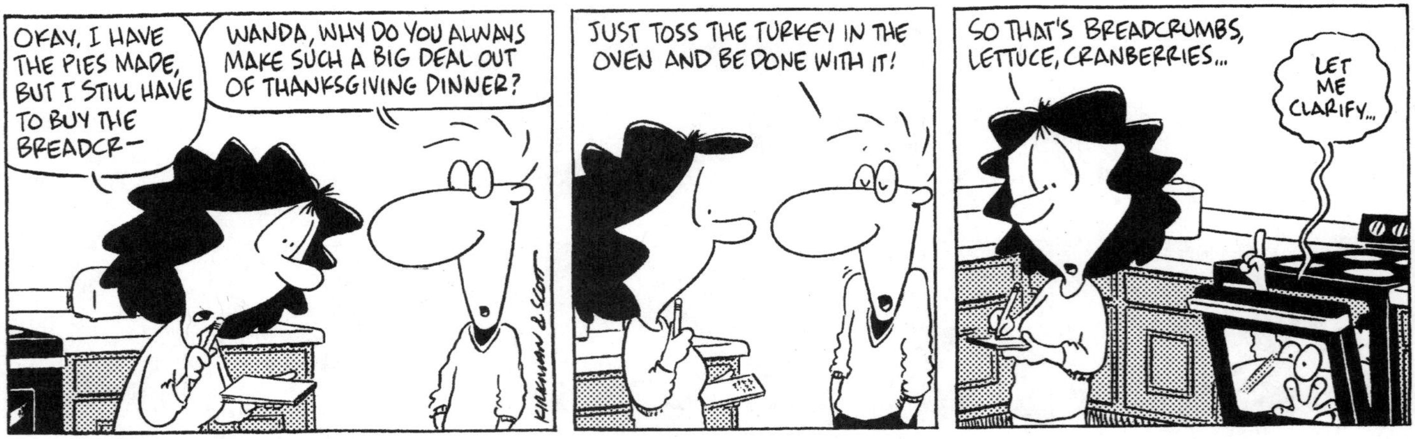
OKAY, I HAVE THE PIES MADE, BUT I STILL HAVE TO BUY THE BREADCR—
WANDA, WHY DO YOU ALWAYS MAKE SUCH A BIG DEAL OUT OF THANKSGIVING DINNER?
JUST TOSS THE TURKEY IN THE OVEN AND BE DONE WITH IT!
SO THAT'S BREADCRUMBS, LETTUCE, CRANBERRIES...
LET ME CLARIFY...

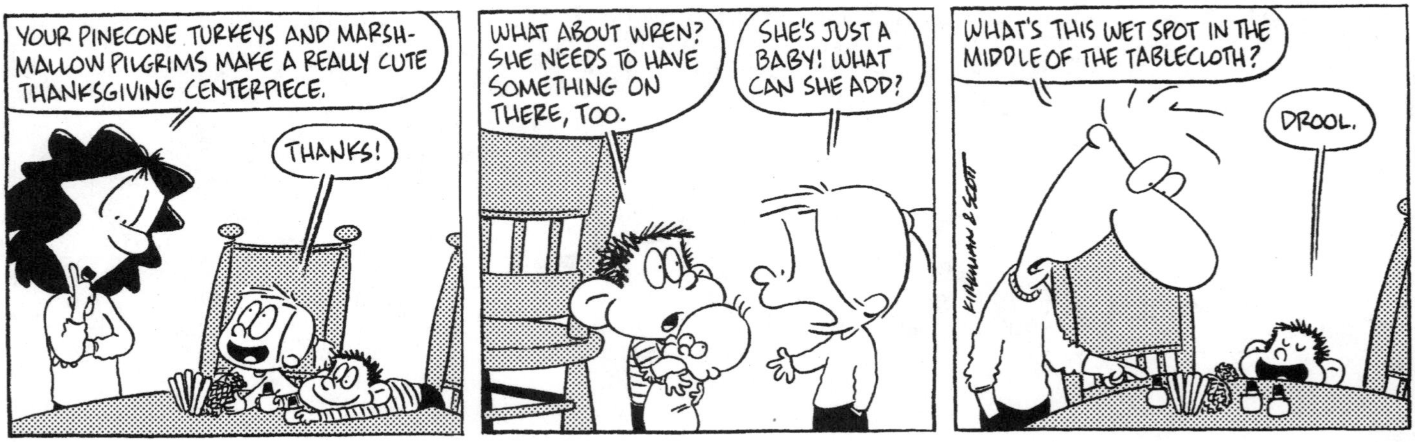
YOUR PINECONE TURKEYS AND MARSH-MALLOW PILGRIMS MAKE A REALLY CUTE THANKSGIVING CENTERPIECE.
THANKS!
WHAT ABOUT WREN? SHE NEEDS TO HAVE SOMETHING ON THERE, TOO.
SHE'S JUST A BABY! WHAT CAN SHE ADD?
WHAT'S THIS WET SPOT IN THE MIDDLE OF THE TABLECLOTH?
DROOL.

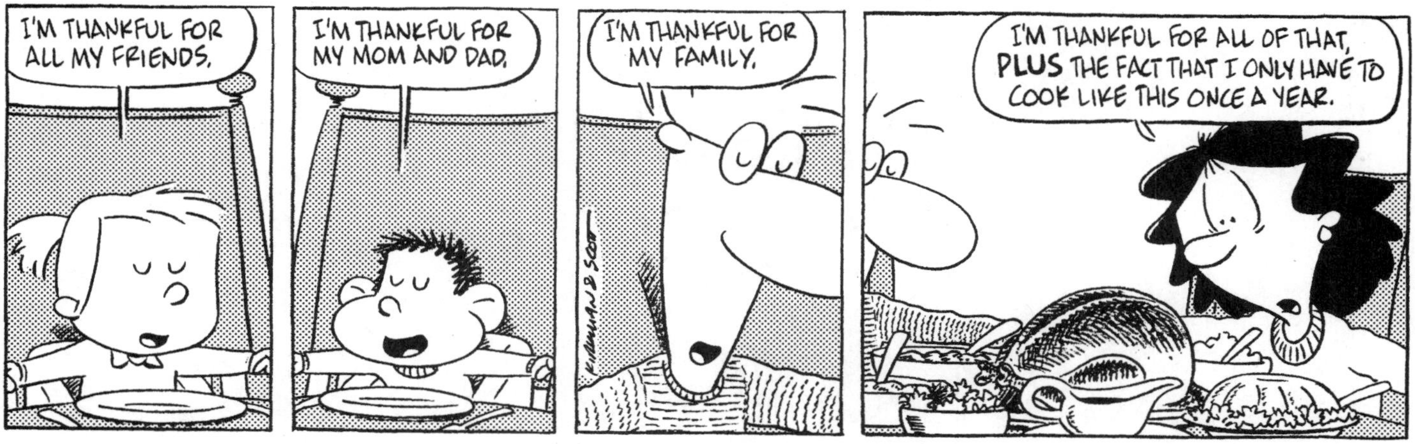
I'M THANKFUL FOR ALL MY FRIENDS.
I'M THANKFUL FOR MY MOM AND DAD.
I'M THANKFUL FOR MY FAMILY.
I'M THANKFUL FOR ALL OF THAT, **PLUS** THE FACT THAT I ONLY HAVE TO COOK LIKE THIS ONCE A YEAR.

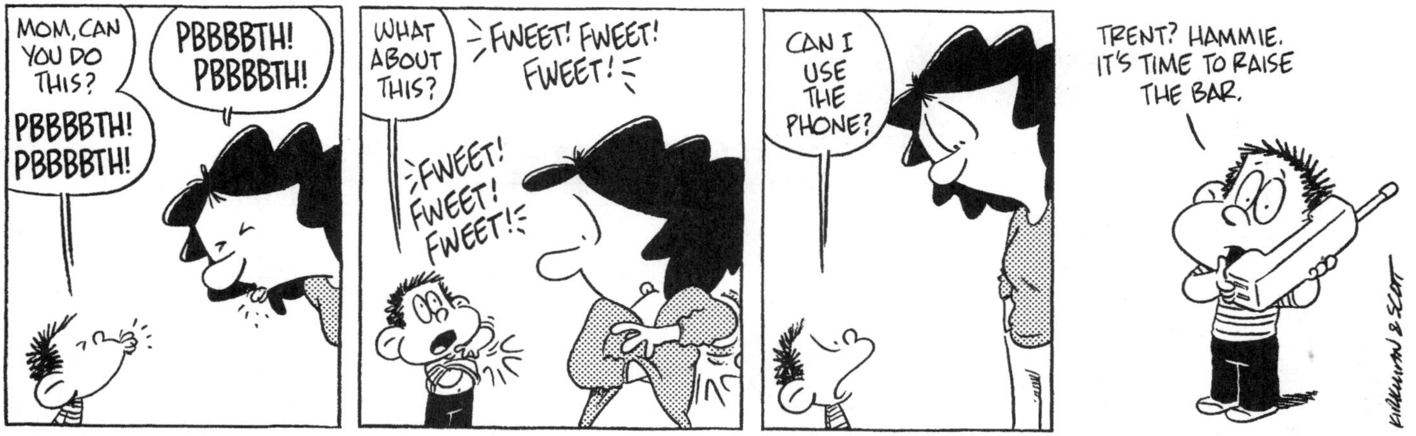
MOM, CAN YOU DO THIS?
PBBBBTH! PBBBBTH!
PBBBBTH! PBBBBTH!
WHAT ABOUT THIS?
FWEET! FWEET! FWEET!
FWEET! FWEET! FWEET!
CAN I USE THE PHONE?
TRENT? HAMMIE. IT'S TIME TO RAISE THE BAR.

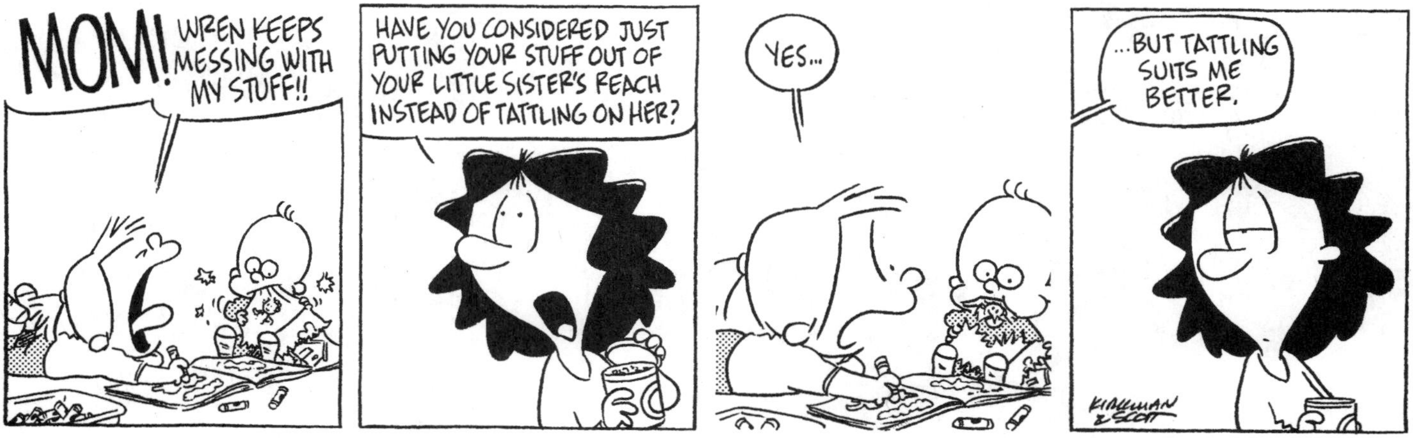
MOM! WREN KEEPS MESSING WITH MY STUFF!!
HAVE YOU CONSIDERED JUST PUTTING YOUR STUFF OUT OF YOUR LITTLE SISTER'S REACH INSTEAD OF TATTLING ON HER?
YES...
...BUT TATTLING SUITS ME BETTER.

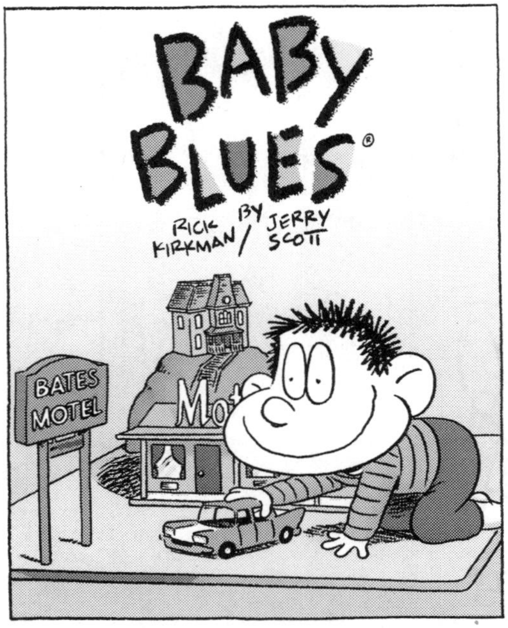
BABY BLUES®
BY RICK KIRKMAN / JERRY SCOTT
BATES MOTEL
Mot

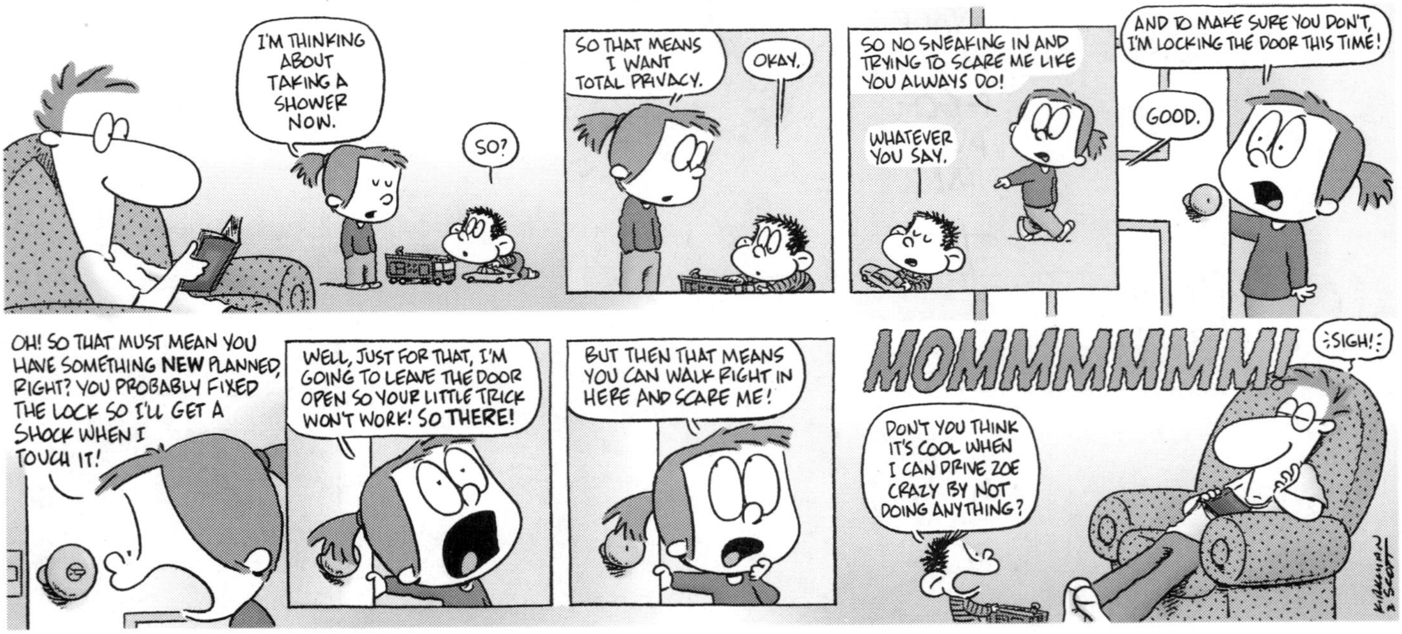
I'M THINKING ABOUT TAKING A SHOWER NOW.
SO?
SO THAT MEANS I WANT TOTAL PRIVACY.
OKAY.
SO NO SNEAKING IN AND TRYING TO SCARE ME LIKE YOU ALWAYS DO!
WHATEVER YOU SAY.
AND TO MAKE SURE YOU DON'T, I'M LOCKING THE DOOR THIS TIME!
GOOD.
OH! SO THAT MUST MEAN YOU HAVE SOMETHING NEW PLANNED, RIGHT? YOU PROBABLY FIXED THE LOCK SO I'LL GET A SHOCK WHEN I TOUCH IT!
WELL, JUST FOR THAT, I'M GOING TO LEAVE THE DOOR OPEN SO YOUR LITTLE TRICK WON'T WORK! SO THERE!
BUT THEN THAT MEANS YOU CAN WALK RIGHT IN HERE AND SCARE ME!
MOMMMMMMM!
SIGH!
DON'T YOU THINK IT'S COOL WHEN I CAN DRIVE ZOE CRAZY BY NOT DOING ANYTHING?

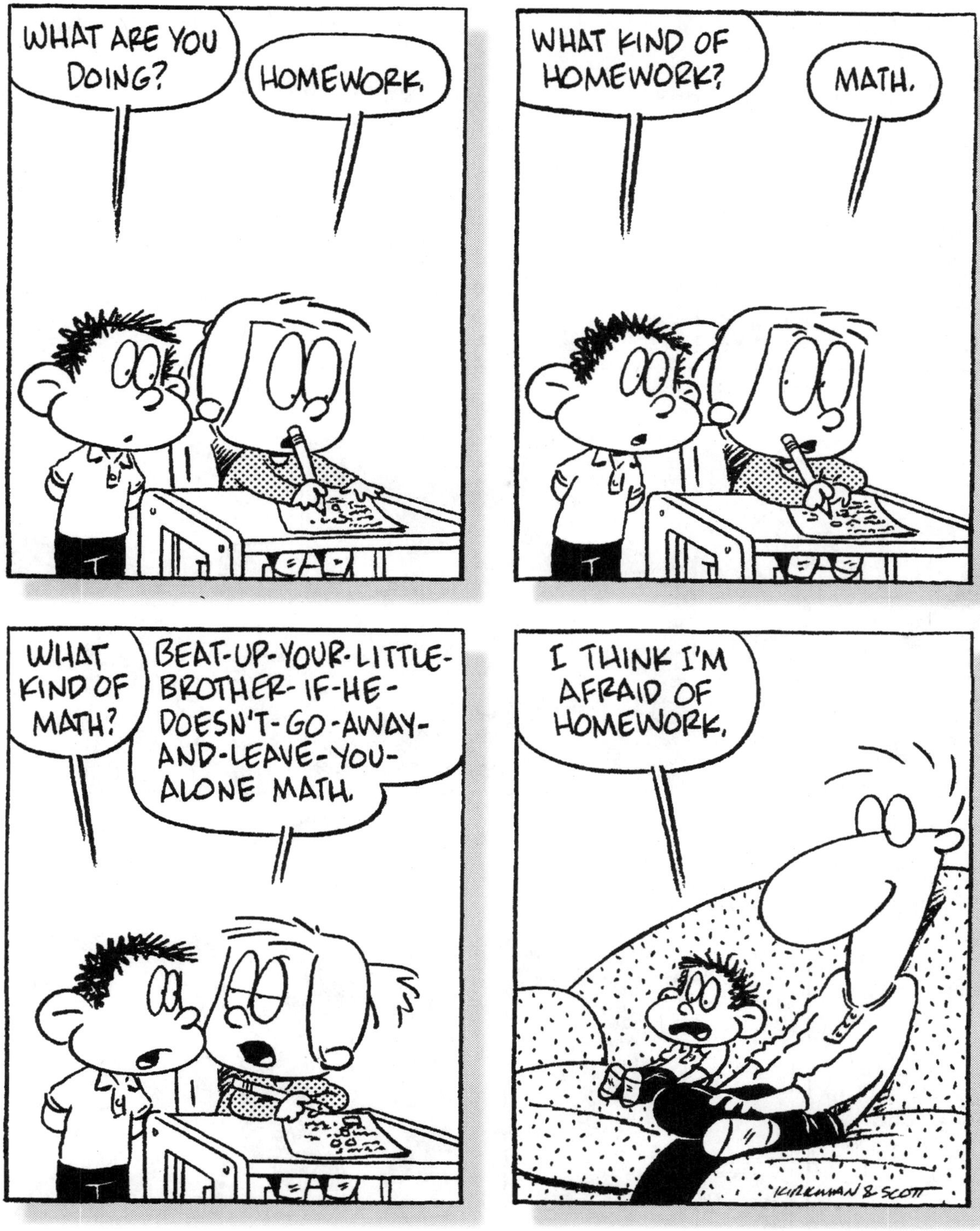
WHAT ARE YOU DOING?
HOMEWORK.
WHAT KIND OF HOMEWORK?
MATH.
WHAT KIND OF MATH?
BEAT-UP-YOUR-LITTLE-BROTHER-IF-HE-DOESN'T-GO-AWAY-AND-LEAVE-YOU-ALONE MATH.
I THINK I'M AFRAID OF HOMEWORK.
KIRKMAN & SCOTT

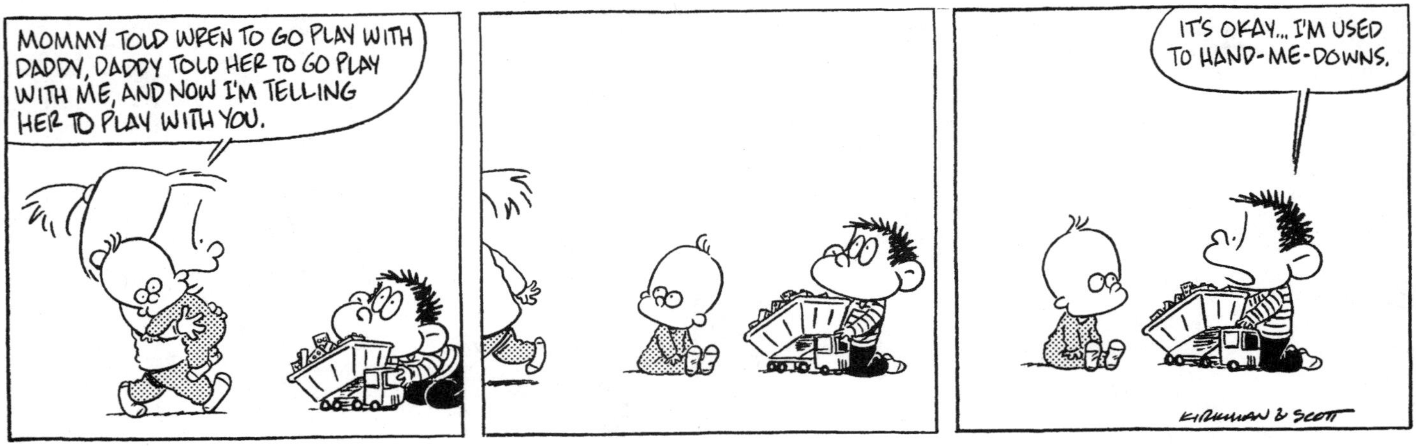
MOMMY TOLD WREN TO GO PLAY WITH DADDY, DADDY TOLD HER TO GO PLAY WITH ME, AND NOW I'M TELLING HER TO PLAY WITH YOU.
IT'S OKAY... I'M USED TO HAND-ME-DOWNS.
KIRKMAN & SCOTT

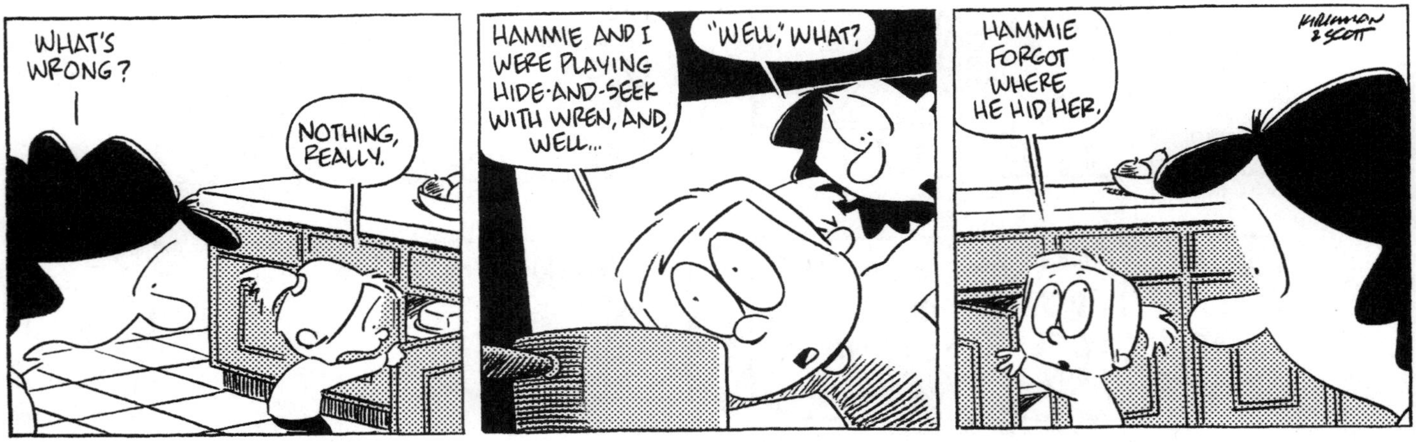
WHAT'S WRONG?
NOTHING, REALLY.
HAMMIE AND I WERE PLAYING HIDE-AND-SEEK WITH WREN, AND, WELL...
"WELL," WHAT?
HAMMIE FORGOT WHERE HE HID HER.
KIRKMAN & SCOTT

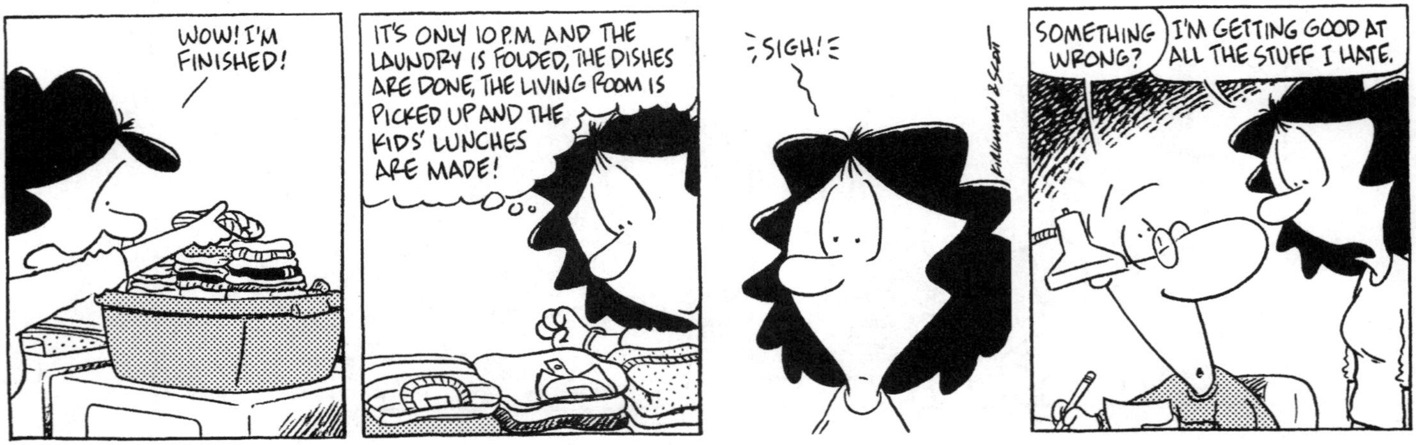
WOW! I'M FINISHED!
IT'S ONLY 10 P.M. AND THE LAUNDRY IS FOLDED, THE DISHES ARE DONE, THE LIVING ROOM IS PICKED UP AND THE KIDS' LUNCHES ARE MADE!
SIGH!
KIRKMAN & SCOTT
SOMETHING WRONG?
I'M GETTING GOOD AT ALL THE STUFF I HATE.

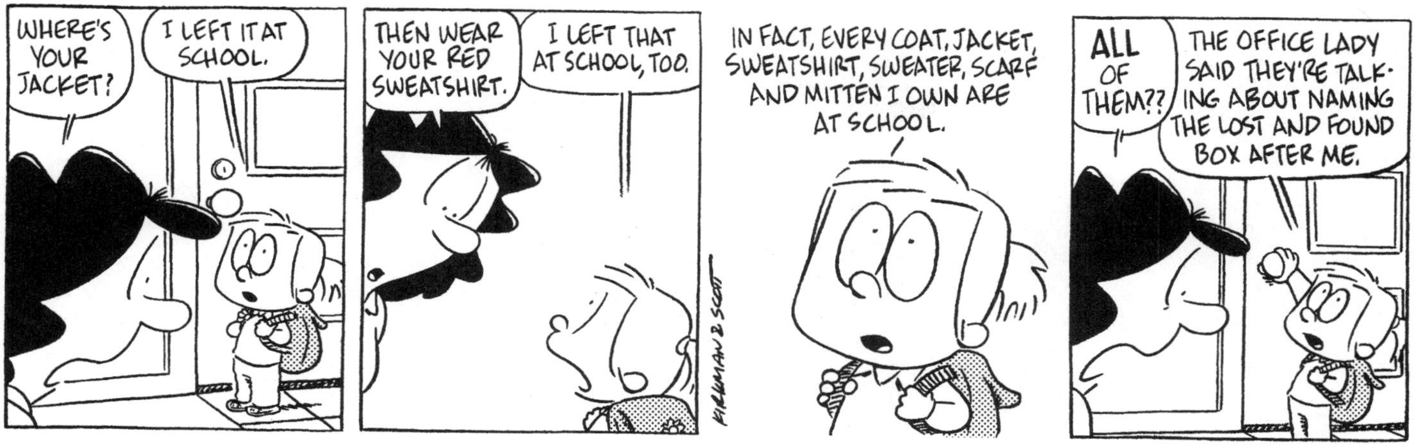
WHERE'S YOUR JACKET?
I LEFT IT AT SCHOOL.
THEN WEAR YOUR RED SWEATSHIRT.
I LEFT THAT AT SCHOOL, TOO.
IN FACT, EVERY COAT, JACKET, SWEATSHIRT, SWEATER, SCARF AND MITTEN I OWN ARE AT SCHOOL.
ALL OF THEM??
THE OFFICE LADY SAID THEY'RE TALKING ABOUT NAMING THE LOST AND FOUND BOX AFTER ME.
KIRKMAN & SCOTT

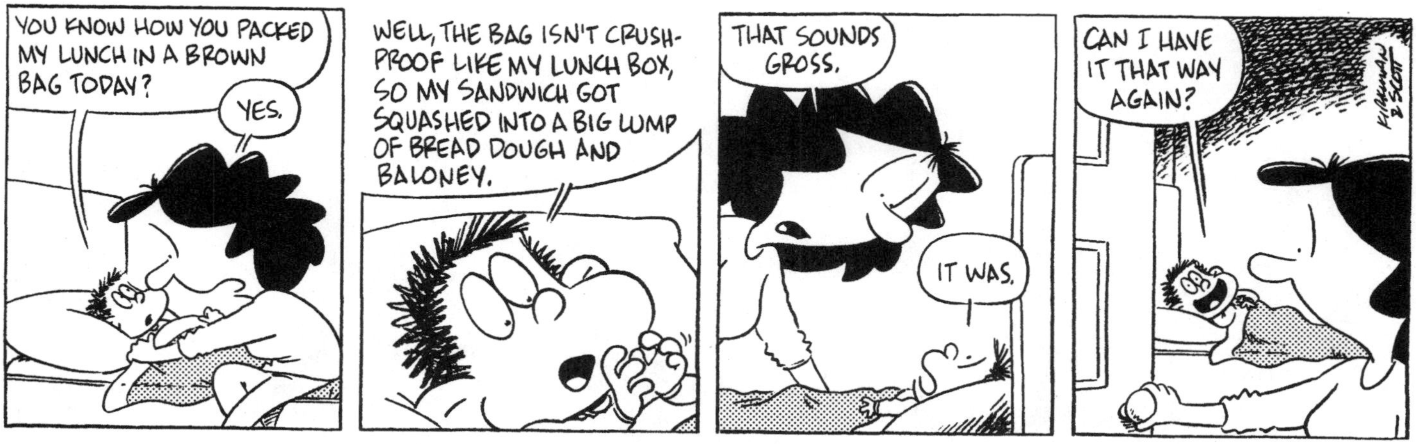
YOU KNOW HOW YOU PACKED MY LUNCH IN A BROWN BAG TODAY?
YES.
WELL, THE BAG ISN'T CRUSH-PROOF LIKE MY LUNCH BOX, SO MY SANDWICH GOT SQUASHED INTO A BIG LUMP OF BREAD DOUGH AND BALONEY.
THAT SOUNDS GROSS.
IT WAS.
CAN I HAVE IT THAT WAY AGAIN?
KIRKMAN & SCOTT

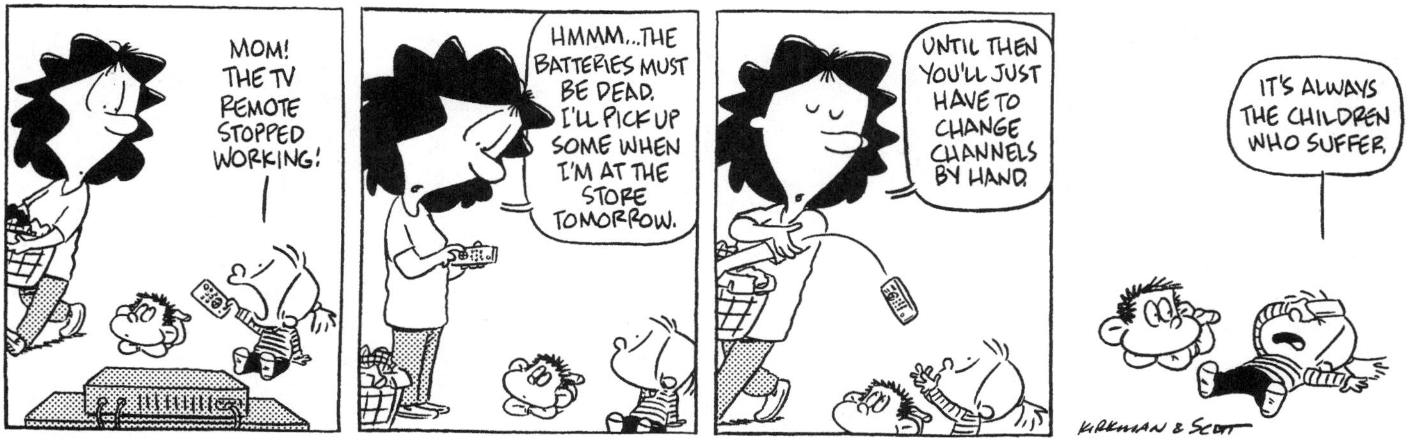
MOM! THE TV REMOTE STOPPED WORKING!
HMMM...THE BATTERIES MUST BE DEAD. I'LL PICK UP SOME WHEN I'M AT THE STORE TOMORROW.
UNTIL THEN YOU'LL JUST HAVE TO CHANGE CHANNELS BY HAND.
IT'S ALWAYS THE CHILDREN WHO SUFFER.
KIRKMAN & SCOTT

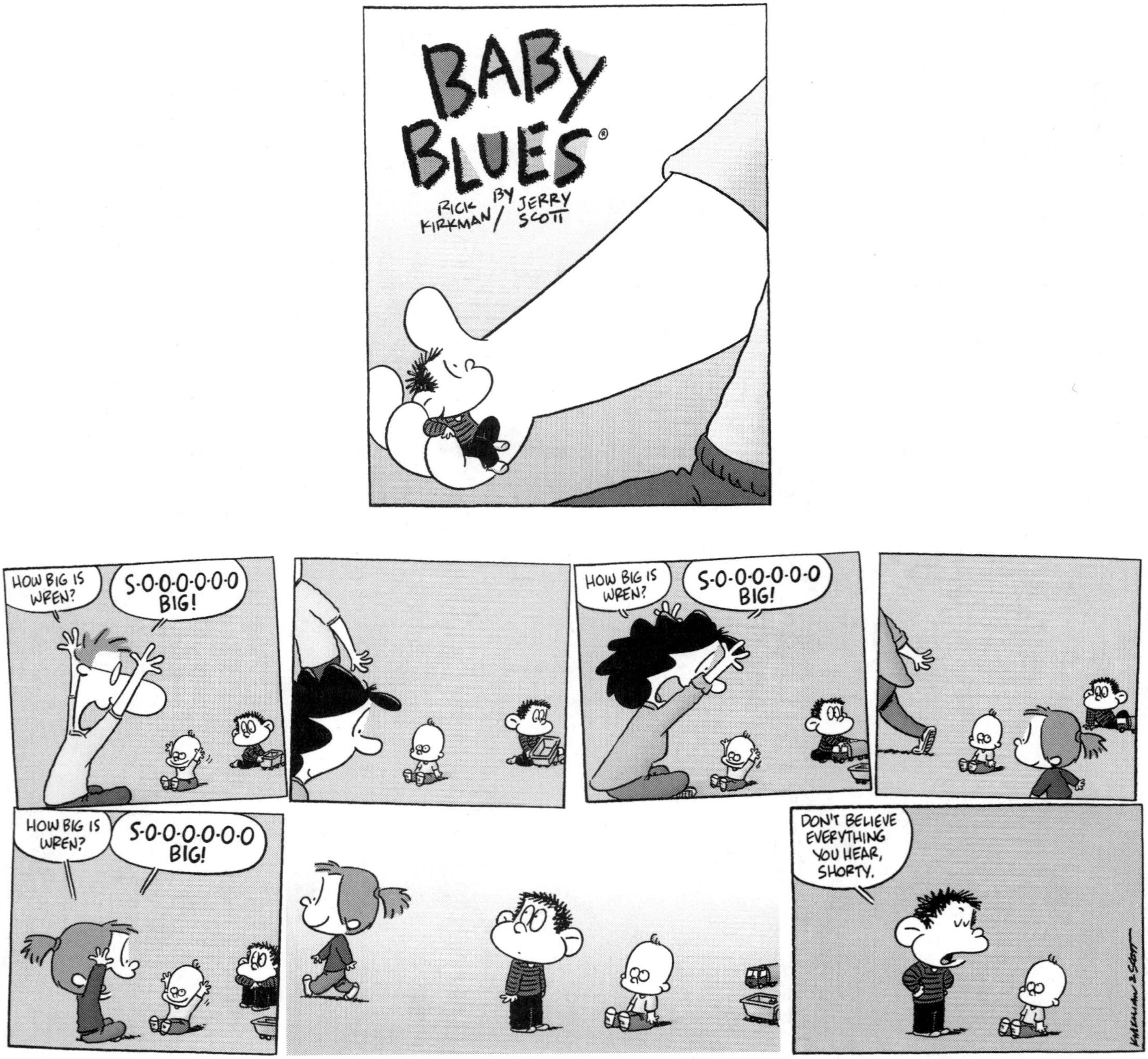
BABY BLUES®
BY RICK KIRKMAN / JERRY SCOTT
HOW BIG IS WREN?
S-O-O-O-O-O-O-O BIG!
HOW BIG IS WREN?
S-O-O-O-O-O-O-O BIG!
HOW BIG IS WREN?
S-O-O-O-O-O-O-O BIG!
DON'T BELIEVE EVERYTHING YOU HEAR, SHORTY.

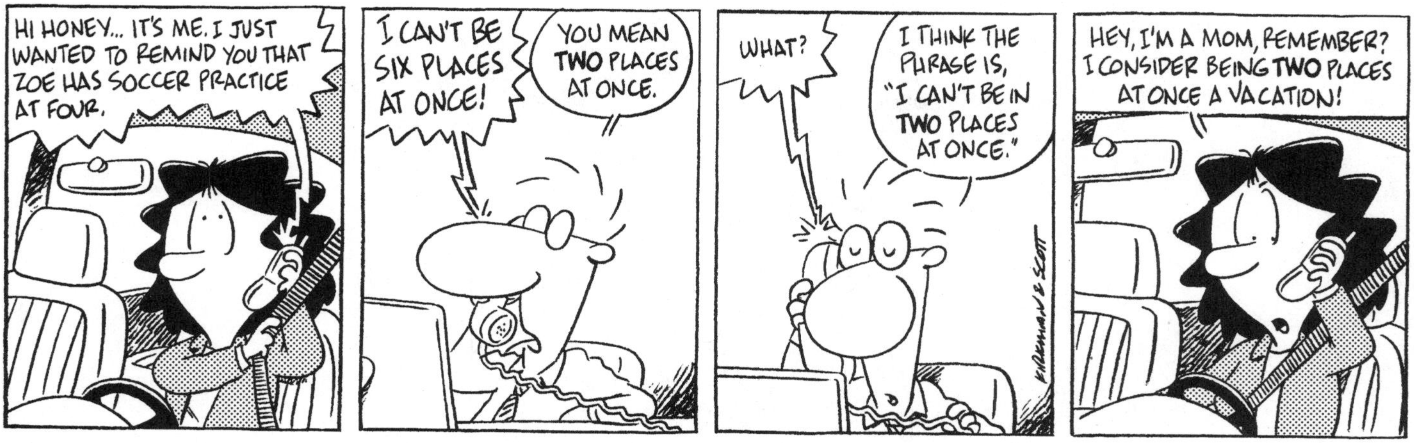
HI HONEY... IT'S ME. I JUST WANTED TO REMIND YOU THAT ZOE HAS SOCCER PRACTICE AT FOUR.
I CAN'T BE SIX PLACES AT ONCE!
YOU MEAN **TWO** PLACES AT ONCE.
WHAT?
I THINK THE PHRASE IS, "I CAN'T BE IN **TWO** PLACES AT ONCE."
KIRKMAN & SCOTT
HEY, I'M A MOM, REMEMBER? I CONSIDER BEING **TWO** PLACES AT ONCE A VACATION!

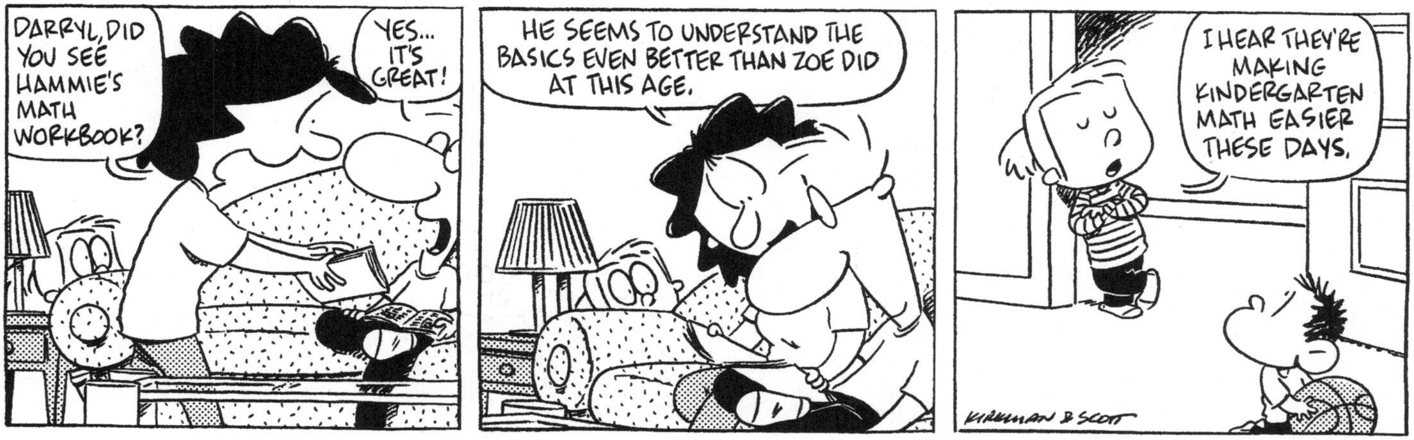
DARRYL, DID YOU SEE HAMMIE'S MATH WORKBOOK?
YES... IT'S GREAT!
HE SEEMS TO UNDERSTAND THE BASICS EVEN BETTER THAN ZOE DID AT THIS AGE.
I HEAR THEY'RE MAKING KINDERGARTEN MATH EASIER THESE DAYS.
KIRKMAN & SCOTT

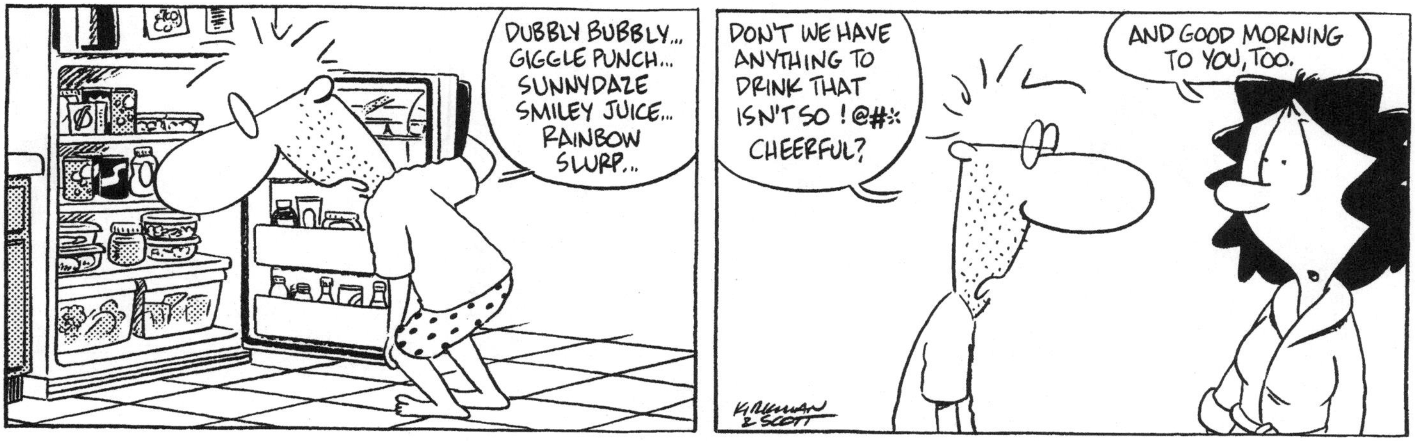
DUBBLY BUBBLY... GIGGLE PUNCH... SUNNYDAZE SMILEY JUICE... RAINBOW SLURP...
DON'T WE HAVE ANYTHING TO DRINK THAT ISN'T SO !@#※ CHEERFUL?
AND GOOD MORNING TO YOU, TOO.
KIRKMAN & SCOTT

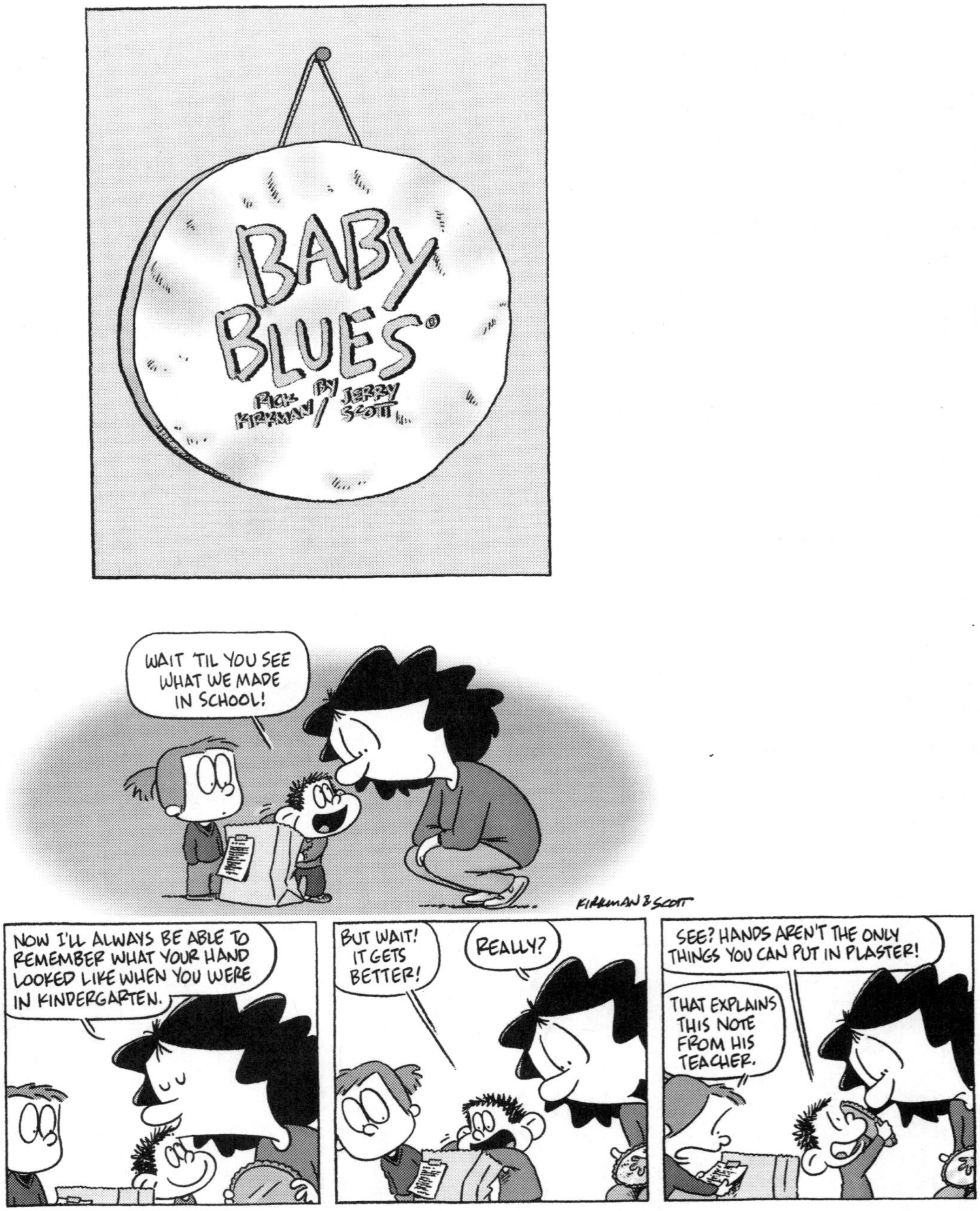
BABY BLUES®
BY RICK KIRKMAN / JERRY SCOTT
WAIT 'TIL YOU SEE WHAT WE MADE IN SCHOOL!
KIRKMAN & SCOTT
TAA-DAAAH!
OH! IT'S A PLASTER HANDPRINT!
NOW I'LL ALWAYS BE ABLE TO REMEMBER WHAT YOUR HAND LOOKED LIKE WHEN YOU WERE IN KINDERGARTEN.
BUT WAIT! IT GETS BETTER!
REALLY?
SEE? HANDS AREN'T THE ONLY THINGS YOU CAN PUT IN PLASTER!
THAT EXPLAINS THIS NOTE FROM HIS TEACHER.

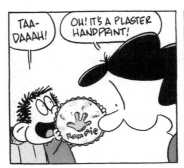

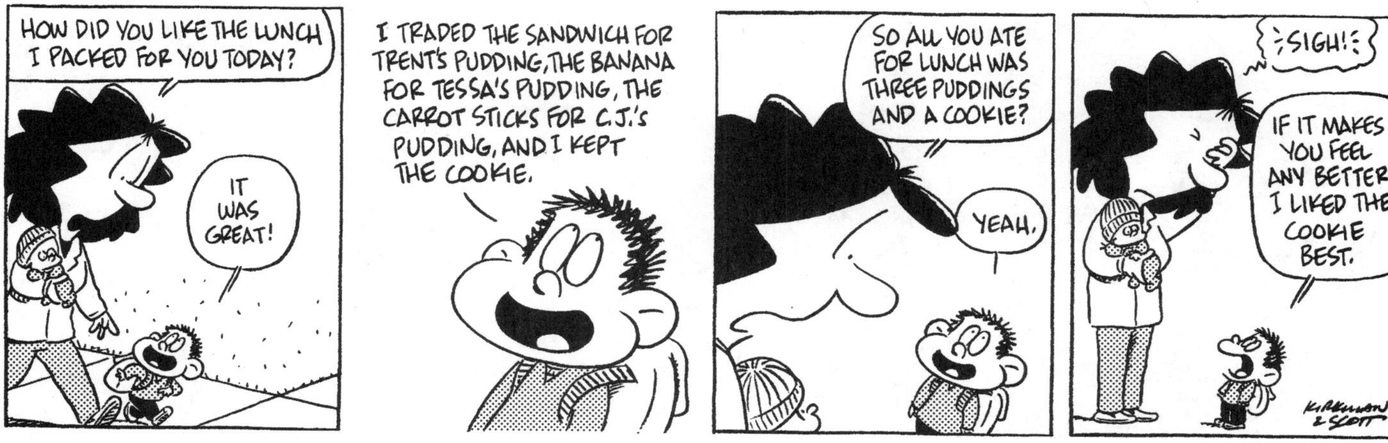
HOW DID YOU LIKE THE LUNCH I PACKED FOR YOU TODAY?
IT WAS GREAT!
I TRADED THE SANDWICH FOR TRENT'S PUDDING, THE BANANA FOR TESSA'S PUDDING, THE CARROT STICKS FOR C.J.'s PUDDING, AND I KEPT THE COOKIE.
SO ALL YOU ATE FOR LUNCH WAS THREE PUDDINGS AND A COOKIE?
YEAH.
SIGH!
IF IT MAKES YOU FEEL ANY BETTER, I LIKED THE COOKIE BEST.
KIRKMAN & SCOTT

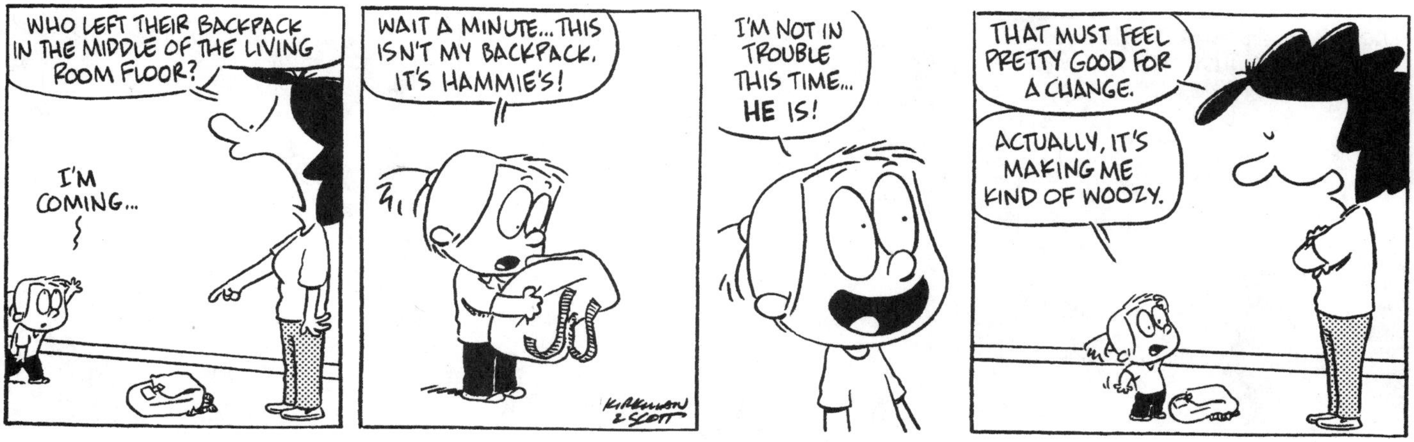
WHO LEFT THEIR BACKPACK IN THE MIDDLE OF THE LIVING ROOM FLOOR?
I'M COMING...
WAIT A MINUTE... THIS ISN'T MY BACKPACK. IT'S HAMMIE'S!
KIRKMAN & SCOTT
I'M NOT IN TROUBLE THIS TIME... HE IS!
THAT MUST FEEL PRETTY GOOD FOR A CHANGE.
ACTUALLY, IT'S MAKING ME KIND OF WOOZY.

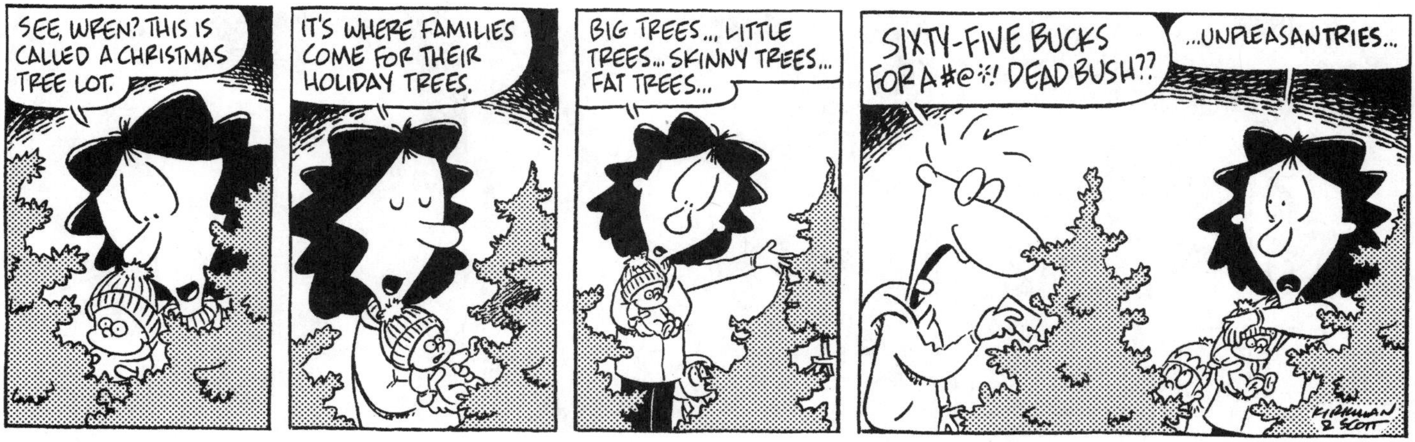
SEE, WREN? THIS IS CALLED A CHRISTMAS TREE LOT.
IT'S WHERE FAMILIES COME FOR THEIR HOLIDAY TREES.
BIG TREES... LITTLE TREES... SKINNY TREES... FAT TREES...
SIXTY-FIVE BUCKS FOR A #@*! DEAD BUSH??
...UNPLEASANTRIES...
KIRKMAN & SCOTT

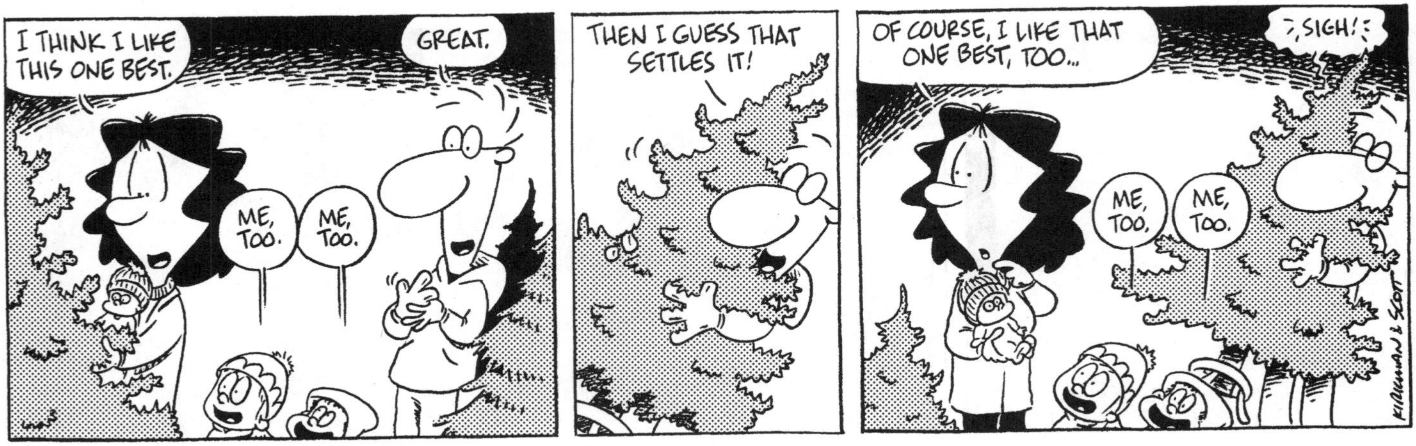
I THINK I LIKE THIS ONE BEST.
ME, TOO.
ME, TOO.
GREAT.
THEN I GUESS THAT SETTLES IT!
OF COURSE, I LIKE THAT ONE BEST, TOO...
ME, TOO.
ME, TOO.
SIGH!
KIRKMAN & SCOTT

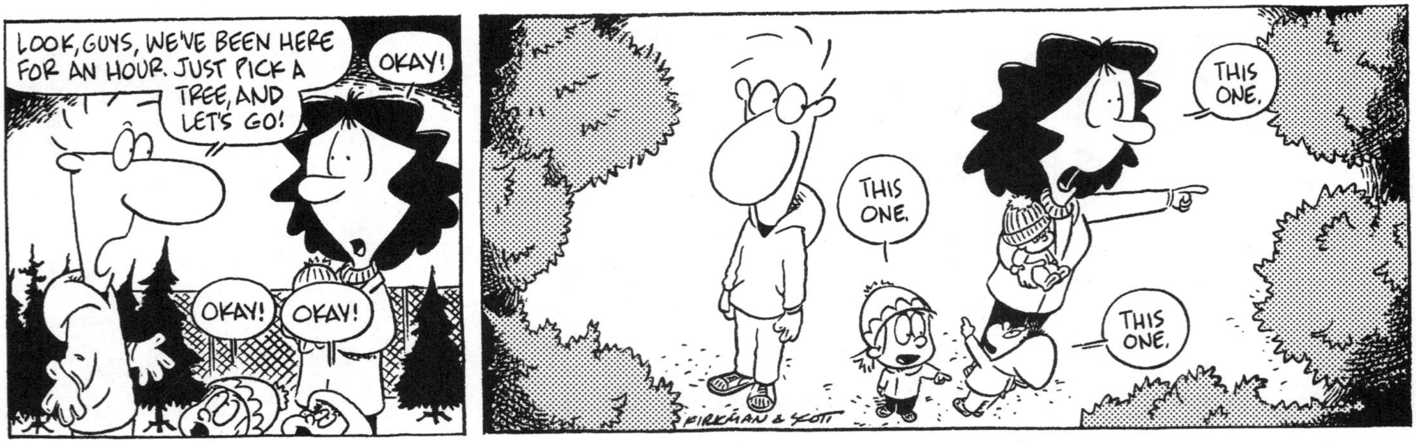
LOOK, GUYS, WE'VE BEEN HERE FOR AN HOUR. JUST PICK A TREE, AND LET'S GO!
OKAY!
OKAY!
OKAY!
THIS ONE.
THIS ONE.
THIS ONE.
KIRKMAN & SCOTT

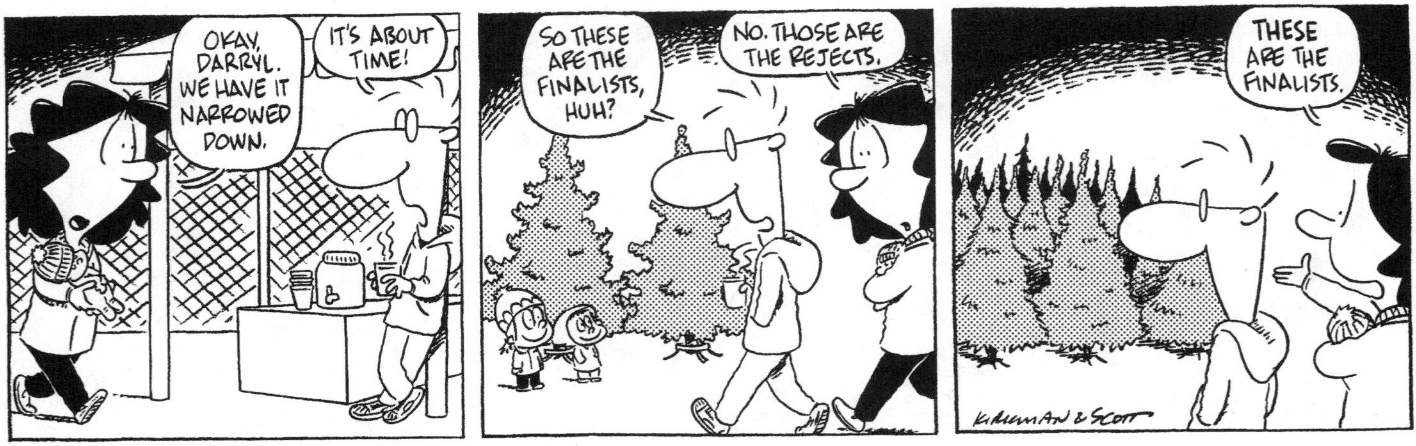
OKAY, DARRYL. WE HAVE IT NARROWED DOWN.
IT'S ABOUT TIME!
SO THESE ARE THE FINALISTS, HUH?
NO. THOSE ARE THE REJECTS.
THESE ARE THE FINALISTS.
KIRKMAN & SCOTT

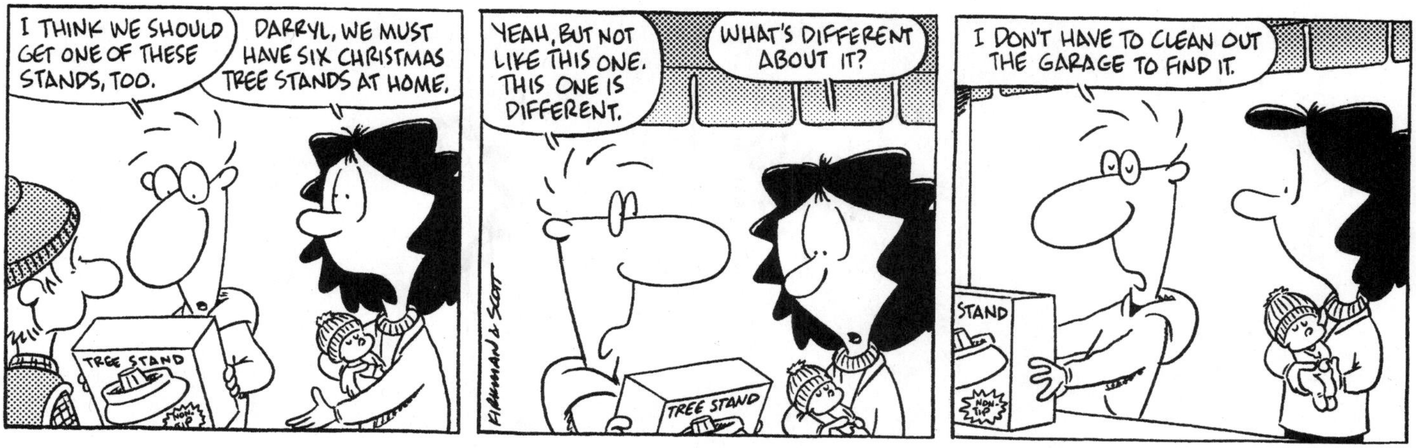
I THINK WE SHOULD GET ONE OF THESE STANDS, TOO.
DARRYL, WE MUST HAVE SIX CHRISTMAS TREE STANDS AT HOME.
TREE STAND
YEAH, BUT NOT LIKE THIS ONE. THIS ONE IS DIFFERENT.
WHAT'S DIFFERENT ABOUT IT?
TREE STAND
KIRKMAN & SCOTT
I DON'T HAVE TO CLEAN OUT THE GARAGE TO FIND IT.
STAND

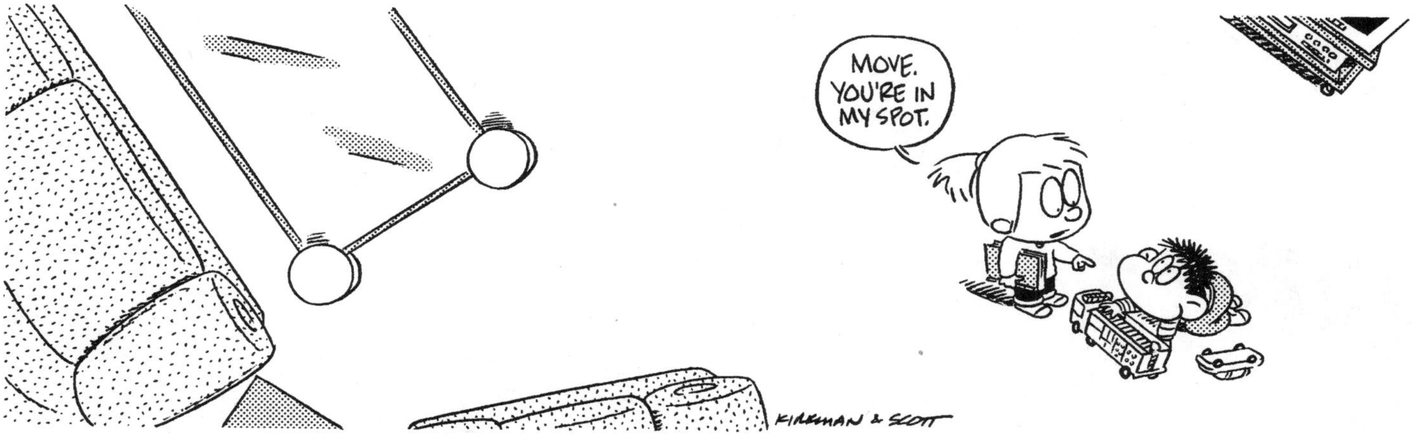
MOVE. YOU'RE IN MY SPOT.
KIRKMAN & SCOTT

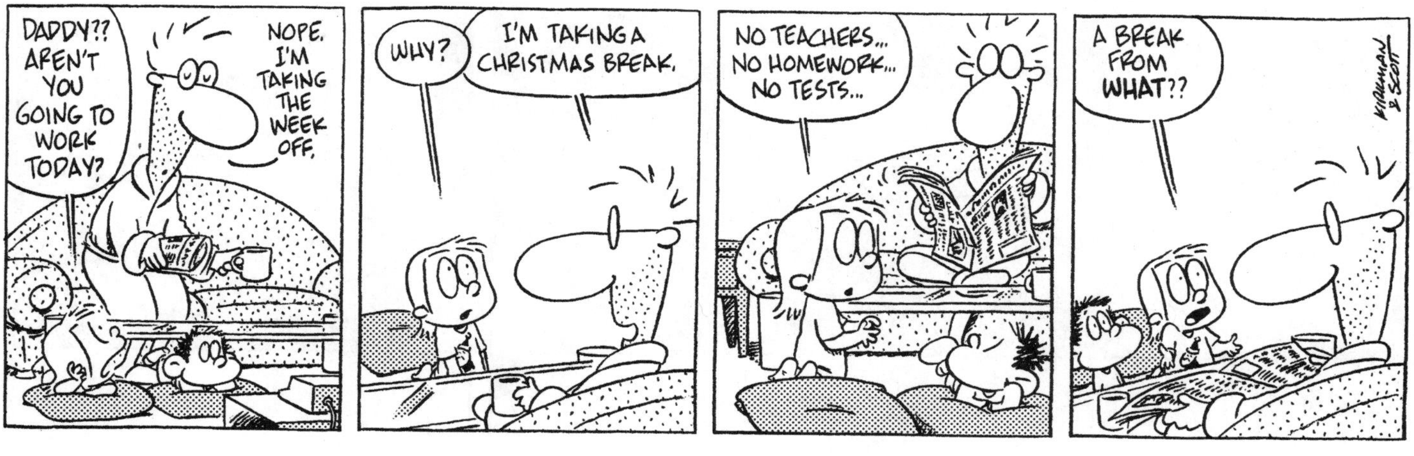
DADDY?? AREN'T YOU GOING TO WORK TODAY?
NOPE. I'M TAKING THE WEEK OFF.
WHY?
I'M TAKING A CHRISTMAS BREAK.
NO TEACHERS... NO HOMEWORK... NO TESTS...
A BREAK FROM **WHAT**??
KIRKMAN & SCOTT

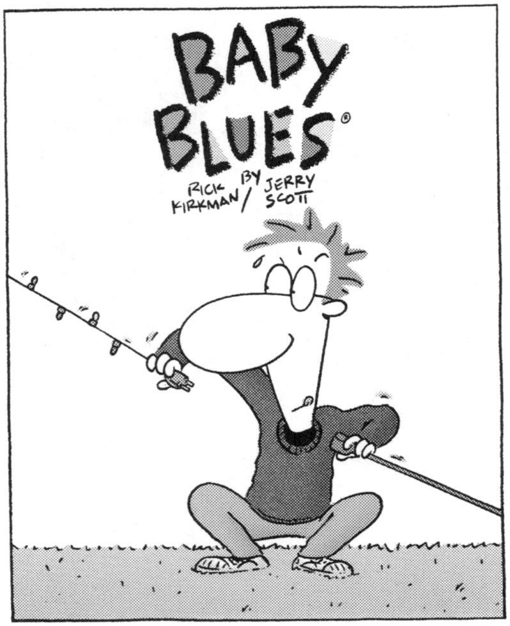
BABY BLUES®
BY RICK KIRKMAN / JERRY SCOTT

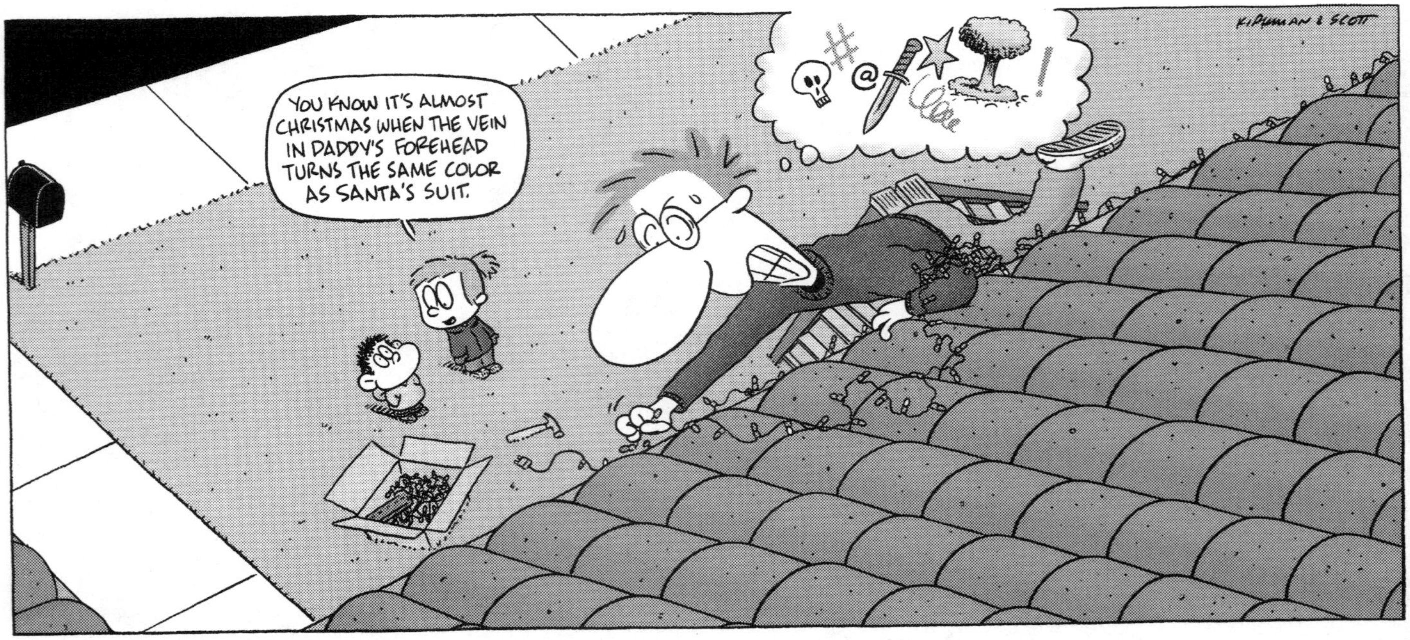
KIRKMAN & SCOTT
YOU KNOW IT'S ALMOST CHRISTMAS WHEN THE VEIN IN DADDY'S FOREHEAD TURNS THE SAME COLOR AS SANTA'S SUIT.

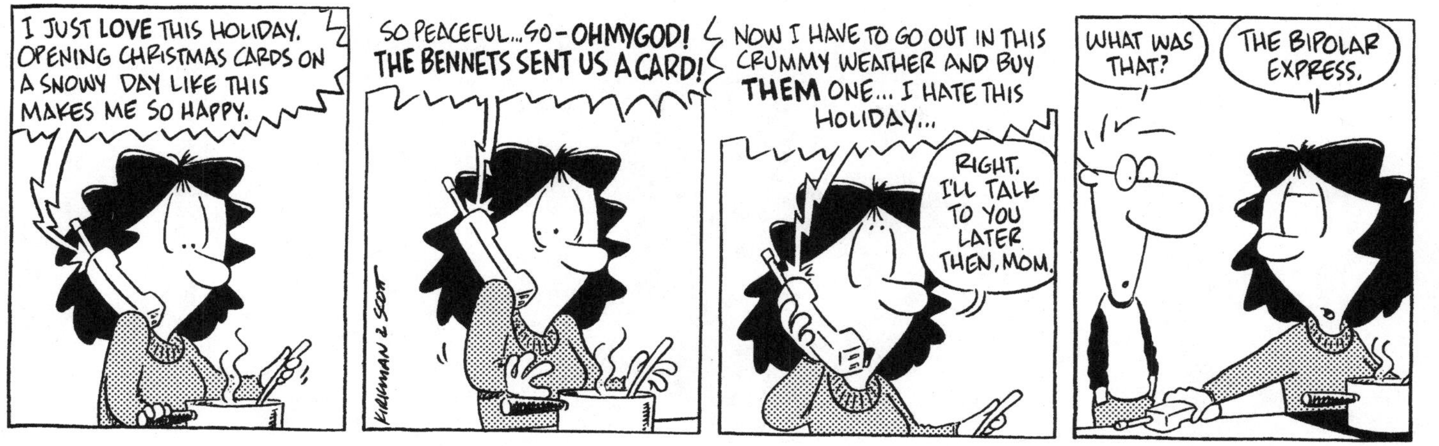
I JUST LOVE THIS HOLIDAY. OPENING CHRISTMAS CARDS ON A SNOWY DAY LIKE THIS MAKES ME SO HAPPY.
SO PEACEFUL...SO-OHMYGOD! THE BENNETS SENT US A CARD!
NOW I HAVE TO GO OUT IN THIS CRUMMY WEATHER AND BUY THEM ONE... I HATE THIS HOLIDAY...
RIGHT. I'LL TALK TO YOU LATER THEN, MOM.
WHAT WAS THAT?
THE BIPOLAR EXPRESS.

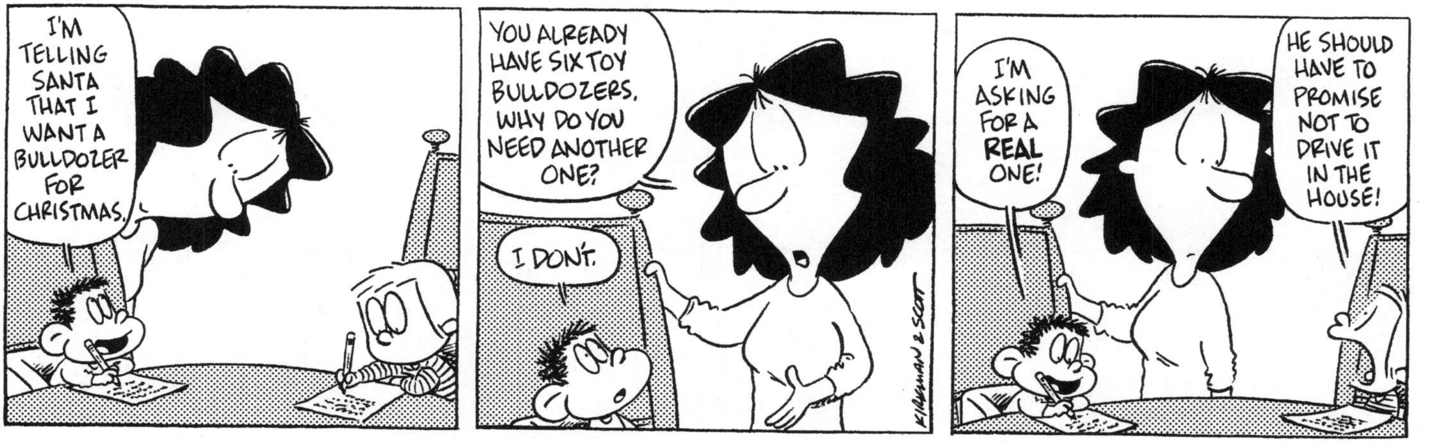
I'M TELLING SANTA THAT I WANT A BULLDOZER FOR CHRISTMAS.
YOU ALREADY HAVE SIX TOY BULLDOZERS. WHY DO YOU NEED ANOTHER ONE?
I DON'T.
I'M ASKING FOR A REAL ONE!
HE SHOULD HAVE TO PROMISE NOT TO DRIVE IT IN THE HOUSE!

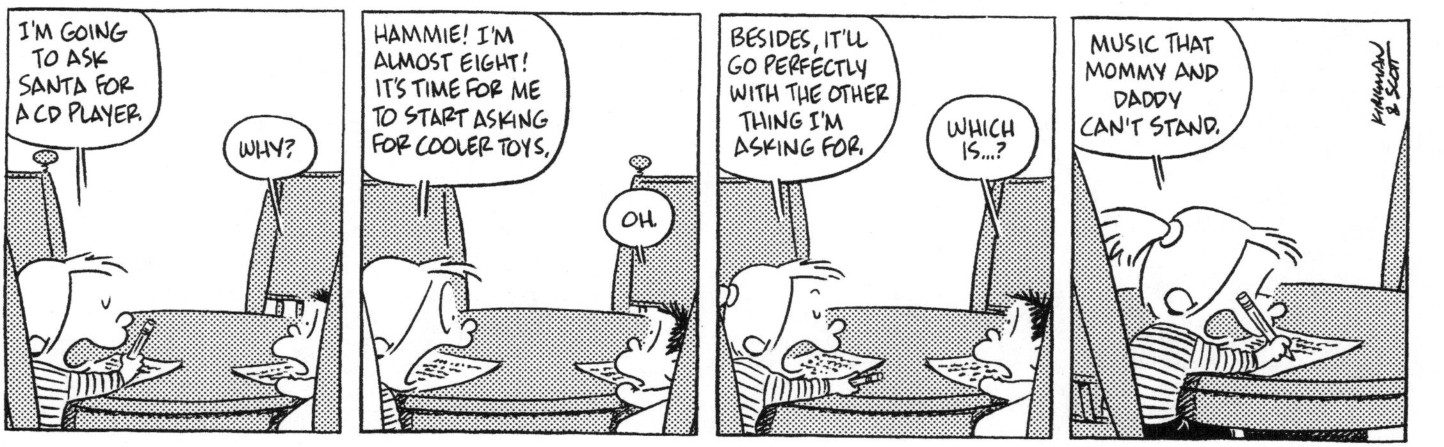
I'M GOING TO ASK SANTA FOR A CD PLAYER.
WHY?
HAMMIE! I'M ALMOST EIGHT! IT'S TIME FOR ME TO START ASKING FOR COOLER TOYS.
OH.
BESIDES, IT'LL GO PERFECTLY WITH THE OTHER THING I'M ASKING FOR.
WHICH IS...?
MUSIC THAT MOMMY AND DADDY CAN'T STAND.

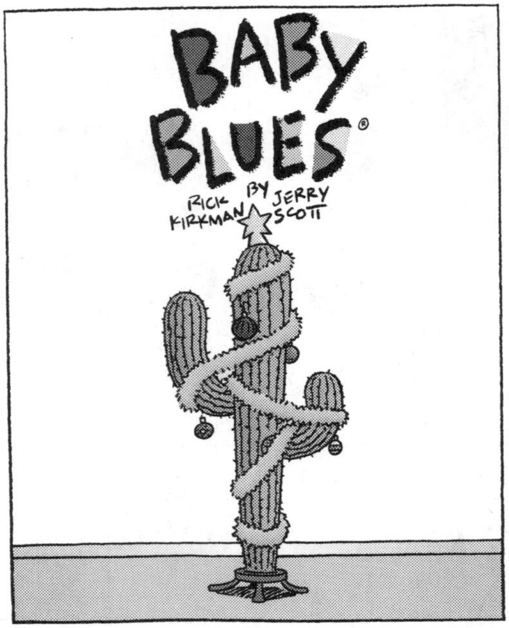

BABY BLUES®
BY
RICK KIRKMAN
JERRY SCOTT

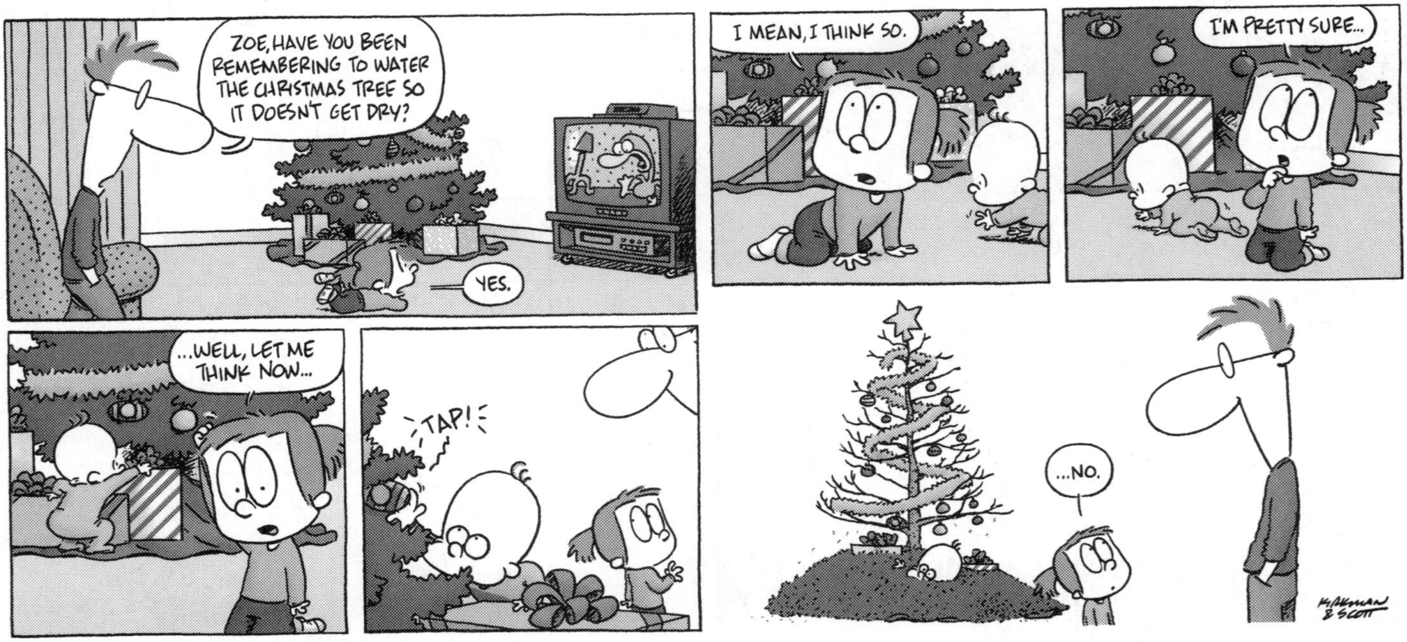

ZOE, HAVE YOU BEEN REMEMBERING TO WATER THE CHRISTMAS TREE SO IT DOESN'T GET DRY?
YES.
I MEAN, I THINK SO.
I'M PRETTY SURE...
...WELL, LET ME THINK NOW...
TAP!
...NO.
KIRKMAN & SCOTT

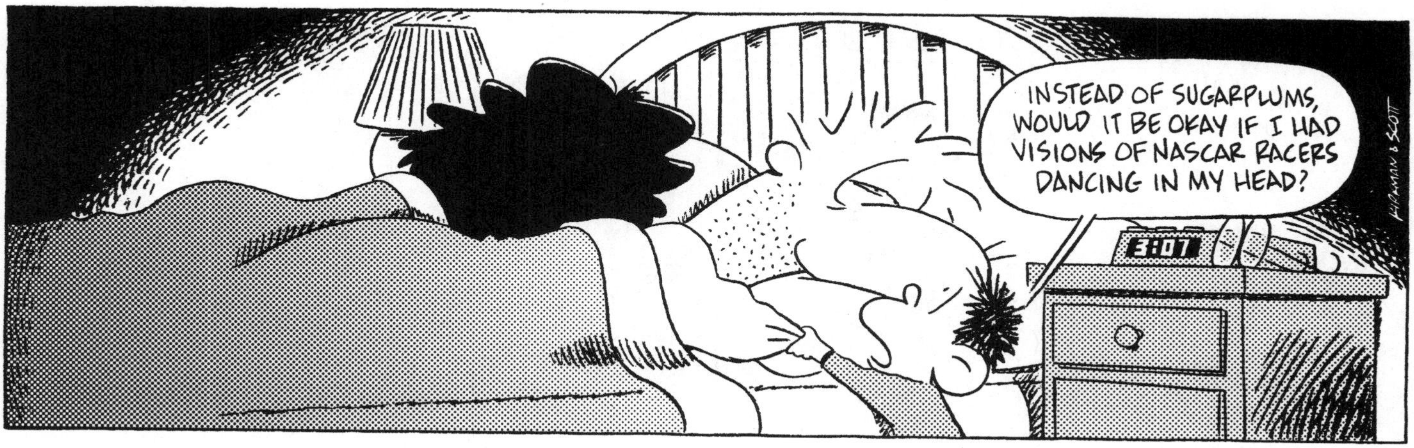
INSTEAD OF SUGARPLUMS, WOULD IT BE OKAY IF I HAD VISIONS OF NASCAR RACERS DANCING IN MY HEAD?
3:07
KIRKMAN & SCOTT

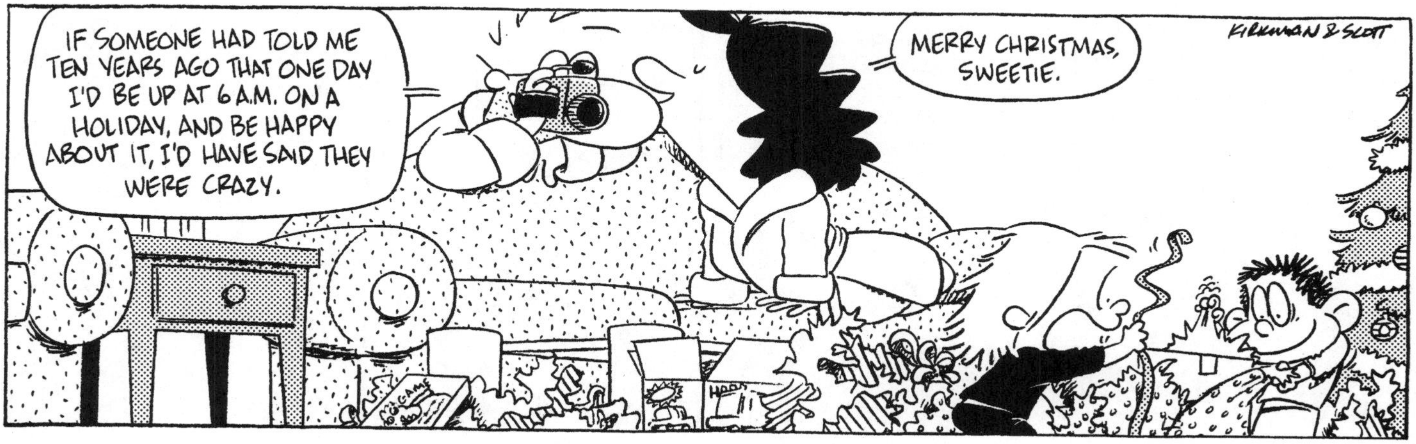
KIRKMAN & SCOTT
IF SOMEONE HAD TOLD ME TEN YEARS AGO THAT ONE DAY I'D BE UP AT 6 A.M. ON A HOLIDAY, AND BE HAPPY ABOUT IT, I'D HAVE SAID THEY WERE CRAZY.
MERRY CHRISTMAS, SWEETIE.

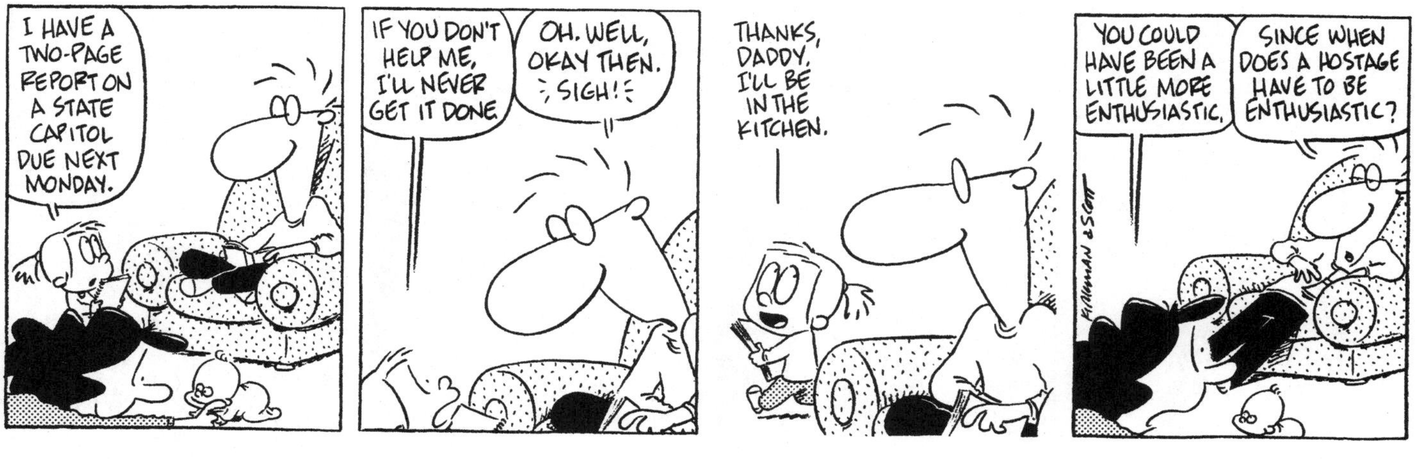
I HAVE A TWO-PAGE REPORT ON A STATE CAPITOL DUE NEXT MONDAY.
IF YOU DON'T HELP ME, I'LL NEVER GET IT DONE.
OH. WELL, OKAY THEN.
SIGH!
THANKS, DADDY. I'LL BE IN THE KITCHEN.
KIRKMAN & SCOTT
YOU COULD HAVE BEEN A LITTLE MORE ENTHUSIASTIC.
SINCE WHEN DOES A HOSTAGE HAVE TO BE ENTHUSIASTIC?

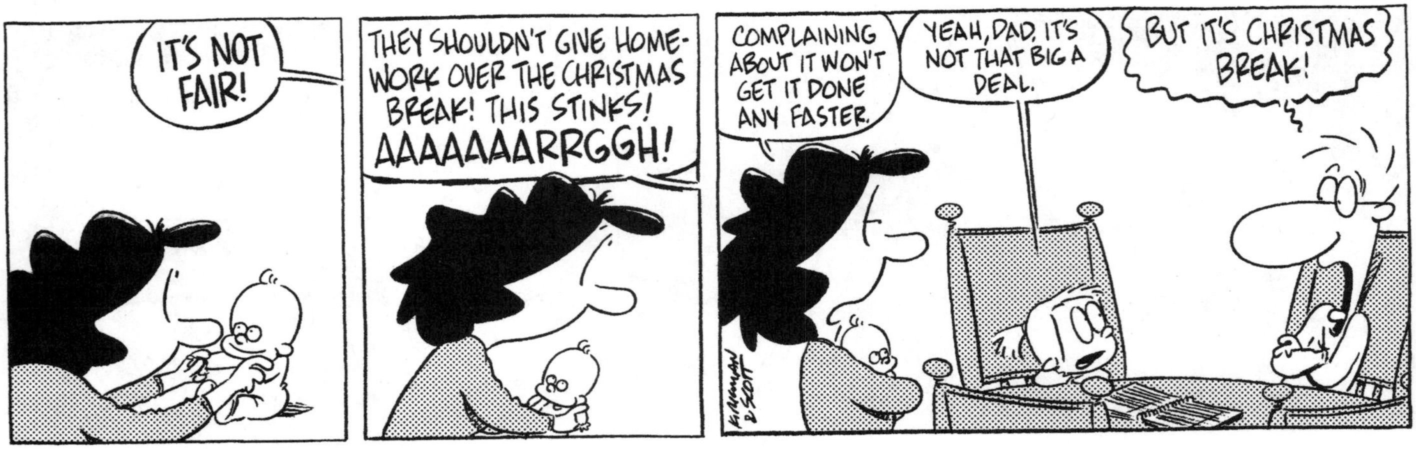
IT'S NOT FAIR!
THEY SHOULDN'T GIVE HOME-WORK OVER THE CHRISTMAS BREAK! THIS STINKS! AAAAAAARRGGH!
COMPLAINING ABOUT IT WON'T GET IT DONE ANY FASTER.
YEAH, DAD, IT'S NOT THAT BIG A DEAL.
BUT IT'S CHRISTMAS BREAK!

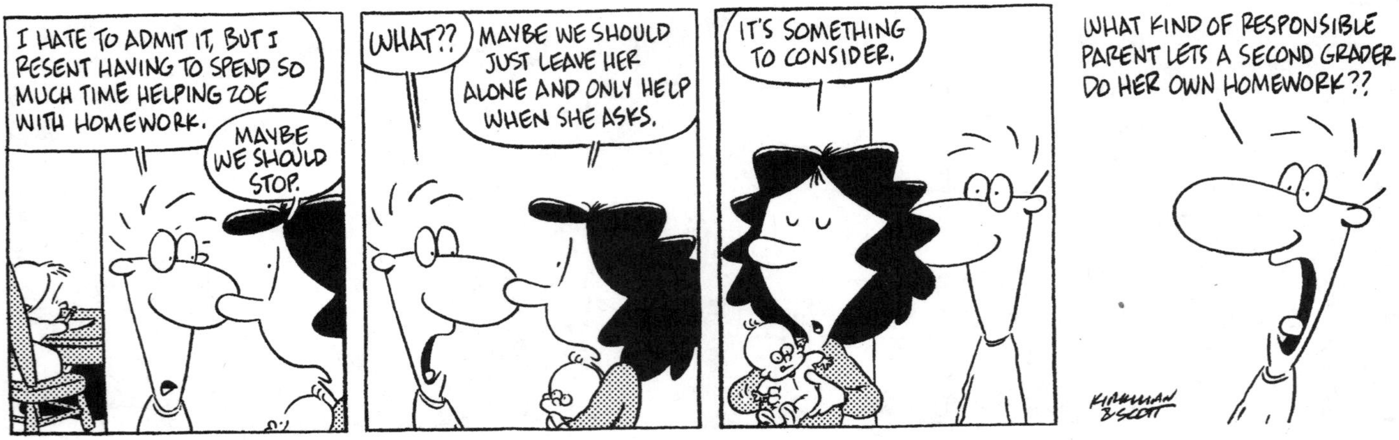
I HATE TO ADMIT IT, BUT I RESENT HAVING TO SPEND SO MUCH TIME HELPING ZOE WITH HOMEWORK.
MAYBE WE SHOULD STOP.
WHAT??
MAYBE WE SHOULD JUST LEAVE HER ALONE AND ONLY HELP WHEN SHE ASKS.
IT'S SOMETHING TO CONSIDER.
WHAT KIND OF RESPONSIBLE PARENT LETS A SECOND GRADER DO HER OWN HOMEWORK??

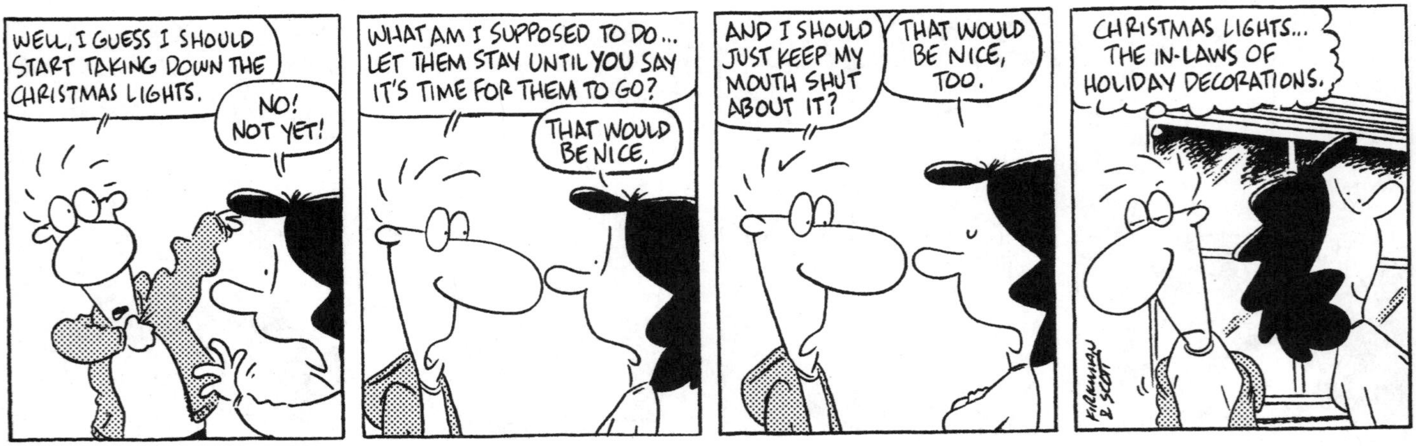
WELL, I GUESS I SHOULD START TAKING DOWN THE CHRISTMAS LIGHTS.
NO! NOT YET!
WHAT AM I SUPPOSED TO DO... LET THEM STAY UNTIL YOU SAY IT'S TIME FOR THEM TO GO?
THAT WOULD BE NICE.
AND I SHOULD JUST KEEP MY MOUTH SHUT ABOUT IT?
THAT WOULD BE NICE, TOO.
CHRISTMAS LIGHTS... THE IN-LAWS OF HOLIDAY DECORATIONS.

BABY BLUES®
BY RICK KIRKMAN / JERRY SCOTT

I'M COLD!
WHY DON'T YOU GO PUT ON A SWEATSHIRT?
OKAY.
BETTER?
NOT REALLY. NOW I'M KIND OF HOT.
KIRKMAN & SCOTT

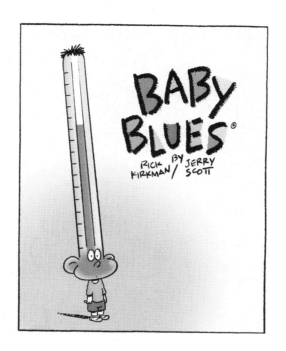

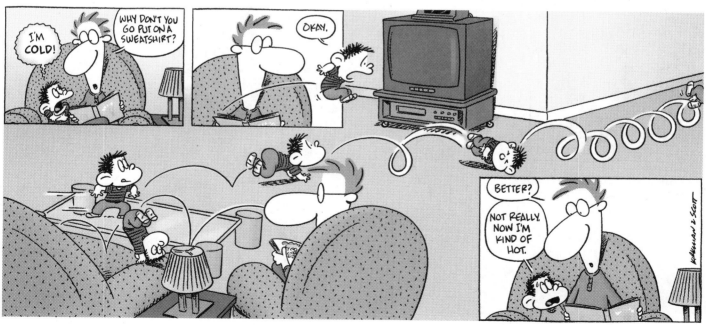

BABY BLUES®
BY RICK KIRKMAN / JERRY SCOTT
The Daily Current

I NEED TO WRITE A CURRENT EVENT REPORT.
OKAY.
WHAT KIND OF CURRENT EVENT?
I DON'T KNOW. THE REGULAR KIND, I GUESS.
JUST AS LONG AS IT'S CURRENT, AND AN EVENT.
I WANT TO DO A GOOD JOB, SO WE SHOULD MAKE IT EXTRA-CURRENT.
AND SUPER-EVENTY... LET'S NOT SCRIMP ON THAT, EITHER!
KIRKMAN & SCOTT
YOU DON'T HAVE ANY IDEA WHAT A CURRENT EVENT IS, DO YOU?
DO YOU THINK THAT WILL AFFECT MY GRADE?

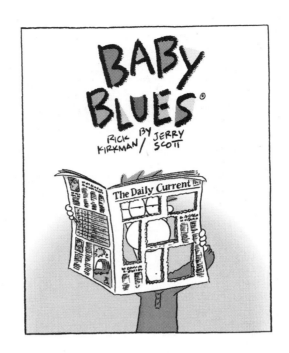

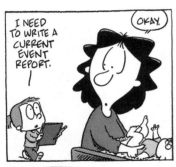

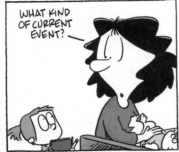

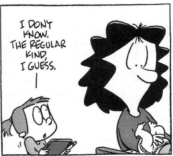

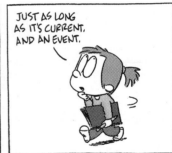

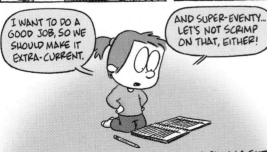

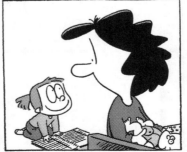

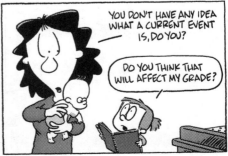

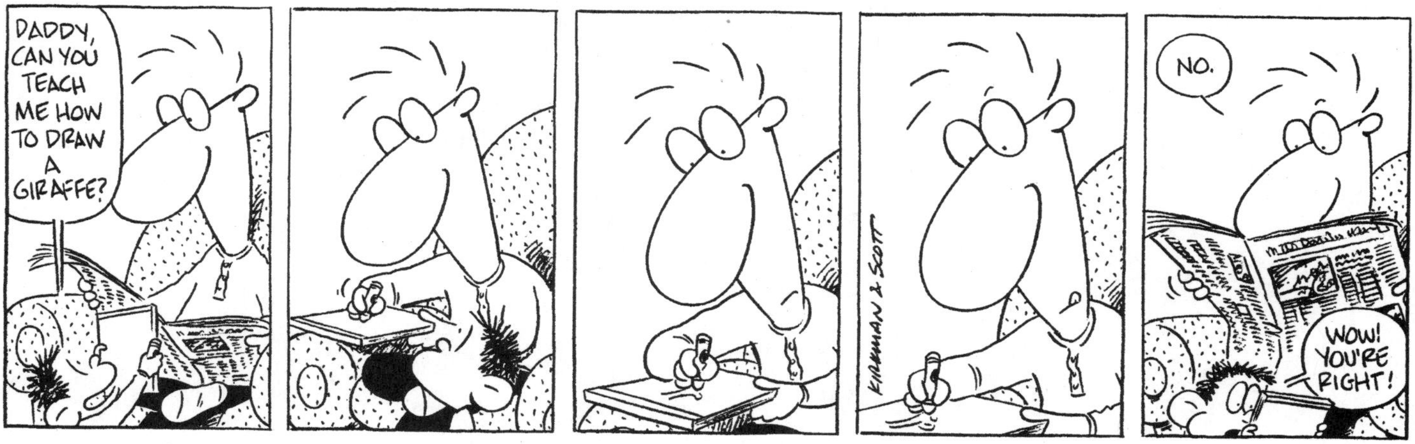
DADDY, CAN YOU TEACH ME HOW TO DRAW A GIRAFFE?
KIRKMAN & SCOTT
NO.
WOW! YOU'RE RIGHT!

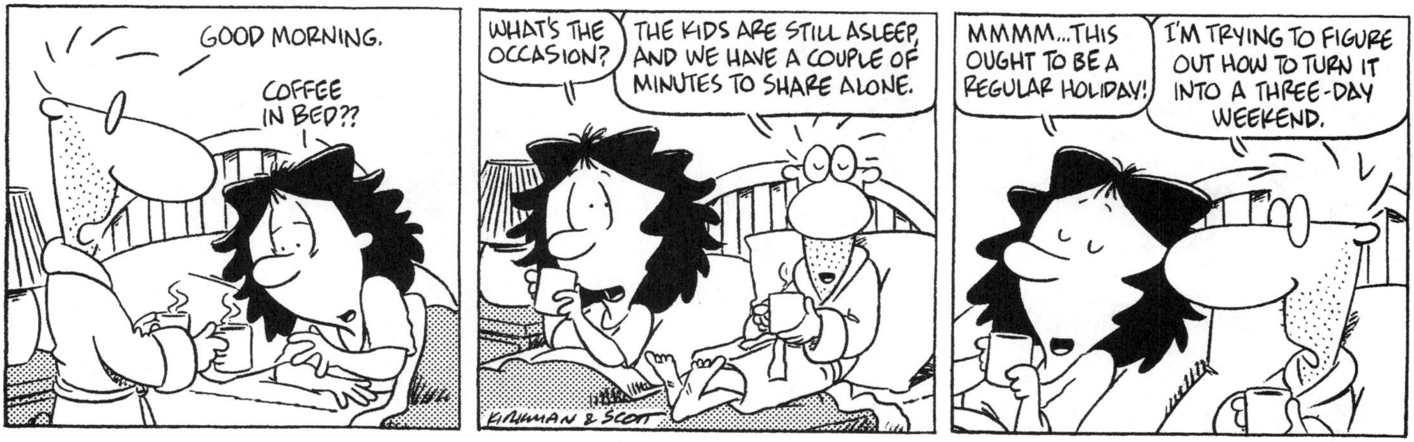
GOOD MORNING.
COFFEE IN BED??
WHAT'S THE OCCASION?
THE KIDS ARE STILL ASLEEP, AND WE HAVE A COUPLE OF MINUTES TO SHARE ALONE.
KIRKMAN & SCOTT
MMMM...THIS OUGHT TO BE A REGULAR HOLIDAY!
I'M TRYING TO FIGURE OUT HOW TO TURN IT INTO A THREE-DAY WEEKEND.

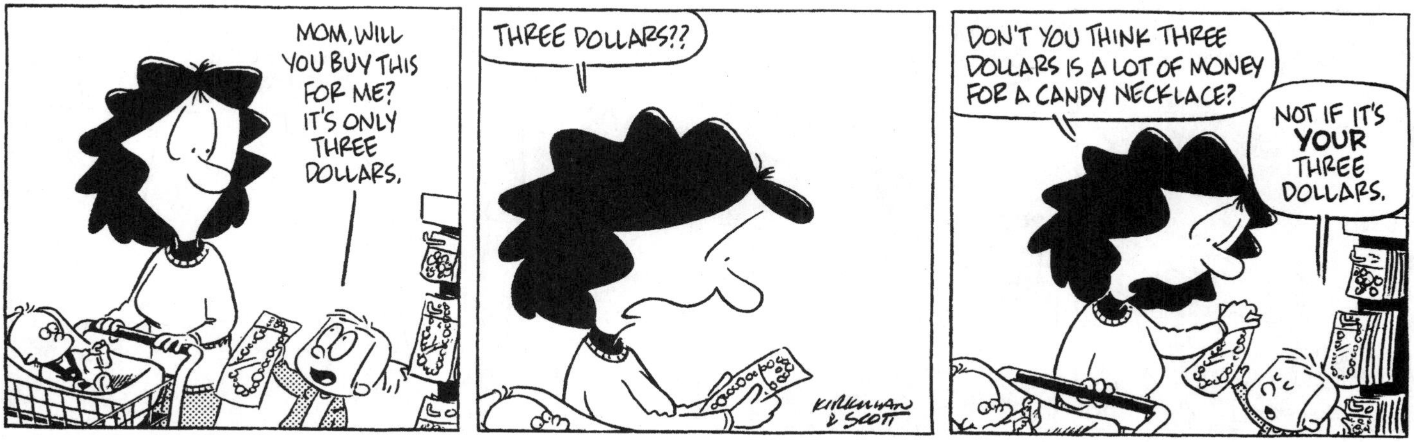
MOM, WILL YOU BUY THIS FOR ME? IT'S ONLY THREE DOLLARS.
THREE DOLLARS??
KIRKMAN & SCOTT
DON'T YOU THINK THREE DOLLARS IS A LOT OF MONEY FOR A CANDY NECKLACE?
NOT IF IT'S YOUR THREE DOLLARS.

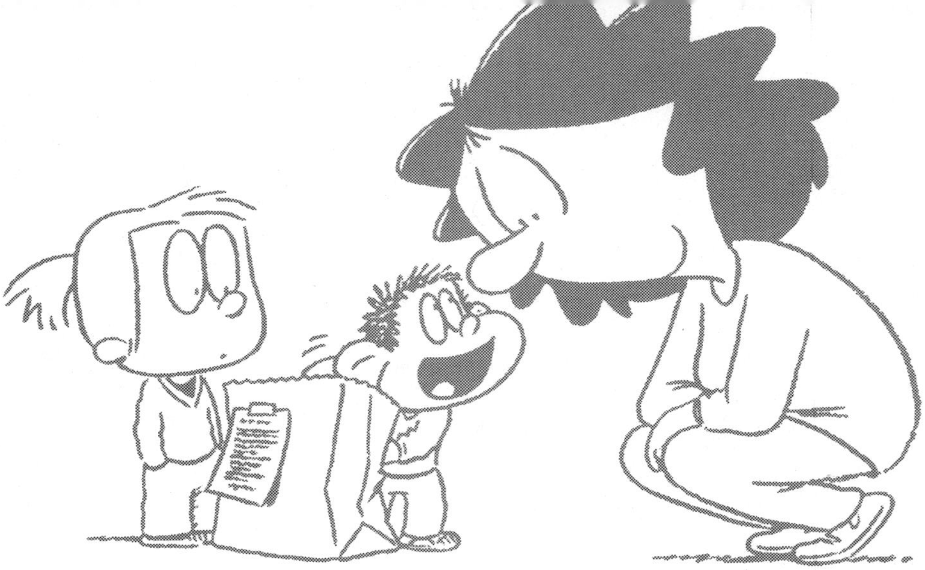

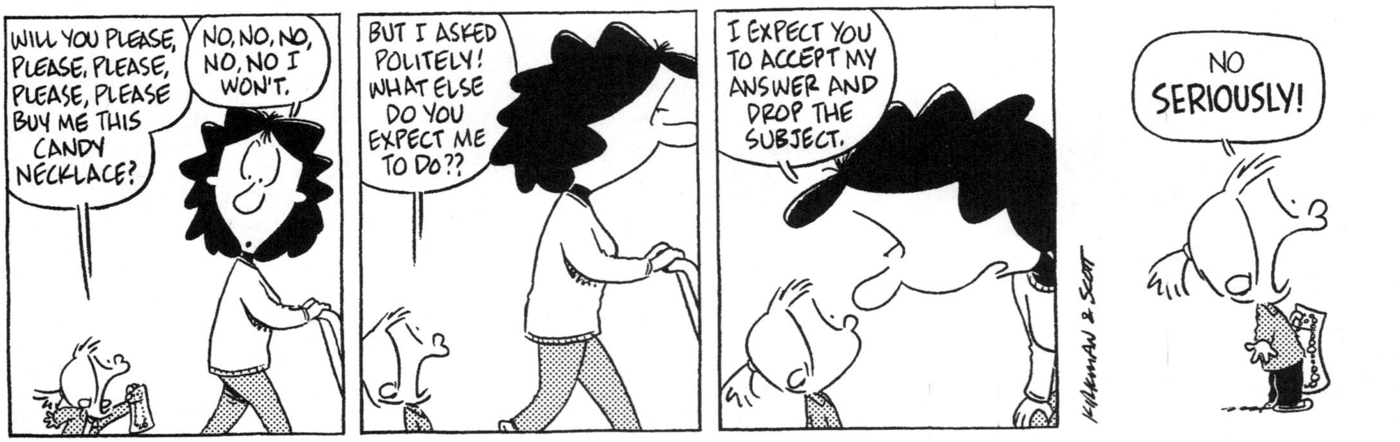
WILL YOU PLEASE, PLEASE, PLEASE, PLEASE, PLEASE BUY ME THIS CANDY NECKLACE?
NO, NO, NO, NO, NO I WON'T.
BUT I ASKED POLITELY! WHAT ELSE DO YOU EXPECT ME TO DO??
I EXPECT YOU TO ACCEPT MY ANSWER AND DROP THE SUBJECT.
KIRKMAN & SCOTT
NO SERIOUSLY!

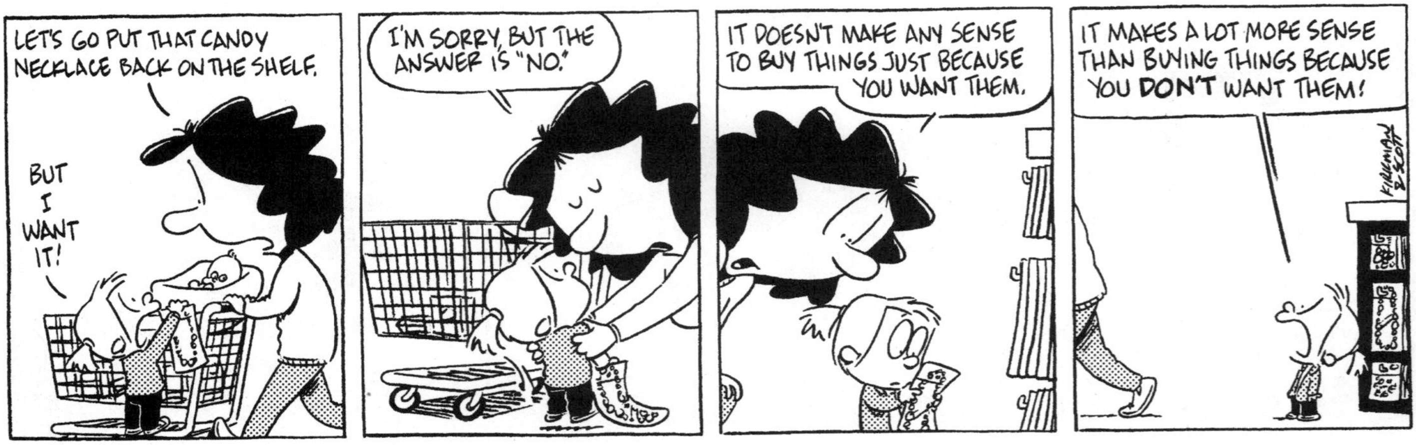
LET'S GO PUT THAT CANDY NECKLACE BACK ON THE SHELF.
BUT I WANT IT!
I'M SORRY, BUT THE ANSWER IS "NO."
IT DOESN'T MAKE ANY SENSE TO BUY THINGS JUST BECAUSE YOU WANT THEM.
IT MAKES A LOT MORE SENSE THAN BUYING THINGS BECAUSE YOU **DON'T** WANT THEM!
KIRKMAN & SCOTT

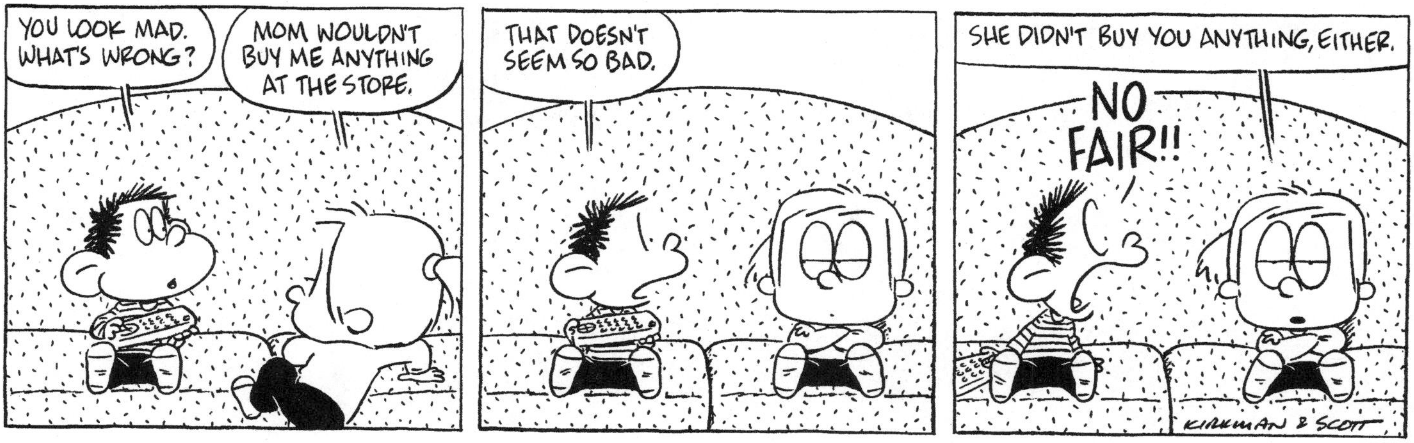
YOU LOOK MAD. WHAT'S WRONG?
MOM WOULDN'T BUY ME ANYTHING AT THE STORE.
THAT DOESN'T SEEM SO BAD.
SHE DIDN'T BUY YOU ANYTHING, EITHER.
NO FAIR!!
KIRKMAN & SCOTT

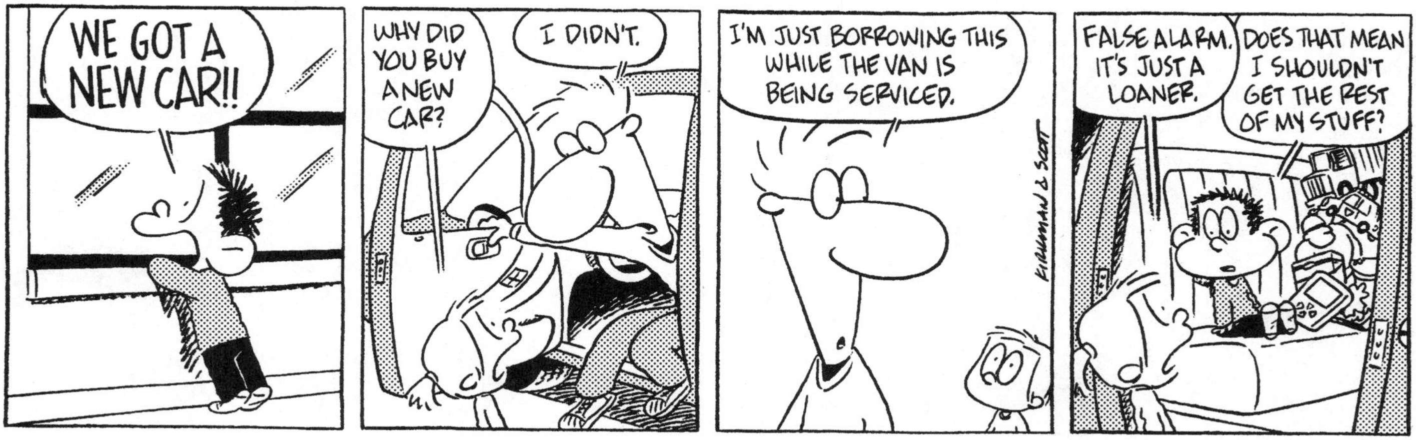
WE GOT A NEW CAR!!
WHY DID YOU BUY A NEW CAR?
I DIDN'T.
I'M JUST BORROWING THIS WHILE THE VAN IS BEING SERVICED.
KIRKMAN & SCOTT
FALSE ALARM. IT'S JUST A LOANER.
DOES THAT MEAN I SHOULDN'T GET THE REST OF MY STUFF?

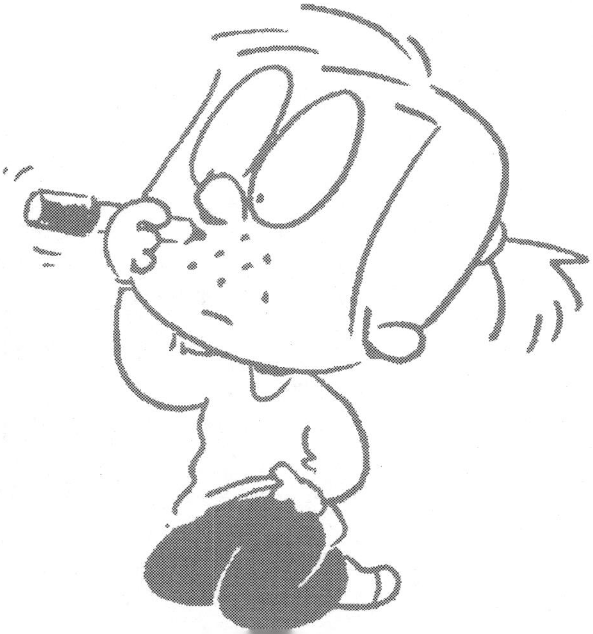

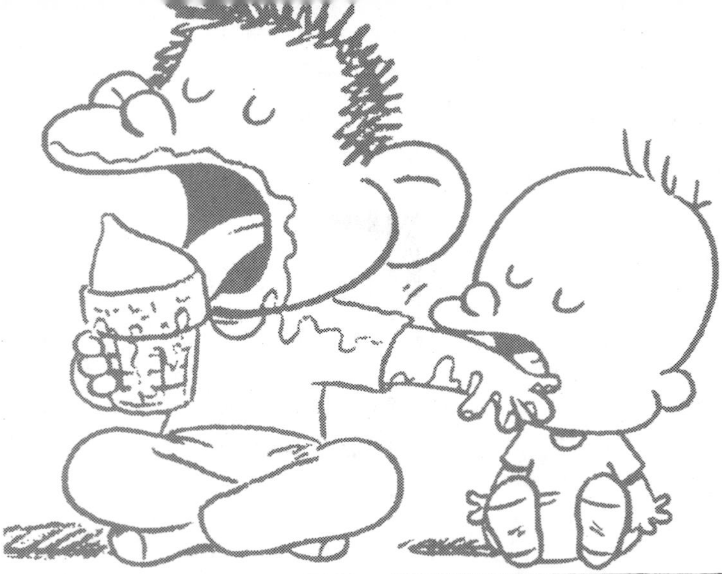

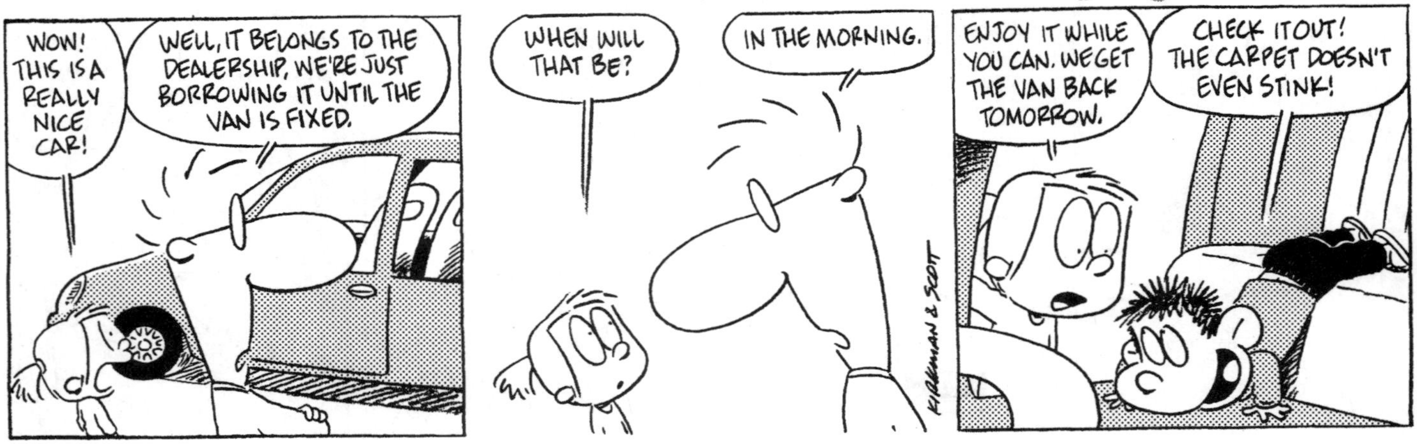

WOW! THIS IS A REALLY NICE CAR!
WELL, IT BELONGS TO THE DEALERSHIP. WE'RE JUST BORROWING IT UNTIL THE VAN IS FIXED.
WHEN WILL THAT BE?
IN THE MORNING.
ENJOY IT WHILE YOU CAN. WE GET THE VAN BACK TOMORROW.
CHECK IT OUT! THE CARPET DOESN'T EVEN STINK!
KIRKMAN & SCOTT

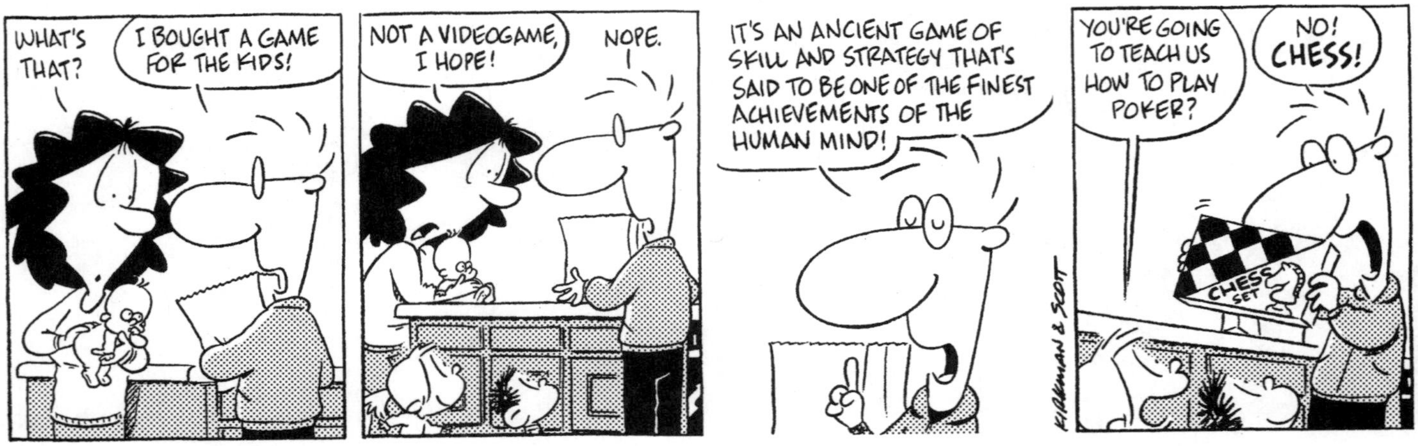

WHAT'S THAT?
I BOUGHT A GAME FOR THE KIDS!
NOT A VIDEOGAME, I HOPE!
NOPE.
IT'S AN ANCIENT GAME OF SKILL AND STRATEGY THAT'S SAID TO BE ONE OF THE FINEST ACHIEVEMENTS OF THE HUMAN MIND!
YOU'RE GOING TO TEACH US HOW TO PLAY POKER?
NO! CHESS!
CHESS SET
KIRKMAN & SCOTT

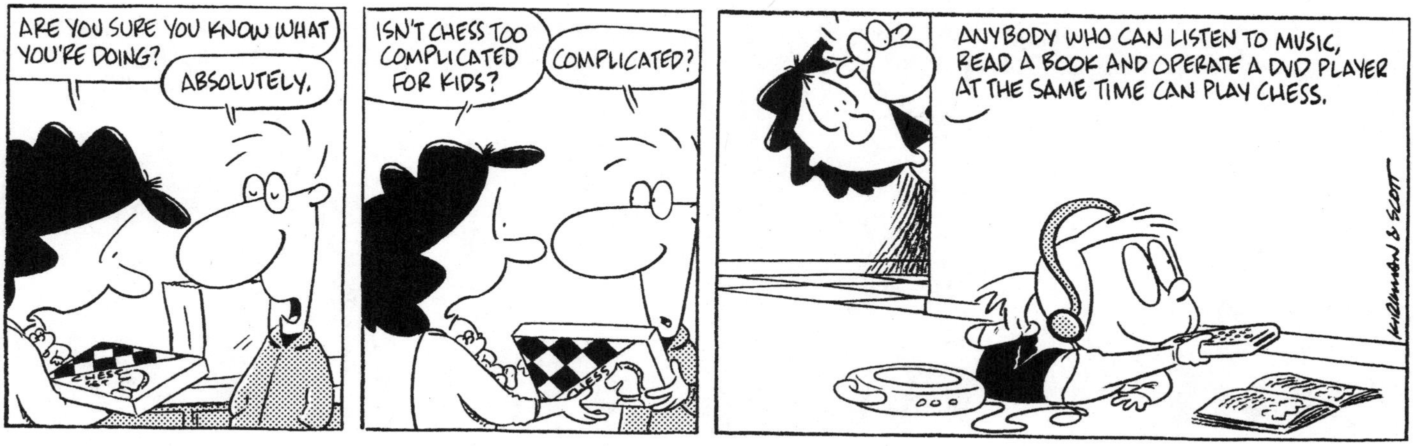
ARE YOU SURE YOU KNOW WHAT YOU'RE DOING?
ABSOLUTELY.
ISN'T CHESS TOO COMPLICATED FOR KIDS?
COMPLICATED?
ANYBODY WHO CAN LISTEN TO MUSIC, READ A BOOK AND OPERATE A DVD PLAYER AT THE SAME TIME CAN PLAY CHESS.
KIRKMAN & SCOTT

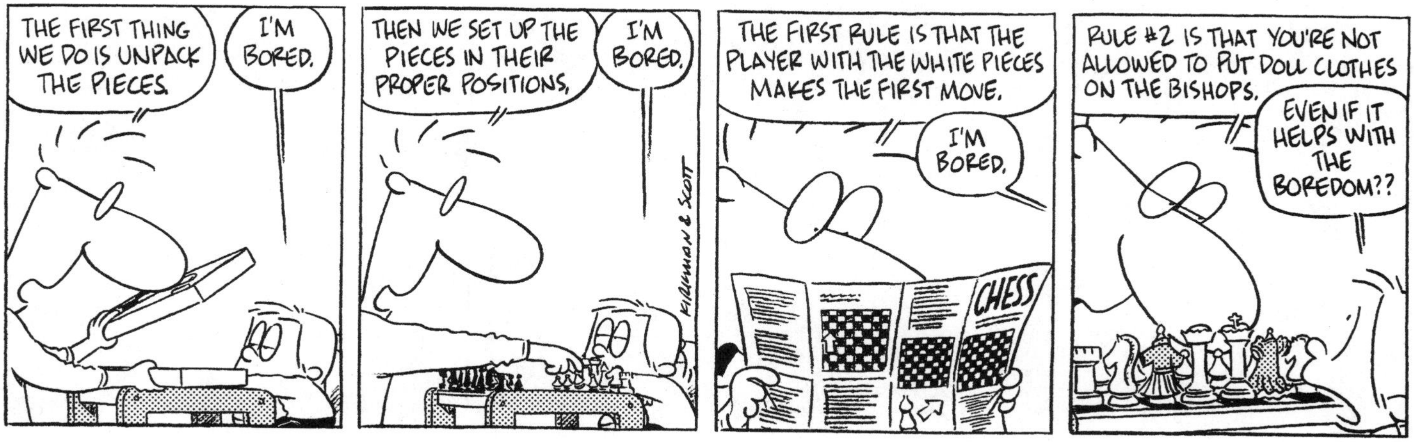
THE FIRST THING WE DO IS UNPACK THE PIECES.
I'M BORED.
THEN WE SET UP THE PIECES IN THEIR PROPER POSITIONS,
I'M BORED.
KIRKMAN & SCOTT
THE FIRST RULE IS THAT THE PLAYER WITH THE WHITE PIECES MAKES THE FIRST MOVE.
I'M BORED.
CHESS
RULE #2 IS THAT YOU'RE NOT ALLOWED TO PUT DOLL CLOTHES ON THE BISHOPS.
EVEN IF IT HELPS WITH THE BOREDOM??

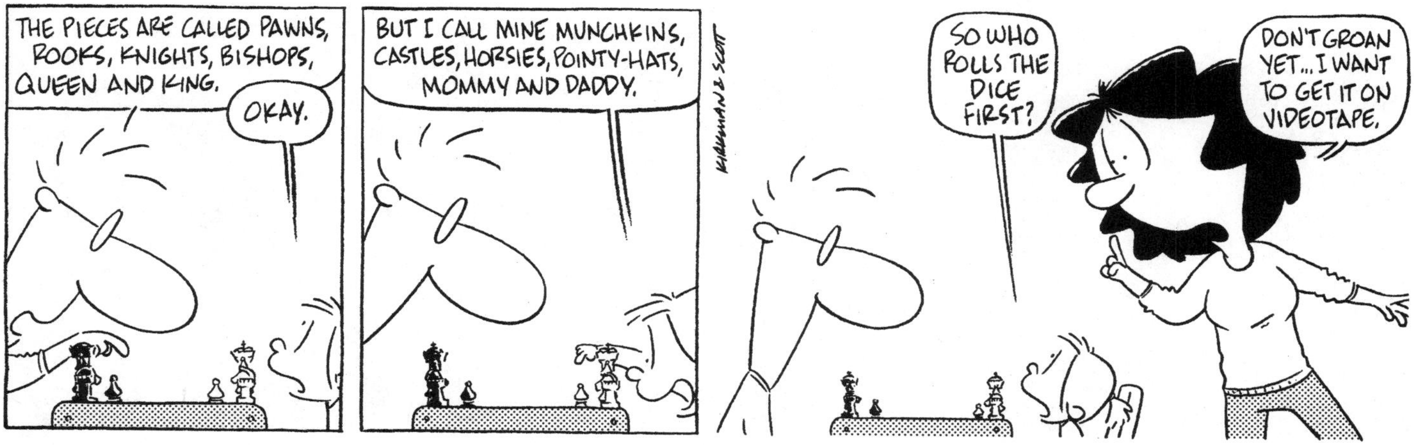
THE PIECES ARE CALLED PAWNS, ROOKS, KNIGHTS, BISHOPS, QUEEN AND KING.
OKAY.
BUT I CALL MINE MUNCHKINS, CASTLES, HORSIES, POINTY-HATS, MOMMY AND DADDY.
KIRKMAN & SCOTT
SO WHO ROLLS THE DICE FIRST?
DON'T GROAN YET... I WANT TO GET IT ON VIDEOTAPE.

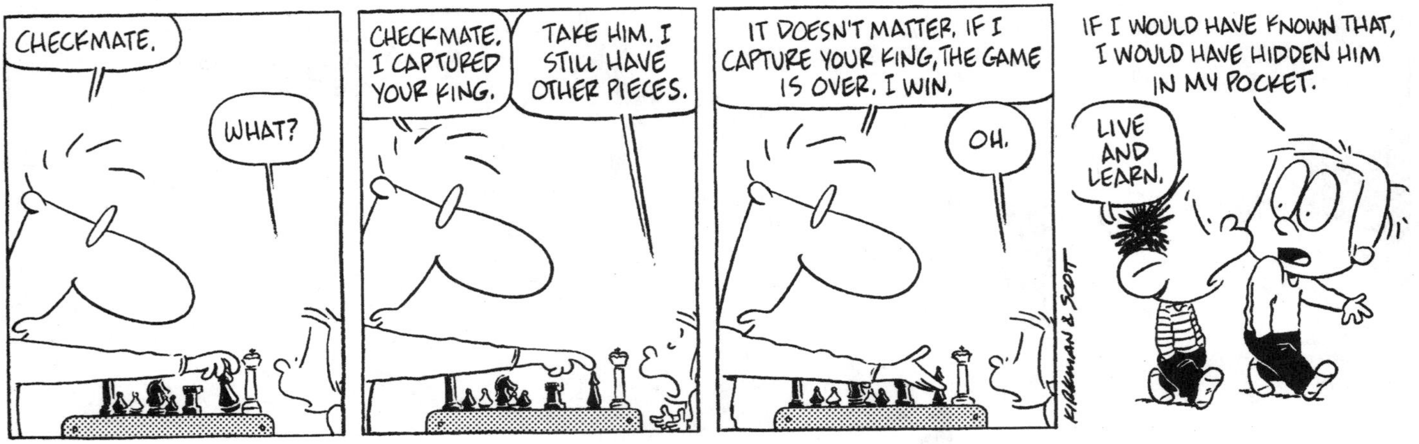
CHECKMATE.
WHAT?
CHECKMATE. I CAPTURED YOUR KING.
TAKE HIM. I STILL HAVE OTHER PIECES.
IT DOESN'T MATTER. IF I CAPTURE YOUR KING, THE GAME IS OVER. I WIN.
OH.
LIVE AND LEARN.
IF I WOULD HAVE KNOWN THAT, I WOULD HAVE HIDDEN HIM IN MY POCKET.
KIRKMAN & SCOTT

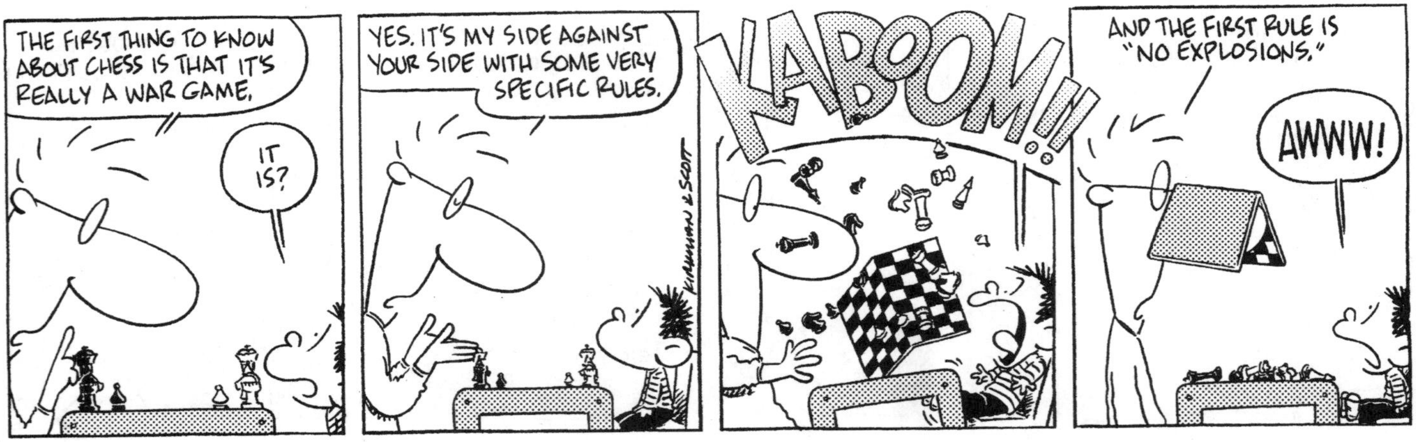
THE FIRST THING TO KNOW ABOUT CHESS IS THAT IT'S REALLY A WAR GAME.
IT IS?
YES. IT'S MY SIDE AGAINST YOUR SIDE WITH SOME VERY SPECIFIC RULES.
KIRKMAN & SCOTT
KABOOM!!
AND THE FIRST RULE IS "NO EXPLOSIONS."
AWWW!

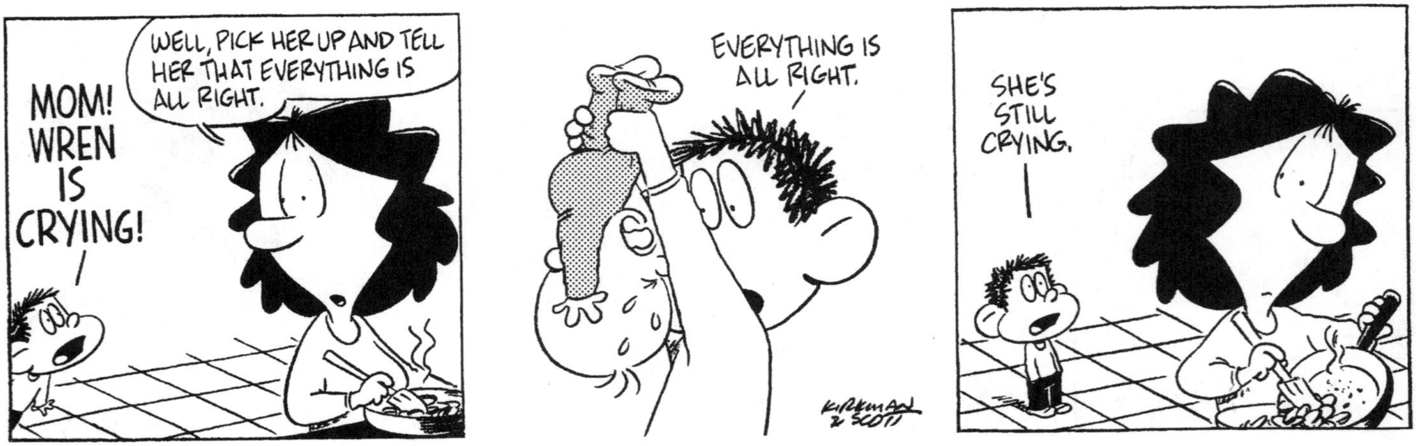
MOM! WREN IS CRYING!
WELL, PICK HER UP AND TELL HER THAT EVERYTHING IS ALL RIGHT.
EVERYTHING IS ALL RIGHT.
KIRKMAN & SCOTT
SHE'S STILL CRYING.

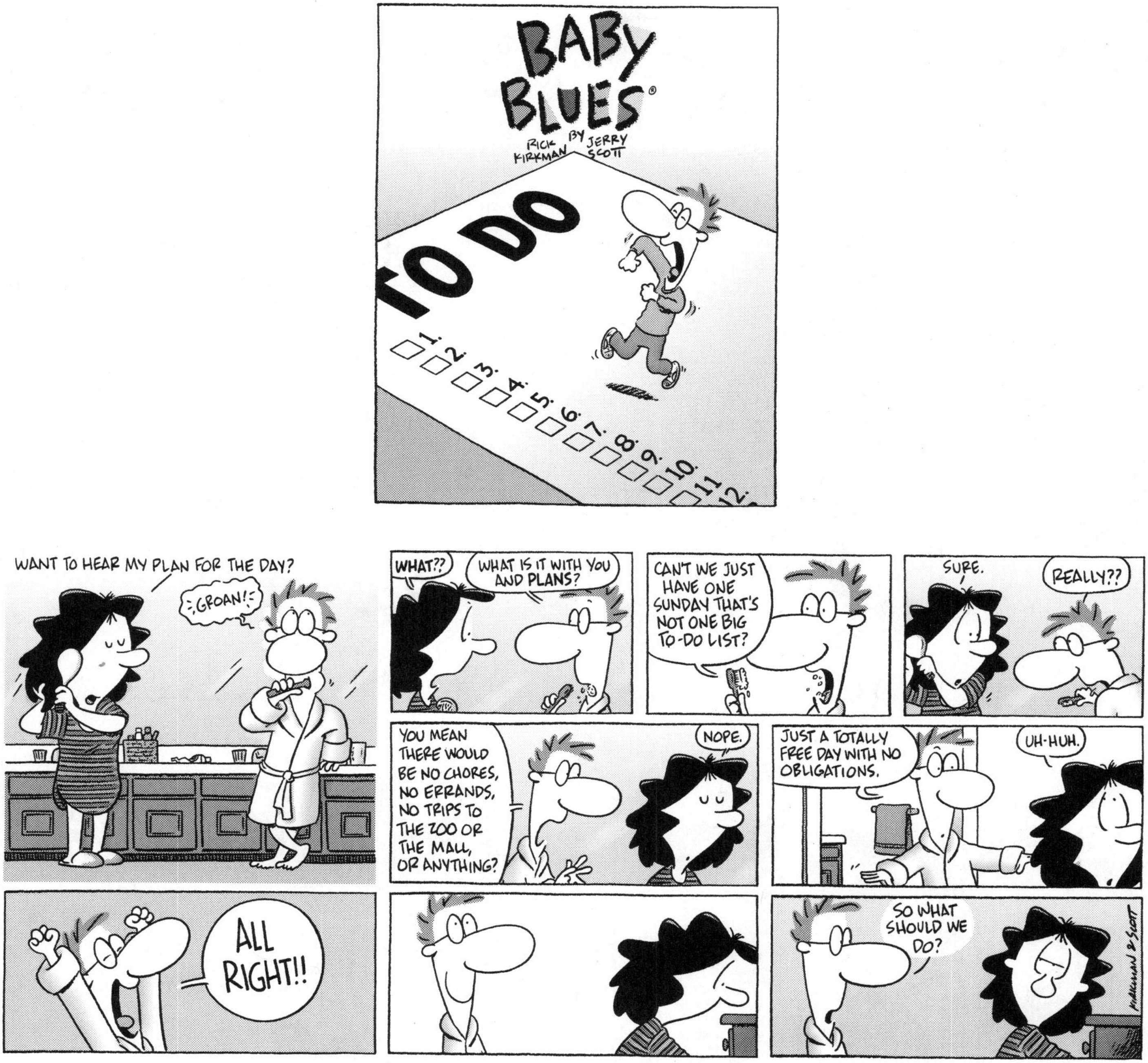
BABY BLUES®
BY RICK KIRKMAN JERRY SCOTT
TO DO
1. 2. 3. 4. 5. 6. 7. 8. 9. 10. 11. 12.
WANT TO HEAR MY PLAN FOR THE DAY?
GROAN!
WHAT??
WHAT IS IT WITH YOU AND PLANS?
CAN'T WE JUST HAVE ONE SUNDAY THAT'S NOT ONE BIG TO-DO LIST?
SURE.
REALLY??
YOU MEAN THERE WOULD BE NO CHORES, NO ERRANDS, NO TRIPS TO THE ZOO OR THE MALL, OR ANYTHING?
NOPE.
JUST A TOTALLY FREE DAY WITH NO OBLIGATIONS.
UH-HUH.
ALL RIGHT!!
SO WHAT SHOULD WE DO?

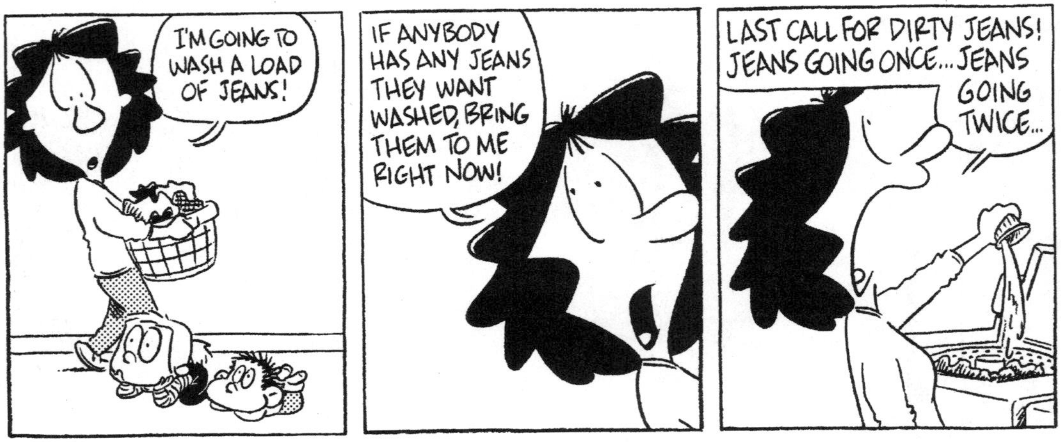
I'M GOING TO WASH A LOAD OF JEANS!
IF ANYBODY HAS ANY JEANS THEY WANT WASHED, BRING THEM TO ME RIGHT NOW!
LAST CALL FOR DIRTY JEANS! JEANS GOING ONCE... JEANS GOING TWICE...
NEXT MORNING–
THERE'S NOTHING TO WEAR. WHY DON'T YOU EVER WASH MY JEANS?
KIRKMAN & SCOTT

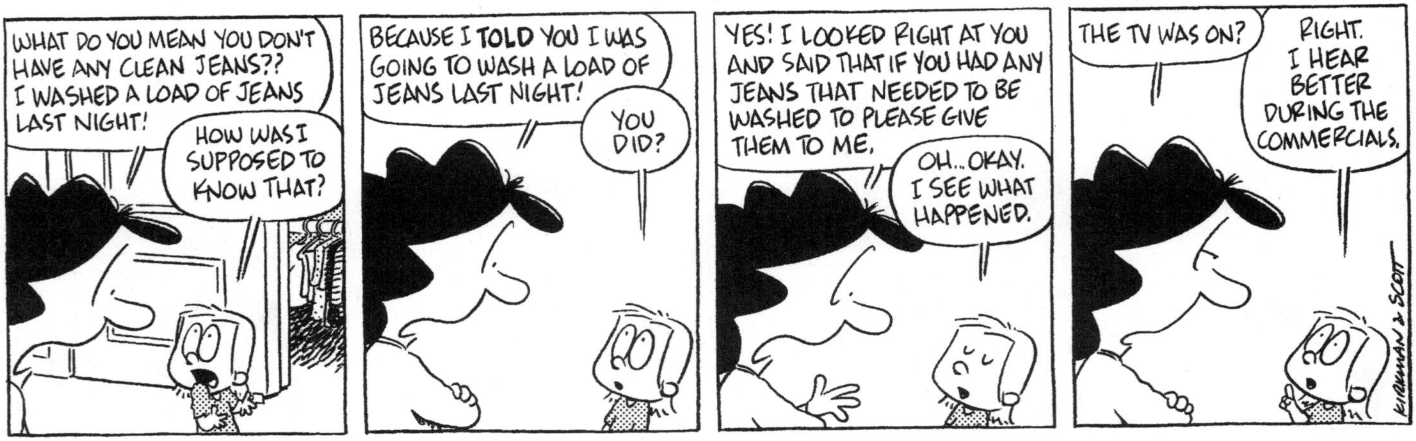
WHAT DO YOU MEAN YOU DON'T HAVE ANY CLEAN JEANS?? I WASHED A LOAD OF JEANS LAST NIGHT!
HOW WAS I SUPPOSED TO KNOW THAT?
BECAUSE I TOLD YOU I WAS GOING TO WASH A LOAD OF JEANS LAST NIGHT!
YOU DID?
YES! I LOOKED RIGHT AT YOU AND SAID THAT IF YOU HAD ANY JEANS THAT NEEDED TO BE WASHED TO PLEASE GIVE THEM TO ME.
OH... OKAY. I SEE WHAT HAPPENED.
THE TV WAS ON?
RIGHT. I HEAR BETTER DURING THE COMMERCIALS.
KIRKMAN & SCOTT

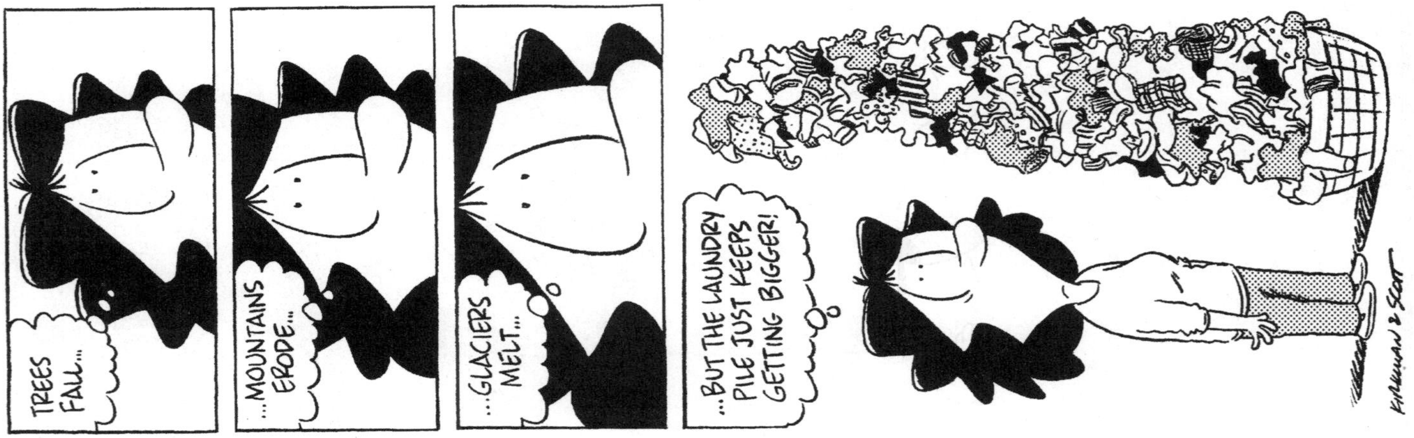
TREES FALL...
...MOUNTAINS ERODE...
...GLACIERS MELT...
...BUT THE LAUNDRY PILE JUST KEEPS GETTING BIGGER!
KIRKMAN & SCOTT

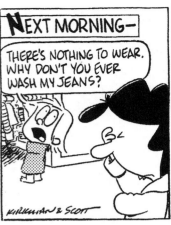

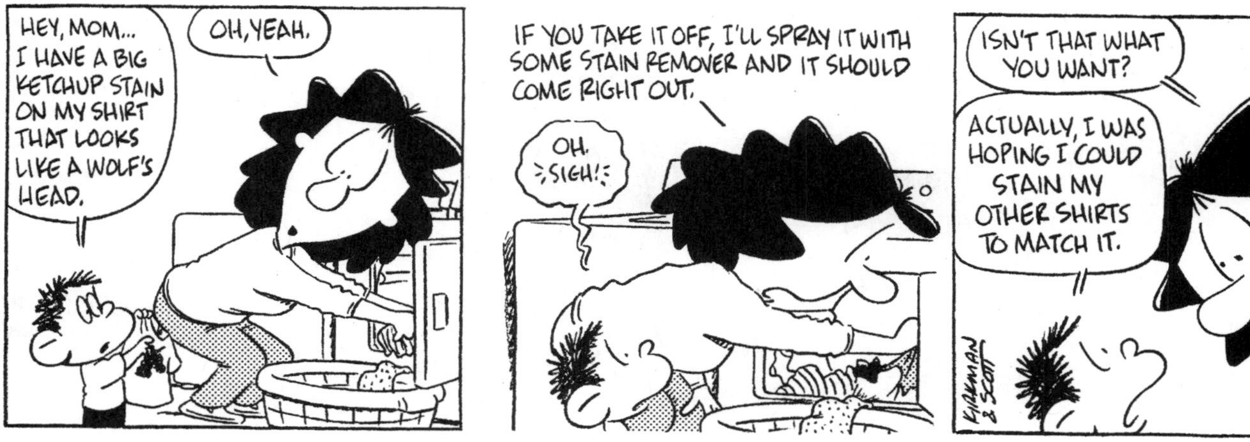
HEY, MOM... I HAVE A BIG KETCHUP STAIN ON MY SHIRT THAT LOOKS LIKE A WOLF'S HEAD.
OH, YEAH.
IF YOU TAKE IT OFF, I'LL SPRAY IT WITH SOME STAIN REMOVER AND IT SHOULD COME RIGHT OUT.
OH. ✱SIGH!✱
ISN'T THAT WHAT YOU WANT?
ACTUALLY, I WAS HOPING I COULD STAIN MY OTHER SHIRTS TO MATCH IT.
KIRKMAN & SCOTT

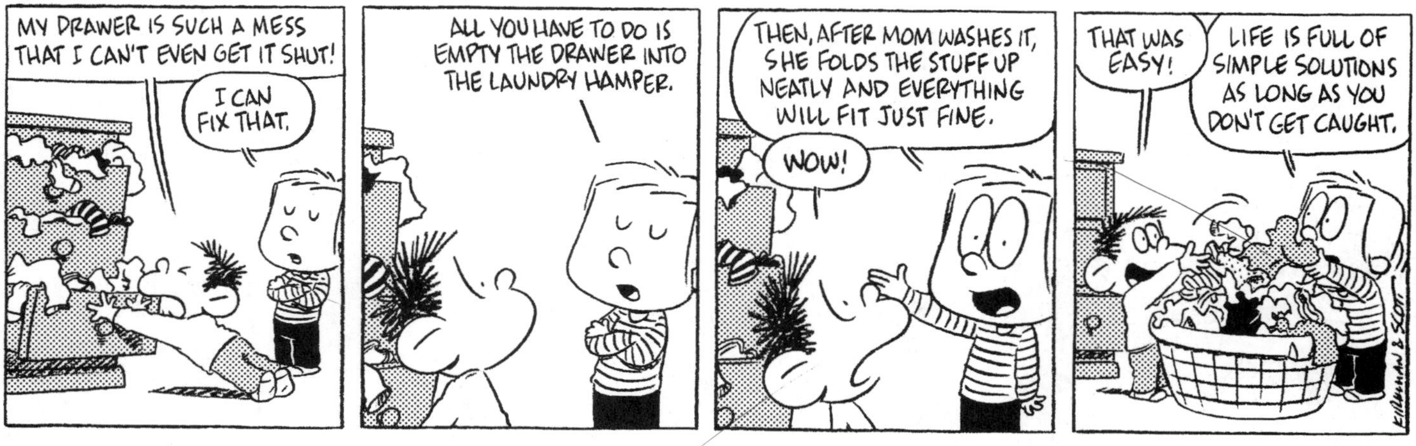
MY DRAWER IS SUCH A MESS THAT I CAN'T EVEN GET IT SHUT!
I CAN FIX THAT.
ALL YOU HAVE TO DO IS EMPTY THE DRAWER INTO THE LAUNDRY HAMPER.
THEN, AFTER MOM WASHES IT, SHE FOLDS THE STUFF UP NEATLY AND EVERYTHING WILL FIT JUST FINE.
WOW!
THAT WAS EASY!
LIFE IS FULL OF SIMPLE SOLUTIONS AS LONG AS YOU DON'T GET CAUGHT.
KIRKMAN & SCOTT

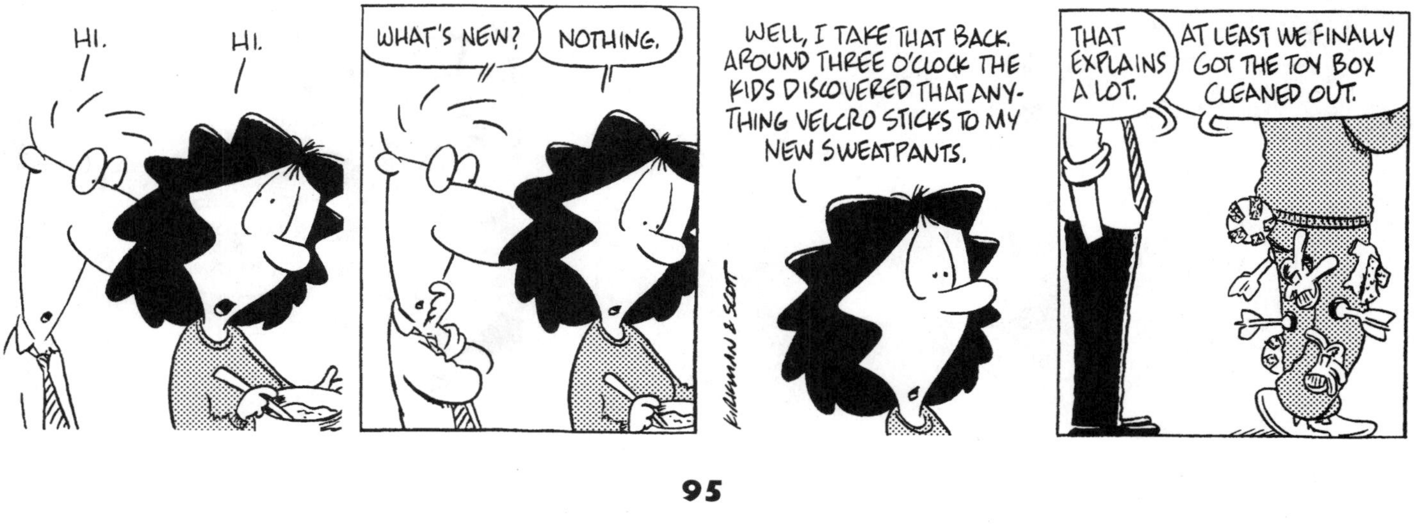
HI.
HI.
WHAT'S NEW?
NOTHING.
KIRKMAN & SCOTT
WELL, I TAKE THAT BACK. AROUND THREE O'CLOCK THE KIDS DISCOVERED THAT ANY-THING VELCRO STICKS TO MY NEW SWEATPANTS.
THAT EXPLAINS A LOT.
AT LEAST WE FINALLY GOT THE TOY BOX CLEANED OUT.

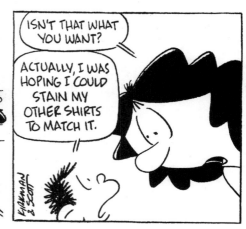

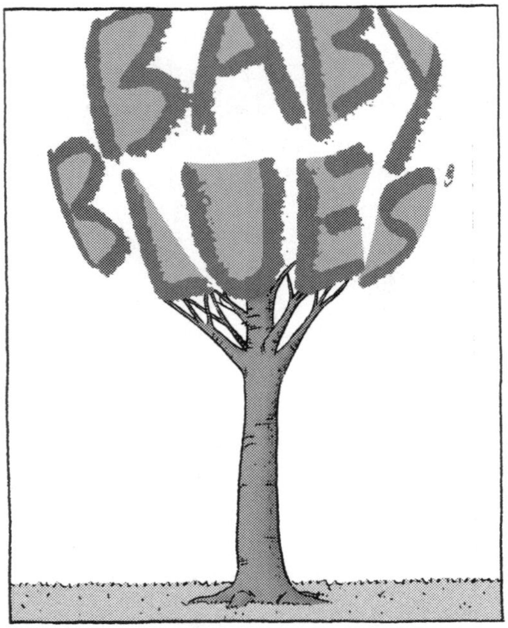
BABY BLUES

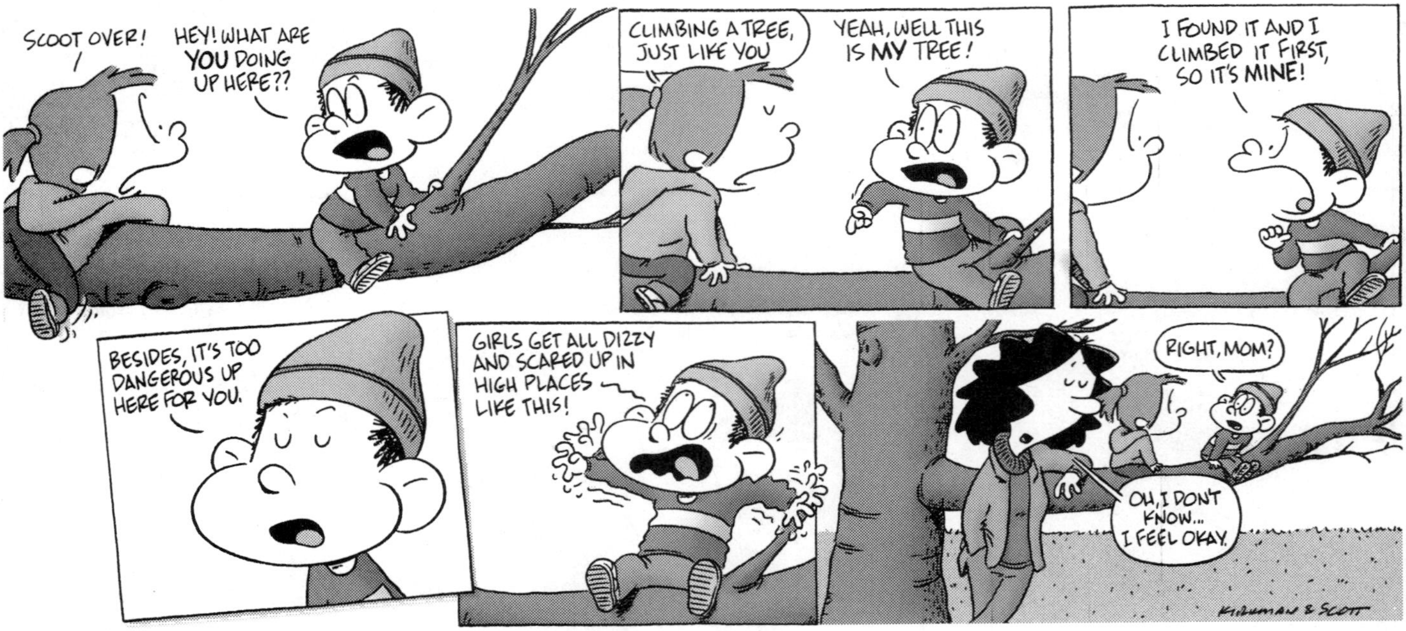
SCOOT OVER!
HEY! WHAT ARE YOU DOING UP HERE??
CLIMBING A TREE, JUST LIKE YOU
YEAH, WELL THIS IS MY TREE!
I FOUND IT AND I CLIMBED IT FIRST, SO IT'S MINE!
BESIDES, IT'S TOO DANGEROUS UP HERE FOR YOU.
GIRLS GET ALL DIZZY AND SCARED UP IN HIGH PLACES LIKE THIS!
RIGHT, MOM?
OH, I DON'T KNOW... I FEEL OKAY.
KIRKMAN & SCOTT

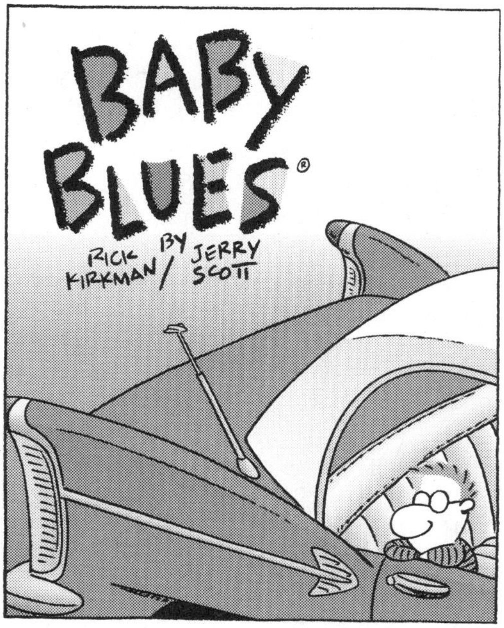
BABY BLUES®
BY RICK KIRKMAN / JERRY SCOTT

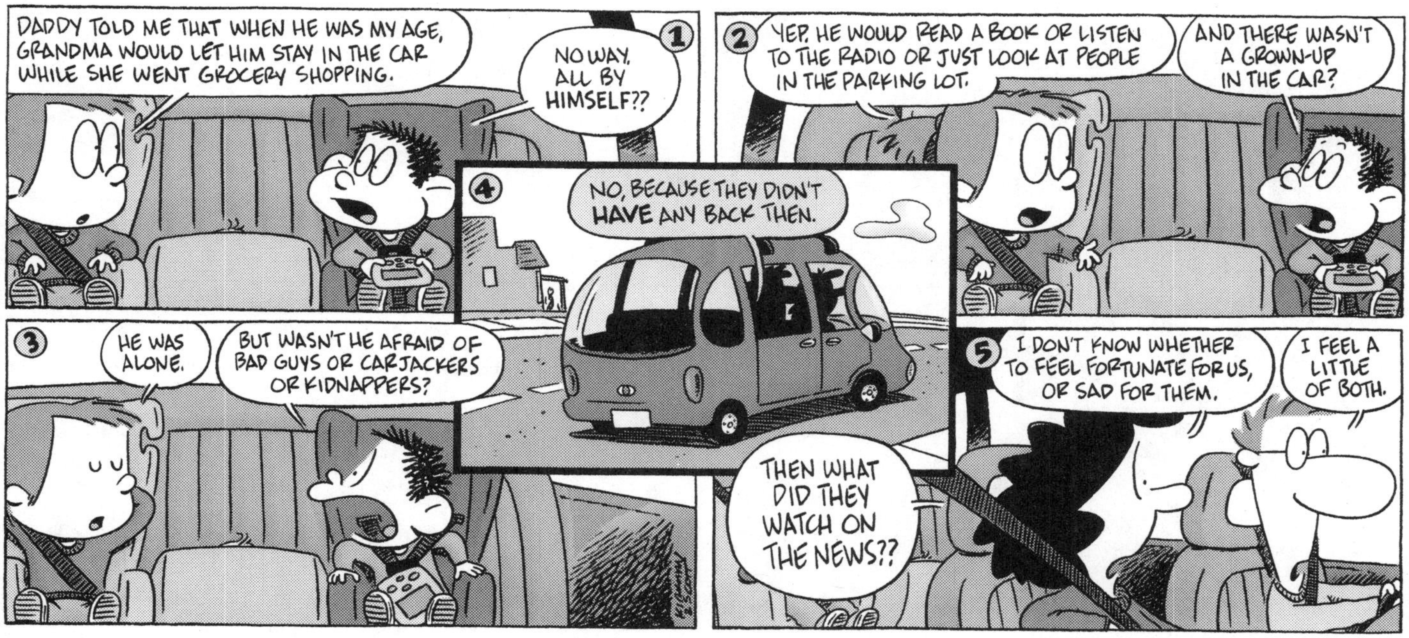
DADDY TOLD ME THAT WHEN HE WAS MY AGE, GRANDMA WOULD LET HIM STAY IN THE CAR WHILE SHE WENT GROCERY SHOPPING.
NO WAY. ALL BY HIMSELF??
YEP. HE WOULD READ A BOOK OR LISTEN TO THE RADIO OR JUST LOOK AT PEOPLE IN THE PARKING LOT.
AND THERE WASN'T A GROWN-UP IN THE CAR?
HE WAS ALONE.
BUT WASN'T HE AFRAID OF BAD GUYS OR CARJACKERS OR KIDNAPPERS?
NO, BECAUSE THEY DIDN'T HAVE ANY BACK THEN.
THEN WHAT DID THEY WATCH ON THE NEWS??
I DON'T KNOW WHETHER TO FEEL FORTUNATE FOR US, OR SAD FOR THEM.
I FEEL A LITTLE OF BOTH.

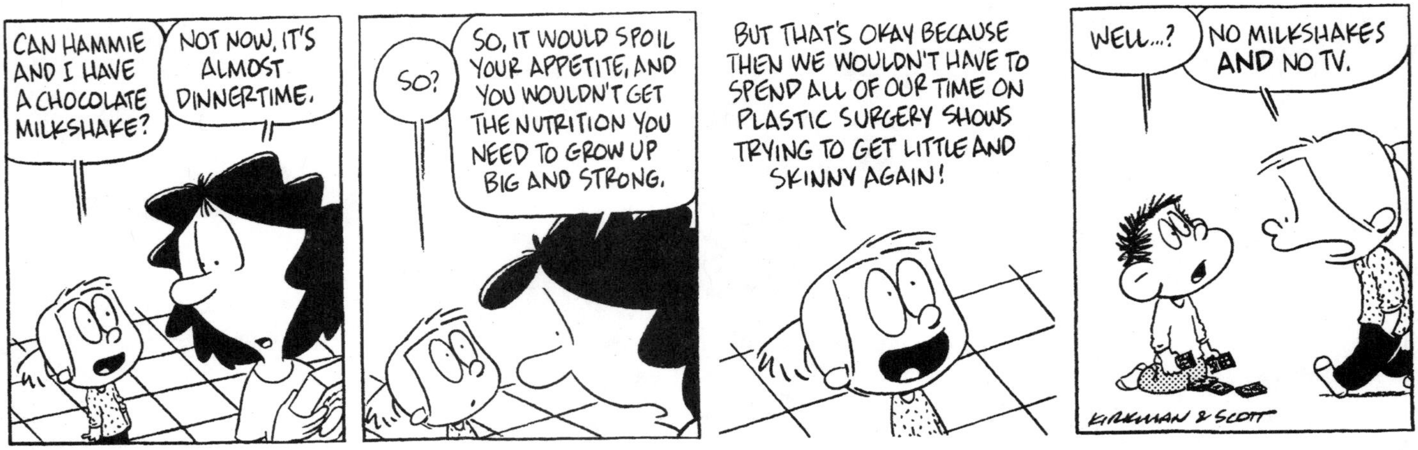
CAN HAMMIE AND I HAVE A CHOCOLATE MILKSHAKE?
NOT NOW, IT'S ALMOST DINNERTIME.
SO?
SO, IT WOULD SPOIL YOUR APPETITE, AND YOU WOULDN'T GET THE NUTRITION YOU NEED TO GROW UP BIG AND STRONG.
BUT THAT'S OKAY BECAUSE THEN WE WOULDN'T HAVE TO SPEND ALL OF OUR TIME ON PLASTIC SURGERY SHOWS TRYING TO GET LITTLE AND SKINNY AGAIN!
WELL...?
NO MILKSHAKES AND NO TV.
KIRKMAN & SCOTT

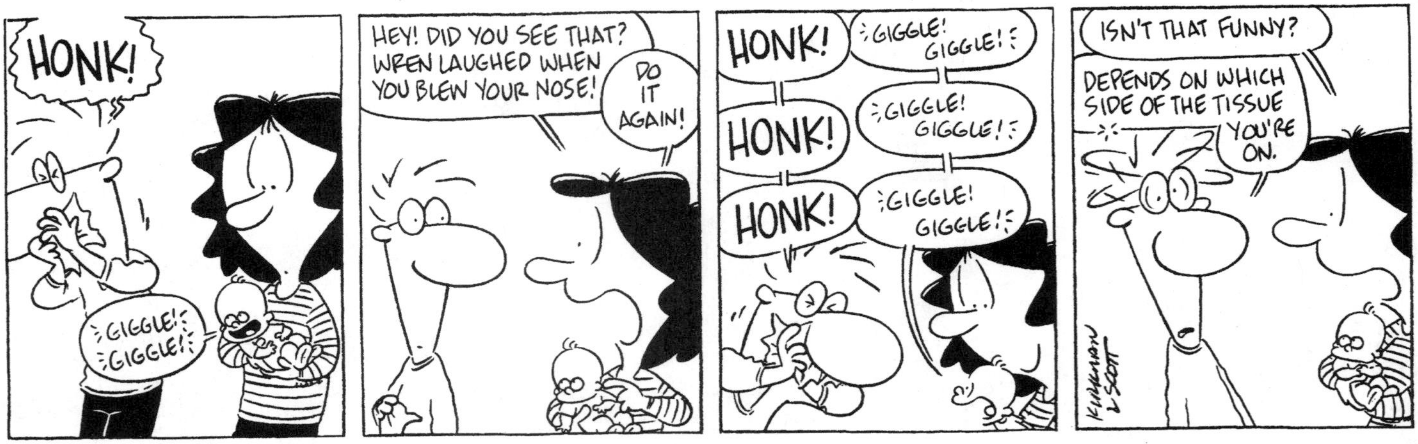
HONK!
GIGGLE! GIGGLE!
HEY! DID YOU SEE THAT? WREN LAUGHED WHEN YOU BLEW YOUR NOSE!
DO IT AGAIN!
HONK!
GIGGLE! GIGGLE!
HONK!
GIGGLE! GIGGLE!
HONK!
GIGGLE! GIGGLE!
KIRKMAN & SCOTT
ISN'T THAT FUNNY?
DEPENDS ON WHICH SIDE OF THE TISSUE YOU'RE ON.

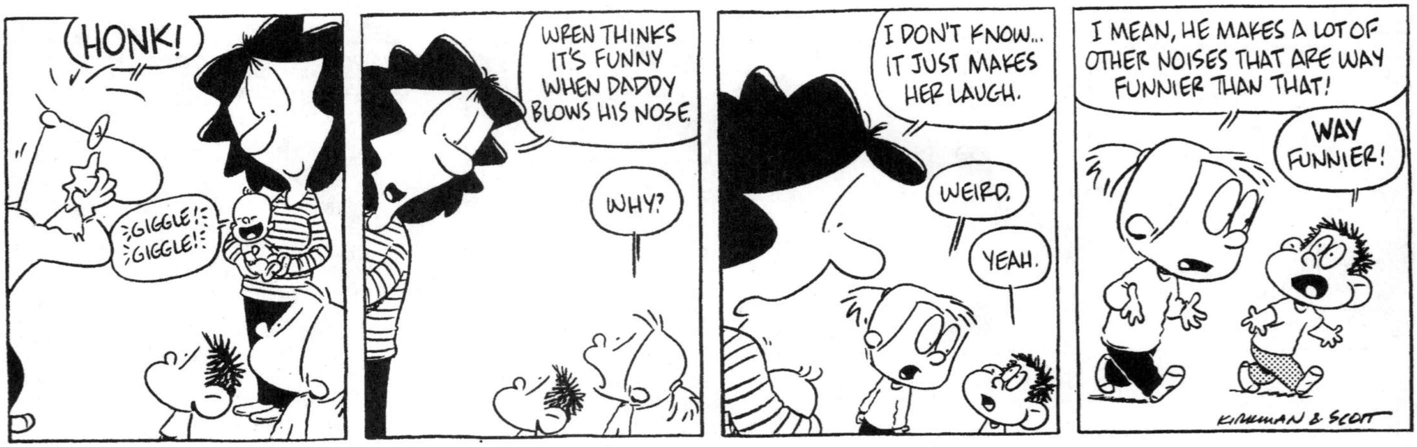
HONK!
GIGGLE! GIGGLE!
WREN THINKS IT'S FUNNY WHEN DADDY BLOWS HIS NOSE.
WHY?
I DON'T KNOW... IT JUST MAKES HER LAUGH.
WEIRD.
YEAH.
I MEAN, HE MAKES A LOT OF OTHER NOISES THAT ARE WAY FUNNIER THAN THAT!
WAY FUNNIER!
KIRKMAN & SCOTT

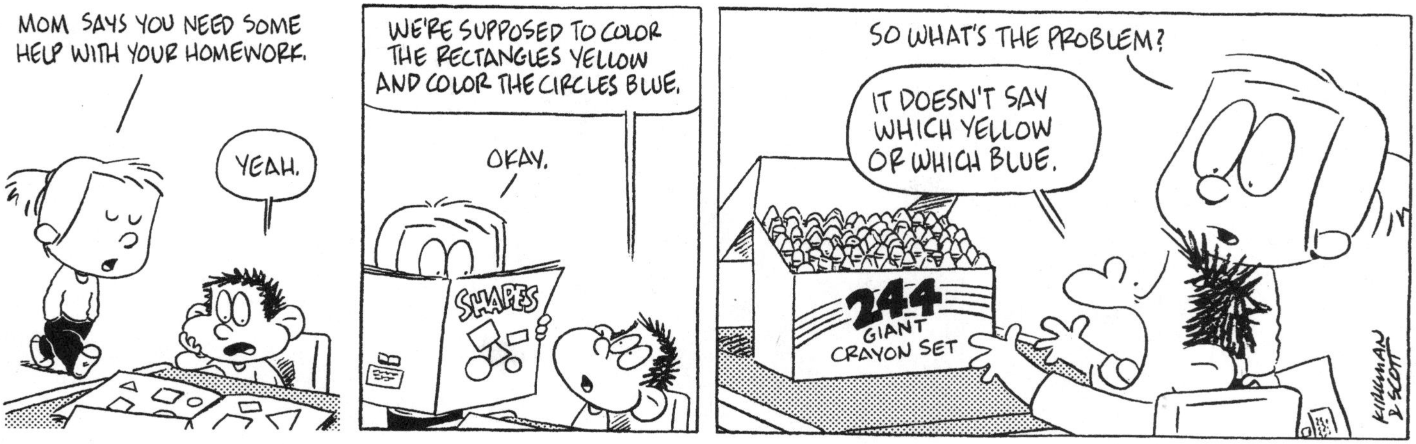
MOM SAYS YOU NEED SOME HELP WITH YOUR HOMEWORK.
YEAH.
WE'RE SUPPOSED TO COLOR THE RECTANGLES YELLOW AND COLOR THE CIRCLES BLUE.
OKAY.
SHAPES
SO WHAT'S THE PROBLEM?
IT DOESN'T SAY WHICH YELLOW OR WHICH BLUE.
244 GIANT CRAYON SET

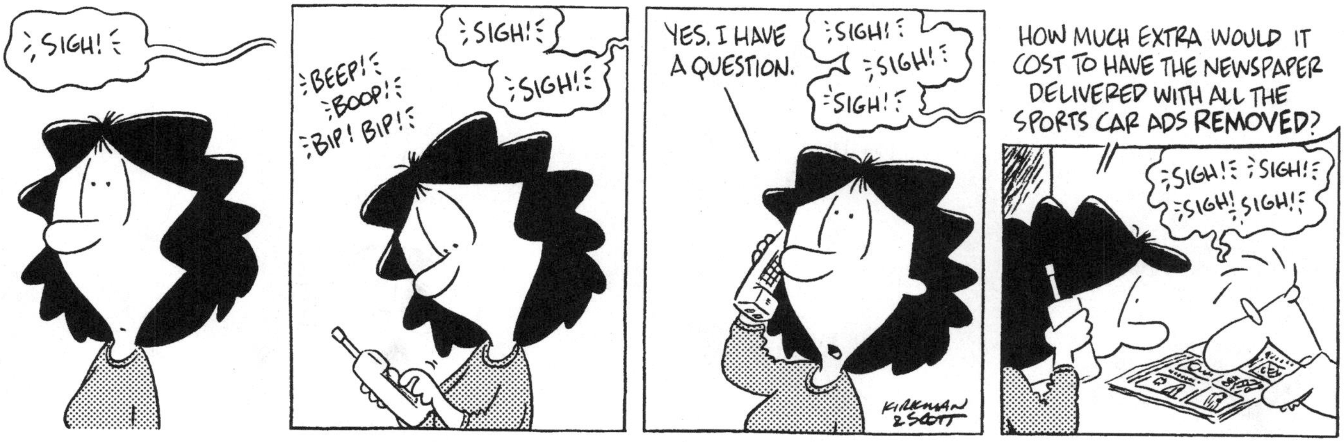
SIGH!
SIGH!
SIGH!
BEEP! BOOP! BIP! BIP!
YES. I HAVE A QUESTION.
SIGH! SIGH! SIGH!
HOW MUCH EXTRA WOULD IT COST TO HAVE THE NEWSPAPER DELIVERED WITH ALL THE SPORTS CAR ADS **REMOVED**?
SIGH! SIGH! SIGH! SIGH!

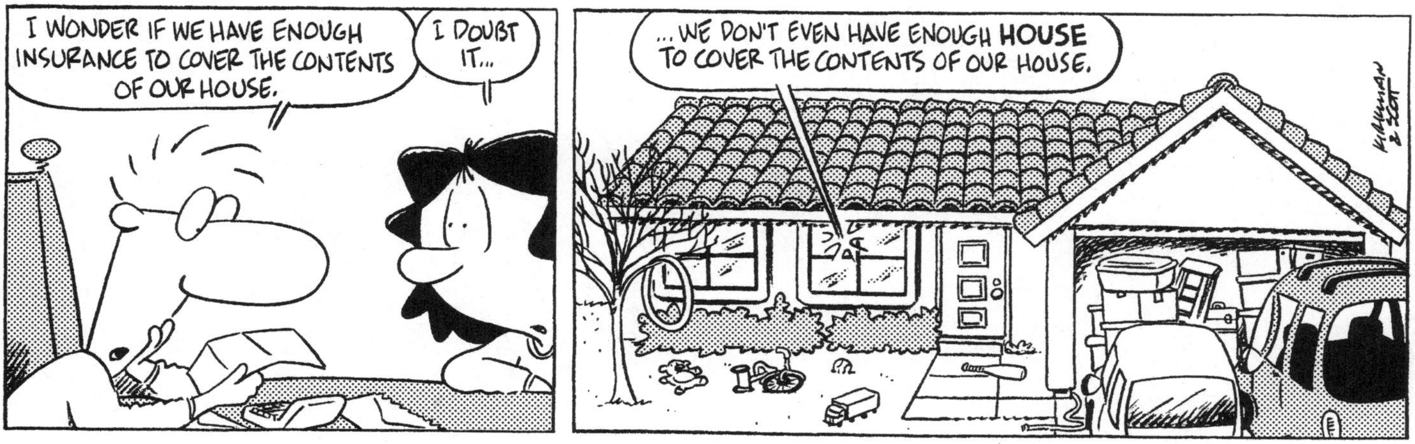
I WONDER IF WE HAVE ENOUGH INSURANCE TO COVER THE CONTENTS OF OUR HOUSE.
I DOUBT IT...
...WE DON'T EVEN HAVE ENOUGH **HOUSE** TO COVER THE CONTENTS OF OUR HOUSE.

BABY BLUES®
BY RICK KIRKMAN / JERRY SCOTT

YOU KNOW HOW I CRAVE CHOCOLATE WHEN I'M FEELING DEPRESSED, RIGHT?
UH-HUH.
WELL, NOW I KNOW WHY.
IT TURNS OUT THAT CHOCOLATE HAS ANTI-DEPRESSIVE QUALITIES, AND IT REALLY CAN MAKE YOU FEEL BETTER WHEN YOU'RE DOWN.
YEAH. I READ ABOUT THAT, TOO.
ALL THE DRIVING, HOMEWORK, AND KID STUFF I'VE BEEN DOING IS MAKING ME FEEL A LITTLE OVERWHELMED, SO I THOUGHT THIS MIGHT BE A GOOD TIME TO MAKE A BATCH OF FUDGE.
GREAT!
ISN'T THAT MORE THAN—?
IT'S A LONG SCHOOL YEAR. I'LL NEED BACKUP FUDGE.
KIRKMAN & SCOTT

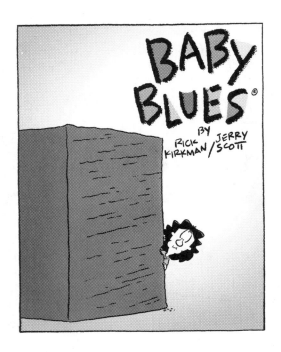

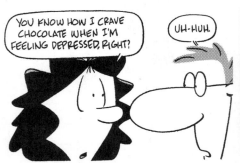

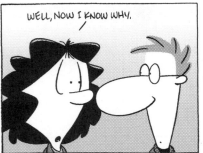

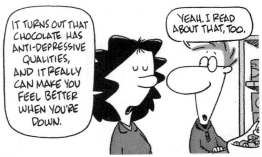

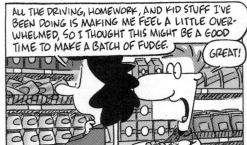

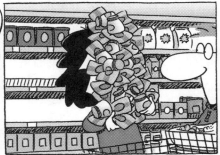

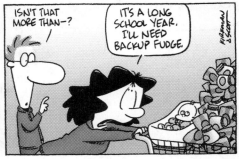

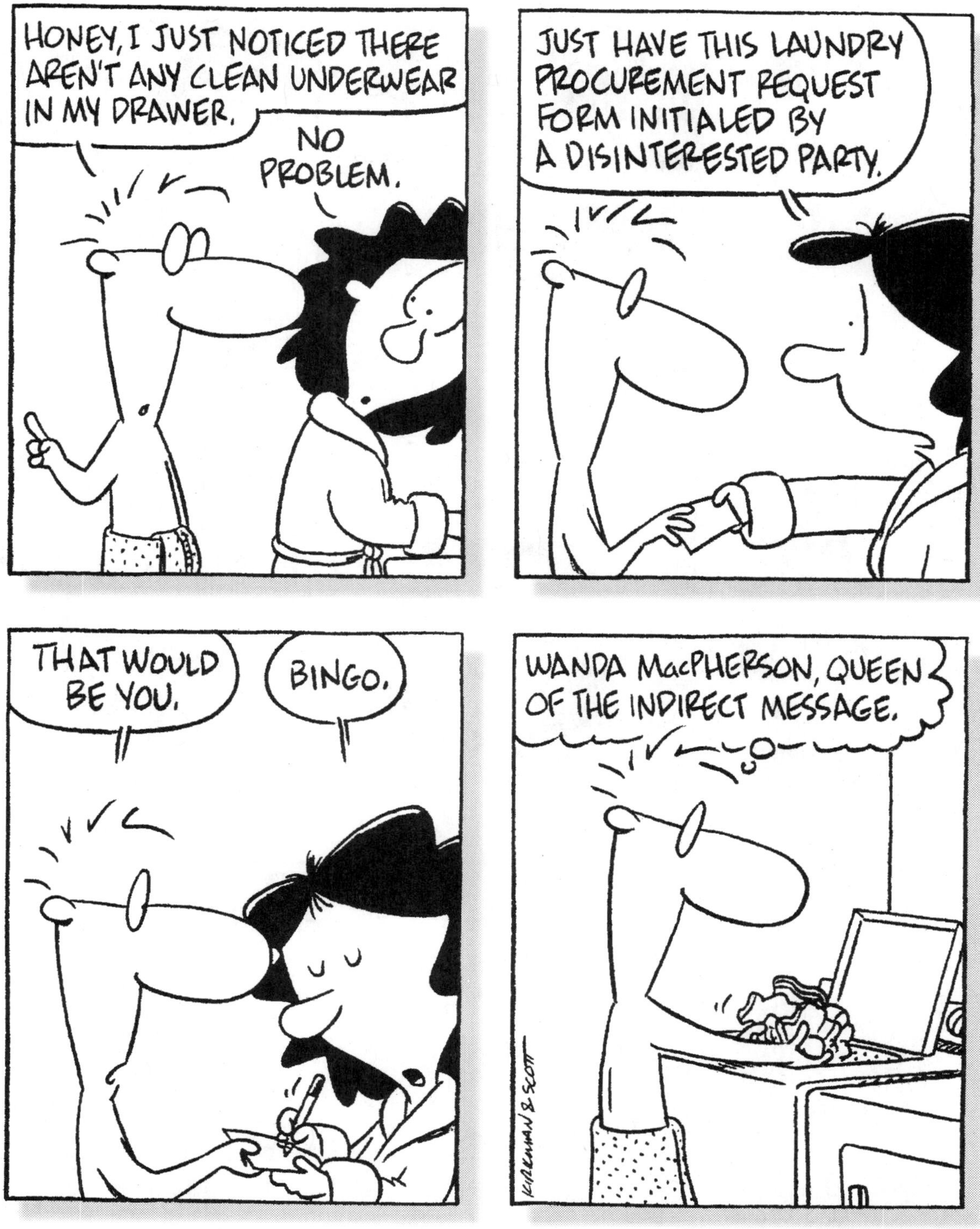
HONEY, I JUST NOTICED THERE AREN'T ANY CLEAN UNDERWEAR IN MY DRAWER.
NO PROBLEM.
JUST HAVE THIS LAUNDRY PROCUREMENT REQUEST FORM INITIALED BY A DISINTERESTED PARTY.
THAT WOULD BE YOU.
BINGO.
WANDA MacPHERSON, QUEEN OF THE INDIRECT MESSAGE.
KIRKMAN & SCOTT

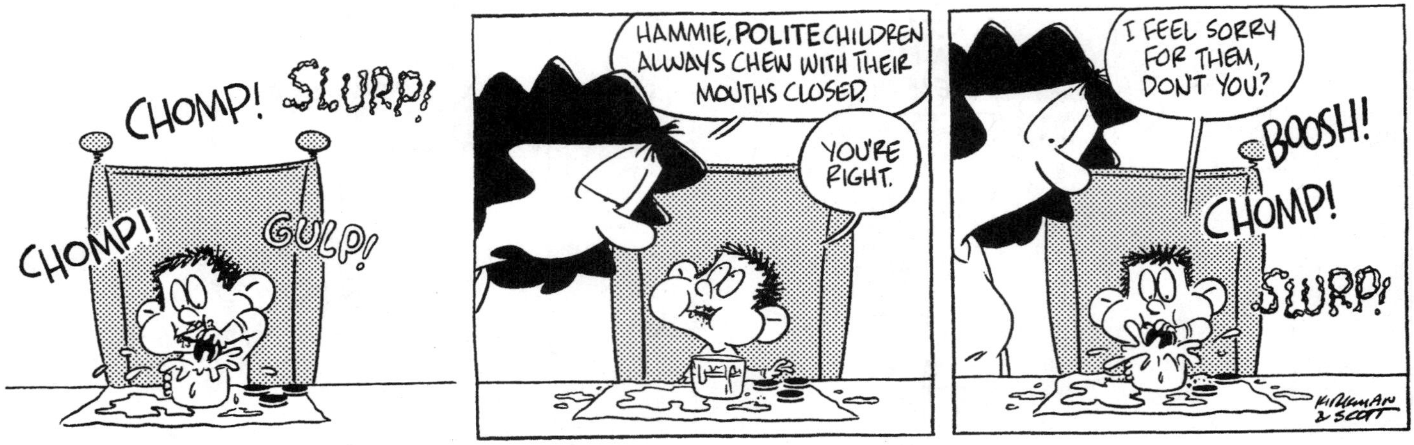
CHOMP! SLURP!
CHOMP!
GULP!
HAMMIE, POLITE CHILDREN ALWAYS CHEW WITH THEIR MOUTHS CLOSED.
YOU'RE RIGHT.
I FEEL SORRY FOR THEM, DON'T YOU?
BOOSH!
CHOMP!
SLURP!
KIRKMAN & SCOTT

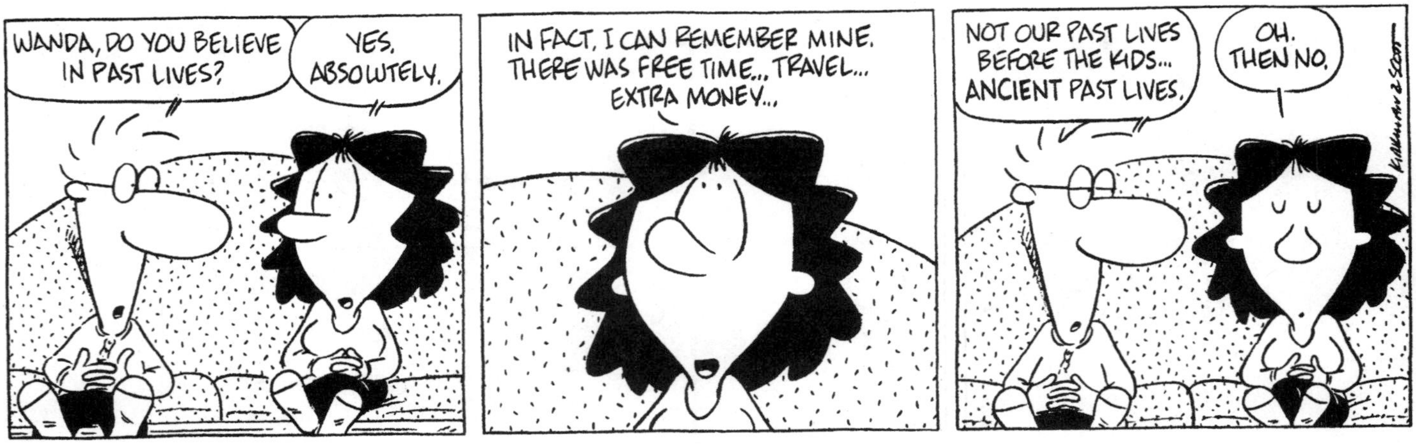
WANDA, DO YOU BELIEVE IN PAST LIVES?
YES. ABSOLUTELY.
IN FACT, I CAN REMEMBER MINE. THERE WAS FREE TIME... TRAVEL... EXTRA MONEY...
NOT OUR PAST LIVES BEFORE THE KIDS... ANCIENT PAST LIVES.
OH. THEN NO.
KIRKMAN & SCOTT

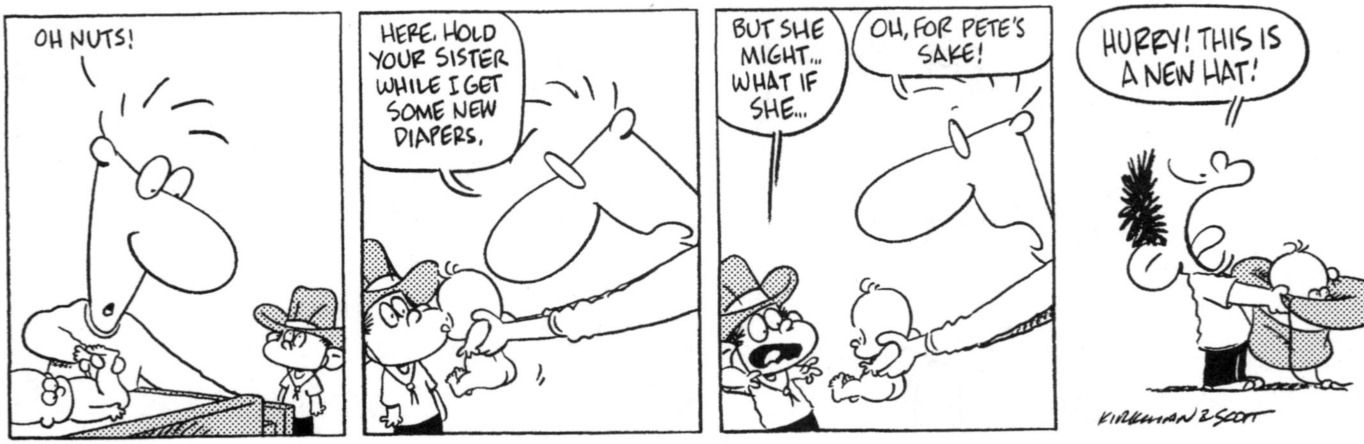
OH NUTS!
HERE. HOLD YOUR SISTER WHILE I GET SOME NEW DIAPERS.
BUT SHE MIGHT... WHAT IF SHE...
OH, FOR PETE'S SAKE!
HURRY! THIS IS A NEW HAT!
KIRKMAN & SCOTT

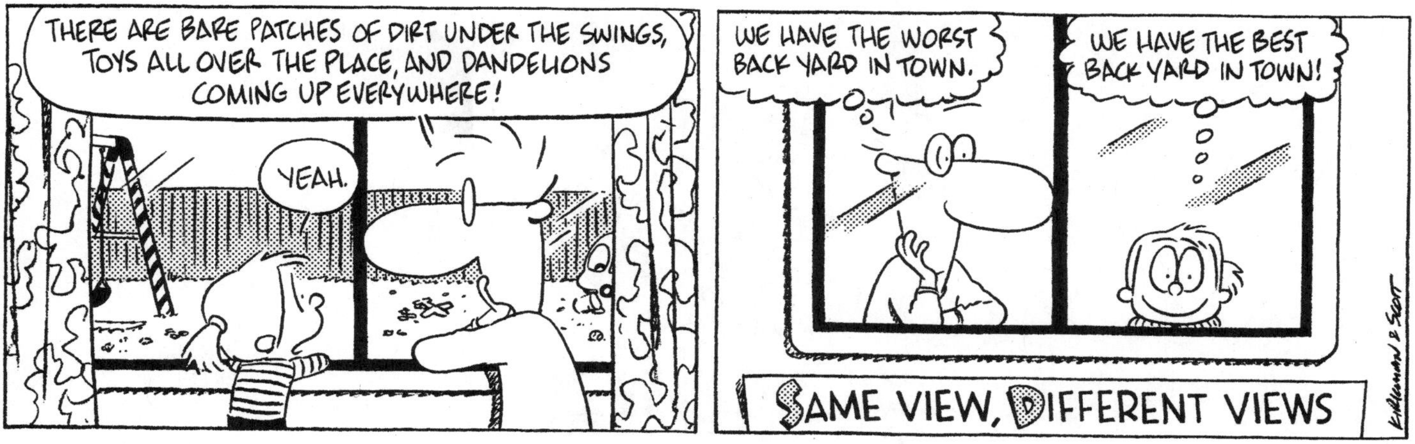
THERE ARE BARE PATCHES OF DIRT UNDER THE SWINGS, TOYS ALL OVER THE PLACE, AND DANDELIONS COMING UP EVERYWHERE!
YEAH.
WE HAVE THE WORST BACK YARD IN TOWN.
WE HAVE THE BEST BACK YARD IN TOWN!
SAME VIEW, DIFFERENT VIEWS
KIRKMAN & SCOTT

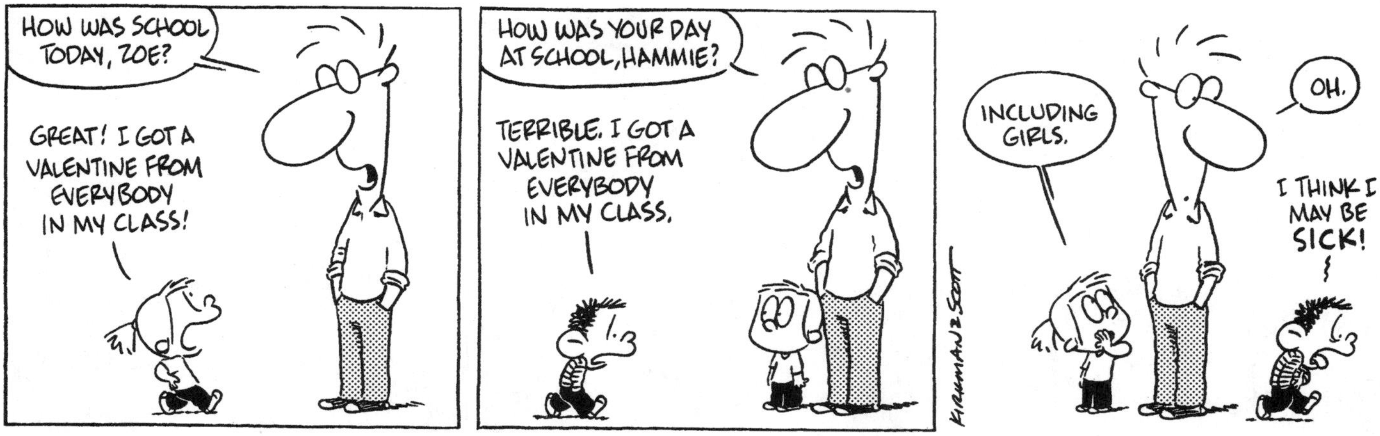
HOW WAS SCHOOL TODAY, ZOE?
GREAT! I GOT A VALENTINE FROM EVERYBODY IN MY CLASS!
HOW WAS YOUR DAY AT SCHOOL, HAMMIE?
TERRIBLE. I GOT A VALENTINE FROM EVERYBODY IN MY CLASS.
KIRKMAN & SCOTT
INCLUDING GIRLS.
OH.
I THINK I MAY BE SICK!

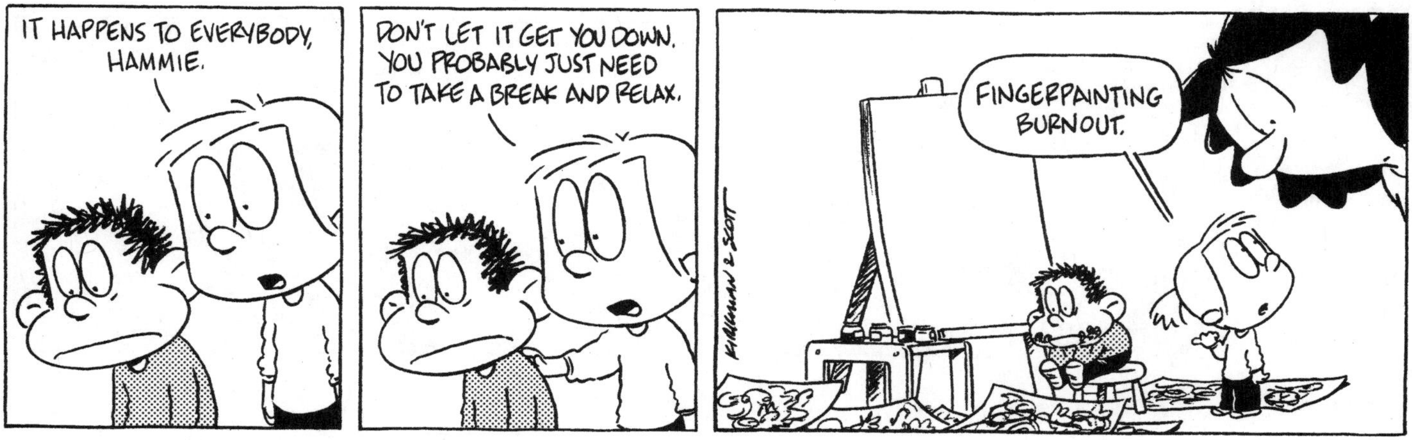
IT HAPPENS TO EVERYBODY, HAMMIE.
DON'T LET IT GET YOU DOWN. YOU PROBABLY JUST NEED TO TAKE A BREAK AND RELAX.
KIRKMAN & SCOTT
FINGERPAINTING BURNOUT.

BABY BLUES®

BY RICK KIRKMAN / JERRY SCOTT

MOM IS GOING TO **LOVE** THIS VALENTINE!
JUST LOOK AT HOW SMOOTH THE EDGES ARE!!
PASS THE GLUE.
AND THE LACE ALL AROUND THE EDGES MAKES IT LOOK VERY FEMININE.
GLITTER.
WHEN YOU ADD THE CUTE LITTLE POEM I WROTE...WELL!
MORE GLUE. AND SOME OF THOSE CANDY HEARTS, TOO.
THIS MAY BE THE MOST PERFECT VALENTINE I EVER MADE!
MINE'S HEAVIER.

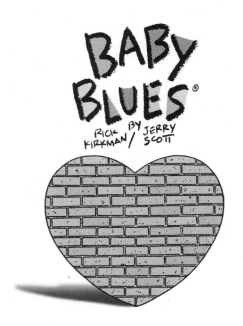

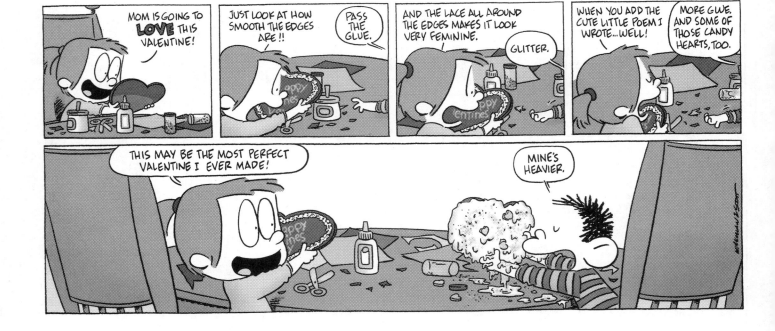

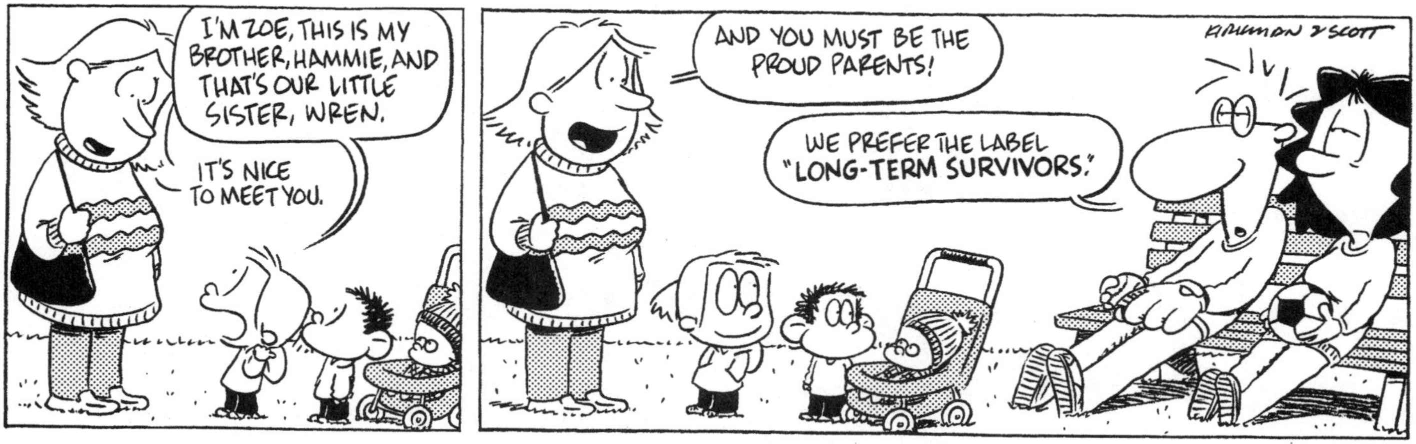
I'M ZOE, THIS IS MY BROTHER, HAMMIE, AND THAT'S OUR LITTLE SISTER, WREN.
IT'S NICE TO MEET YOU.
AND YOU MUST BE THE PROUD PARENTS!
WE PREFER THE LABEL "LONG-TERM SURVIVORS."
KIRKMAN & SCOTT

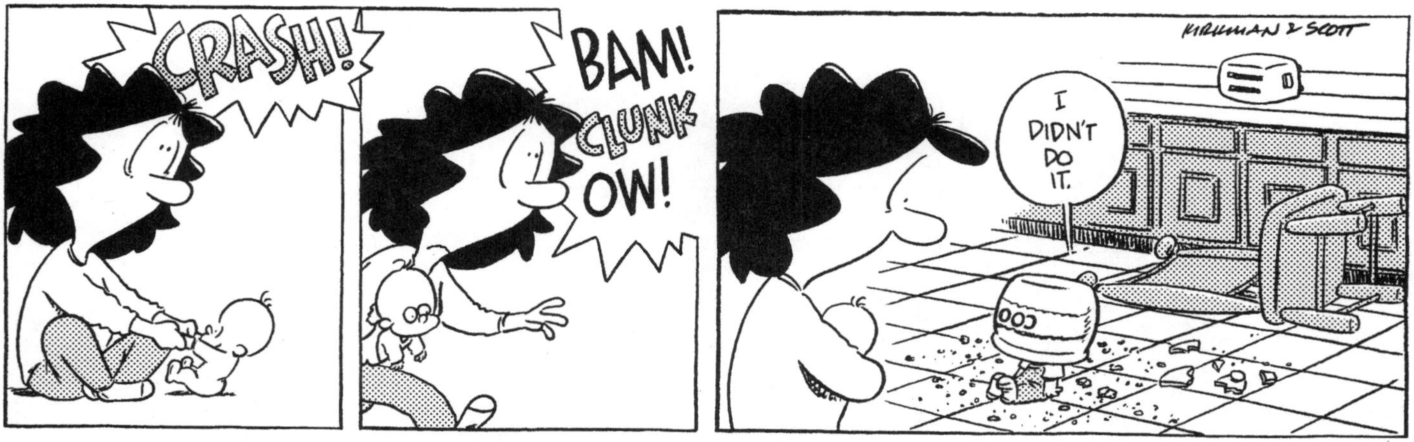
CRASH!
BAM!
CLUNK
OW!
KIRKMAN & SCOTT
I DIDN'T DO IT.

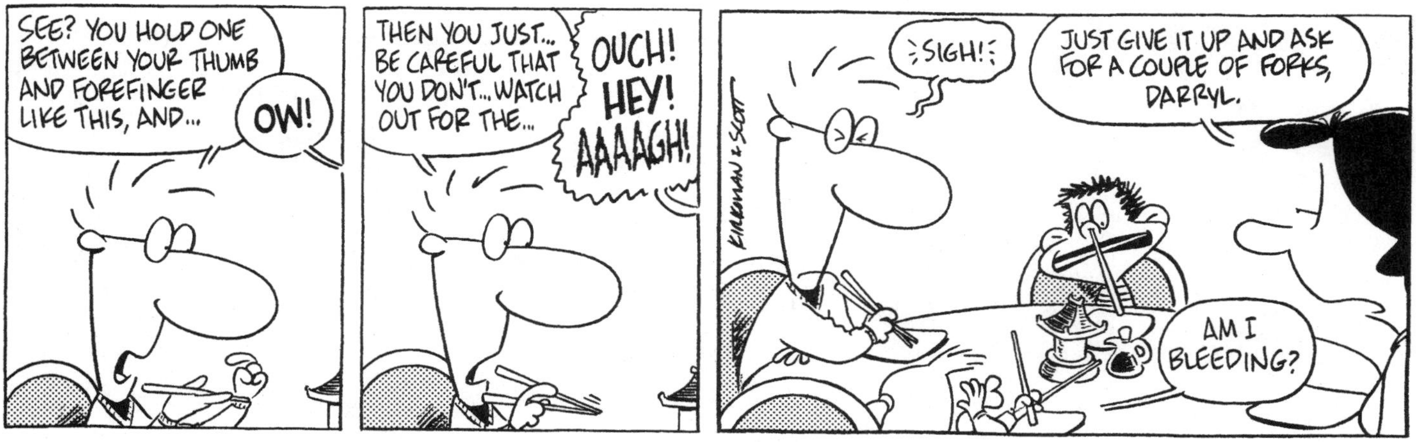
SEE? YOU HOLD ONE BETWEEN YOUR THUMB AND FOREFINGER LIKE THIS, AND...
OW!
THEN YOU JUST... BE CAREFUL THAT YOU DON'T... WATCH OUT FOR THE...
OUCH! HEY! AAAAGH!
KIRKMAN & SCOTT
SIGH!
JUST GIVE IT UP AND ASK FOR A COUPLE OF FORKS, DARRYL.
AM I BLEEDING?

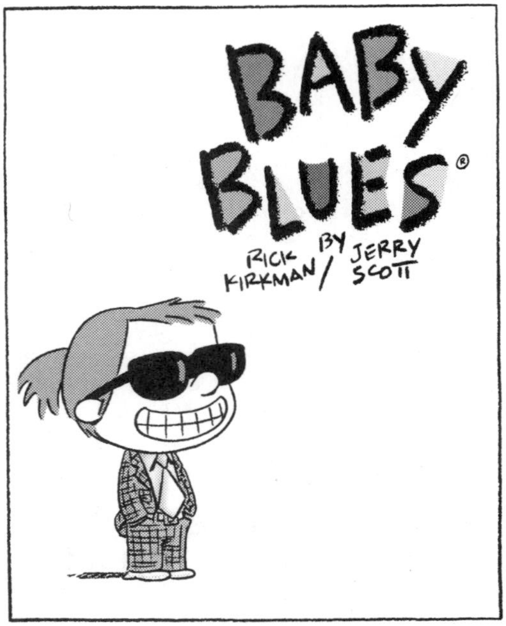
BABY BLUES®
BY RICK KIRKMAN / JERRY SCOTT

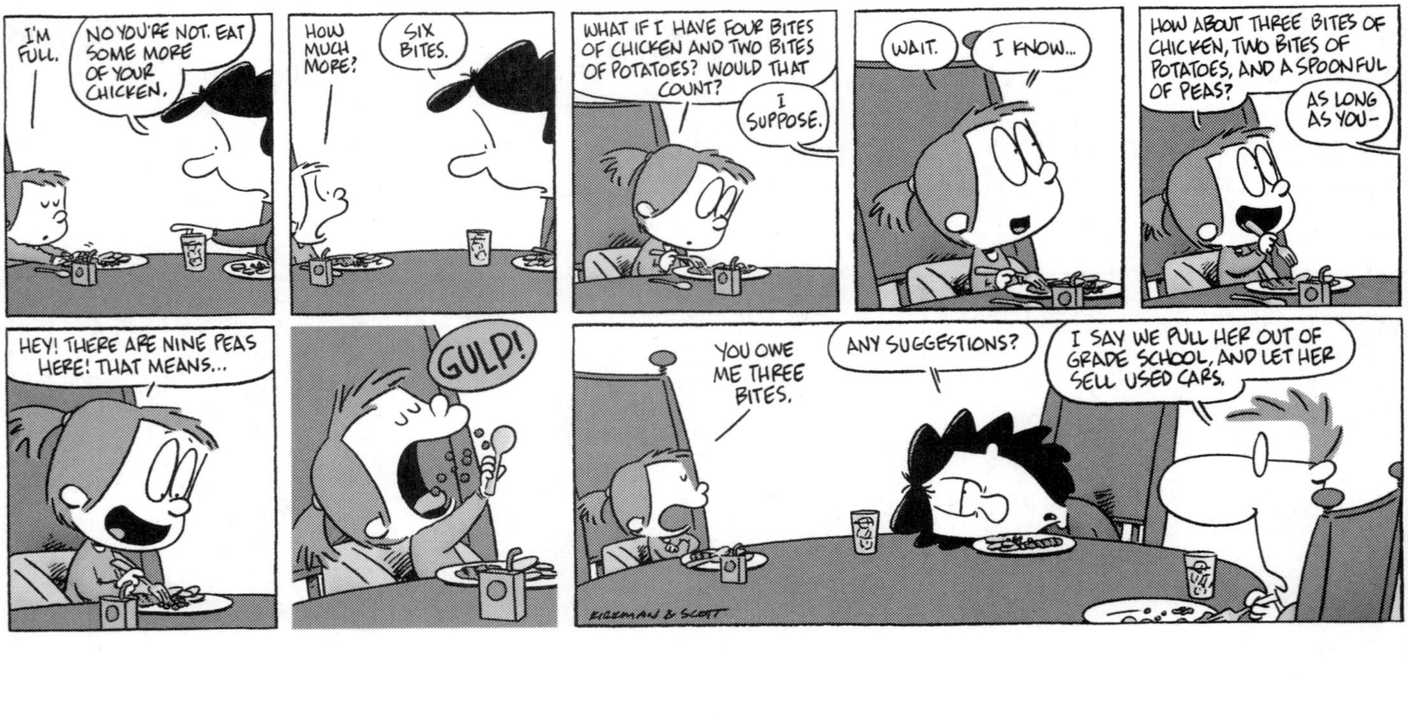
I'M FULL.
NO YOU'RE NOT. EAT SOME MORE OF YOUR CHICKEN.
HOW MUCH MORE?
SIX BITES.
WHAT IF I HAVE FOUR BITES OF CHICKEN AND TWO BITES OF POTATOES? WOULD THAT COUNT?
I SUPPOSE.
WAIT.
I KNOW...
HOW ABOUT THREE BITES OF CHICKEN, TWO BITES OF POTATOES, AND A SPOONFUL OF PEAS?
AS LONG AS YOU–
HEY! THERE ARE NINE PEAS HERE! THAT MEANS...
GULP!
YOU OWE ME THREE BITES.
ANY SUGGESTIONS?
I SAY WE PULL HER OUT OF GRADE SCHOOL, AND LET HER SELL USED CARS.
KIRKMAN & SCOTT

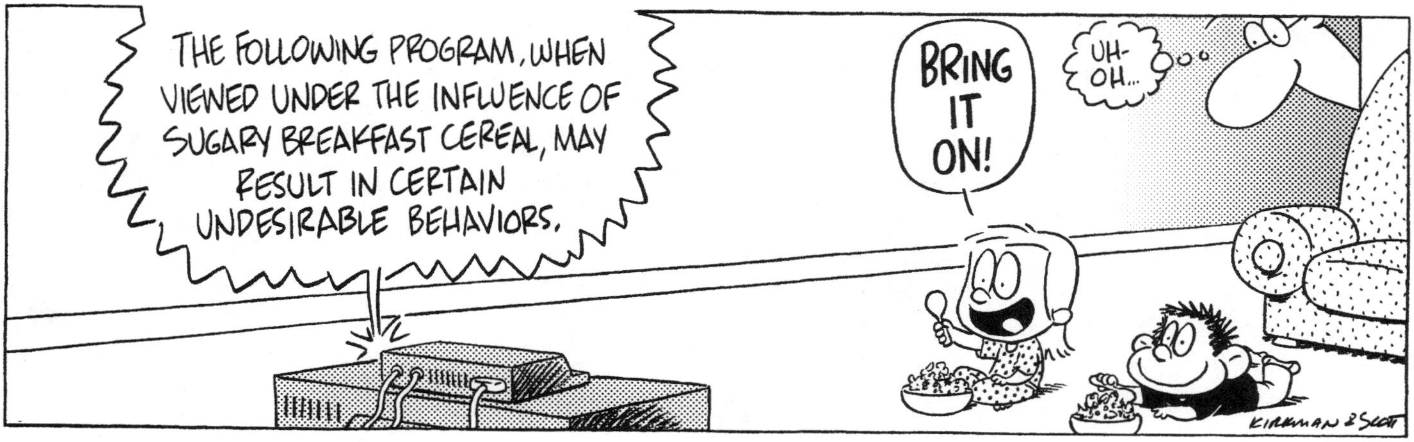
THE FOLLOWING PROGRAM, WHEN VIEWED UNDER THE INFLUENCE OF SUGARY BREAKFAST CEREAL, MAY RESULT IN CERTAIN UNDESIRABLE BEHAVIORS.
BRING IT ON!
UH-OH...
KIRKMAN & SCOTT

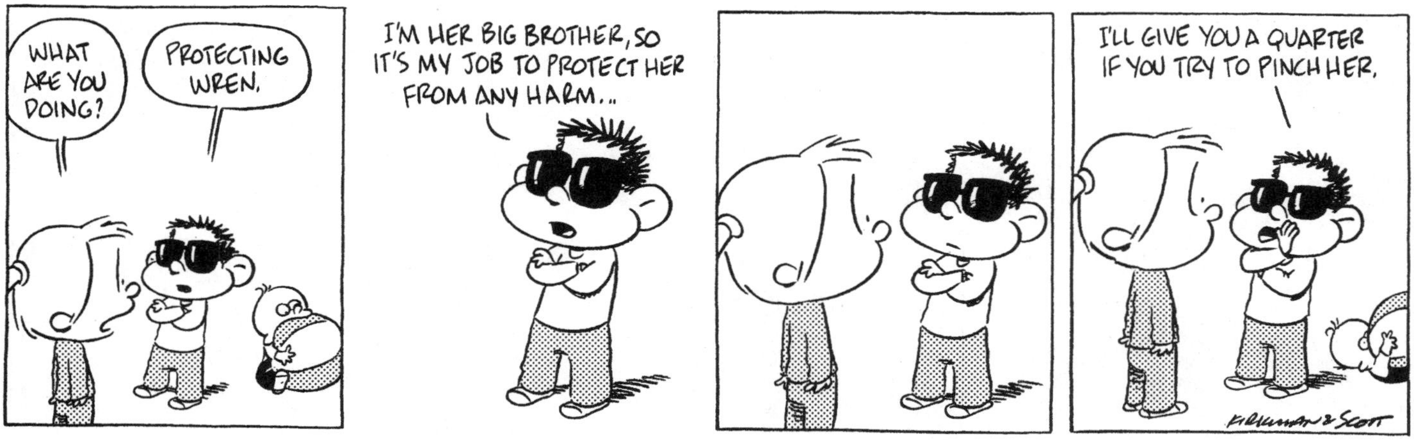
WHAT ARE YOU DOING?
PROTECTING WREN.
I'M HER BIG BROTHER, SO IT'S MY JOB TO PROTECT HER FROM ANY HARM...
I'LL GIVE YOU A QUARTER IF YOU TRY TO PINCH HER.
KIRKMAN & SCOTT

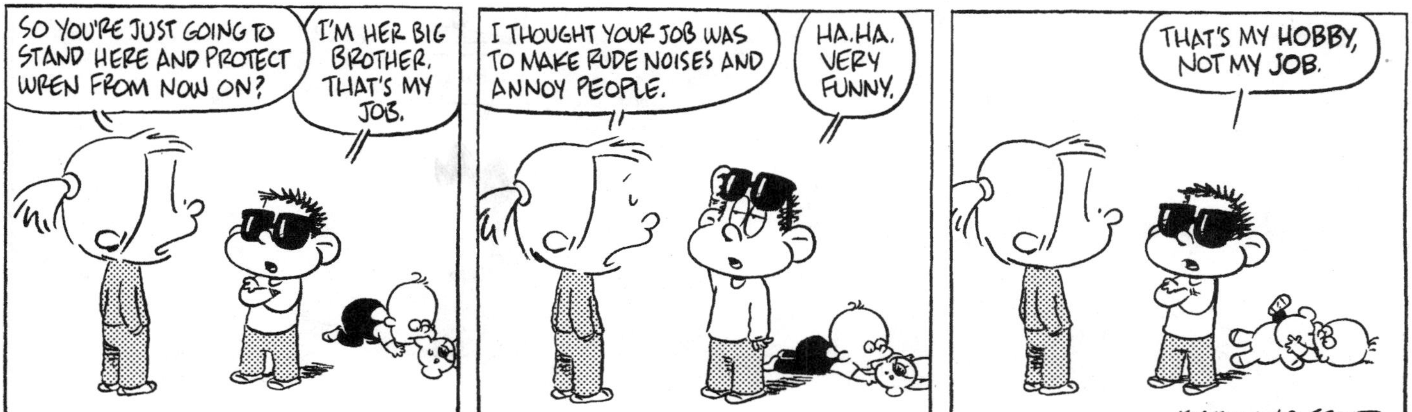
SO YOU'RE JUST GOING TO STAND HERE AND PROTECT WREN FROM NOW ON?
I'M HER BIG BROTHER. THAT'S MY JOB.
I THOUGHT YOUR JOB WAS TO MAKE RUDE NOISES AND ANNOY PEOPLE.
HA.HA. VERY FUNNY.
THAT'S MY HOBBY, NOT MY JOB.
KIRKMAN & SCOTT

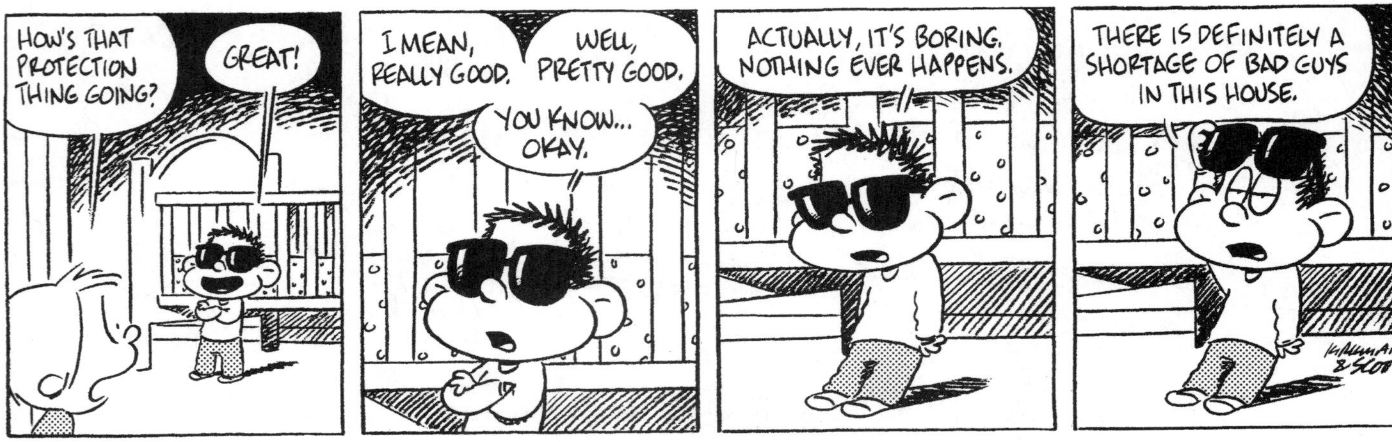
HOW'S THAT PROTECTION THING GOING?
GREAT!
I MEAN, REALLY GOOD.
WELL, PRETTY GOOD.
YOU KNOW... OKAY.
ACTUALLY, IT'S BORING. NOTHING EVER HAPPENS.
THERE IS DEFINITELY A SHORTAGE OF BAD GUYS IN THIS HOUSE.
KIRKMAN & SCOTT

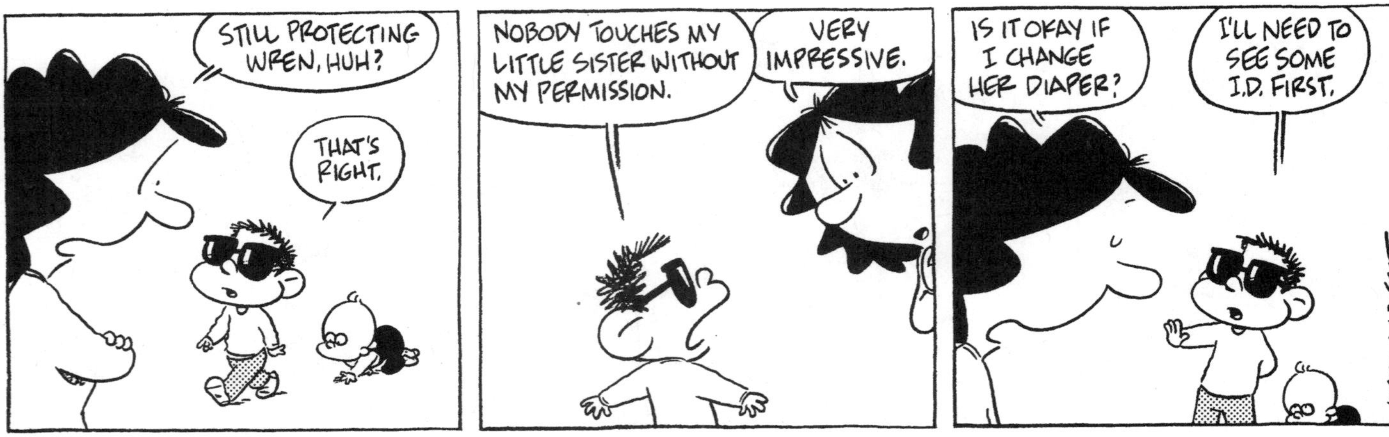
STILL PROTECTING WREN, HUH?
THAT'S RIGHT.
NOBODY TOUCHES MY LITTLE SISTER WITHOUT MY PERMISSION.
VERY IMPRESSIVE.
IS IT OKAY IF I CHANGE HER DIAPER?
I'LL NEED TO SEE SOME I.D. FIRST.
KIRKMAN & SCOTT

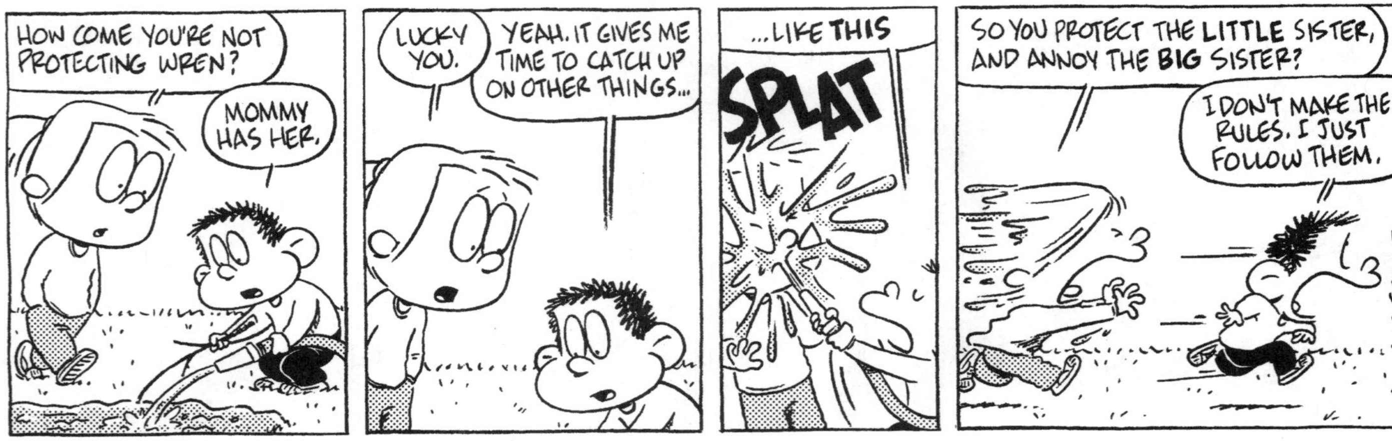
HOW COME YOU'RE NOT PROTECTING WREN?
MOMMY HAS HER.
LUCKY YOU.
YEAH. IT GIVES ME TIME TO CATCH UP ON OTHER THINGS...
...LIKE **THIS**
SPLAT
SO YOU PROTECT THE **LITTLE** SISTER, AND ANNOY THE **BIG** SISTER?
I DON'T MAKE THE RULES. I JUST FOLLOW THEM.
KIRKMAN & SCOTT

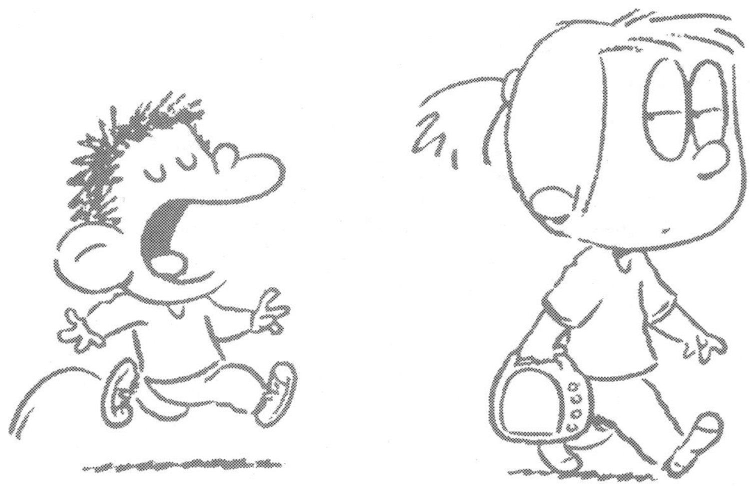

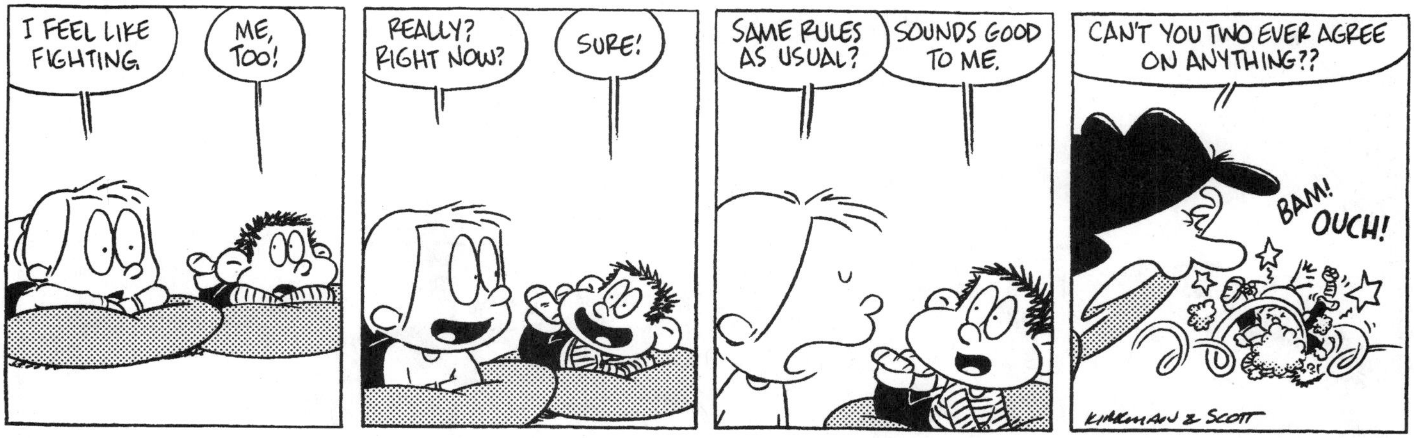

I FEEL LIKE FIGHTING.
ME, TOO!
REALLY? RIGHT NOW?
SURE!
SAME RULES AS USUAL?
SOUNDS GOOD TO ME.
CAN'T YOU TWO EVER AGREE ON ANYTHING??
BAM!
OUCH!
KIRKMAN & SCOTT

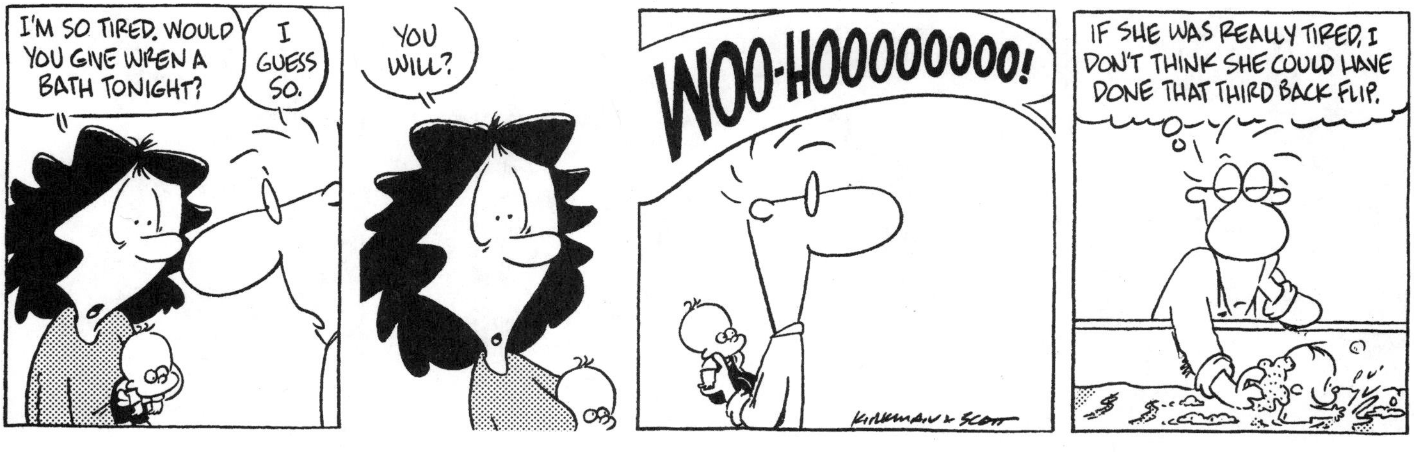

I'M SO TIRED. WOULD YOU GIVE WREN A BATH TONIGHT?
I GUESS SO.
YOU WILL?
WOO-HOOOOOOOO!
KIRKMAN & SCOTT
IF SHE WAS REALLY TIRED, I DON'T THINK SHE COULD HAVE DONE THAT THIRD BACK FLIP.

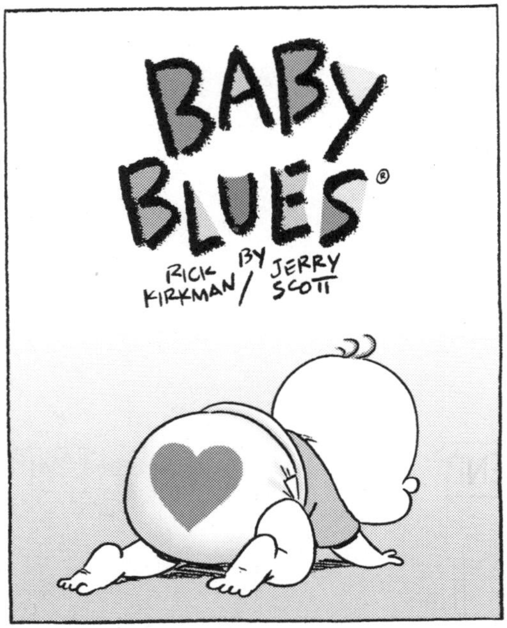
BABY BLUES®
BY RICK KIRKMAN / JERRY SCOTT

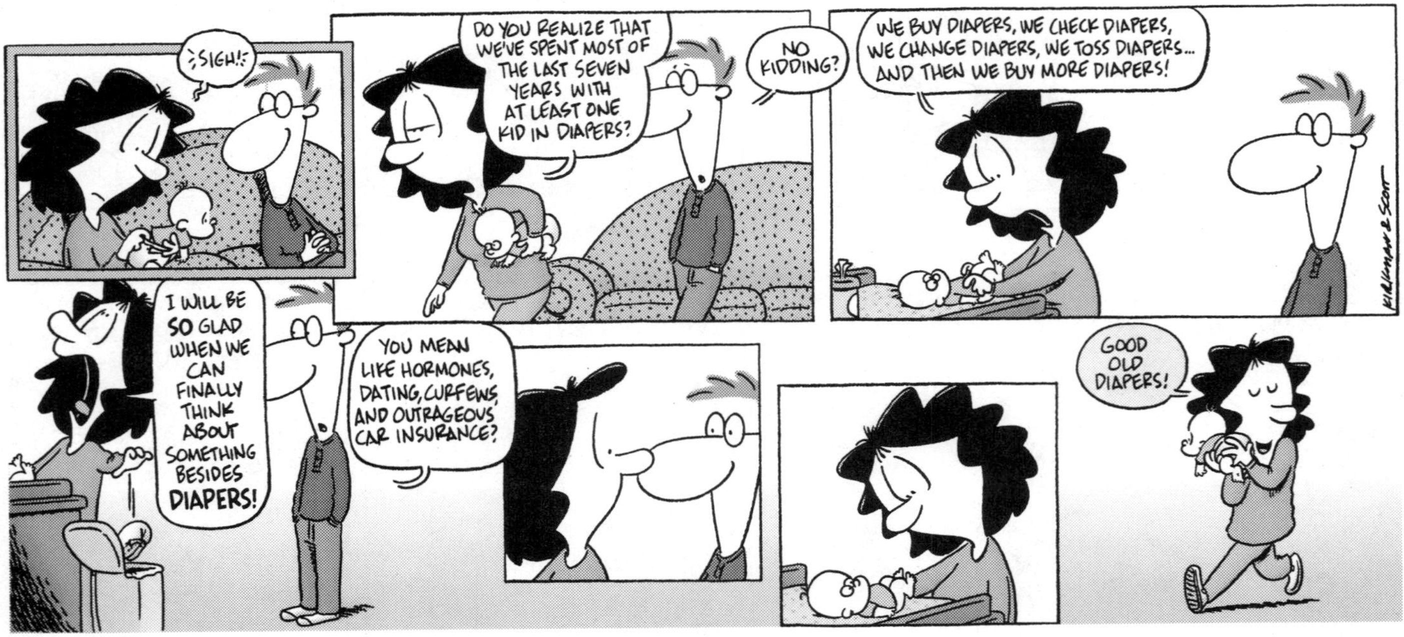
SIGH!
DO YOU REALIZE THAT WE'VE SPENT MOST OF THE LAST SEVEN YEARS WITH AT LEAST ONE KID IN DIAPERS?
NO KIDDING?
WE BUY DIAPERS, WE CHECK DIAPERS, WE CHANGE DIAPERS, WE TOSS DIAPERS... AND THEN WE BUY MORE DIAPERS!
KIRKMAN & SCOTT
I WILL BE SO GLAD WHEN WE CAN FINALLY THINK ABOUT SOMETHING BESIDES DIAPERS!
YOU MEAN LIKE HORMONES, DATING, CURFEWS AND OUTRAGEOUS CAR INSURANCE?
GOOD OLD DIAPERS!

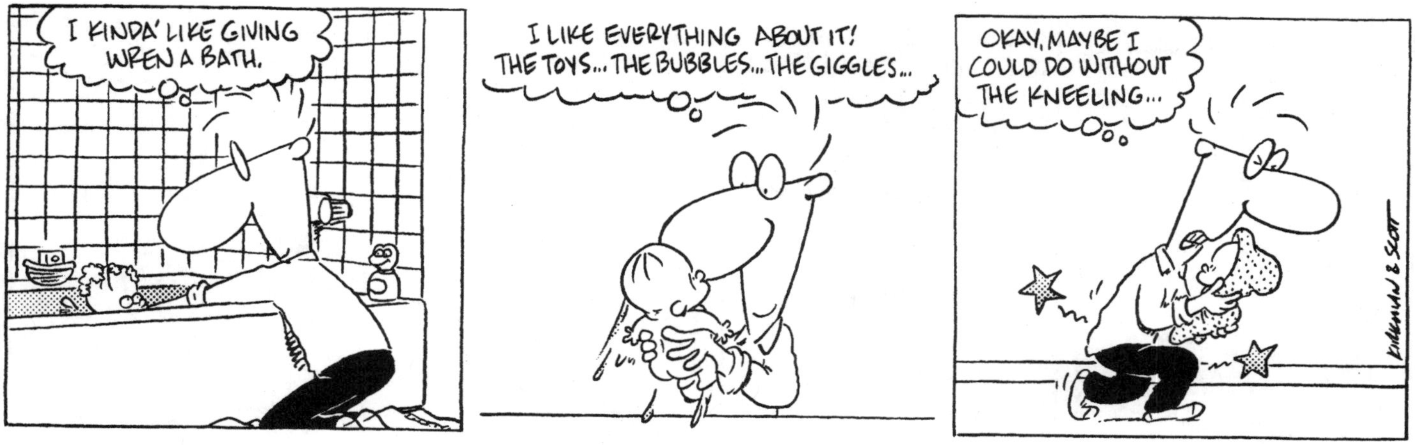
I KINDA' LIKE GIVING WREN A BATH.
I LIKE EVERYTHING ABOUT IT! THE TOYS... THE BUBBLES... THE GIGGLES...
OKAY, MAYBE I COULD DO WITHOUT THE KNEELING...
KIRKMAN & SCOTT

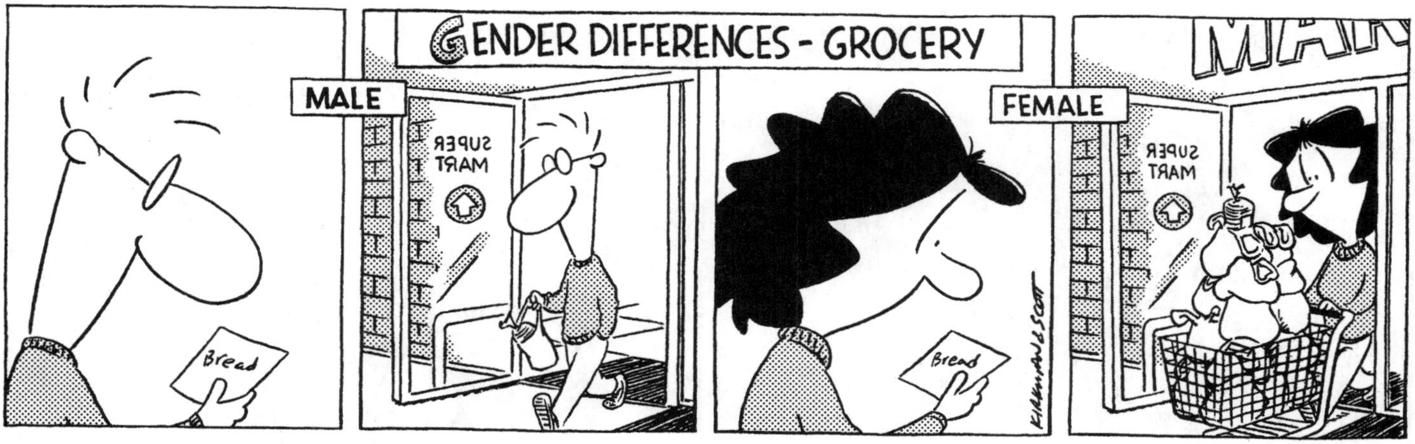
GENDER DIFFERENCES - GROCERY
MALE
Bread
SUPER MART
FEMALE
Bread
KIRKMAN & SCOTT
SUPER MART

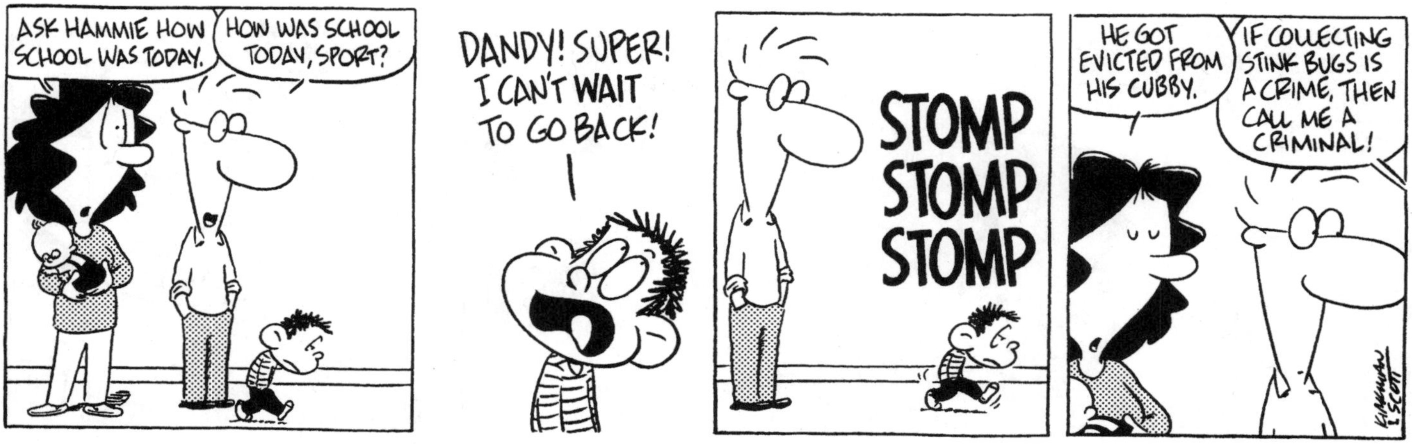
ASK HAMMIE HOW SCHOOL WAS TODAY.
HOW WAS SCHOOL TODAY, SPORT?
DANDY! SUPER! I CAN'T WAIT TO GO BACK!
STOMP STOMP STOMP
HE GOT EVICTED FROM HIS CUBBY.
IF COLLECTING STINK BUGS IS A CRIME, THEN CALL ME A CRIMINAL!
KIRKMAN & SCOTT

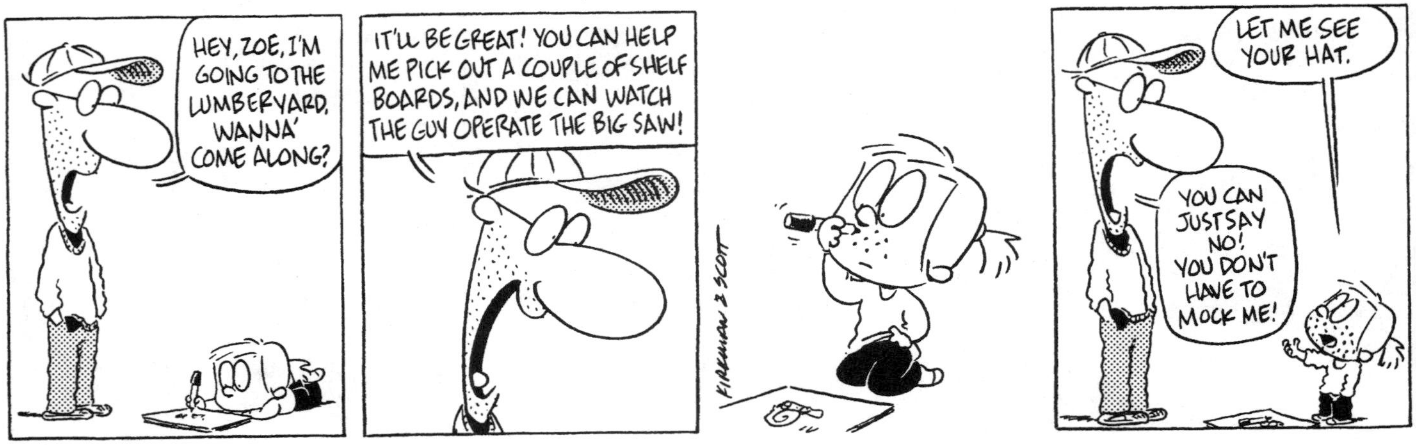
HEY, ZOE, I'M GOING TO THE LUMBERYARD. WANNA' COME ALONG?
IT'LL BE GREAT! YOU CAN HELP ME PICK OUT A COUPLE OF SHELF BOARDS, AND WE CAN WATCH THE GUY OPERATE THE BIG SAW!
KIRKMAN & SCOTT
LET ME SEE YOUR HAT.
YOU CAN JUST SAY NO! YOU DON'T HAVE TO MOCK ME!

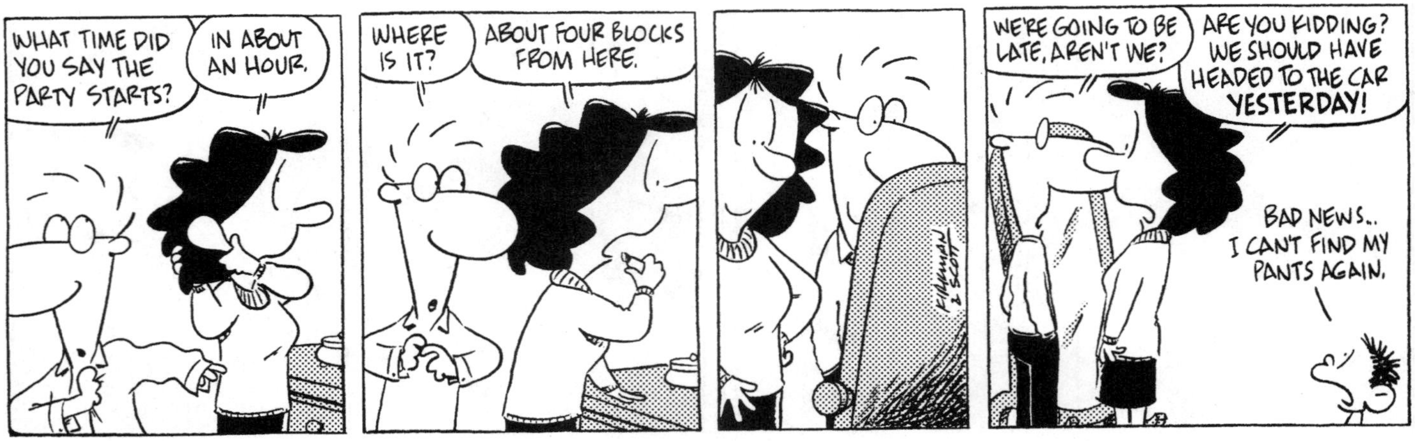
WHAT TIME DID YOU SAY THE PARTY STARTS?
IN ABOUT AN HOUR.
WHERE IS IT?
ABOUT FOUR BLOCKS FROM HERE.
KIRKMAN & SCOTT
WE'RE GOING TO BE LATE, AREN'T WE?
ARE YOU KIDDING? WE SHOULD HAVE HEADED TO THE CAR **YESTERDAY!**
BAD NEWS... I CAN'T FIND MY PANTS AGAIN.

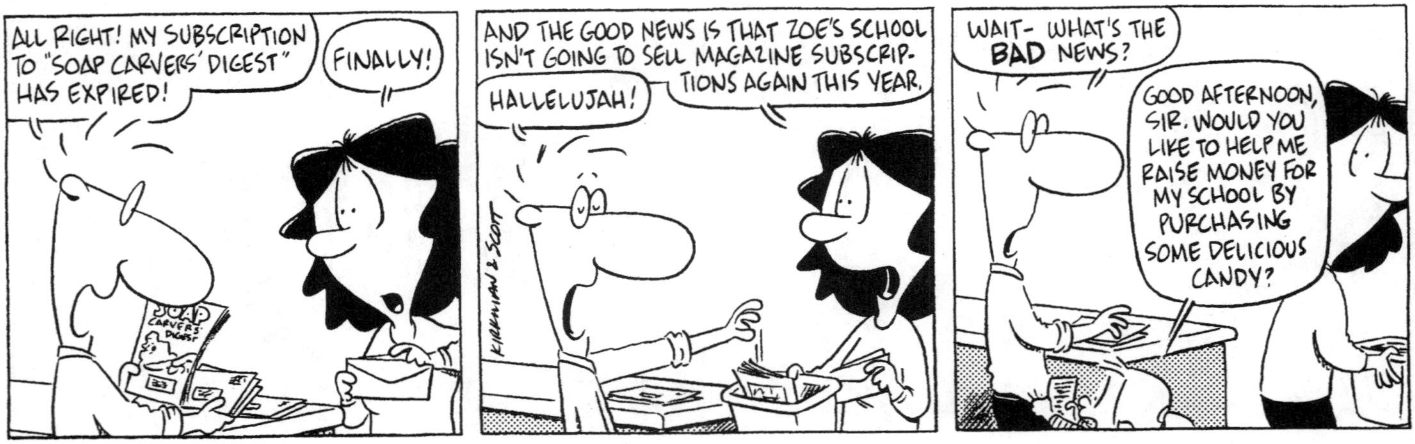
ALL RIGHT! MY SUBSCRIPTION TO "SOAP CARVERS' DIGEST" HAS EXPIRED!
FINALLY!
SOAP CARVERS' DIGEST
AND THE GOOD NEWS IS THAT ZOE'S SCHOOL ISN'T GOING TO SELL MAGAZINE SUBSCRIPTIONS AGAIN THIS YEAR.
HALLELUJAH!
KIRKMAN & SCOTT
WAIT- WHAT'S THE **BAD** NEWS?
GOOD AFTERNOON, SIR. WOULD YOU LIKE TO HELP ME RAISE MONEY FOR MY SCHOOL BY PURCHASING SOME DELICIOUS CANDY?

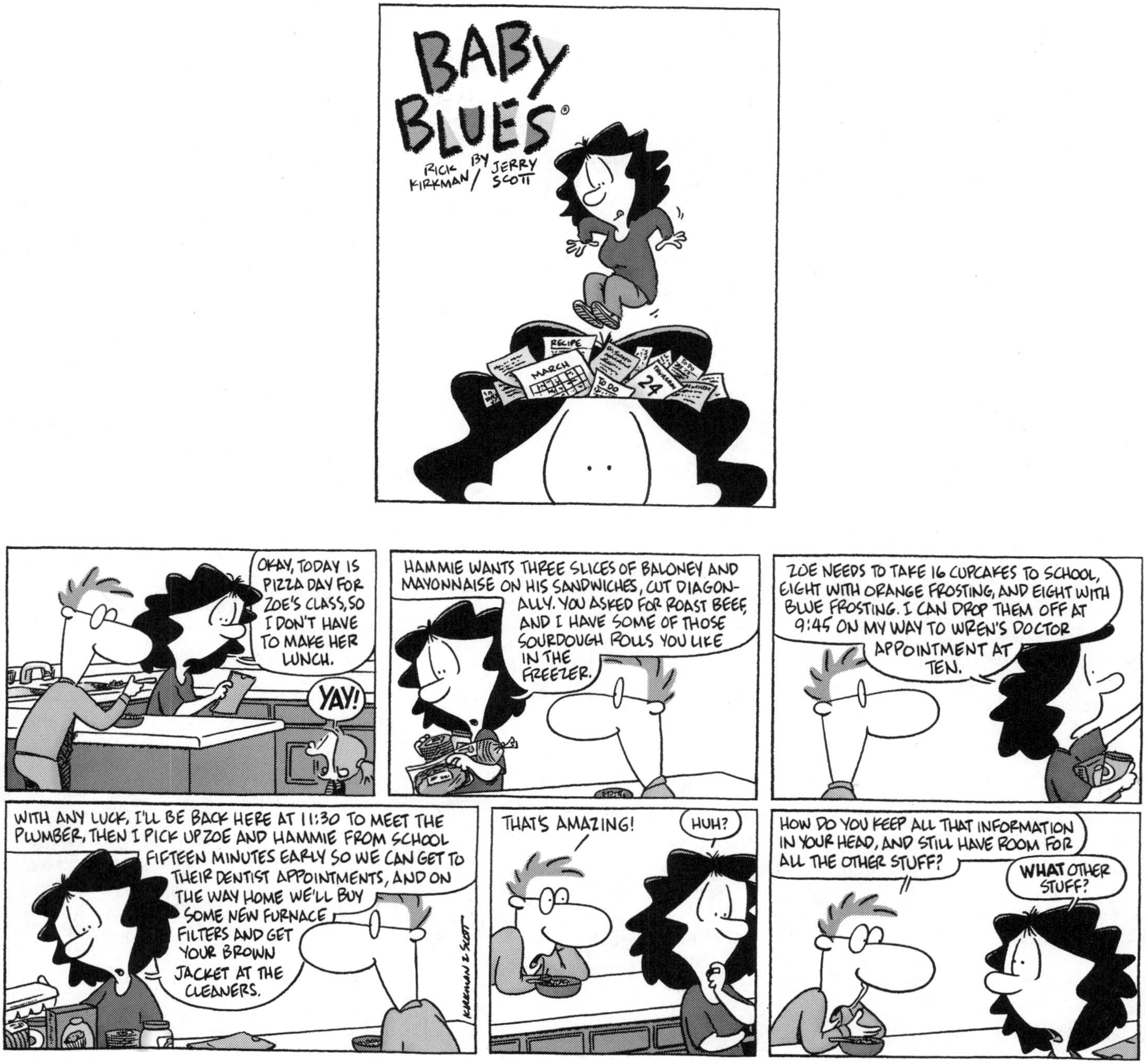
BABY BLUES®
BY RICK KIRKMAN / JERRY SCOTT
RECIPE
MARCH
TO DO
24
OKAY, TODAY IS PIZZA DAY FOR ZOE'S CLASS, SO I DON'T HAVE TO MAKE HER LUNCH.
YAY!
HAMMIE WANTS THREE SLICES OF BALONEY AND MAYONNAISE ON HIS SANDWICHES, CUT DIAGONALLY. YOU ASKED FOR ROAST BEEF, AND I HAVE SOME OF THOSE SOURDOUGH ROLLS YOU LIKE IN THE FREEZER.
ZOE NEEDS TO TAKE 16 CUPCAKES TO SCHOOL, EIGHT WITH ORANGE FROSTING, AND EIGHT WITH BLUE FROSTING. I CAN DROP THEM OFF AT 9:45 ON MY WAY TO WREN'S DOCTOR APPOINTMENT AT TEN.
WITH ANY LUCK, I'LL BE BACK HERE AT 11:30 TO MEET THE PLUMBER, THEN I PICK UP ZOE AND HAMMIE FROM SCHOOL FIFTEEN MINUTES EARLY SO WE CAN GET TO THEIR DENTIST APPOINTMENTS, AND ON THE WAY HOME WE'LL BUY SOME NEW FURNACE FILTERS AND GET YOUR BROWN JACKET AT THE CLEANERS.
KIRKMAN & SCOTT
THAT'S AMAZING!
HUH?
HOW DO YOU KEEP ALL THAT INFORMATION IN YOUR HEAD, AND STILL HAVE ROOM FOR ALL THE OTHER STUFF?
WHAT OTHER STUFF?

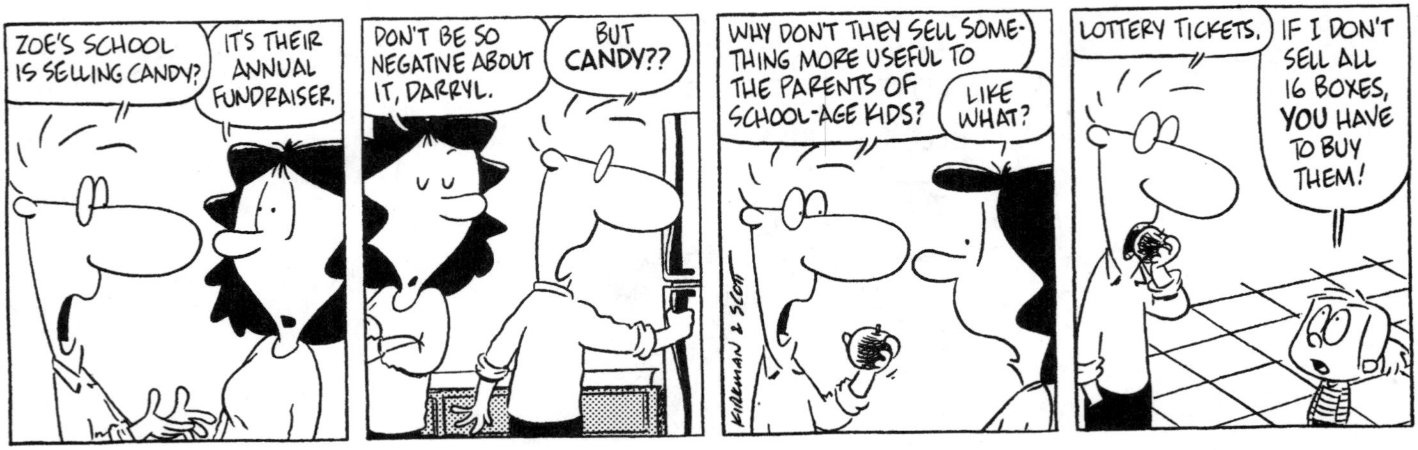
ZOE'S SCHOOL IS SELLING CANDY?
IT'S THEIR ANNUAL FUNDRAISER.
DON'T BE SO NEGATIVE ABOUT IT, DARRYL.
BUT **CANDY??**
WHY DON'T THEY SELL SOMETHING MORE USEFUL TO THE PARENTS OF SCHOOL-AGE KIDS?
LIKE WHAT?
KIRKMAN & SCOTT
LOTTERY TICKETS.
IF I DON'T SELL ALL 16 BOXES, **YOU** HAVE TO BUY THEM!

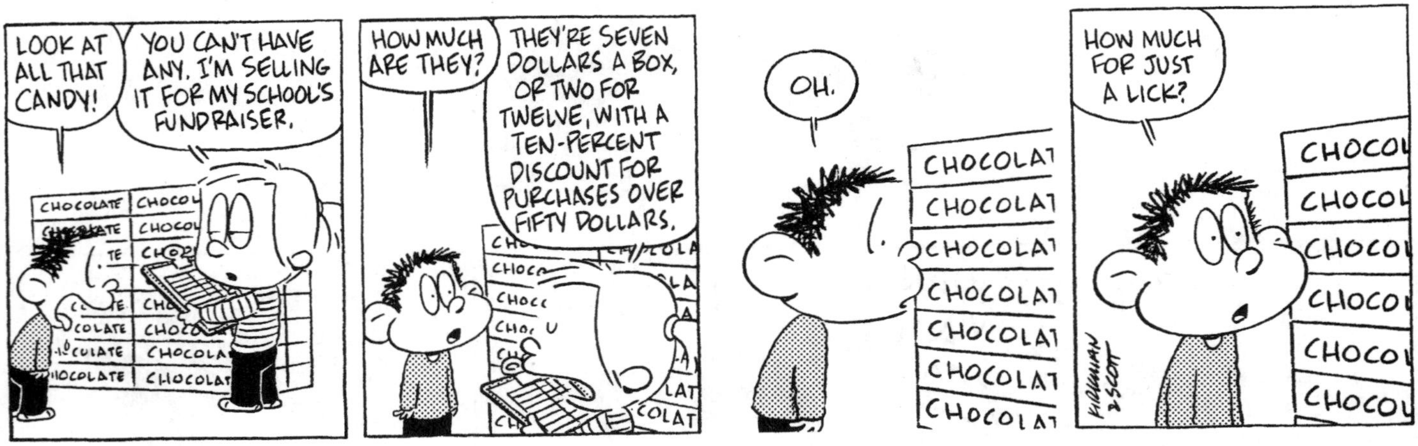
LOOK AT ALL THAT CANDY!
YOU CAN'T HAVE ANY. I'M SELLING IT FOR MY SCHOOL'S FUNDRAISER.
HOW MUCH ARE THEY?
THEY'RE SEVEN DOLLARS A BOX, OR TWO FOR TWELVE, WITH A TEN-PERCENT DISCOUNT FOR PURCHASES OVER FIFTY DOLLARS.
OH.
HOW MUCH FOR JUST A LICK?
KIRKMAN & SCOTT

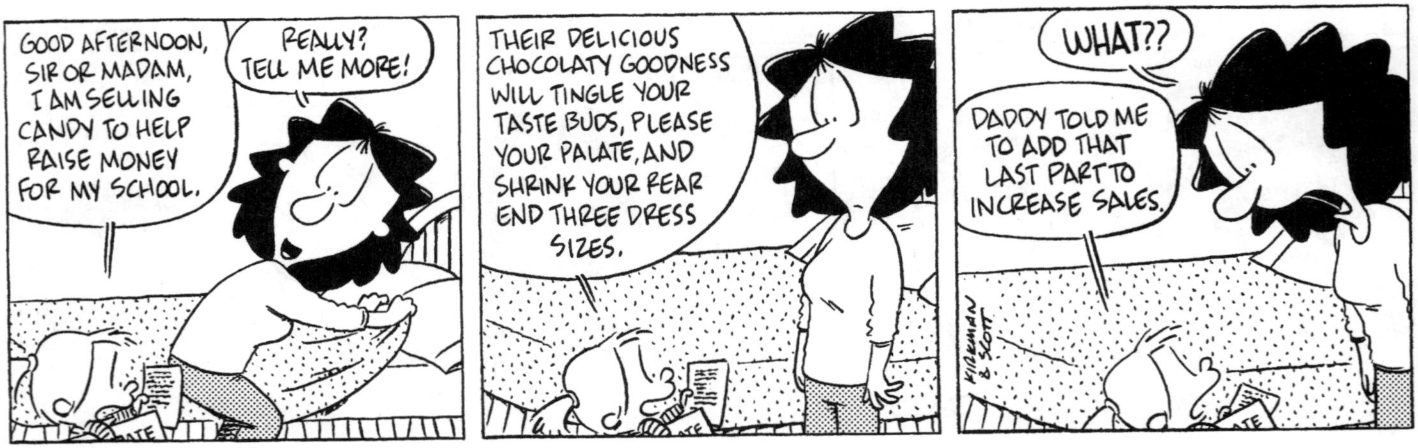
GOOD AFTERNOON, SIR OR MADAM, I AM SELLING CANDY TO HELP RAISE MONEY FOR MY SCHOOL.
REALLY? TELL ME MORE!
THEIR DELICIOUS CHOCOLATY GOODNESS WILL TINGLE YOUR TASTE BUDS, PLEASE YOUR PALATE, AND SHRINK YOUR REAR END THREE DRESS SIZES.
KIRKMAN & SCOTT
WHAT??
DADDY TOLD ME TO ADD THAT LAST PART TO INCREASE SALES.

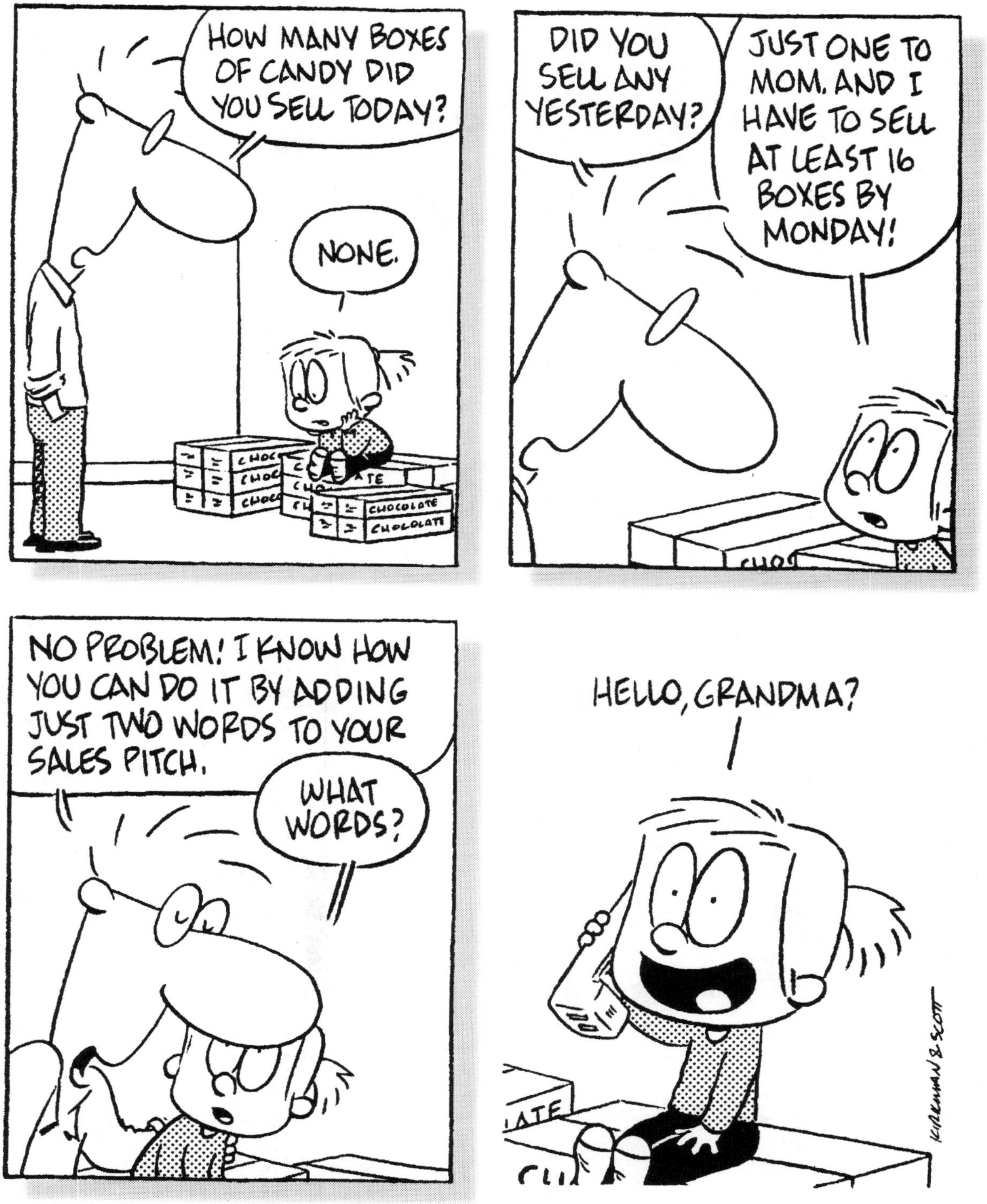
HOW MANY BOXES OF CANDY DID YOU SELL TODAY?
NONE.
CHOCOLATE
DID YOU SELL ANY YESTERDAY?
JUST ONE TO MOM. AND I HAVE TO SELL AT LEAST 16 BOXES BY MONDAY!
NO PROBLEM! I KNOW HOW YOU CAN DO IT BY ADDING JUST TWO WORDS TO YOUR SALES PITCH.
WHAT WORDS?
HELLO, GRANDMA?
KIRKMAN & SCOTT

BABY BLUES®
BY RICK KIRKMAN / JERRY SCOTT

ZOE, CAN YOU KEEP AN EYE ON WREN WHILE I GO GET HER SHOES AND SOCKS?
NO PROBLEM.
JUST TRY TO KEEP HER IN THE LIVING ROOM IF POSSIBLE!
OKAY.
I DON'T EXPECT MIRACLES... JUST DO THE BEST YOU CAN!
I WILL
OKAY, I'LL TAKE OVER FROM–
–HERE.
SHE'S SITTING EXACTLY WHERE I LEFT HER!
I KNOW. I'M PRETTY GOOD WITH KIDS.
HOW DID YOU DO IT?
EASY. IT JUST TAKES LOVE, PATIENCE...
...AND PLENTY OF DOUBLE-STICK TAPE.
KIRKMAN & SCOTT

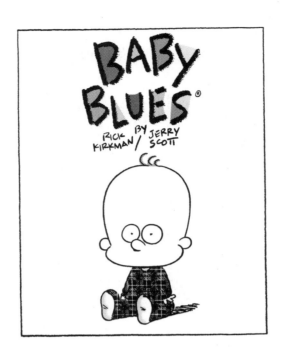

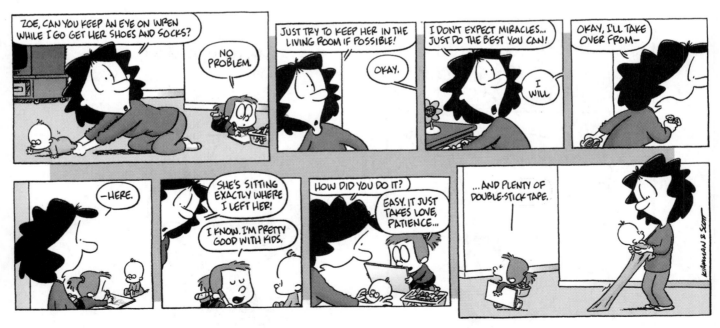

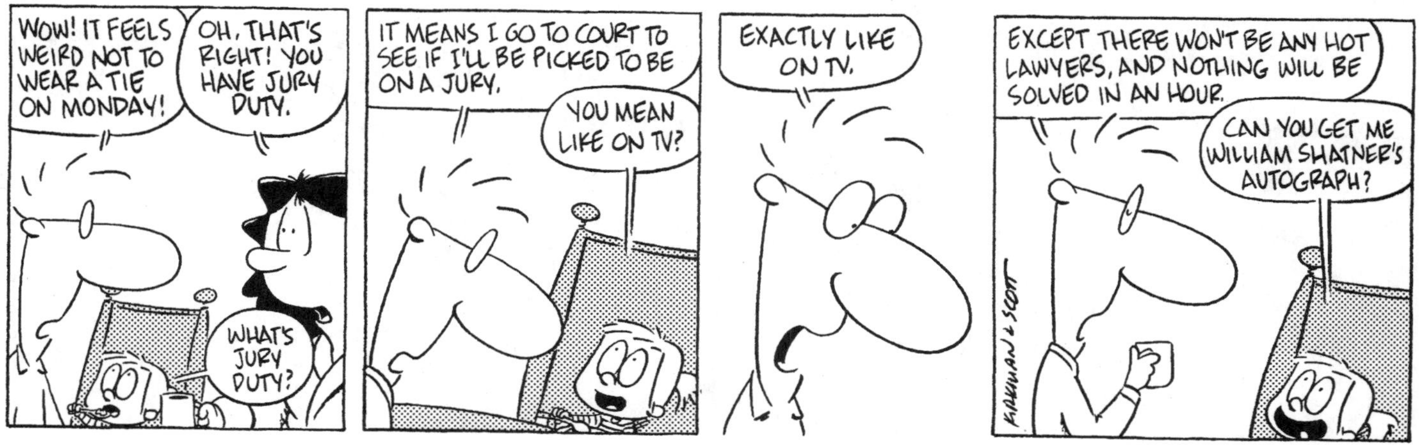
WOW! IT FEELS WEIRD NOT TO WEAR A TIE ON MONDAY!
OH, THAT'S RIGHT! YOU HAVE JURY DUTY.
WHAT'S JURY DUTY?
IT MEANS I GO TO COURT TO SEE IF I'LL BE PICKED TO BE ON A JURY.
YOU MEAN LIKE ON TV?
EXACTLY LIKE ON TV.
EXCEPT THERE WON'T BE ANY HOT LAWYERS, AND NOTHING WILL BE SOLVED IN AN HOUR.
CAN YOU GET ME WILLIAM SHATNER'S AUTOGRAPH?
KIRKMAN & SCOTT

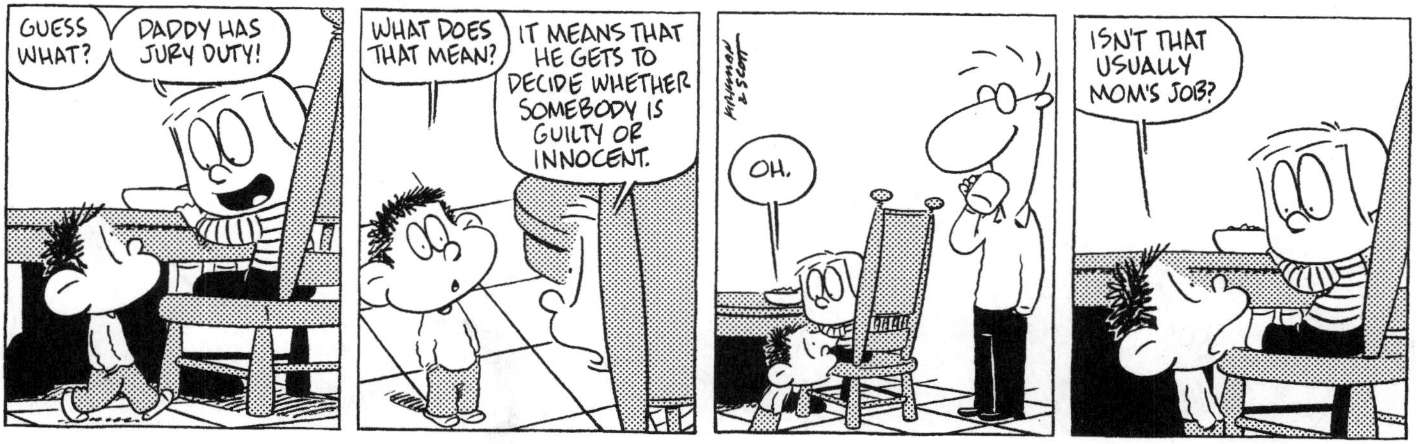
GUESS WHAT?
DADDY HAS JURY DUTY!
WHAT DOES THAT MEAN?
IT MEANS THAT HE GETS TO DECIDE WHETHER SOMEBODY IS GUILTY OR INNOCENT.
OH.
KIRKMAN & SCOTT
ISN'T THAT USUALLY MOM'S JOB?

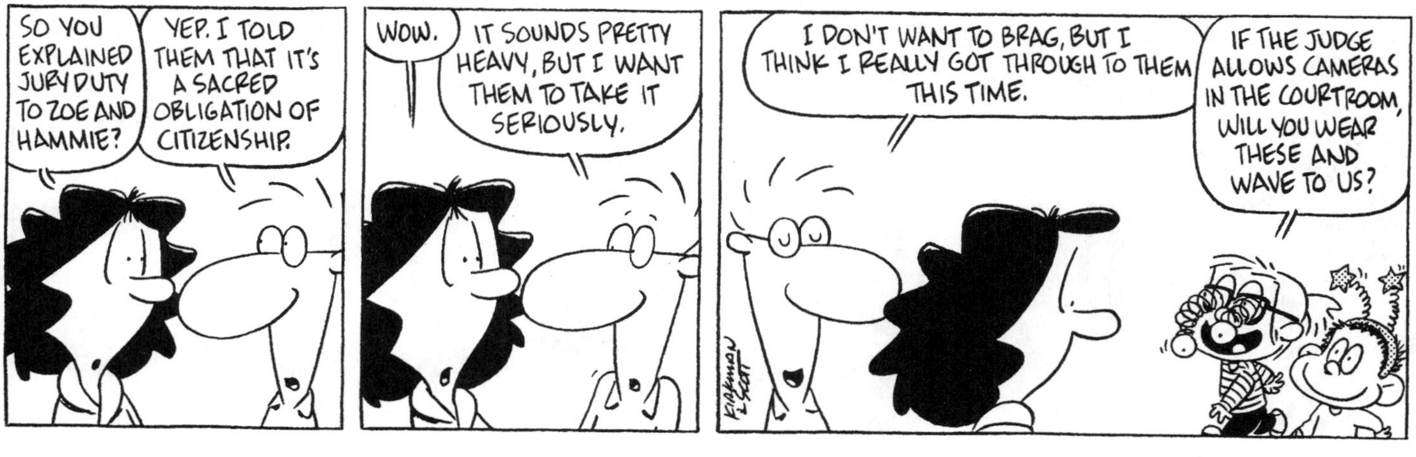
SO YOU EXPLAINED JURY DUTY TO ZOE AND HAMMIE?
YEP. I TOLD THEM THAT IT'S A SACRED OBLIGATION OF CITIZENSHIP.
WOW.
IT SOUNDS PRETTY HEAVY, BUT I WANT THEM TO TAKE IT SERIOUSLY.
I DON'T WANT TO BRAG, BUT I THINK I REALLY GOT THROUGH TO THEM THIS TIME.
IF THE JUDGE ALLOWS CAMERAS IN THE COURTROOM, WILL YOU WEAR THESE AND WAVE TO US?
KIRKMAN & SCOTT

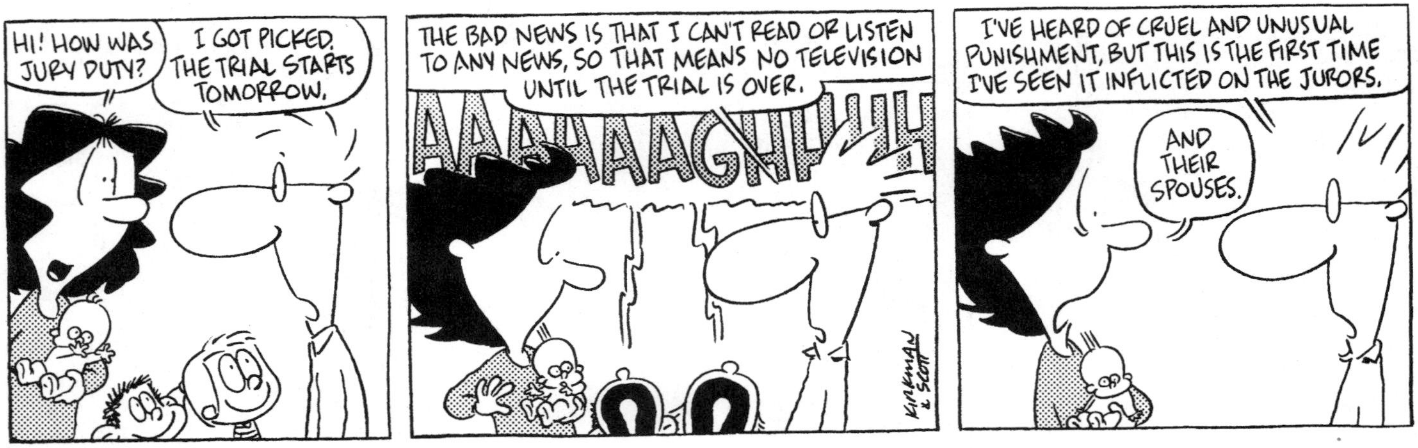
HI! HOW WAS JURY DUTY?
I GOT PICKED. THE TRIAL STARTS TOMORROW.
THE BAD NEWS IS THAT I CAN'T READ OR LISTEN TO ANY NEWS, SO THAT MEANS NO TELEVISION UNTIL THE TRIAL IS OVER.
AAAAAAAGHHHH
KIRKMAN & SCOTT
I'VE HEARD OF CRUEL AND UNUSUAL PUNISHMENT, BUT THIS IS THE FIRST TIME I'VE SEEN IT INFLICTED ON THE JURORS.
AND THEIR SPOUSES.

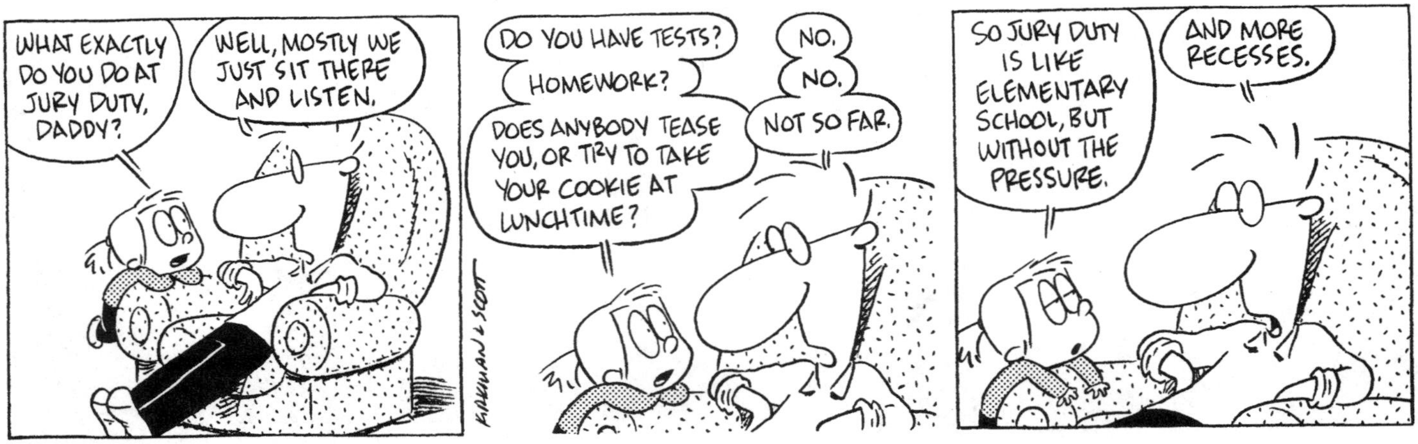
WHAT EXACTLY DO YOU DO AT JURY DUTY, DADDY?
WELL, MOSTLY WE JUST SIT THERE AND LISTEN.
KIRKMAN & SCOTT
DO YOU HAVE TESTS?
NO.
HOMEWORK?
NO.
DOES ANYBODY TEASE YOU, OR TRY TO TAKE YOUR COOKIE AT LUNCHTIME?
NOT SO FAR.
SO JURY DUTY IS LIKE ELEMENTARY SCHOOL, BUT WITHOUT THE PRESSURE.
AND MORE RECESSES.

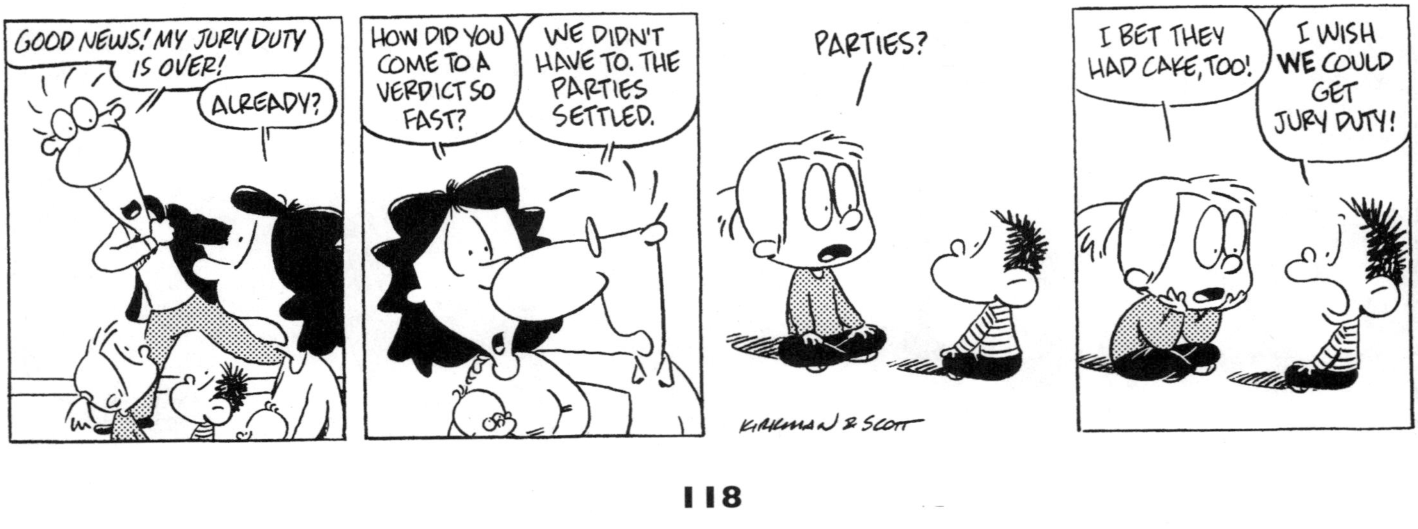
GOOD NEWS! MY JURY DUTY IS OVER!
ALREADY?
HOW DID YOU COME TO A VERDICT SO FAST?
WE DIDN'T HAVE TO. THE PARTIES SETTLED.
PARTIES?
KIRKMAN & SCOTT
I BET THEY HAD CAKE, TOO!
I WISH WE COULD GET JURY DUTY!

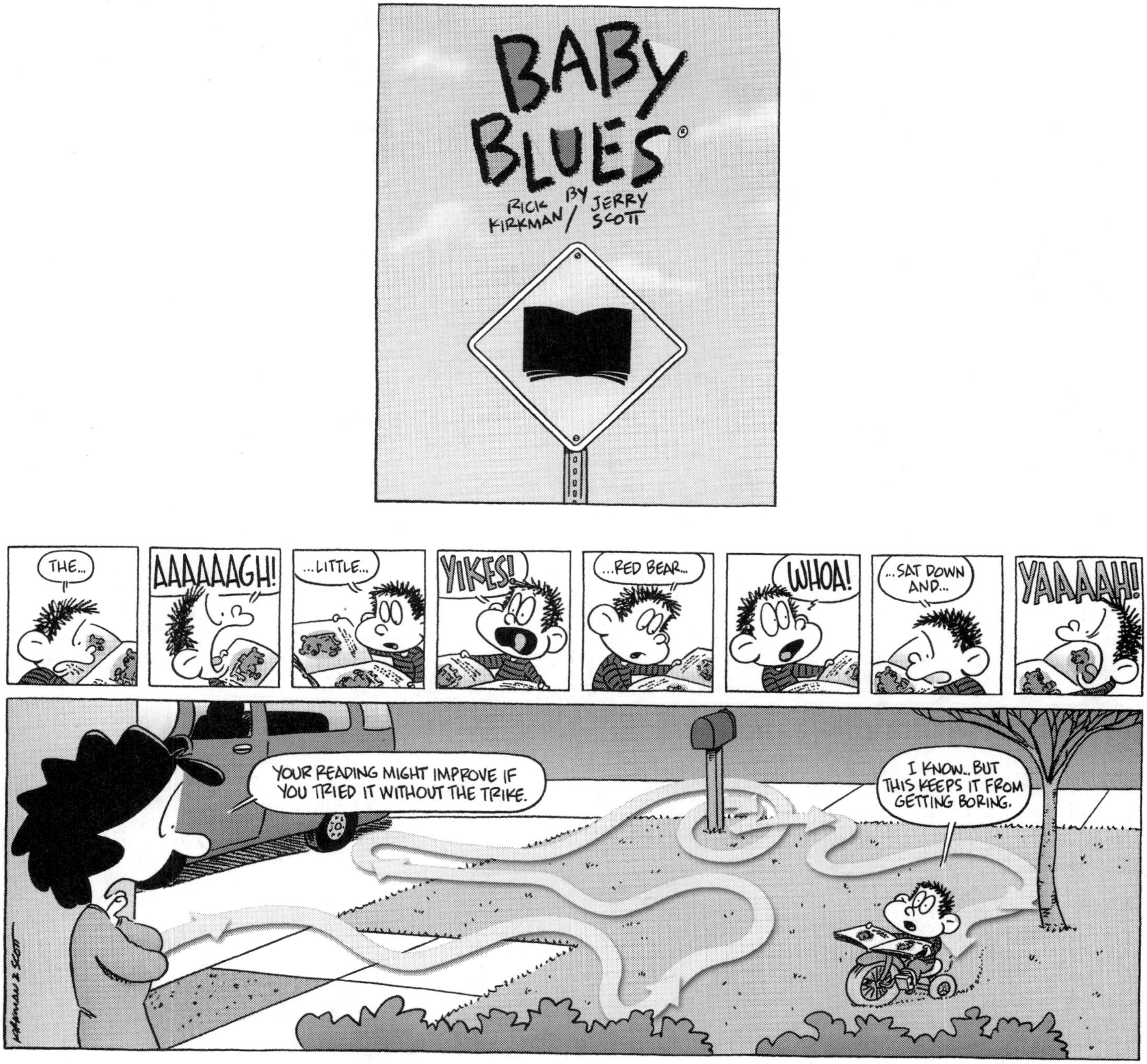

BABY BLUES®
BY RICK KIRKMAN / JERRY SCOTT
THE...
AAAAAAGH!
...LITTLE...
YIKES!
...RED BEAR...
WHOA!
...SAT DOWN AND...
YAAAAH!
YOUR READING MIGHT IMPROVE IF YOU TRIED IT WITHOUT THE TRIKE.
I KNOW... BUT THIS KEEPS IT FROM GETTING BORING.
KIRKMAN & SCOTT

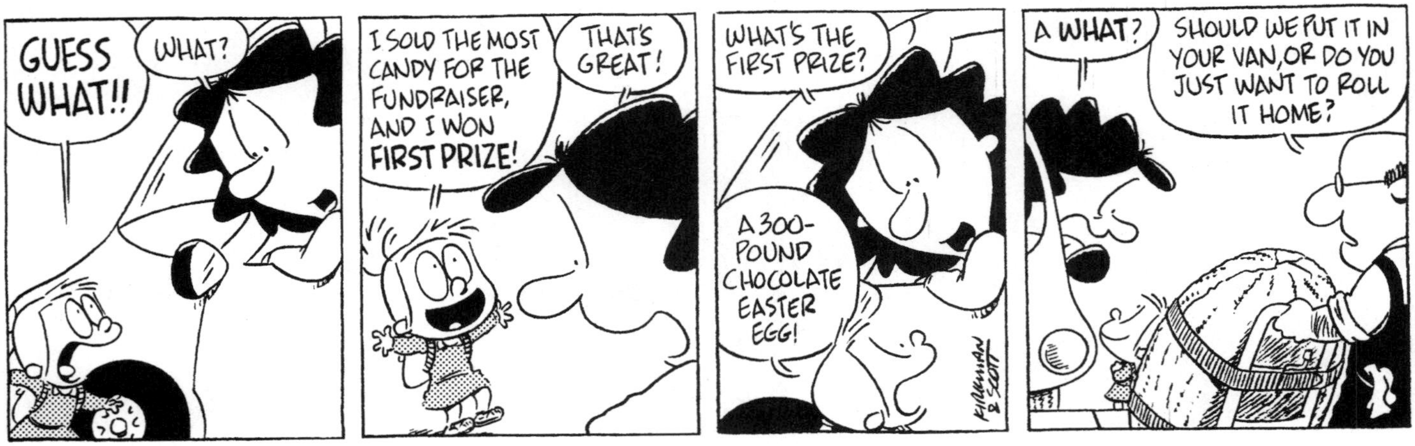
GUESS WHAT!!
WHAT?
I SOLD THE MOST CANDY FOR THE FUNDRAISER, AND I WON **FIRST PRIZE**!
THAT'S GREAT!
WHAT'S THE FIRST PRIZE?
A 300-POUND CHOCOLATE EASTER EGG!
A **WHAT**?
SHOULD WE PUT IT IN YOUR VAN, OR DO YOU JUST WANT TO ROLL IT HOME?

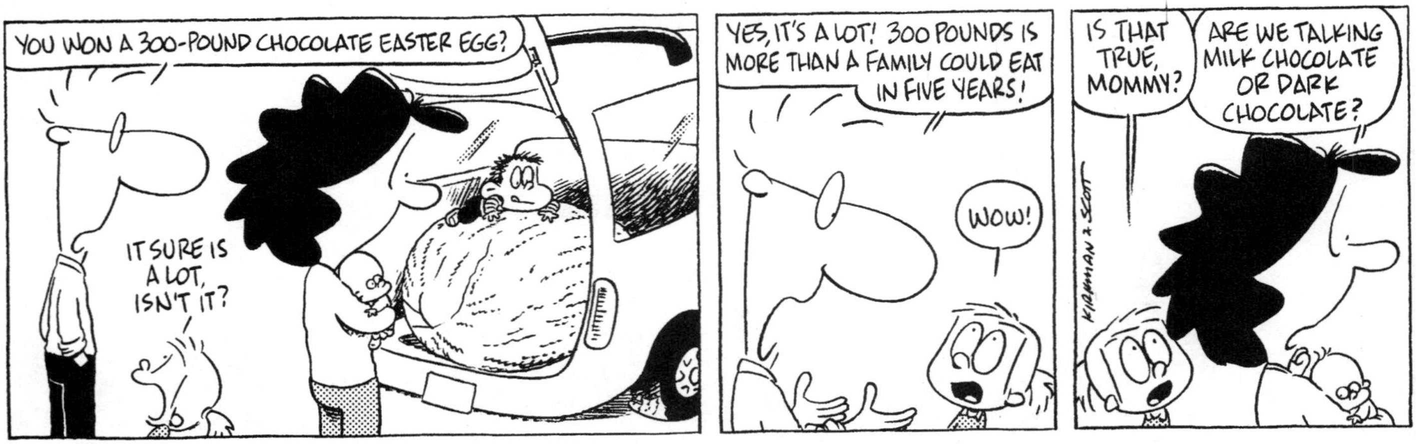
YOU WON A 300-POUND CHOCOLATE EASTER EGG?
IT SURE IS A LOT, ISN'T IT?
YES, IT'S A LOT! 300 POUNDS IS MORE THAN A FAMILY COULD EAT IN FIVE YEARS!
WOW!
IS THAT TRUE, MOMMY?
ARE WE TALKING MILK CHOCOLATE OR DARK CHOCOLATE?

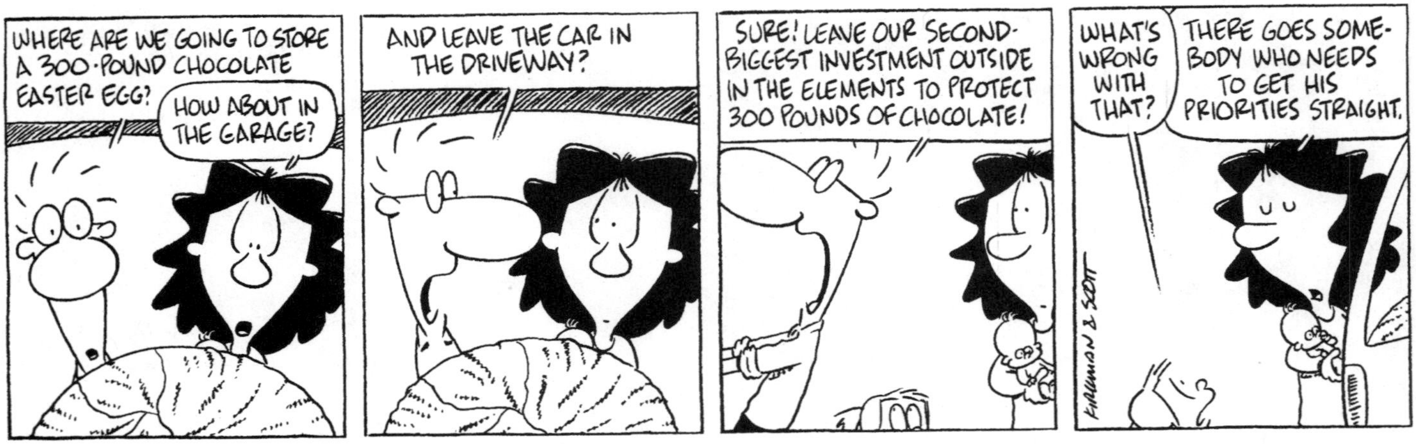
WHERE ARE WE GOING TO STORE A 300-POUND CHOCOLATE EASTER EGG?
HOW ABOUT IN THE GARAGE?
AND LEAVE THE CAR IN THE DRIVEWAY?
SURE! LEAVE OUR SECOND-BIGGEST INVESTMENT OUTSIDE IN THE ELEMENTS TO PROTECT 300 POUNDS OF CHOCOLATE!
WHAT'S WRONG WITH THAT?
THERE GOES SOMEBODY WHO NEEDS TO GET HIS PRIORITIES STRAIGHT.

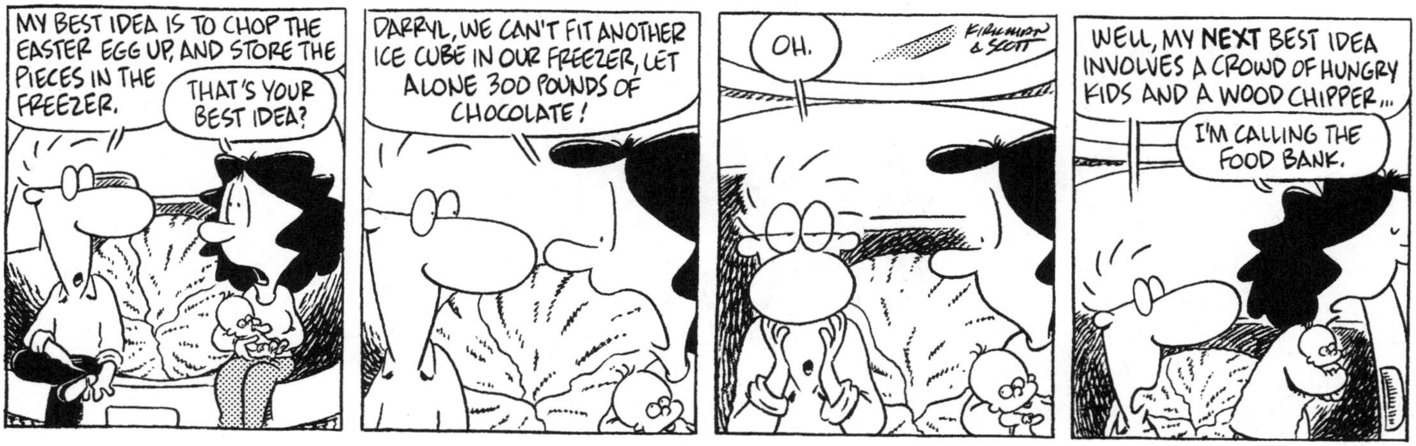
MY BEST IDEA IS TO CHOP THE EASTER EGG UP, AND STORE THE PIECES IN THE FREEZER.
THAT'S YOUR BEST IDEA?
DARRYL, WE CAN'T FIT ANOTHER ICE CUBE IN OUR FREEZER, LET ALONE 300 POUNDS OF CHOCOLATE!
OH.
KIRKMAN & SCOTT
WELL, MY **NEXT** BEST IDEA INVOLVES A CROWD OF HUNGRY KIDS AND A WOOD CHIPPER...
I'M CALLING THE FOOD BANK.

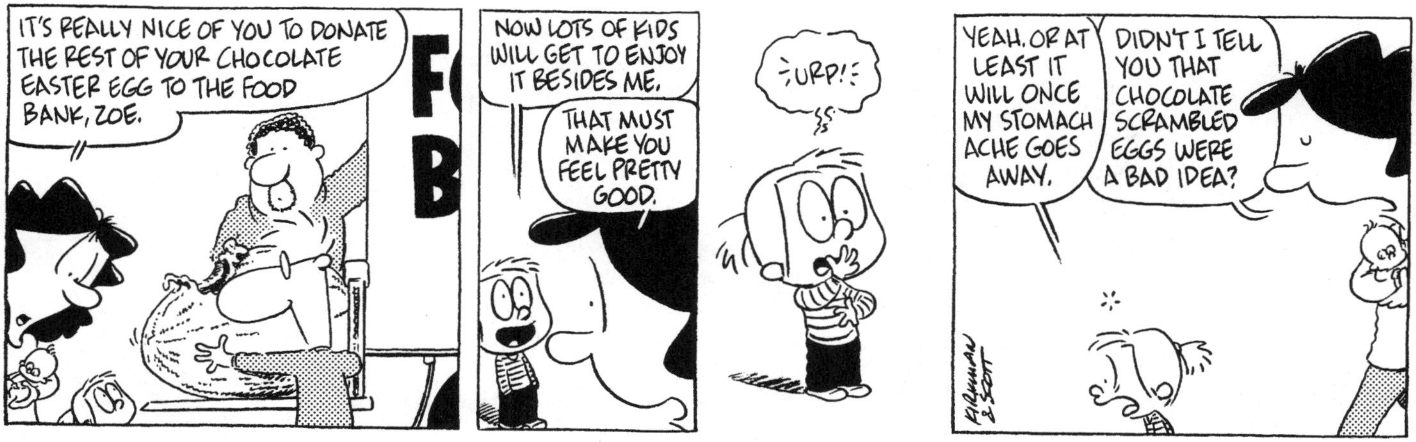
IT'S REALLY NICE OF YOU TO DONATE THE REST OF YOUR CHOCOLATE EASTER EGG TO THE FOOD BANK, ZOE.
NOW LOTS OF KIDS WILL GET TO ENJOY IT BESIDES ME.
THAT MUST MAKE YOU FEEL PRETTY GOOD.
URP!
YEAH. OR AT LEAST IT WILL ONCE MY STOMACH ACHE GOES AWAY.
DIDN'T I TELL YOU THAT CHOCOLATE SCRAMBLED EGGS WERE A BAD IDEA?
KIRKMAN & SCOTT

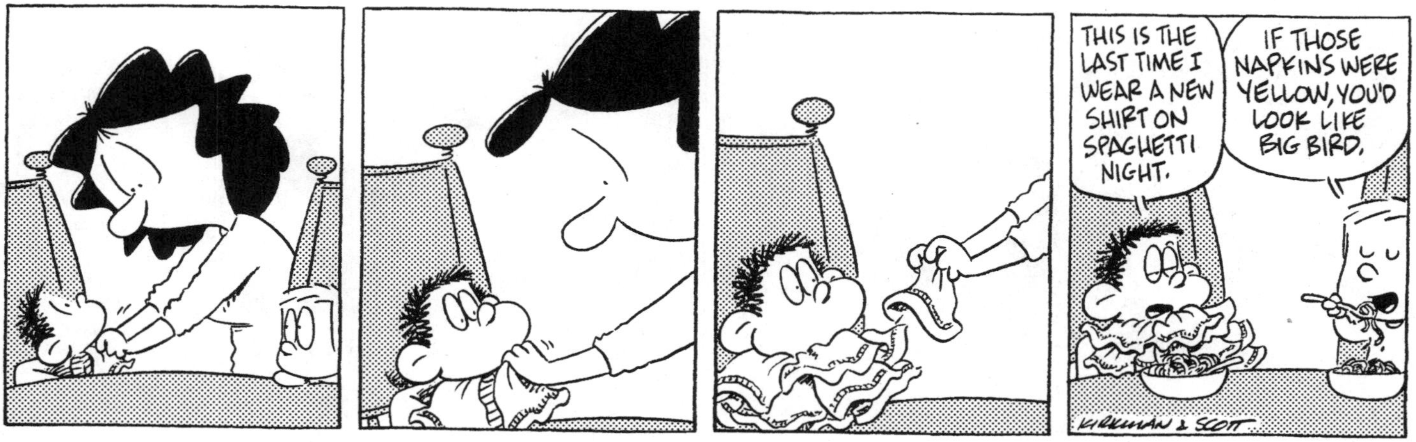
THIS IS THE LAST TIME I WEAR A NEW SHIRT ON SPAGHETTI NIGHT.
IF THOSE NAPKINS WERE YELLOW, YOU'D LOOK LIKE BIG BIRD.
KIRKMAN & SCOTT

BABY BLUES®
BY RICK KIRKMAN / JERRY SCOTT
I FOUND ONE!
ME, TOO!
OH, WOW! THERE'S A BIG ONE!
HERE'S ONE BEHIND THE TREE!
THERE ARE THREE UNDER THIS BUSH!
SAVE ONE FOR ME!
WE ALREADY HAD THE EASTER EGG HUNT, AND WE DID THE EASTER EGG ROLL...
SO WHAT'S ALL THIS?
A BRAND NEW TRADITION.
DADDY IS PAYING US 10¢ APIECE FOR EVERY DANDELION WE FIND!
THE "EASTER WEED PULL"?
I MAY APPLY FOR THE TRADEMARK.

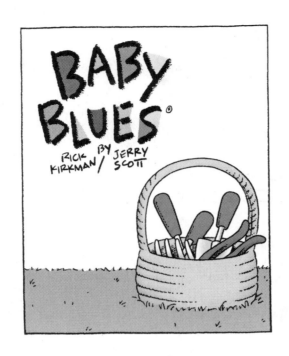

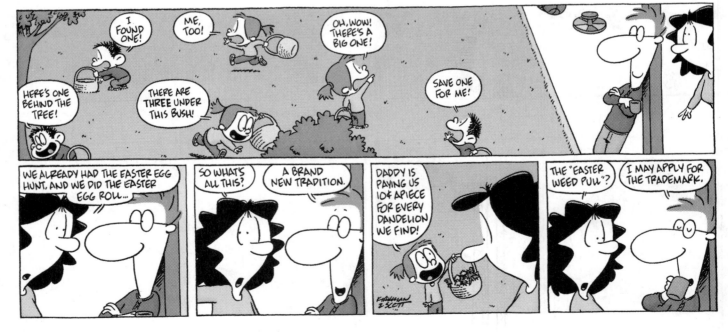

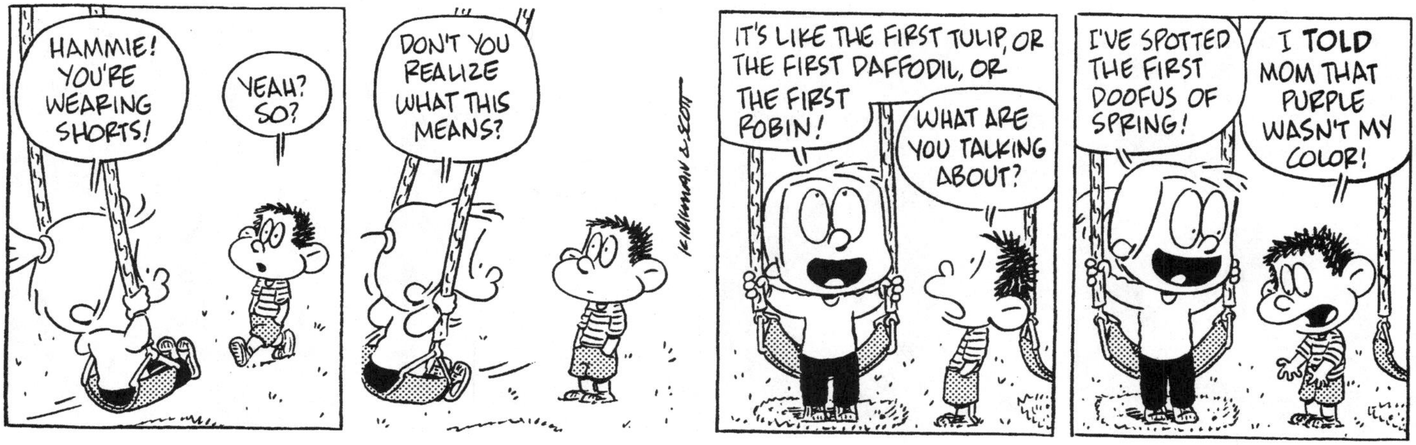
HAMMIE! YOU'RE WEARING SHORTS!
YEAH? SO?
DON'T YOU REALIZE WHAT THIS MEANS?
KIRKMAN & SCOTT
IT'S LIKE THE FIRST TULIP, OR THE FIRST DAFFODIL, OR THE FIRST ROBIN!
WHAT ARE YOU TALKING ABOUT?
I'VE SPOTTED THE FIRST DOOFUS OF SPRING!
I TOLD MOM THAT PURPLE WASN'T MY COLOR!

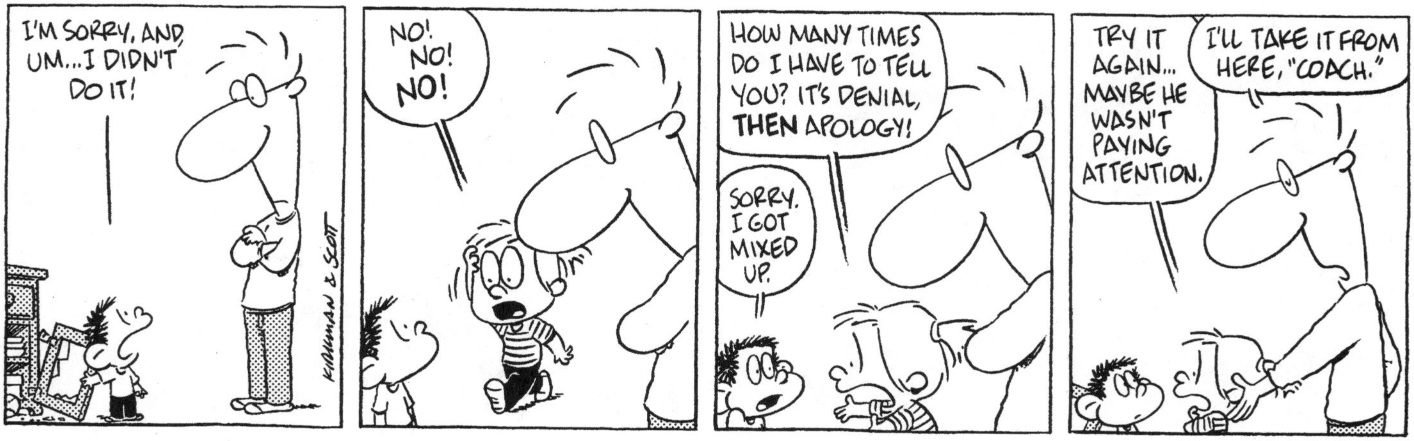
I'M SORRY, AND, UM...I DIDN'T DO IT!
KIRKMAN & SCOTT
NO! NO! NO!
HOW MANY TIMES DO I HAVE TO TELL YOU? IT'S DENIAL, THEN APOLOGY!
SORRY. I GOT MIXED UP.
TRY IT AGAIN... MAYBE HE WASN'T PAYING ATTENTION.
I'LL TAKE IT FROM HERE, "COACH."

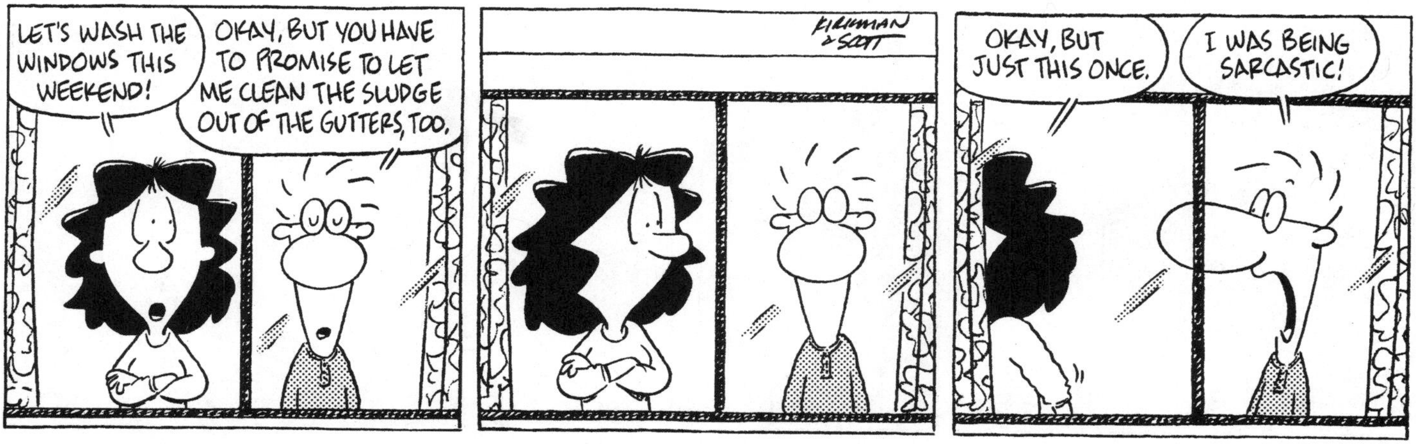
LET'S WASH THE WINDOWS THIS WEEKEND!
OKAY, BUT YOU HAVE TO PROMISE TO LET ME CLEAN THE SLUDGE OUT OF THE GUTTERS, TOO.
KIRKMAN & SCOTT
OKAY, BUT JUST THIS ONCE.
I WAS BEING SARCASTIC!

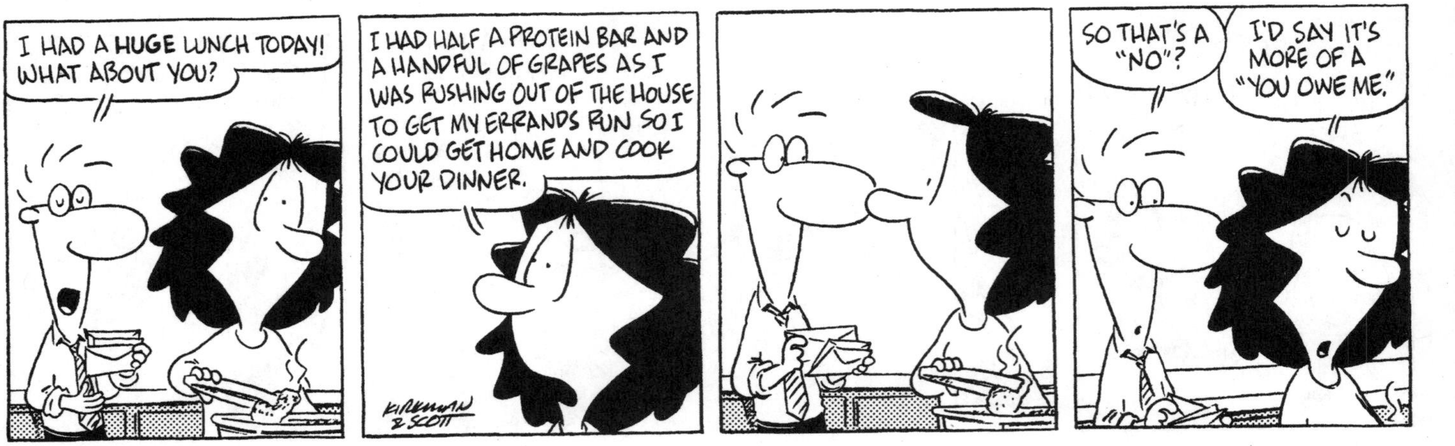
I HAD A **HUGE** LUNCH TODAY! WHAT ABOUT YOU?
I HAD HALF A PROTEIN BAR AND A HANDFUL OF GRAPES AS I WAS RUSHING OUT OF THE HOUSE TO GET MY ERRANDS RUN SO I COULD GET HOME AND COOK YOUR DINNER.
KIRKMAN & SCOTT
SO THAT'S A "NO"?
I'D SAY IT'S MORE OF A "YOU OWE ME."

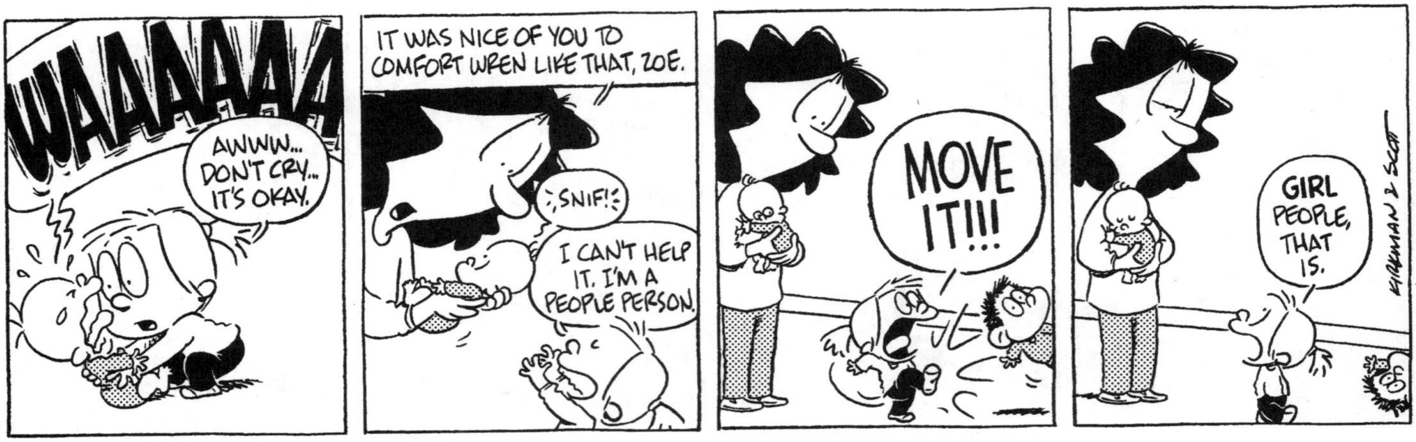
WAAAAAAA
AWWW... DON'T CRY... IT'S OKAY.
IT WAS NICE OF YOU TO COMFORT WREN LIKE THAT, ZOE.
SNIF!
I CAN'T HELP IT. I'M A PEOPLE PERSON.
MOVE IT!!!
GIRL PEOPLE, THAT IS.
KIRKMAN & SCOTT

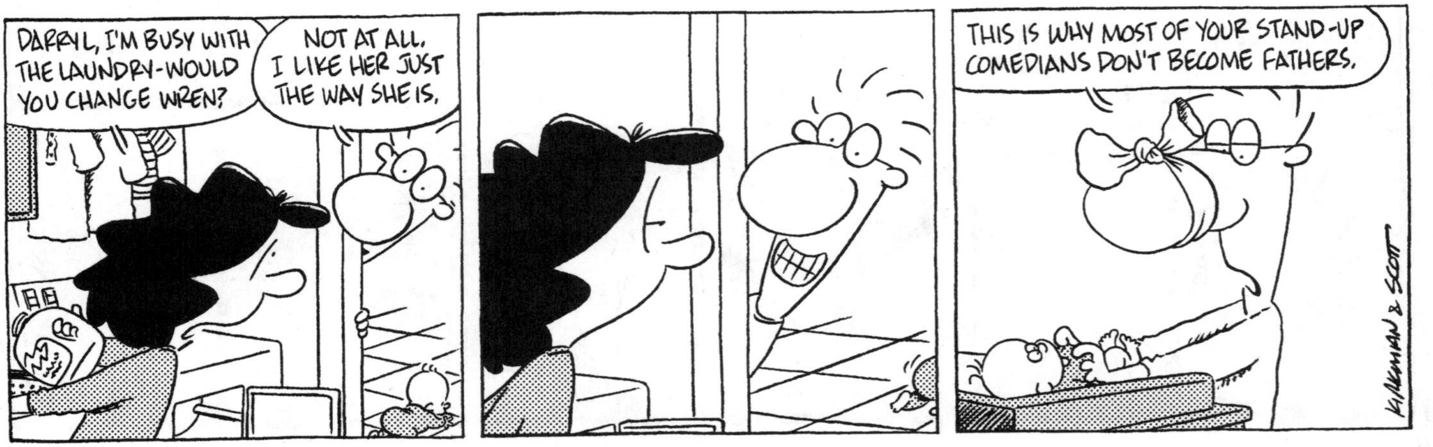
DARRYL, I'M BUSY WITH THE LAUNDRY-WOULD YOU CHANGE WREN?
NOT AT ALL. I LIKE HER JUST THE WAY SHE IS.
THIS IS WHY MOST OF YOUR STAND-UP COMEDIANS DON'T BECOME FATHERS.
KIRKMAN & SCOTT

BABY BLUES®
BY RICK KIRKMAN/ JERRY SCOTT

Z
PANT! SCHOOL DAYS OUGHT TO BE AN OLYMPIC EVENT.
YEAH. IT'S ABOUT TIME THERE WAS A SPORT DOMINATED BY MIDDLE-AGED WOMEN.
KIRKMAN & SCOTT

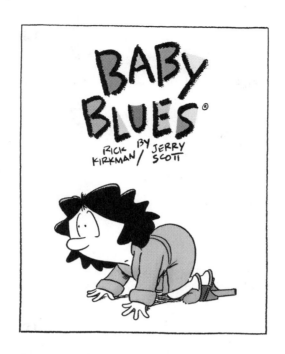

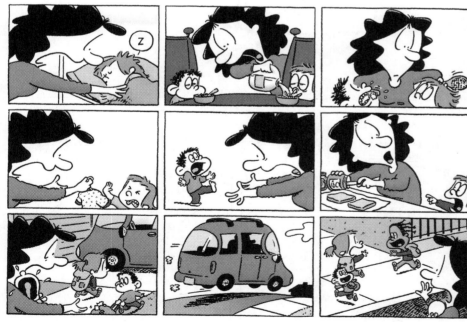

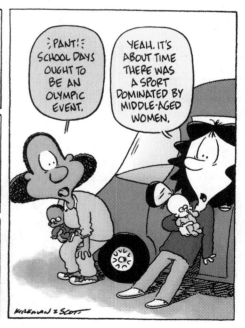

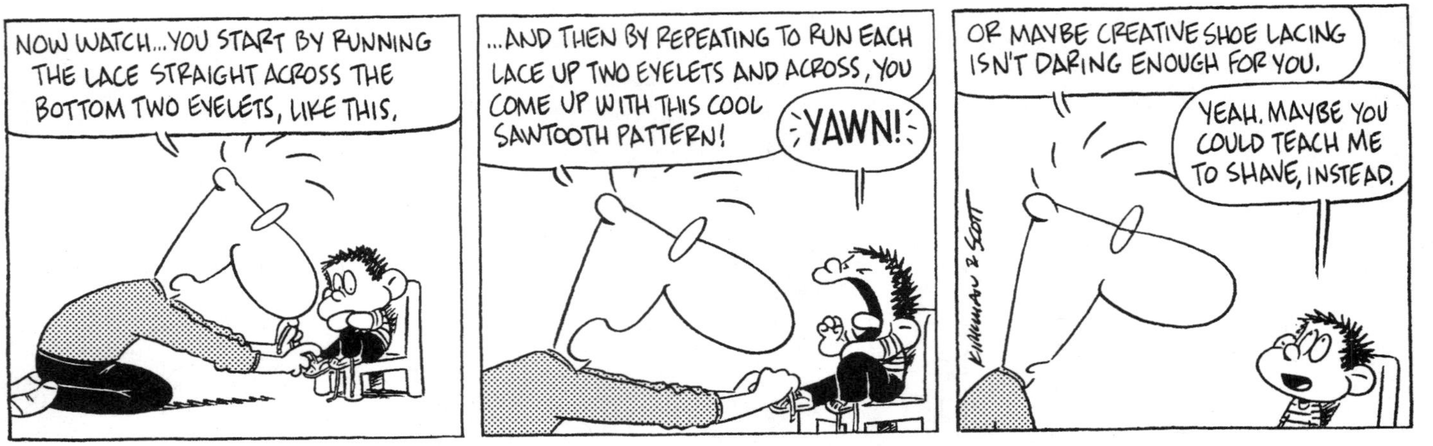
NOW WATCH...YOU START BY RUNNING THE LACE STRAIGHT ACROSS THE BOTTOM TWO EYELETS, LIKE THIS.
...AND THEN BY REPEATING TO RUN EACH LACE UP TWO EYELETS AND ACROSS, YOU COME UP WITH THIS COOL SAWTOOTH PATTERN!
YAWN!
KIRKMAN & SCOTT
OR MAYBE CREATIVE SHOE LACING ISN'T DARING ENOUGH FOR YOU.
YEAH. MAYBE YOU COULD TEACH ME TO SHAVE, INSTEAD.

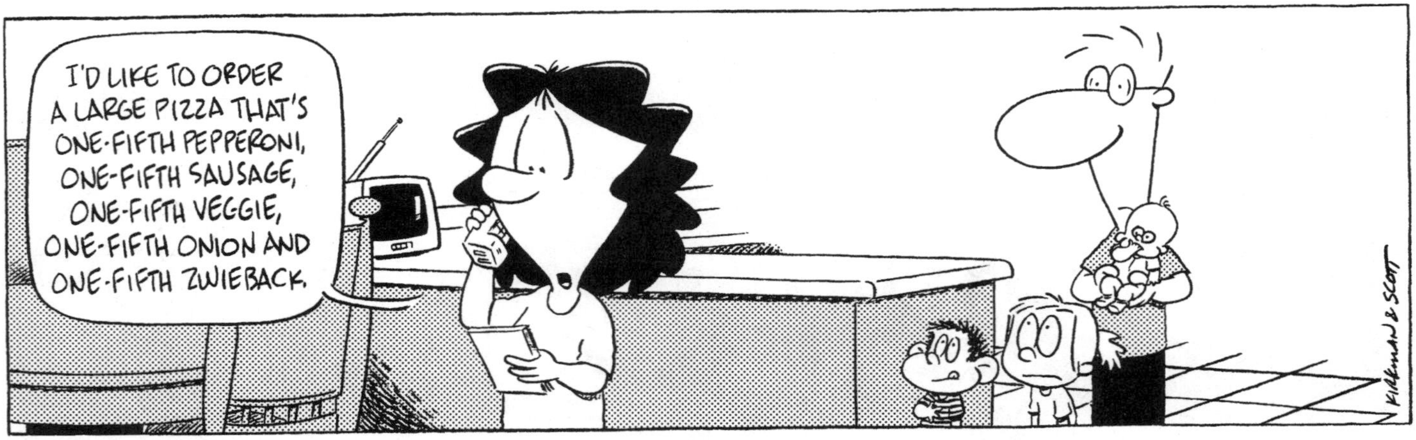
I'D LIKE TO ORDER A LARGE PIZZA THAT'S ONE-FIFTH PEPPERONI, ONE-FIFTH SAUSAGE, ONE-FIFTH VEGGIE, ONE-FIFTH ONION AND ONE-FIFTH ZWIEBACK.
KIRKMAN & SCOTT

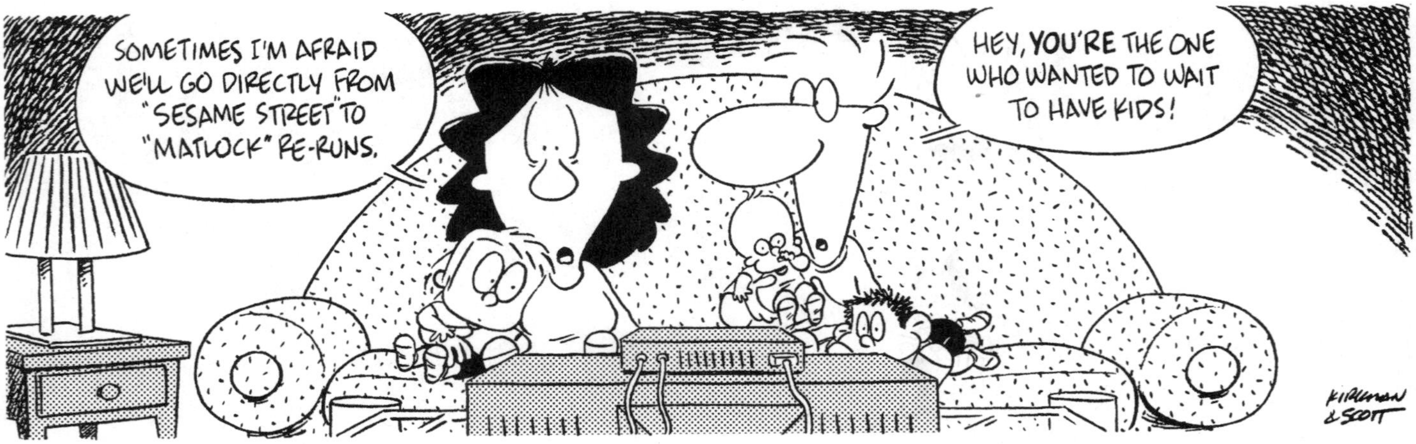
SOMETIMES I'M AFRAID WE'LL GO DIRECTLY FROM "SESAME STREET" TO "MATLOCK" RE-RUNS.
HEY, YOU'RE THE ONE WHO WANTED TO WAIT TO HAVE KIDS!
KIRKMAN & SCOTT

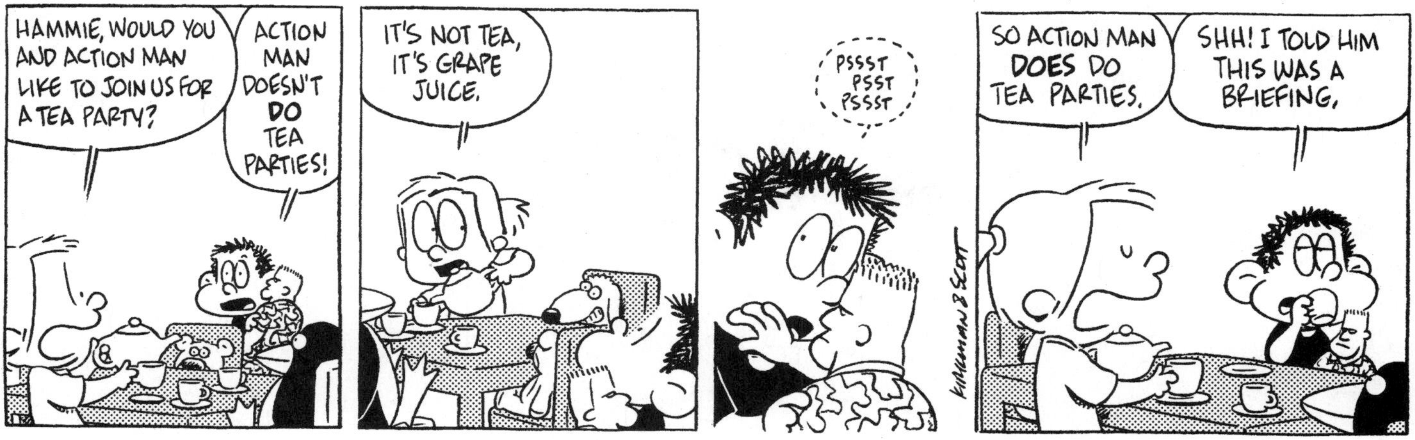
HAMMIE, WOULD YOU AND ACTION MAN LIKE TO JOIN US FOR A TEA PARTY?
ACTION MAN DOESN'T **DO** TEA PARTIES!
IT'S NOT TEA, IT'S GRAPE JUICE.
PSSST PSST PSSST
KIRKMAN & SCOTT
SO ACTION MAN **DOES** DO TEA PARTIES.
SHH! I TOLD HIM THIS WAS A BRIEFING.

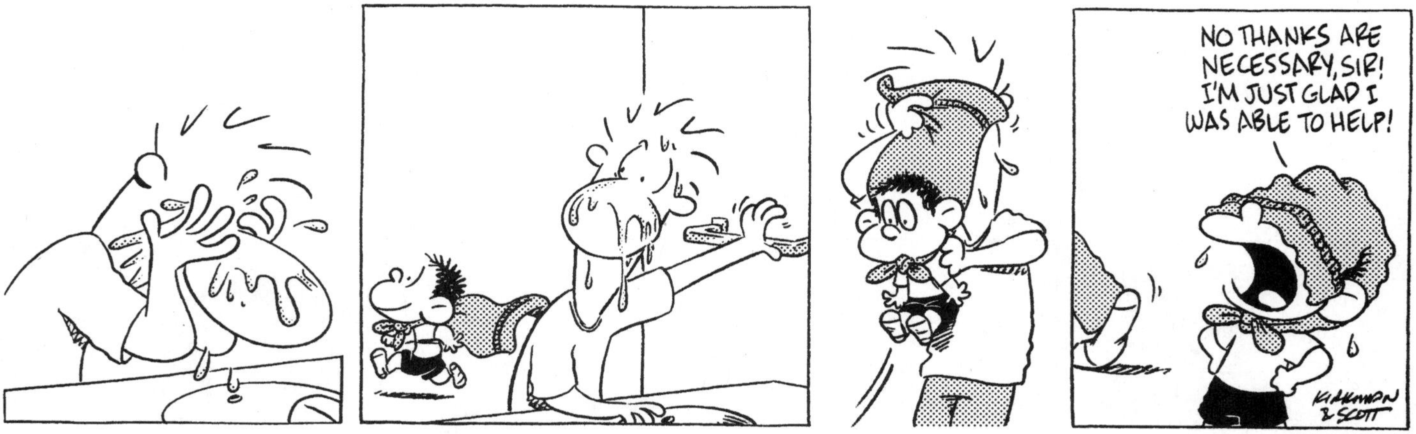
NO THANKS ARE NECESSARY, SIR! I'M JUST GLAD I WAS ABLE TO HELP!
KIRKMAN & SCOTT

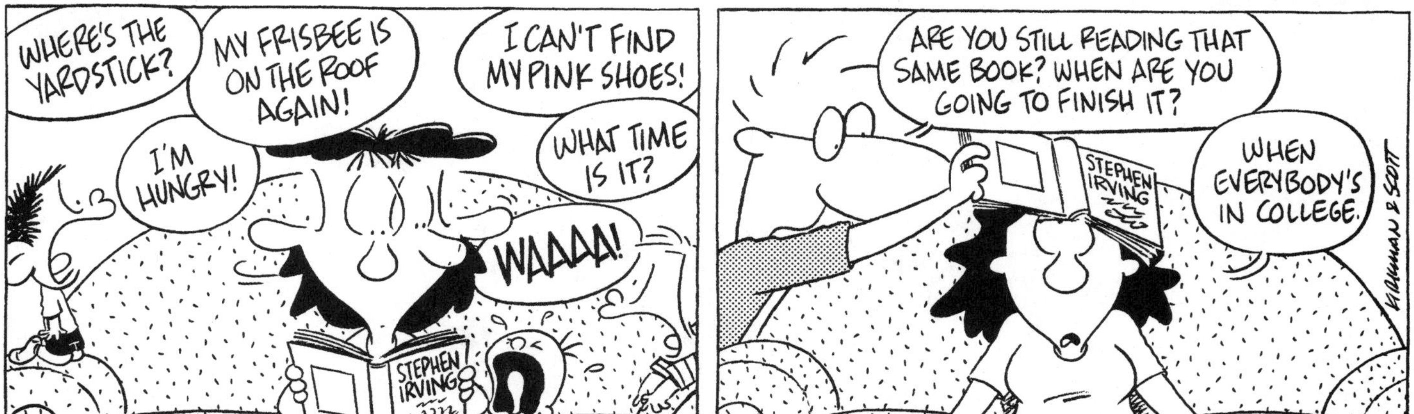
WHERE'S THE YARDSTICK?
MY FRISBEE IS ON THE ROOF AGAIN!
I CAN'T FIND MY PINK SHOES!
I'M HUNGRY!
WHAT TIME IS IT?
WAAAA!
STEPHEN IRVING
ARE YOU STILL READING THAT SAME BOOK? WHEN ARE YOU GOING TO FINISH IT?
STEPHEN IRVING
WHEN EVERYBODY'S IN COLLEGE.
KIRKMAN & SCOTT

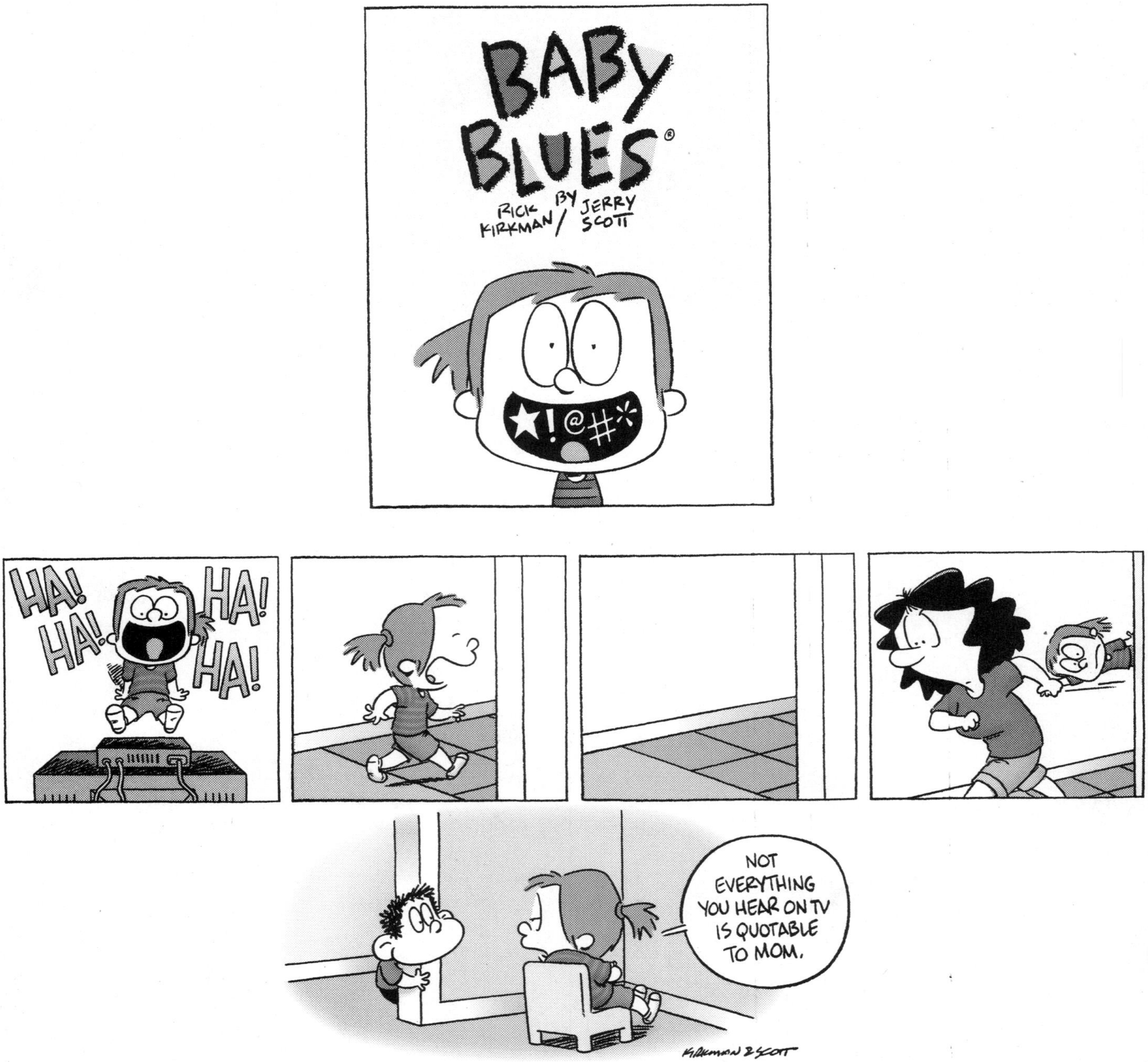
BABY BLUES®
BY RICK KIRKMAN / JERRY SCOTT
HA! HA! HA! HA!
NOT EVERYTHING YOU HEAR ON TV IS QUOTABLE TO MOM.
KIRKMAN & SCOTT